Arctic Migrants/Arctic Villagers

The Transformation of
Inuit Settlement in the Central Arctic

In recent years the view has emerged that the Inuit were coerced by the Canadian government into abandoning life in scattered camps for centres of habitation. In *Arctic Migrants/Arctic Villagers* David Damas demonstrates that for many years government policies helped maintain dispersed settlement, but that eventually concerns over health, housing, and education and welfare brought about policy changes that inevitably led to centralization.

Damas shows that while there were cases of government-directed relocation to centres, centralization was largely voluntary as the Inuit accepted the advantages of village living. In examining archives, anthropological writings, and the results of field research from an anthropological perspective, Damas provides fresh insights into the policies and developments that led to the centralization of Inuit settlement during the 1950s and 1960s.

DAVID DAMAS, professor emeritus of the Department of Anthropology, McMaster University, is the author of *Bountiful Island: A Study of Land Tenure on a Micronesian Atoll,* and a contributing editor to *Handbook of North American Indians, Volume 5: Arctic.*

MCGILL-QUEEN'S NATIVE AND NORTHERN SERIES
BRUCE G. TRIGGER, EDITOR

Arctic Migrants/ Arctic Villagers

The Transformation of Inuit Settlement in the Central Arctic

David Damas

McGill-Queen's University Press

Montreal & Kingston · London · Ithaca

© McGill-Queen's University Press 2002
ISBN 0-7735-2404-5

Legal deposit fourth quarter 2002
Bibliothèque nationale du Québec

Printed in Canada on acid-free paper that is 100%
ancient forest free (100% post-consumer recycled),
processed chlorine free.

This book has been published with the help of a grant
from the Humanities and Social Sciences Federation of
Canada, using funds provided by the Social Sciences
and Humanities Research Council of Canada.

McGill-Queen's University Press acknowledges the support of the Canada Council for the Arts for our publishing program. We also acknowledge the financial
support of the Government of Canada through the
Book Publishing Industry Development (BPIDP) for
our publishing activities.

National Library of Canada Cataloguing in Publication

Damas, David, 1926-
    Arctic migrants/Arctic villagers: the transformation of
    Inuit settlement in the central Arctic/David Damas.
    (McGill-Queen's native and northern series; 32)
    Includes bibliographical references and index.
    ISBN 0-7735-2404-5

    1. Inuit – Nunavut – History. 2. Land settlement –
    Nunavut – History. 3. Inuit – Nunavut – Government
    relations. 4. Inuit-Nunavut – Social conditions. I. Title.
    II. Series.
    E99.E7D337 2002   971.9'50049712   C2002-901695-9

This book was typeset by Dynagram Inc.
in 10/12 Baskerville

*This book is dedicated to the memory of James W. VanStone.
The extensiveness of the geographical scope and time depth
of his researches, together with his mastery of the methods
of archaeology, ethnohistory, and ethnology, provide direction
and inspiration to all scholars of the North.*

Contents

Maps and Tables

Acknowledgments

It was during field research in the period 1960–68 that I became aware of the transformation of Inuit settlement and the beginnings of the social and cultural consequences of this great change. During that period I benefitted from the helpful cooperation of a large number of Inuit, many of whom are now deceased. The field research was supported first by the United States Institute of Health and Welfare, and later by the National Museum of Canada, now the Canadian Museum of Civilization.

The second phase of my research on problems of centralization of settlement in the Central Arctic involved exploration of archival materials. This brought me to the National Archives of Canada in Ottawa, the Hudson's Bay Company collection in the Public Archives of Manitoba, and the Prince of Wales Northern Heritage Centre in Yellowknife, NWT. I wish to thank the staffs of these archival centres for their assistance. Research in these archives was supported in large part by the Social Sciences and Humanities Research Council of Canada and by travel grants from the Arts Research Board of McMaster University. I also wish to thank Ernest S. Burch, Jr., George W. Wenzel, and anonymous readers for many helpful suggestions. I am grateful for the help of Jacqueline Crerar and Janis Weir for converting amorphous and rough earlier versions into readable form. Mr and Mrs Geoffrey Humphrys' help in indexing is also greatly appreciated. Karen M. McCoullough for the Arctic Institute of North America and Paula Cardwell for Smithsonian Institution granted permission for the maps used in the book, as did Louis-Jacques Dorais for material previously published in *Études/Inuit/Studies*. I am also grateful to Lesley Barry for her editorial improvements.

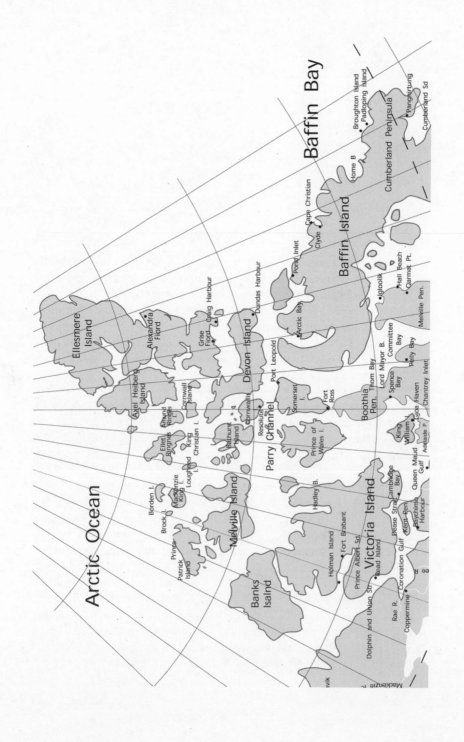

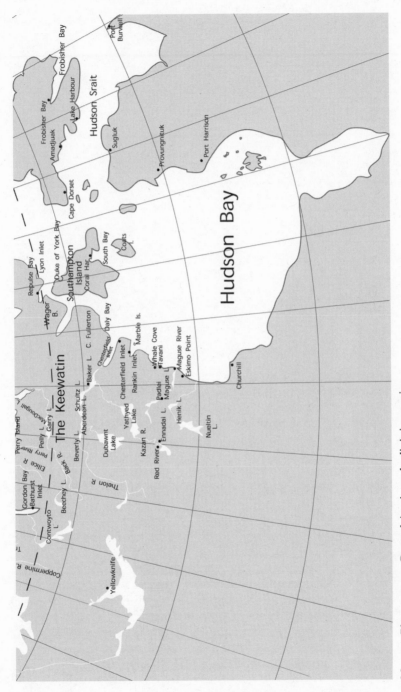

Map 1   Place names: Central Arctic and adjoining regions

Arctic Migrants/Arctic Villagers

Introduction

The shift from dispersed to centralized settlement in Arctic Canada brought on profound economic, social, and cultural changes for the Inuit.[1] Inuit have moved from small all-native hunting-trapping base camps[2] to much larger mixed ethnic villages and in doing so have experienced drastically altered social environments. For the most part this transformation in settlement took place during the 1950s and 1960s. Vallee and his associates have in broad terms listed the factors that they felt led toward centralization of settlement during those years: "Population concentration has been a product of several factors: the collapse of the fur trade; federal government policies to introduce effective administration of educational health and welfare programs; subsidized housing; mechanization of hunting practices; and the gradual acquisition of urban preferences by Native people."[3]

The chief objectives here are to explore these and other factors in specific examples of centralization and to assess their relative importance in each case, while paying particular attention to the impact of government policies on the shifting patterns of Inuit settlement. These policies were the driving force that for years maintained scattered populations in the Canadian Arctic, as well as contributing to the ingathering that later took place.

Two sorts of movements of resettlement must be distinguished. Lieber provides a useful distinction: "We can distinguish two types of resettled communities on the basis of the processes by which communities come to be resettled: planned movement of a group of people, whose destination is determined by some outside agency, and movement undertaken by individuals without the intervention of an outside agency. The first process is ... termed 'relocation'; the second is 'migration.'"[4] As discussion of individual cases of centralization will indicate, at some places the two processes were combined. In Arctic

Canada *migrations* have had a long history.[5] This process can be detected from archaeological periods through aboriginal and early contact times into the second half of the twentieth century.

With regard to *relocation*, some Inuit were moved within the eastern Canadian Arctic as early as the whaling era at the beginning of the century. Later, especially during the 1920s and 1930s, traders relocated people to new hunting-trapping locales. During the 1950s, the Canadian government engineered other relocation schemes. These latter movements of Inuit were subject to considerable analysis and criticism during the 1990s,[6] so much so that it might easily be assumed that this process dominated over migration in the formation of new communities in the 1950s and 1960s. This study considers both relocation and migration.

The study takes the approach of ethnohistory, an orientation that differs from other historical studies in three important respects.[7] First, there is more extensive use of anthropological sources, including archaeological as well as ethnological reports when appropriate. Second, anthropological concepts are employed when they explicate historical processes. Third, the ethnohistorian brings to bear the less tangible but equally important elements of an anthropological perspective. This perspective arises from direct contact with native people. It seeks to avoid both ethnocentric evaluations and romanticized portrayals of the subjects of study. In my view, a proper ethnohistoric study should strive to embody the scholarly ideals of objectivity and balance, and eschew excessively polemic or partisan positions.

Turning, then, to the sources used, I have enlisted the relevant published and unpublished materials concerning specific communities. The study focuses on the Central Arctic regions of Canada, which exclude the Mackenzie region as well as the Quebec–Labrador Peninsula.[8] These latter areas have had separate histories and, more recently, different administration. The regions selected correspond almost exactly to the Territory of Nunavut,[9] which emerged in 1999. Community studies by anthropologists and other researchers are cited, as are observations from personal field research during the 1960s. The reader will note considerable reliance on archival records. The reason for this emphasis relates to the main thrust of this work – the role of policy in the dispersal and, later, the concentration of Inuit populations. It is largely in archival documents that the discussions and debates that formulated these policies are available. The reports of RCMP officers[10] and, later, Northern Service officers reveal how the policies were implemented in the Arctic. There is correspondence and discussion regarding the policies not only among various government agencies but also with nongovernmental bodies; the Hudson's Bay

Company, the missions, and certain other private bodies were involved in policy formation, though their involvement was often secondary to that of the government.

Chapter 1 uses mainly published historical, archaeological, and ethnological materials to build a background of Inuit settlement practices. The discussion includes the observations of explorers and the role of whalers, and special attention is devoted to the major change in the distribution of Inuit brought on by the expansion of the trade in arctic fox. In chapter 2 I trace the advent and development of a government policy that sought to maintain scattered settlement. Here, correspondence between government officials and representatives of the Hudson's Bay Company is especially relevant. Also important for this era, which was dominated by the fur trade, are the reports of meetings of the Northwest Territories Council.

Chapters 3 and 4 examine how adherence to this Policy of Dispersal continued through the 1950s, with a comprehensive survey of each of the localities where the process of in-gathering either had begun or was on the horizon. Chapter 5 addresses the dramatic shift in policy that began in the fifties and culminated in the sixties. This new policy was characterized by a relaxation of resistance to centralization, and it espoused the humanitarian goals of the Welfare State. The following two chapters treat this policy's implementation during the 1960s, using the case-by-case survey used for the decade of the fifties to document the in-gathering process, which reached virtual completion by the end of the sixties.

The final chapter draws together material presented in earlier chapters to trace the road to centralization. I also treat variant views of the process of concentration of the Inuit population. Finally, the nature of the communities that were formed in the fifties and sixties are depicted again at the century's end.

CHAPTER ONE

Early Settlement in the Central Arctic

A number of anthropological sources have dealt with the cultures of the Inuit of the Central Arctic and of their predecessors.[1] Consequently, there is a large body of literature covering many aspects of the traditional lives of the people concerned, including their material culture, yearly economic cycles, mythology and religion, kinship and social organization, and language. In this study, I focus on patterns of settlement, in terms of location, duration, and size of local groupings. As background for the main period of the study, it is appropriate to assess the circumstances of Inuit settlement over a significant period of time: while established settlement practices have characterized certain phases of history, these practices can be seen to have been dynamic when viewed over several centuries.

ARCHAEOLOGY

Archaeologists agree that the bearers of the Thule culture were the biological, linguistic, and cultural ancestors of all Canadian Inuit. These people entered the Central Arctic about 1000 A.D. and spread rapidly eastward to Greenland. The most visible evidence of their presence are the remains of stone and sod houses, often raftered with bones of large whales.[2] On Thule settlement, McGhee writes: "Most Thule sites consist of from one to four winter houses, and at the larger sites which may have several dozen houses, there is little evidence that more than a few houses were occupied simultaneously" and "perhaps 10 to 50 people ... they built their houses wherever a summer kill of whales was made and they also hunted land animals."[3] The generalizations regarding house sites apply only to winter dwellings; other site types have been discovered for other seasons. These include traces of kill sites, caches, and tent encampments, which were bases for hunting excursions.[4] Generalizations regarding the importance of whales apply largely to the regions bordering Parry Channel (see map 1 for geographical and place names). These regions were on the route of the original migration and settlement of Thule people. A second phase of migration brought people southward, and by 1200–1300 A.D.[5] most of the regions that were eventually inhabited by Central Eskimo were occupied. Along the Arctic coast of North America and adjoining regions, the chief game was the caribou and most sites occurred at places where that animal could be expected to migrate. Since these regions were outside the range of the large whales, winter dwellings were either raftered with driftwood or had roofs made of slabs of flat stone.[6]

By about 1500 A.D. the whaling areas to the north were abandoned. It is now accepted that the migration out of those regions was occasioned by climatic changes that interfered with the movement of whales.[7] Climatic changes also resulted in the abandonment of permanent winter houses,[8] signifying a more nomadic settlement pattern.

Location of settlements showed variation over time and according to local resources. In the whaling areas winter sites could be found where the pursuit of whales could be carried out within a convenient radius. Further south, after the second expansion of Thule, winter houses were located near caribou migration paths. Location at other seasons was more random, radiating outward from the winter villages according to the distribution of game. Duration of settlement relates to both seasonal and longer term residences. A defining marker of Thule was the permanent structures that were occupied during the winter period. It is impossible to discern from the archaeological record just how many months of occupancy was typical for these villages. It is clear that several less permanent sites were occupied during each year. Difficult to judge is the length of time over several years that the main winter sites were occupied continuously. There is, however, evidence to indicate that houses were at times abandoned and later reoccupied. There has been some controversy regarding the size of Thule local groupings. As the culture progressed there is the likelihood that the snowhouse sealing villages of the aboriginal–early contact period, set on the sea ice, became the typical winter gathering. If this was the case, these aggregations could have been larger than most of the winter villages, having more substantial structures. As is indicated in the next section, these sea ice encampments could have housed 100 people.

THE ABORIGINAL – EARLY CONTACT PERIOD

Moving forward in time, away from the archaeological record, an aboriginal–early contact phase of history can be designated.[9] This is the period when our information comes mainly from the accounts of explorers and the logs of whalers. In the later phases of the era, or after its end, ethnologists either witnessed cultures and societies that represented the period or sought to reconstruct them on the basis of statements of informants. It would be desirable to present a truly aboriginal picture of settlement practices, but in many cases this is not possible because in some regions the earliest accounts come from a time when considerable European contact, either direct or indirect, had already taken place.

Coming as they did from European seaports, the earliest explorers made contact with the Inuit of the Central Arctic at the eastern margins of the area. First contacts, subsequent to possible encounters between Norse from Greenland and the Inuit, came with explorers of the sixteenth century and early seventeenth century, including Martin Frobisher, John Davis, and William Baffin, who made brief and often hostile contact with the Inuit of Baffin Island.[10] We learn little of settlement practices from these accounts, though from the accounts of the Frobisher expeditions we get depictions of winter and summer dwellings.[11]

Whalers were the next to enter the east Central Arctic, beginning as early as the eighteenth century. After about 1820, whalers expanded their operations to the western parts of Davis Strait and Baffin Bay. After 1853, whaling ships began to overwinter in the Cumberland Sound region, and later, year-round shore stations were established at some Baffin Island locations.[12] Regarding the nature of whaling contacts in the east Central Arctic, W. Gillies Ross writes: "In its simplest terms, the evolving geography of whaling influence was characterized by nucleation, first at a number of localities where kreng, drift whales, and wrecks came ashore or where whaling vessels tended to stop for a few weeks in summer, later a smaller number of harbours where ships customarily wintered, and finally at a few whaling stations where whaling and trading were year-round and endured for a period of years. This trend toward centralization had its effect on the distribution of Eskimo population, and it brought about important regional disparities in the acculturative process."[13]

The account of American explorer Charles Francis Hall of his visit to Frobisher Bay over 1860–62 reports encampments of Inuit not far from overwintering whaling ships. Especially interesting in terms of Inuit settlement patterns is the observation: "the inhabitants of both villages have gone away to Frobisher Bay, where they hoped more success would attend their exertions to procure food. Indeed, I understand that not less than a hundred Inuit were located in one place and doing well."[14] Here is a suggestion of smaller local groupings abandoning hunting locales in close proximity to a whaling vessel to congregate in another place, where aggregation apparently represented an advantage for hunting.

The geographer-anthropologist Franz Boas spent the year 1883–84 in the Cumberland Sound region, where he produced a census for December 1883 of eight settlements ranging in size from ten to twenty-nine persons, and one larger settlement of eighty-two located at a whaling station.[15] However, this pattern represents a situation already affected by whaling operations in the region. Boas's most important contribution describes more truly aboriginal settlement conditions: "There are only a few districts where the proximity of open water favors walrus hunting during the winter and all of those have neighboring floes on which seals may be hunted with the harpoons ... As to the remainder, the Eskimo lives altogether independent of the open water during the winter. Generally speaking, two conditions are required for winter settlement, viz, the existence of extensive floe and smooth ice." On aggregations, he writes: "The natives who lived in large settlements during the winter are spread over the whole country in order that every one may have a better chance of travelling over his own hunting ground."[16]

For the Pond Inlet region to the north, there is a brief description of Inuit settlement in the account of the English explorer Sir Leopold McClintock from 1857. There larger groups are described as aggregating for winter sea-mammal hunting, with dispersal for fishing and caribou hunting in the warmer seasons. By the time of McClintock's visit, however, aggregations were also occurring at the coast, "awaiting the arrival of whaling ships for trade."[17] Whaling operations had by the mid nineteenth century also interrupted whatever seasonal cycle of settlement had existed on the Hudson Strait shore of Baffin Island. Inuit in this region made summer trips from their camps in order to trade with whalers.[18] Little is known of their sites or patterns of habitation at other seasons.

In the region of Hudson Bay, explorers and, later, crews of Hudson's Bay Company (HBC) sloops out of Churchill encountered people along the west shore of the Bay in the eighteenth century. Groups of thirty to forty were met in early summer on islands along the coast.[19] These Inuit moved inland about the beginning of autumn to hunt caribou, having lived earlier in the year on sea mammals. Little is known of their movements at other seasons during this period.[20] A movement inland of greater magnitude and permanence began about the end of the eighteenth century and gradually penetrated further inland until "during the eighteen forties, some began to live inland on a year-round basis."[21] Later, their essential subsistence source gave rise to their designation as the Caribou Eskimos.[22] Burch indicates that musk oxen were also important, especially during the nineteenth century.[23]

Observations of travellers during the late nineteenth century give some indication of the distributions and movements of this population, as well as the size of groupings. For instance, Lofthouse, who travelled along the west shore of the Bay as far north as Marble Island, encountered groups as large as 150 people.[24] Some were hunting sea mammals, but others were traveling from trading at Churchill. As well, other Caribou Eskimo, particularly a northern group, the Qairnirmiut, began in 1860 to camp where whaling vessels were frozen in during winters.[25] Other encounters were made in the interior by Schwatka in 1878–79,[26] J.W. and J.B. Tyrrell in 1893 and 1894,[27] and by Hanbury in 1901–02,[28] and their accounts give some indication of locations and sizes of groups. An especially well-populated region was along the Kazan River, where J.B. Tyrrell encountered frequent encampments in 1894, some of which were quite large. These observations of the Caribou Eskimo came at a time of peak populations. During the period of 1915–25 a drastic decline in numbers occurred,[29] which upsets our ability to determine the nature of groupings in the area. Indeed, by the time of the visit of the Fifth Thule Expedition in 1922–24, no more than half and possibly one-third of past peak numbers remained. One can gain some sense of the nature of groupings for the early 1920s from Birket-Smith when he writes, "the most conspicuous thing about the settlements on the Barren Grounds is their temporary character," and "that to give a universal list of the settlements of the Caribou Eskimos is therefore simply an impossibility."[30] Birket-Smith does, however, explore the question of locations of groups in some detail, listing a number of factors. For example, he writes, "the big caribou crossing places act as magnets on the population."[31]

Other factors cited were the presence of good house-building snow in winter, and in summer, rocky hills where mosquitos were kept away by the wind. Good fishing locales were also places of residence. For those who traveled to the coast in summer, off-lying islands and sand spits were favoured places of access to sea mammals.[32] Birket-Smith cites fifty people or "about ten families" as being the largest aggregations.[33] This figure may have been too low for the earlier period of larger populations.

Information on settlement patterns for northwestern Hudson Bay comes from a number of accounts provided by nineteenth-century explorers. The first of these was from the Parry–Lyon expedition, which wintered in Repulse Bay in 1821–22.[34] They reported a snowhouse village of sixty-four people built near their ships. The location is accounted for not only by the presence of the ships, *Fury* and *Hecla*,

Map 2   Aboriginal ranges of major Central Eskimo groups. Adapted from
vol. 5, *Arctic, Handbook of North American Indians.*

but also in view of access to floe edge and breathing-hole sealing.
Mathiassen[35] abstracted a seasonal cycle from the accounts of Lyon,
Parry, Rae,[36] and an Inuit informant, deriving a picture of late winter
gathering on the sea ice that at times included the entire population
of the region. These groups split in spring into dispersed hunting
groups, and reunited during the late autumn and early winter at
cache sites before descending again to the sea ice for breathing-hole
sealing. ·

After 1860, the range of the Inuit of the Repulse Bay region (the Aivilingmiut) was extended southward as American whalers drew them to the Cape Fullerton–Marble Island region, where the ships spent winters. Largely in service of the whalers, men hunted at the floe edge for seals and walrus. Inland hunts were devoted to caribou for meat and winter clothing,[37] and for the musk oxen, whose fur was valuable in trade. Beginning also in the 1860s elements of Netsilik Eskimo[38] moved down to northwestern Hudson Bay from their normal ranges to the north and northwest for sea-mammal hunting and to trade with the whaling crews. W.G. Ross indicates that from 50 to 200 people lived near the overwintering whaling vessels.[39]

For the Iglulik region at the north end of Melville Peninsula, again the accounts of Parry and Lyon,[40] who wintered there in 1822–23, give a basis for our understanding of yearly settlement cycles. These descriptions were supplemented by the work of Mathiassen for a period that can be considered aboriginal.[41] Iglulik Island was the locus of aggregation and the bulk of the Iglulingmiut population lived there from early autumn to mid winter. Usually sometime in January one or two large encampments formed on the sea ice, with hunters engaged in sealing or hunting walrus from the floe edge. As with the Aivilingmiut, the large winter gatherings split in the spring for a period of surface sealing. Later, as in the Repulse Bay region, further splitting took place, with younger men going inland to hunt caribou. Older men hunted in kayaks in the sea before coalescence again took place, in the autumn when the period of living from stores began.[42]

The heart of the Central Arctic, the regions inhabited by the Netsilik Eskimo, was first penetrated by the expedition of Sir John Ross in his *Victory*.[43] This expedition wintered for three years on the east shore of Boothia Peninsula. Ross's descriptions of the Inuit of the region are more useful than those of many other explorers who entered the region in search of the Franklin expedition. However, combining information from these various sources with later accounts of the parties of Amundsen (1903–05) and Rasmussen (1923–24)[44] help fill out the picture.

The Netsilik area extended from Pelly Bay in the east and included Boothia Peninsula, King William Island, and the mainland westward to Perry River and adjoining areas of sea ice that were hunted on during winters. Nearly all Netsiliks spent much of their winters in large groups on the sea ice engaged in breathing-hole sealing. The groups began to split in late winter. Only around Pelly Bay was surface sealing widely practiced.[45] Fishing was the most prominent activity in spring, before people began to move inland in small, extended family groups for caribou hunting. The major contrast with groups further east, the Iglulik and Baffinland Eskimo, was that there was no sea-mammal hunting during the warmer seasons. Some shore sites were inhabited if they happened to be localities where fishing streams entered the sea.[46] Fishing was indeed more highly developed than further east. As was the case further east, the winter sealing villages were the largest sorts of gathering, with up to 100 people often aggregating for at least part of most winters.

In the Copper Eskimo regions, most of the nineteenth-century explorers followed coastal routes in summers, a season when people hunted inland.[47] The account of Collinson gives some indication of year-round habitation practices. However, our most reliable accounts come from Stefansson, who arrived in the area in 1910 when the basic culture and cycle of settlement were still intact, and from Jenness, who in 1914–16 observed situations where only minimal change had taken place.[48]

Stefansson's first encounter with Copper Eskimo in the spring of 1910 provides an interesting model of winter movements of people on the ice of Dolphin and Union Strait: "As we understood dimly then and know definitely now, each village ... should be about ten miles from the next preceding, and should be about a month more recent ... in a month or so the hunters of a single village will have killed off all the seals within a radius of about five miles, they must then move camp about ten miles so that a five mile radius circle around their next camp shall be tangent to the five-mile circle about their last one, for if the circle overlapped there would be that much waste territory within the new circle of activities. If, then, you are following such a trail and come to a village about four months old you will expect to find the people who made it not more than forty miles off."[49]

His model of winter movements of western elements of the Copper Eskimo can probably be applied throughout the entire range of Copper Eskimo, as well as of most Netsilik Eskimo. Jenness observed in the winter of 1914–15 a pattern of movements that largely confirms the observations of Stefansson.[50] Jenness did find that during December and January camps were not moved, though afterwards the monthly movements described by Stefansson took place. The largest aggregations occurred during this early winter period, after which they were split.

Stefansson and Jenness also observed settlement practices of western elements of Copper Eskimo during the warmer seasons. Especially enlightening was Jenness's accompaniment of a small group during the spring, summer, and autumn of 1915.[51] The group fluctuated in membership from three to nineteen according to the fortunes of hunting and fishing. Jenness also indicated a period that "corresponds roughly with our month of November"[52] when the Copper Eskimo lived largely on stores while the winter clothing was being sewn, before the move was made to the sea ice for the period of winter sealing. A map in Jenness's monograph shows the location of these sewing places where Inuit convened each year.[53] This practice and the associated settlement, usually at points of land, was common throughout the Central Arctic, while the period during which stores supplied the main food varied from region to region.

For eastern elements of Copper Eskimo, Rasmussen provides a similar picture of the yearly cycle of subsistence and settlement patterns.[54] One exception were those Inuit on the mainland south of Coronation and Queen Maud Gulfs, who spent longer periods in the interior hunting caribou.

I have indicated the difficulty of deriving a truly aboriginal picture of Inuit settlement practices in parts of the Central Arctic. It is nevertheless necessary to attempt such a depiction in order that a baseline be established for the later settlement situations that are the focus of this study.

In drawing together the material presented thus far, I return to the basic concepts that illuminate the dimensions of settlement patterns: location, duration, and size of groupings. With regard to location, some circumstances have universal or near universal relevance in the Central Arctic. There was a tendency to locate at sites of large game takes for periods of living largely from stores accumulated in caches. Wherever large kill sites occurred in a scattered fashion we would expect that settlement for such periods would also be scattered. However, examples from some regions show that stores from the kills could be transported to places of habitual aggregation.

Throughout the entire Central Arctic area there was also a tendency to form aggregations at sites of caribou drives and at especially favourable fishing places. Also, during warmer months some of the Iglulik and Baffinland groups lived at locales where hunting of sea mammals from watercraft could be carried out. In some of the same societies accessibility to floe edges in winter was a consideration in settlement location. This was especially true in those locales where walrus were hunted through newly formed ice off the margins of the floe edges. Elsewhere, Boas's association between annually dispersing land-fast ice and Inuit habitation relates to the practice of breathing-hole sealing. In most of the Central Arctic, location of summer encampments was largely opportunistic for those groups who hunted inland, depending upon the requirements of the hunt. As well, dislocations from normal ranges of habitation were not unusual. In the case of the Copper Eskimo, for example, long journeys were made to wooded areas lying at the margins of or outside normal hunting ranges.

Duration of settlement varied widely. At one extreme is the case of the Iglulingmiut, who spent up to five months settled in one place during the autumn and early winter. This practice is associated with having unusually large stores of meat and fat, particularly those from the walrus, which abounded in the region. This meat and fat would be accumulated during the summer months. The other extreme can be seen in Jenness's description of the summer settlement habits of certain Copper Eskimo groups: "On both sides of Dolphin and Union strait ... the traveller will find scattered families roaming about from place to place, here today, and gone tomorrow in their restless search for game. Days of feasting alternate with days of fasting according to their failure or success. No fowl of the air, no creature of the land, no fish in the water is too great or too small to attract their notice at this time."[55] Other elements of Central Eskimo groups may have approached this degree of mobility during the more nomadic phases of their yearly cycles, but this is probably the extreme. Intermediate, but closer to the Iglulik example, was the location of Caribou Eskimo in the fall and part of each winter at sites of large caribou kills.

The Copper Eskimo groupings represented both extremes of size. Jenness's account indicates splitting to as low as three individuals, while Stefansson estimated that a trading village on Dolphin and Union Strait had housed 200 people when occupied.[56] He also visited an encampment of 150 on the ice of Prince Albert Sound.[57] There the inhabitants were traveling from winter hunting regions and living on meat carried along. Both of these aggregations were portrayed as being of fleeting duration. Of the Caribou Eskimo, in more populous times there were groups reported to be in excess of the maximum fifty posted by Birket-Smith. I have used the figure of 100 as being a typical maximal number for the winter sealing villages of much of the area,[58] but it appears that groups of such size did not endure throughout entire winters.

Economic factors were vital in influencing the location, duration, and size of local groups. Location of resources was, of course, crucial to the location of aggregations of whatever size. Places where fishing could be carried out, sites of lakes and streams where caribou crossed, land-fast ice and floe edges for sea-mammal hunting are examples. Duration of settlement lasted as long as game was available: when game failed, people moved. Under some circumstances, especially when land game is scarce, dispersal of population is advantageous. In other cases, such as at caribou drives, fish runs, or breathing-hole sealing, larger groupings have economic advantage.

If economic factors are the most visible and amenable to explanatory use, other factors are involved. Anecdotal information, the observations of earlier visitors to the Central Arctic, and even behaviour observable as late as the 1960s, indicate that social-psychological factors also shaped settlement practices. In hunting societies aggregations have the advantage of fostering social and ceremonial events. In the case of the Inuit of Central Arctic, games, singing, dancing, and shamanistic performances provided important integrating functions. The renewal of ties of kinship beyond the family also provided motives for aggregations of people, as did affirmation in a number of voluntary associations.

While larger aggregations provide the best opportunities for such interaction, fragmentation also had its advantages in easing social tensions. Among the Central Eskimo the most prominent of these tensions were the threats of blood feud and of witchcraft, but these were not the only sources of friction. Taken together, both the economic and social-psychological factors produced advantages to periodic coalescence and dispersals.

Other characteristics of local groups fall outside those of settlement patterns and belong instead to the realm of community patterns or social organization. Chief among these characteristics is the composition of groups. In much of the Central Arctic the chief building block was a patrilocal extended family, that is, a unit headed by a senior male and including adult sons, the wives of these men, and the younger children of the couples. This form of family organization has been reported for Baffinlanders,[59] the Iglulik,[60] the Netsilik,[61] and the Caribou Eskimo.[62] Only among the Copper Eskimo was this unit all but lacking, with the isolation of the nuclear family being quite pronounced.[63] In all regions of the Central Arctic, in the larger groupings, families of either description were linked with others through ties of affinity and consanguinity to form continuous or near continuous chains of kin.

While features of composition may seem to be remote from settlement patterns, they do enter into the segmentation and coalescences of groups over time. For example, in the case of the Copper Eskimo, where the nuclear family was relatively isolated, at times these families would operate as independent units for certain periods of the yearly cycle. In the Netsilik area there was seldom splitting of the extended family over this cycle. This also seemed to be the case for the Caribou Eskimo, groups. For the Igluliks and possibly Baffinlanders, the extended family was also an important minimal local unit, but for part of the year's cycle there was an age-youth split. Older men, usually related heads of extended families, joined in pairs for hunting in the sea. The adult sons of the extended family, with their spouses and children, hunted inland together. Eventually the results of both hunts were shared within the extended family when reunited.

Another feature of Central Eskimo social organization must be mentioned: leadership status, that of the *Isumataaq* or *Ihumataaq*. All of the major Central Eskimo groupings recognized this form of leadership except, again, the Copper Eskimo.[64] For most of the major area this designation was usually accorded the heads of extended families and passed down to the eldest sons on the death of the elder. For the Igluliks, and perhaps elsewhere, this designation was extended to one man who was regarded as heading the larger aggregations.[65]

Turning to settlement situations occasioned by early contact with Europeans, the trading journeys to Churchill during the nineteenth century upset normal patterns of movements for the natives who lived west of Hudson Bay. These journeys created apparently large groups during these trips. However, often these gatherings were within the normal hunting ranges of the Inuit concerned. They were usually of shorter duration than those that grew either at the sites of frozen-in whaling ships or at whaling stations. In describing the effect of whaling activities on settlement, Ross points to the process of centralization, the major concern of this study: "The pre-contact pattern of dispersed settlement was an inconvenience to the whaleman: In order to utilize Inuit as an effective arm of the industry they had to alter the traditional dispersal of population and the nomadic annual cycle of food procurement. Demographic centralization was as essential to whaling in the nineteenth century as it has been to government services since the World War."[66] In later chapters I shall examine this latter relationship, but at this point it is well to note that the settlement situations attributed to whaler contact did not obtain for the west Central Arctic, the regions of the Copper and Netsilik groupings, except for the movement of elements of the Netsiliks to northwestern Hudson Bay.

After whaling operations ended in the second decade of the twentieth century, other factors brought on another set of settlement practices.

THE CONTACT – TRADITIONAL PERIOD

Following upon the aboriginal–early contact period came the era designated as the contact-traditional horizon.[67] Relations with the Inuit of the Central Arctic during this period were restricted mainly to missionaries, traders, and, as representatives of the Canadian government in the north, the Royal Canadian Mounted Police. Fur traders were the most influential agents of change on settlement patterns. Indeed, the onset of the horizon can be set at the establishment of trading posts within or close to traditional ranges of habitation of the various elements of Central Eskimo. Less regularized trade had, however, existed prior to the founding of these posts and deserves treatment in providing background for the contact-traditional patterns of trapping and trading.

Trade began with the Inuit along the west coast of Hudson Bay by the third decade of the eighteenth century,[68] and was carried out intermittently until 1750–90 when it became more regular as sloops moved northward from Churchill. Andrew Graham, our chief source for this latter period, describes items brought to the trade by the Inuit of the region: "we take from them train oil, and blubber, whalebone, and two or three foxe's skins."[69]

After the sloop trade ceased and the Inuit began to travel to Churchill for the goods they desired, the nature of trade was limited by means of transport: "the trade they brought whenever it is recorded, always consisted of skins – of deer, wolf, wolverine, and fox. ... They did not bring those two old staples of the slooping trade, whalebone and oil or blubber which could not well be carried on a kayak."[70]

Among the skins that later featured in the trade at Churchill (as well as with overwintering whalers) toward the end of the nineteenth century were those of musk oxen. This trade peaked after about 1890 when the bison had been exterminated from the Great Plains and robes of musk oxen hides were substituted in open carriages for buffalo skins.[71] In 1866, the HBC sent its ship *Ocean Nymph* to winter at Marble Island.[72] During the winter of 1866–67 a variety of furs were traded, including 313 white fox. While this expedition was not at the time considered a success, the trading activities of whalers caused the HBC to compete by sending regular summer trading expeditions northward beginning in 1882.[73]

While the contact-traditional fur trade base was the arctic fox, whalers concentrated on other products, even though steel traps were among their inventories.[74] S.I. Robinson writes of the results of the fox trade during the later years of whaling activity in Hudson Bay: "The trapping of arctic fox was just becoming an important commercial enterprise for the Aivilingmiut at the end of the whaling era. It is only after 1900 that fairly consistent records of fox trading occurs. In 1903–04 about 120 fox were traded. In 1904–05 about 172, and in 1910–12 some 421 fox were mentioned as traded."[75]

W.G. Ross compiled a listing of furs and skins traded by whalers in the period of 1900–15, presumably for the entire Central Arctic.[76] American whalers obtained 1,391 fox furs as compared to 2,533 by Scottish whalers, whose area of operations was largely in the Davis Strait–Baffin Bay regions. Also significant in respect to later trading emphases in that region is the listing of 3,310 sealskins and 2,730 walrus hides obtained by Scottish whalers, items all but absent in the records of American whalers. It must not be supposed that these total numbers of fox pelts for the fifteen-year period cited by Ross point to an intensification in that trade. In some years during the heyday of the trade in arctic fox single posts exceeded the number traded by American whalers.[77]

The year 1911 can be said to have marked the advent of the economic focus of the contact-traditional orientation on Baffin Island. In that year the Hudson's Bay Company established its first post on the island at Lake Harbour, and the Sabellum Company founded no fewer than four posts in or about that year on southeastern Baffin Island.[78] The HBC continued to open posts in the following years, at Cape Dorset in 1913, and at Pangnirtung, Pond Inlet, and Amadjuak in 1921.[79] Their operations expanded such that by 1927, when Sabellum left the scene,[80] the HBC had posts at so many points that the Inuit of the island had access to trade within relatively easy reach. While the chief emphasis in contact-traditional trade was on the arctic fox, sealskins continued to be important at most posts on Baffin Island.

The year 1911 also saw the beginning of developed trade in arctic fox for the regions to the west of and in northwestern Hudson Bay with the founding of the HBC post at Chesterfield Inlet.[81] The company set up trading stations at the eastern entrance to Baker Lake in 1914[82] (later moved to the north shore of the lake), at Repulse Bay in 1920,[83] at Eskimo Point in 1921,[84] and Coral Harbour in 1924.[85] Posts were established at various places in the southern interior west of Hudson Bay during the 1920s.[86] Chief competition for HBC came from the Revillion Frères Company, beginning in the mid 1920s.[87]

The contact-traditional period, with its emphasis on fox trapping and trade, succeeded directly on an aboriginal-early contact base in the west central regions where contact with whalers had not developed. It is true that some of the traders who entered these regions were themselves former whaling men. Captain Joseph Bernard in his small schooner, the *Teddy Bear*, wintered three years (1910–11, 1912–13, and 1913–14) in the Coronation Gulf–Dolphin and Union Strait regions and introduced trade goods to the Copper Eskimo.[88] In 1914 the Canadian Arctic Expedition also engaged in some trade from their base at Bernard Harbour.[89] It was with their departure and the arrival of the HBC at that place in 1916 that regularized trade began in the Copper Eskimo area.[90] Independent traders and white trappers, operating from both 'floating posts' and shore stations, also entered the area at about this time. The Canalaska Company was the chief trading firm competing with the Hudson's Bay Company from 1926.[91] The HBC expanded its operations eastward rapidly with posts at Tree River (1918),[92] Kent Peninsula (1920),[93] and Perry River (1926),[94] and also moved north, founding a post in Prince Albert Sound in 1923.[95] By the mid 1920s traders had spread themselves across the entire coastal expanse of Copper Eskimo country. The Netsilik area was reached in direct trade when the HBC set up a post on King William Island in 1923, followed by Canalaska in 1927.[96]

By the middle of the 1920s nearly all Inuit of the Central Arctic could trade at posts within or near to their normal ranges of habitation. A notable exception were the natives of the Iglulik region at the north end of Melville Peninsula, where for many years round trip journeys of 500 to 600 miles had to be made to Repulse Bay to the south or Pond Inlet to the north. Also, the people of Pelly Bay had a considerable distance to travel to the nearest post at Repulse Bay.

There are two ways in which adoption of fox trapping had the potential for altering aboriginal or early contact settlement practices. More directly, the location of camps could be influenced by favourable trapping locales. Indirectly, with the wide use of firearms, the steady supply of ammunition, and the availability of nets for fishing, hunting and fishing practices changed and in turn so did the locations and durations of habitations. Two patterns of trapping emerged during contact-traditional times. One was the establishment of traplines, which could be very extensive, involving long trips and consequent absences of men from their base camps. The other practice was that of planting traps at meat caches, which were usually located within easy reach of such bases.

We begin our survey of the effects of the fur trade on settlement patterns in eastern Baffin Island. By the early 1920s trading posts had replaced whaling stations as the chief points of contact. Aside from the disappearance of the gatherings that had taken place at the stations – the traders discouraged such aggregations at their posts[97] – there was little change in locations and sizes of habitation places. These were set on coasts where sea-mammal hunting was productive, just as in the time of Boas. Likewise, the number of inhabitants was on about the same scale as during whaling times. For example, an RCMP patrol of 1924 gave an average of about twenty persons per camp for Cumberland Sound.[98] This agrees with Boas's census of December 1883, which gives an average of 18.8 persons in the sites of habitation, exclusive of a large gathering at a whaling station.[99]

The natives of eastern Baffin Island did not adopt the trade in arctic fox completely. The post manager at Pangnirtung in 1939 complained that "the Cumberland Sound native seems to be a pretty fair sealer and whaler, but he is a very poor trapper … After he has secured his one or two foxes to pay his debt he sits back and calls it a day."[100] While there is doubtlessly some exaggeration revealed in the frustration of this trader, maps in Freeman's *Inuit Land Use* show a circular trapping pattern that bespeaks setting traps at meat caches, rather than any extensive traplines in the region.[101]

In general, there appears to have been an indifferent adoption of the trade in arctic fox in much of Baffin Island, together with the maintenance of earlier settlement practices. Sealskins were more often traded in eastern Baffin Island than fox pelts, but each sealskin brought much lower return than did a fox pelt. As an example, at the post at Frobisher Bay in the 1938–39 trading year, 320 fox brought $2,700 while 1,229 sealskins brought less than $900.[102] Of course, sealskins were a product of food-getting pursuits and did not require the extra efforts connected with trapping. Nevertheless, the fox trapping that did occur produced the largest source of trade goods in Baffin Island, as elsewhere in the Central Arctic, during the bulk of the contract-traditional period.

In the Iglulik Eskimo area, more significant changes in economy and settlement patterns accompanied the adoption of the fur trade.[103] In parts of the area, especially around Iglulik Island itself, long periods of sedentary living had been reported as early as the Parry–Lyon sojourn in 1822–23. These periods were extended even further as subsistence practices were enhanced through the use of whaleboats, guns, and ammunition. Settlement came to be located at cache sites along the coasts for much of the year. Breathing-hole sealing, and the former large gatherings on the sea ice associated with the practice, became less frequent, and was gradually replaced by floe edge rifle hunting except in late winter, when stores from summer and autumn hunts ran low and ammunition became scarce. This periodic scarcity occurred for many years until a trading post was established on the island (1939–43, and from 1947 onward).[104]

Trapping around Iglulik itself was largely restricted to the vicinity of cache sites and short lines running along the coasts, largely reachable in a day's travel. For the Iglulik Eskimo regions of north Baffin Island, the long-established pattern of seasonal shifting of settlement was quickly replaced by more sedentary camps along coasts as subsistence was aided through improved technology. In the Pond Inlet region, in particular, longer traplines extended along coasts.[105]

In the southern part of Iglulik Eskimo country, around Repulse Bay, trapping was more extensively adopted and, in addition to coastal traplines, others ran some distance inland and across Melville Peninsula. While the use of wooden boats in sea hunting had for a time enhanced the economy, by the mid 1930s the walrus populations had declined to the extent that there was extensive emigration mainly to the north end of Melville Peninsula.[106] As elsewhere, in the Iglulik Eskimo area camps replaced nomadic bands that had occupied various sites during yearly cycles. The camps were set at favourable hunting sites along the coasts of the region.

In the Netsilik area there was quite some degree of regional variation in the economy as well as in the settlement patterns during the contact-traditional era. Balikci traced the course of change for Pelly Bay.[107] While the trade in arctic fox and trapping activity there never did reach the development found in most parts of the Central Arctic,[108] some trading took place so that, especially, the increased use of firearms brought on significant changes in economy and settlement patterns. By 1926 the range of movements during the yearly economic cycle had more than doubled:[109] with increased subsistence success more dogs could be supported, which increased general mobility during much of the year. Caribou hunting in particular was expanded through use of rifles, and for a time the hunt of this animal was extended well into the winter. However, sometime in the 1920s, caribou populations declined drastically and the range of movements decreased. Aboriginal times had a pattern of coalescence in most of each winter for the sealing season; now, with wider use of rifles, floe edge sealing largely replaced the breathing-hole method.[110] As the Pelly Bay mission was established, the majority of people spent more and more of each year nearby. Fishing gained in importance with the use of the now available nets, and dispersal to spring and summer camps was focused on good fishing locales.

For people living on the east shore of Boothia Peninsula there was little change in settlement practices from the time of John Ross's visits in the period 1829–33.[111] Each winter, large snowhouse encampments were formed on the ice of Thom Bay. With the use of rifles some hunting of both seals and polar bear did take place at the floe edge, but this involved only short trips by some of the younger men. Breathing-hole sealing in the immediate vicinity of the camp was the chief occupation. After the diminution of caribou herds on the peninsula, and with wide use of nets, the chief settlement in the warmer seasons centred at good fishing places, usually at the mouths of rivers. This picture of economy and settlement continued well into the 1960s, as will be seen when later periods of Netsilik history are discussed.

The people of King William Island found their most productive fishing at lakes in the interior of the island.[112] As in Netsilik regions to the east, the decline and, in this case, virtual disappearance of caribou forced considerable reliance on fishing, although hunting of seals from small wooden boats was also important in summer. Most of the year was spent in small camps set on the east coast of King William Island. As stores of fish and seal meat and fat ran low during the winter, hunters from two or more of these camps converged for winter sealing through the ice. People in both Boothia and King William Island trapped extensively. The chief concentration of traplines was across the neck of Boothia Peninsula, but long lines also ran along the east coast of the peninsula. After the establishment of Fort Ross in 1937 on Bellot Strait, lines also ran along the shores of Somerset and Prince of Wales Islands.

In the lower Back River–Chantrey Inlet region, shortly after the Fifth Thule Expedition passed through the country in 1923, the natives ceased moving to the sea ice for the winter sealing.[113] With the availability of nets traded from the post at Gjoa Haven, the Inuit of the region concentrated more and more on fishing. Virtual year-round settlement at chief fishing sites replaced the more nomadic existence of earlier times. With rifles and a steady supply of ammunition, long excursions were made for caribou. In the interior from the Back River westward in Netsilik country, both circular routes, denoting cache-oriented trapping, and traplines of some extent characterized trapping activity.[114] The people of Adelaide Peninsula also hunted caribou during summer and autumn from camps placed on the coast and inland. During much of each winter people in this region moved to the ice of Queen Maud Gulf, a practice that continued through much of the contact-traditional period.[115]

The most complete change in settlement patterns for the entire Central Arctic took place in the Copper Eskimo regions to the south of Queen Maud and Coronation Gulfs. With ready availability of rifles, ammunition, and nets for fishing, inland habitation became practical for longer periods of each year than had been the case earlier.[116] Camps were established within easy reach of the now expanded caches of caribou meat as well as, usually, near good fishing lakes or rivers.[117] It was now possible to delay the descent to the sea for sealing until as late as April in some years, as compared to December or early January in aboriginal times. The larger aggregations on the sea ice did, however, continue during much of the contact-traditional period, though usually for less time than before.[118] Summer locations varied for those who hunted seals in small wooden boats, now available from trading posts, and those who began caribou hunts in the interior earlier in summer. For this mainland Copper Eskimo region there were some long traplines, but a more common trapping orientation also obtained: "Trap lines ... were short, but they generally had as many traps as longer trap lines elsewhere, for with large caches of caribou meat in the vicinity, many foxes could be attracted and caught in the 50 or 75 traps around each cache."[119] Thus, it can be seen that for much of the interior south of Queen Maud and

Coronation Gulfs the trapping industry accommodated itself to the subsistence economy, rather than conversely.

With the cessation of caribou migration to Victoria Island, many of those Inuit who had lived on the western part of the island joined people on the mainland for caribou hunting, and in the winter on the sea ice for sealing. Others, however, remained on the island and adopted the most intensive trapping found in the Central Arctic. In order to devote as much time as possible to trapping in season, great efforts were made to store up meat and fat during the other periods of the year, by sealing from boats in summer and by surface sealing and using seal hooks at breathing holes in spring.[120] While women and children remained in camps, men spent considerable time during the trapping season covering extensive traplines both along the coast and deep into the interior of Victoria Island.[121]

Another area of extensive trapping was the southern interior west of Hudson Bay. A map in Freeman's *Inuit Land Use* shows a tortuous pattern of intersecting and overlapping traplines extending many miles inland from Eskimo Point and from various point in the interior.[122] The other pattern of trapping was also evident: "Traps were placed near the caches of caribou meat that had been made in the previous fall and in fox denning areas. People trapped out from their main camps. The distance travelled and the number of traps set varied greatly. Some trappers had lines as much as 100 miles long and they often spent two weeks or more checking their traps."[123] It may be, as in the case of Copper Eskimo trappers, that the presence of white trappers and the competition between the HBC and other firms, in this case Revillion Frères, stimulated this devotion to the trapping economy. Here, as elsewhere, these patterns of trapping had little direct influence on settlement patterns, as it was only the men who were involved in visiting traps.

For the northern interior west of Hudson Bay, including the regions centred around Baker Lake and the upper Back River, circular routes dominated over linear routes of any length, indicating cache-oriented trapping.[124] The settlement pattern was thus little altered from earlier times. However, the uncertainty of the main source of food, the caribou, ordained that in poor years, caches could be exhausted in late winter or before the spring migrations of caribou occurred. At such times fishing became a stop gag measure. Caribou Eskimo camp size varied, but in general was not larger than the maximum of fifty people noted earlier by Birket-Smith.[125] While trapping might be regarded as a casual occupation, given the usual restricted range covered from camps, records from the Baker Lake HBC post indicate that fox takes were similar to such posts as Eskimo Point, from which long traplines radiated.[126]

From this survey it should be clear that the extent of changes in settlement patterns that characterized the contact-traditional period varied widely from region to region. At one extreme were those Inuit living in eastern Baffin Island whose practices had undergone considerable change during the whaling period but showed continuity from that era. At the other extreme was the shift to a much greater inland orientation among groups of Copper Eskimo. The survey also suggests that it was the indirect rather than direct effects of the fur trade, and the associated trapping methods, that created settlement typical of the period. While trappers exploited their territory to varying degrees, and had correlative periods of absence from base camps, since it was only the men who trapped, base camp locations were not affected. In general, a greater degree of sedentariness prevailed as compared to earlier periods, when entire families shifted residences over yearly cycles.

Aside from the influence of the economy during the fur trade era, other agents of outside society helped change settlement practices. There were certain concentrations of people around missions at Igloolik, Chesterfield, and Pelly Bay, but these occurred only in the later phases of the fur trade era. The missions, or rather the process of conversion, affected the yearly cycle of settlement in that the Christian holidays of Christmas and Easter brought on temporary centralization of people around the centres of trading and worship. To a large extent these gatherings replaced in form and function the earlier aggregations that had occurred at certain phases of the traditional yearly cycles, when economic advantage could be found in congregating, or during periods of living on cached meat. Gatherings of Inuit around whaling ships or stations had also provided such occasions. As in these former cases, aggregation at the mission–trading centres were occasions for reunion of friends and relatives.

With the RCMP, except for brief meetings when people visited or gathered at the points of trade where there were also police detachments, most contacts were during patrols when camps were visited. While some of these visits concerned the breaching of southern Canadian laws, they were often devoted to administering aid in health and welfare and to census taking, and had little to do with law enforcement. I have noted that settlement was, in general, more sedentary during the contact-traditional period than in previous times, but it should also be appreciated that, except for brief visits to the points of trade, interaction was mainly within the Inuit community. That is, the hunting-trapping base camp was all-native in character. Usually only one or two families lived at the posts, those of post servants of trading firms, or in cases where there was a police detachment, native Special Constables.

I have tried to show the extent to which the fur trade affected the location and duration of settlement. In terms of size, a degree of continuity existed during the fur trade era from earlier eras. The all-native hunting-trapping base camps resembled most closely the more dispersed phases of the yearly settlement cycle of aboriginal times. For most of each year the population was spread into units of from one to six families, though there were the exceptions of larger units, especially on seasonal bases. In those regions where breathing-hole sealing villages still formed, larger gatherings were in evidence.

Kinship factors continued to be the primary means of group formation. They were supplemented by a series of voluntary associations, which in the Copper Eskimo area were the chief integrating means. In most regions of the Central Arctic, with the exception again of the Copper Eskimo area, the *Isumataaq* or *Ihumataaq* continued, as before, to coordinate activities. The very dispersal of settlement served to maintain a large degree of autonomy in the base camps. While missionaries strived to influence the moral life of the Inuit, and the RCMP to enforce the legal strictures of southern Canada, the greatest degree of control was in the hands of the local traders. They determined not only the inventory of goods available for trade but, from their headquarters in Winnipeg, both the price of furs and the trade goods themselves. The trader also controlled extension of credit and, at places without an RCMP detachment, issuances of government-derived relief.

It has been possible to point to the advent of the contact-traditional period at individual locations according to the dates that fur trading posts were established, but the decline of that orientation was a process that in most cases extended over a number of years, and was strongly influenced by slowly moving policy changes.

CHAPTER TWO

The Policy of Dispersal

The chief agencies that encouraged and sustained dispersal of Inuit settlement in the Northwest Territories were the trading companies, especially the Hudson's Bay Company, and certain branches or departments of the Canadian federal government. After the trade in arctic fox was fully established in 1910–23, expansion was rapid. By the period of 1920–24 there were 74 posts, with 34 of them belonging to the HBC in the Mackenzie, Keewatin, and Eastern Arctic Districts together.[1] By 1925–29 there were in these districts 117 posts, with the HBC operating 51 of them. Although the police established three posts in those areas as early as 1903, in 1924 there were only seven detachments scattered throughout the Canadian Arctic.[2]

While the RCMP remained the resident representatives of the government in the north, growth of a central agency to administer Canadian Arctic affairs proceeded slowly. In 1905 the Northwest Territories Act provided for a commissioner and a Council of the Northwest Territories, but it was only in 1921 under Commissioner W.W. Cory that the council was actually formed.[3] Six members included, besides the commissioner, the assistant deputy commissioner of Indian Affairs; the commissioner of Crown Lands and the RCMP; the deputy minister of the Department of Mines; the superintendent of Mining Lands and Yukon Branch; and the chief mining inspector of that branch, then O.S. Finnie. In 1923, the Northwest Territories and Yukon Branch was formed under the directorship of Finnie, who continued as a member of the council.[4]

Early meetings of the council dealt with such matters as issuing hunting and trapping licences to white residents of the Territories, and reporting on game and fur takes and on drilling operations.[5] A third meeting held in 1924, set aside six game preserves to be used only by "natives and half-breeds."[6]

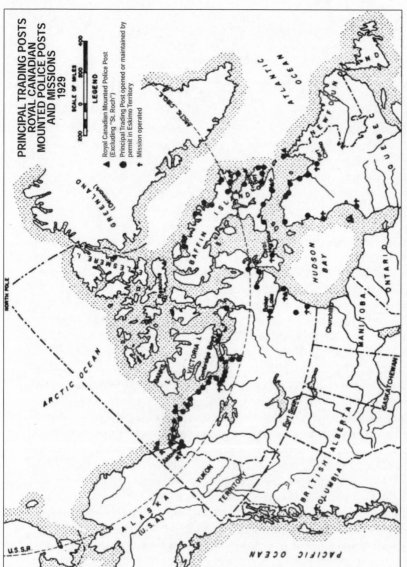

Map 3 Principal trading posts, Royal Canadian Mounted Police posts and missions, 1929.
From Jenness, *Eskimo Administration 2.*

THE HUDSON'S BAY COMPANY, THE GOVERNMENT, AND POPULATION DISPERSAL

In 1924 various complaints about the operations of the HBC reached Ottawa. A number of the complaints revolved around events taking place in the extreme western part of the Northwest Territories, away from the regions of concern here, but others are more relevant.[7] Copies of correspondence from the RCMP regarding these matters were passed to Commissioner Cory, who wrote to Edward Fitzgerald, chairman of the HBC's Canadian Committee, summarizing these complaints. Cory asserted that not only could the department set aside areas where trading posts would not be allowed but that, as in the existing cases of Alaska and Greenland, the government itself could conduct posts.[8]

Shortly afterwards, L.T. Burwash of the Northwest Territories and Yukon Branch submitted a report to Finnie that stirred up conflict between the HBC and Finnie's branch.[9] The aim of Burwash's trip to the eastern Arctic had been primarily to assess game conditions, but part of his report commented on the relations of the HBC with the Inuit. Among his criticisms was the accusation that the HBC moved Inuit from good hunting localities to places that were less well endowed with game but more favourable to trapping. Burwash also charged that the HBC encouraged aggregations around posts, a condition that he saw as detrimental to the hunting economy. These complaints, together with a number of others, were compiled by Finnie, who composed a "Synopsis of Charges made against employees of the Hudson's Bay Company in their dealings with the natives of the Far North, and in some instances of their dealings on the wild life."[10] After circulating among various branches and departments of the government, and with some modifications, the report was cleared by Commissioner Cory and sent to the HBC's Canadian headquarters in Winnipeg.

On 10 April 1925 Chairman Fitzgerald sent a thirteen-page reply that, among other matters, challenged the accusation that the company moved people to poor hunting areas. He wrote, "The Company does not compel the Eskimos to move to new areas in Baffinland supposed to contain fur, but where food is absent. Food for the natives is the first essential of a fur trading post. Where there is a good supply of seal and caribou there is always a supply of fox fur ... The natives themselves suggest to the Company areas which they themselves consider good for food and for fur to which they are anxious to go." On the question of the food supply itself, Fitzgerald added: "Every effort is made to keep the Eskimo to his original habits and mode of life. Foods, such as flour, biscuits, tea and molasses, are imported but only in limited quantities and at the majority of Posts they are not regarded as necessities for the natives. He is a meat eater and as long as meat can be had the purchase of imported food is discouraged as much as possible." Furthermore, "[a]s to keeping large numbers of natives at or near the Post the Company's greatest difficulty at the opening of posts in Baffinland has been to break the natives of this habit, developed by the whalers of congregating in large camps." Fitzgerald also presented the provision of hunting equipment for the Inuit as a company practice. Perhaps as a response to Cory's threat of a government-operated fur trade, he cited the company's role in providing medical services, employment, extension of credit, and relief. He also supplied biographical sketches of some employees who had been criticized, and dealt with accusations of unfair trading practices.[11]

The Hudson's Bay Company was the chief force behind relocation in the period before the 1950s. In view of the question of volition versus compulsion in resettlement in the Canadian Arctic,[12] it is well to cite material from HBC correspondence in this regard.[13] An early example of movement of Inuit in the eastern Central Arctic came in 1923 (after a failed attempt in the previous year), from places in southern Baffin Island to the Clyde River region, which was regarded as being previously uninhabited.[14] It is possible that both migration and relocation, as defined here, were involved in movements of people in this case: it is clear from internal company correspondence that people were moved from the south,[15] while others may have migrated from the north at about the same time, when the post was established at Clyde in 1923. It is impossible now to judge to what extent consultation was carried out with those Inuit involved in relocation in this case. The following statement from the HBC's representative for the eastern Arctic (Ungava District) to its fur trade commissioner tends to contradict Fitzgerald's depiction of volition in such moves: "We do not expect to find everything in that country so nearly in order that we can sit down at once and start trading – if sufficient Eskimos are not where we may want them, we transfer them from somewhere else."[16] While the above statement was applied specifically to the failed establishment of the Pond Inlet and Clyde River posts in 1922, we can suppose that such a policy was applied elsewhere. Another aspect of the establishment of the Clyde River post and the simultaneous movement of people in 1923 is that no approach was made to the government for permission either for operating the post or to transfer natives. Rather, internal HBC correspondence reveals that only permission from company headquarters in London was sought.

There is, then, evidence that Inuit participation in moving from habitual ranges may not have always been voluntary. Some references in journals, however, support Fitzgerald's contention that the company discouraged aggregation around their posts. From the post at Perry River for the spring of 1927: "The hospitality the natives are receiving at the post is gradually getting itself advertised, however, it has also the drawback that once they have tasted it, it seems very hard to get rid of them again."[17] From the post on King William Island in the spring of 1928: "15th of May 'a full settlement and no sign of them pulling out yet' ... 18 May, 'impossible to get natives out' ... 22 May, 'Natives still around, about 14 families.' ... 27 May, '12 families still remain' ... 3 June, 'The large number of natives still remaining in the settlement doing nothing are a source of much annoyance' ... 6 June, 'Still about 15 families camped in the settlement, they have no inclination to hunt or exert themselves but are content to sit around in a state of destitution.'"[18] And from Fort Brabant on Victoria Island for November 1928: "Having a hard time explaining to the natives that they can stay here no longer. I only intend to keep one man and woman."[19] It should be noted that these cases come from an early period and at places where posts had been only recently established – four years in the case of King William Island and Fort Brabant, and only one year at Perry River.[20] Considering the dearth of similar complaints for later years in the post journals, it seems that traders became more successful in discouraging such gatherings. One circumstance, however, did lead the company to encourage some aggregation of people near their posts, according to the comments of the trader at Arctic Bay in his annual report for the trading year 1941–42: "These natives are required annually to work cargo when the ship arrives, and hunt from the post for a few weeks every year. With such a short season of open water it is too bad that these natives have to spend so much time around the post, as it spoils their sealing to some extent which in turn reacts on their winter trapping."[21] This comment is noteworthy, as well, in the clear connection with the ideal yearly economic pattern endorsed by the HBC, that is, the desirability of stockpiling meat during the months when trapping was not carried out, so that more time and energy would be devoted to trapping during season.

As missionaries moved into the Central Arctic they were to be accused by the traders of encouraging clustering of people around their missions. There is some basis for such accusations, since Christmas and Easter became important occasions for gatherings at missions, which were usually sited at the trading posts. Easter often corresponded with the end of the trapping season, when trading peaked. At any rate, as we have seen, periodic coalescence had been customary during the more nomadic phases of Inuit history and served important social and ceremonial functions, some of which continued into the contact-traditional period.

Discouraging aggregation at trading centres was part and parcel of the underlying philosophy of preservationism that dominated these times. This philosophy was conceived in terms of benevolence by both the trading companies and the Canadian government, but as will be explored later, there were practical and, especially, economic motivations at its base.

By the time in the 1920s when relations between the HBC and the government were being clarified, the HBC had acquired considerable influence in the north. This influence was largely due to the late appearance of a central agency to exert control over the Northwest Territories. With the objective of challenging this dominance doubtlessly in mind, Finnie took a strict position regarding the newly established game preserves. Ultimately, this position and later actions by the government were to threaten Inuit settlement patterns, especially in terms of movement of people from normal hunting and trapping ranges.

In a letter to Commissioner Cory, Finnie called for the government to assert control over hunting and trading in the preserves and to expand the then existing Back River Preserve, which would inevitably lead to the closure of the post on King William Island.[22] His suggestion that the natives of the area could trade instead at Kent Peninsula to the west, or at Repulse Bay to the southeast, meant journeys of up to 250 miles, or actual migration from habitual hunting ranges. Such a proposal showed Finnie's lack of knowledge of Arctic conditions. He also proposed that approval from the Advisory Board on Wild Life Protection should be required for new posts, pointing to a concern for wildlife preservation that was to become one of the factors in locations of posts.

Cory's position regarding the preserves was less extreme than Finnie's, for he responded that "it is not the present intention to prevent the Hudson's Bay Company maintaining posts already established, even although they may be in the Game Preserves."[23] Accordingly, Finnie had to amend the statement he was preparing to send to the HBC to read "no *more* posts were to be allowed in any Native preserve."[24]

Correspondence regarding openings and closures of trading posts ensued between Ottawa and Winnipeg. Eventually, a meeting was held between the company's fur trade commissioner and members of the Wild Life Advisory Board.[25] The results of the discussions led to greatly increased governmental control over the HBC and other trading company firms in the Arctic.

Expansion of the Back River Preserve to the Arctic Islands Preserve in 1926, as well as the establishment of the Thelon Game Preserve in the following year, followed upon these discussions.[26] The 1924 resolutions of the Northwest Territories Council regarding the preserves had stated that (1) "no persons other than Indians, Eskimos or halfbreeds" should be allowed to "travel, trade or traffic in game preserves," and (2) "no trading post should be established or maintained without the permission of the Commissioner."[27] Such measures ensured the use of game and fur resources by natives or part natives, but at the same time, if carried out, removed them from reasonable access to trading for items that by then were regarded as necessities.

Despite these probably unrecognized implications, and Cory's more moderate view on the matter of trading posts, plans were set in motion to close or relocate eight to ten posts, "as they are in or adjacent to areas set aside as native hunting and trapping preserves."[28] The King William Island and Cambridge Bay posts were later allowed to remain open,[29] even though they lay within the Arctic Islands Preserve, but others were closed and new ones prevented from opening.

An example of the consequences of removing posts from traditional Inuit hunting grounds can be seen in the case of the Arctic Bay post, which was closed by the government after only two years of operation.[30] Since removal of the post meant longer distances to trading centres, subsequent hardship, including actual starvation, in that region has been attributed to the post's closure. The government thus established its control over locations of trading centres during the 1920s, but over the following decade, a gradual liberalization of policy was seen. Eventually, nearly all of the posts that had been closed according to the strictures regarding preserves were reopened or re-established at points close to the original sites. It would appear that Ottawa had assumed the position that posts should be located in regions that were in or near traditional Inuit ranges of movement. As we will see, other factors were also involved in post closures that resulted in either increased travel for trade or actual migrations of people.

Accommodation between the HBC and the government, as represented by the Northwest Territories Council, came about by the early 1930s largely through governmental concern for austerity brought on by the Great Depression, and partly through the ascendency of Roy A. Gibson as deputy commissioner of the Northwest Territories after the departure of Finnie and Cory in 1931.[31] An example of cooperation and confluence of goals between the government and the HBC can be seen in the transference of Inuit beginning in 1934.[32] During the 1920s the government had established RCMP detachments on Ellesmere Island and at Dundas Harbour on Devon Island.[33] The detachment at Dundas Harbour was removed in 1933, apparently as part of the expression of the austerity policies of the time.[34] With continued concern for sovereignty, during the following winter the Department of the Interior actually invited the HBC to establish a post on Devon Island. The offer was accepted and a permit granted. In granting this permit, the deputy minister of the department wrote on 15 March 1934 to Winnipeg with the stipulation that the HBC would have to "assume full responsibility for the welfare and maintenance of the said natives" who were to be transferred to the region as the post was opened. He wrote further that "in the event of the Company withdrawing from Devon Island the Company agrees to return the natives to their homes at its own expense or to transfer them to such other trapping grounds as may be designated by the Department."[35]

Indeed, the move was in the nature of an experiment conducted by the government and phrased in terms of moving Inuit as part of "a general plan of northern migration and settlement where game is abundant." Consequently, four families were brought from Cape Dorset, three from Pangnirtung, and four from Pond Inlet – a total of fifty-two people.[36] It is interesting to note that in 1923 internal HBC correspondence cited an RCMP report on Devon and Ellesmere Islands that indicated "a good report of white and blue fox." This circumstance occasioned the remark in the correspondence that "it may well to bear this information in mind, for, at some future date, we may consider it advisable to remove natives there from our more southern posts."[37] This removal plan and its execution is remarkable not only because it represented a coincidence of aims between the HBC and the government but also because it represented one of the first departures from the policy of forbidding posts on the Arctic Islands.

Hunting conditions on Devon Island proved unfavourable for the relocated people and they were removed to Admiralty Inlet.[38] This movement lay within the directives laid down by the deputy minister. Also consistent with these directives was the return of two families to the Pangnirtung district.[39] Some of the people involved in the original transference from other parts of Baffin Island now moved to Somerset Island, where they were joined by North Baffinlanders who had previously traded at Port Leopold at the north end of that island. That post had been closed during the 1920s when the policy of restricting posts on the islands was in full force. Both groups were now moved to the Bellot Strait region at the south end of the island "where they say they are quite content to remain." Later, in 1937, Fort Ross was founded there as a trading station for these immigrants.[40] This post had been established with the precondition, reported in government records, that a total of about 350 people now living on Prince of Wales and Somerset Islands and northern Boothia Peninsula had no place to trade other than King William Island,[41] some distance to the south.

It is evident as well that people of the Netsilik group had migrated to the region of northern Boothia and Somerset and Prince of Wales Islands, since the total estimate of 300 to 400 people for those regions at the time of the founding of Fort Ross far exceeds the number of immigrants from Baffin Island.[42] The maps in Freeman's *Inuit Land Use* show this general region as being hunted over for caribou, musk oxen, polar bear, and sea mammals at this period.

The founding of Fort Ross is an example of where the HBC sought to exploit the fur resources of a region that had already been used as hunting grounds by some Inuit from nearby regions. It also involved relocation of people from southern Baffin Island and Pond Inlet and had stipulated return of the people if they so desired.[43] This stipulation was not honoured. Internal correspondence in HBC files indicates that in January 1943, twenty-four of the Dorset peoples who had been trading at Fort Ross wanted to be moved to Lake Harbour.[44] The manager of the eastern Arctic (Ungava District) wrote to the manager of the Fur Trade Department that "in 1941 a Peterhead boat had been sold to Dorset people in order to allow them to return home via Fury and Hecla Strait" and "with this arrangement we thought to free ourselves of the obligation of carrying them on the Nascopie."[45] The arrangement was entirely impractical, given that the strait had never been navigated by ship.

Ice conditions hampered the operation of the Fort Ross post and it was closed in 1943–44 due to failure of supply. It reopened again until 1948, when it was abandoned.[46] This closure meant for difficulties for those natives hunting and trapping in the surrounding region. Further, internal HBC correspondence indicates that in November 1947, when closure of Ross was being planned, there were seventeen adults and twenty children of the Dorset group in the region. "Only one was actually to return to Dorset" while the others "should go to Spence Bay or Arctic Bay regions."[47] No transportation was provided for them, and some of the people moved to the coasts of Boothia Peninsula. They, as well as those who stayed north, all began to trade at Spence Bay.

Meanwhile, further relocations and migrations had continued to Clyde River. Ralph Parsons, then the HBC's fur trade commissioner, wrote to Roy A. Gibson on 24 February 1940 requesting permission for movement of people from Frobisher Bay.[48] Permission was granted,[49] "on the understanding that the Eskimos affected are satisfied, and that the Company assumes full responsibility for their maintenance. Should these Eskimos desire to return to Frobisher Bay it is assumed that the same transportation facilities will be provided."[50] There was some uncertainty within the HBC management as to whether such responsibility should be assumed,[51] which suggests that some moves to Clyde River, and perhaps to other destinations, were still being carried out without the government's permission. Company officials eventually agreed to accept the responsibilities outlined by Gibson.

Nevertheless, the manager of the Ungava District wrote to the manager of the Fur Trade Department that "fundamentally, of course, the proposed transfer of natives from Frobisher Bay and Lake Harbour to Clyde is not desirable from the food supply point of view."[52] It is clear that here, and perhaps in other casess, the HBC's motivation for relocation was the fur trade. On the other hand, at this time the government conceived of relocations in terms of redistributing the population for subsistence advantages. In the same company correspondence there is reference to other correspondence from Gibson regarding his concern for "thinning out of the population of New Quebec by transfer to the Northwest Territories."[53] It was indicated that the HBC had in 1941 moved people "from Sugluk to Southampton Island" and that "in 1942 about a dozen natives from Port Burwell and a couple from Sugluk" were moved to the island in accordance with the concern of Gibson. "... [a] process that must be gradually and cautiously undertaken."[54]

As it was, however, relocation to Southampton Island already had a history of over two decades, most of which movement appears to have been made without seeking the government's permission. On the basis of the following description by Mathiassen, it appears that the repopulation of Southampton Island involved both migration as conceived here and a very early example of relocation. Writing in the 1920s, he notes: "*Southampton Island* is a recent acquisition of the Aivilik Eskimos but nevertheless is now their most important possession. Until 1902 it was inhabited by the Sadlermiut, who were very unfriendly towards the Aiviliks with whom they did not have very much intercourse until the later years. It seems, however, that even before then the Aiviliks visited the northern part of the island fairly frequently, from which the Sadlermiut had disappeared ... After the Sadlermiut had died off in 1902–03 a number of Aiviliks Eskimos settled on the island, which is a splendid hunting district."[55] At the time of Mathiassen's visit to the island in 1922–23 both South Bay and Duke of York Bay at the north end of the island were favourite places of habitation, but much of the interior was also hunted over by the Aiviliks. While the actual date of first occupation by the Aivilingmiut from the Repulse Bay region is uncertain, a relocation engineered by the HBC followed in 1924, when people who had been previously moved to Coats Island in 1918 were moved to the south shore of the island with the shifting of the trading post there to Coral Harbour.[56]

Manning reports that there was circulation of people during the 1920s and 1930s between Southampton Island and those points to the east that the immigrants came from.[57] He gives a population of 120 on the island for 1938, one-third of whom he estimates as being "Oko-miut," or people from these eastern points. However, this immigration and possible return is not mentioned in government archives, and probably did not involve seeking permission from the government as would be the case in the 1940s.[58]

Southampton Island became the site of a U.S. military base in 1942.[59] During the summer of that year, the next wave of immigrants from the east arrived and began to cluster around the post at Coral Harbour.[60] The HBC manager complained that "there is a tendency to hang around the post and the Construction Camp, chief attraction being, we believe, the mess hall and moving pictures at the Camp."[61] However, this in-gathering brought on by the presence of the military base was apparently short-lived, for by January of 1943 the HBC manager indicated "all natives who were transferred from other sections of the country to Southampton Island are distributed amongst the Native camps."[62]

While the air base represented a disruption in settlement and contributed to habitation being largely confined to the south coast and capes of the island, this region had been the focus of population during both the Sadlirmiut occupation and by the Aivilingmiut who had come later. Actual concentration of people at Coral Harbour was to be a product of conditions in later years. The Southampton example does, however, introduce the concept of contraction, which was to become a factor in settlement at other places, and which was at odds with the Policy of Dispersal.

Another locale of World War II activity was at Frobisher Bay, which was to become the largest settlement in the Central Arctic during the decade of the fifties. A 1943 RCMP report indicated that while fifty-three Inuit were employed in the construction of the U.S. Army weather station, after the construction was completed only one native family was employed.[63] Further success was experienced in discouraging people from "hanging around" the base. Indeed, at war's end, in May 1945, an RCMP patrol reported that they had visited the seven Eskimo camps "that comprise the total population of Frobisher Bay natives."[64] For the most part this dispersal of population persisted well into the 1950s, while gatherings during the summer months for temporary employment became an annual pattern for much of the local population.

I have emphasized to perhaps too great an extent the instances of relocation, as defined here, on the basis of its predominance in much of the correspondence of 1930s and early 1940s in government and HBC records. In succeeding chapters, as I consider local settlement situations, I try to assess the relative importance of relocation as opposed to migration in the movements of Inuit in the Central Arctic. For the period before about 1940 when the HBC moved people, largely without assent from the federal government, it is difficult to sort out the degree to which each of these two factors were involved in specific movements. It would be remarkable, however, if more than one-quarter of the total population of the eastern Central Arctic was involved in relocation movements. For the regions of Melville Peninsula, western Hudson Bay, and the Arctic coast and adjacent insular regions west of Melville Peninsula, there is no evidence of relocations. As indicated above, the situation for the Somerset Island–northern Boothia Peninsula region was a complex of both migration and relocation. The relocations that were to take place in the Keewatin began only in the late 1950s.

THE NEGLECTED PEOPLE AND THE SEEDS OF SOCIAL CONSCIOUSNESS

I have elsewhere characterized the contact-traditional era as one of generally enhanced economic conditions. Changes in material conditions were cyclical, rather than steadily declining, as has sometimes been posed.[65] It was a period of stability in several aspects of society and culture, but welfare, health care, and education stagnated. Some very minimal provisions for welfare had early been in effect. Government relief was ideally "supplied by the local trader of the Hudson's Bay Company on order from the R.C. M. Police."[66] Of course, this system could operate only in those few places where police detachments were on the scene. More often than not, the traders issued relief supplies without such consultation. Traders also issued credit, another form of rudimentary welfare. That relief, when issued by traders, comprised lesser amounts than credit can be seen in some examples. At Lake Harbour for the year 1939–40, $188.50 was issued in relief as compared to $1,087 being advanced as credit.[67] At Cape Dorset for 1940–41, $213.27 was given in relief and $1,536 as credit.[68] At Arctic Bay in 1939–40 no relief was issued, but $731 was extended on credit.[69] In connection with the meagre relief issuances at Frobisher Bay in the year 1939–40, the HBC manager commented: "It will be seen ... that a firm hand has been kept on issuing of relief, and it is worthy of note although native earnings were less than half of that of the previous year, the destitute account is greatly reduced this outfit."[70] As issued by the HBC, relief usually comprised food and clothing, while credit consisted of rifles, ammunition, fish nets, traps, and other equipment directly related to economic pursuits. There was a concerted effort to stimulate hunting rather than increase dependence on store food. This position was consistent with maintaining a hunting-trapping economy and the dispersed settlement that at that time was associated with these pursuits.

While both relief and credit were extended to the Inuit by the HBC at times of visits to posts, the police also provided relief during the course of their patrols from detachment bases. The amount of relief supplies that could be carried on dogsled patrols was limited by the need to carry personal equipment and supplies, as well as dog feed. Nevertheless, the aid that could be supplied could provide the margin between life and death, or at least extreme conditions of want, in the dispersed camps. An example of sled patrol issuances can be drawn from the account of a patrol from Baker Lake in April and May of 1931.[71] At a camp on the Kazan River where several families were "more or less in a starving state" the following supplies were left: 100 pounds of flour, 50 pounds of biscuits, 5 pounds of lard, 4 pounds of baking powder, 2 gallons of coal oil, 5 pounds of tea. At times the amounts required for relief by the police were greater than those issued by the local HBC trader. For instance, in 1939 the destitute issuances of the RCMP detachment at Baker Lake totalled $335.49 and the police report stated that "over half" of this amount was given to two families that were "permanently destitute" and "were unable to get any credit from the trading company and had no fur with which to get on credit to purchase the necessary supplies."[72] It is virtually impossible to know how widespread was this close grip on HBC issuances, but it is clear that control was left in the hands of the trader, except in such cases as the above where police were present.

While relief issuances were to be given under hardship conditions, social legislation assistance was designed to provide a basis for steady support, and to be distributed at regular intervals without regard for local circumstances. The Old Age Pension Act was passed in 1927 and was to include people of the Northwest Territories as well as the provinces.[73] The act provided for pensions not to exceed $240 annually per pensioner. However, even this minimal sum did not reach the Inuit for many years after the act was passed. In 1929 only one such pensioner was paid in the Territories for a total of $168[74] and as late as 1939 there were only seven recipients, who were paid a total of $1,753.13.[75] While the act was amended in 1937 to include the blind, there is no indication that any payments reached the Inuit or other remote groups of native people in the Territories.[76] It was only with the Family Allowances Act of 1944, or rather, sometime later, when it was actually substantially implemented in the Canadian Arctic, that significant social legislation support came to the Inuit.

Concern with health and health care was, as with welfare, only rudimentarily developed before the end of World War II. The introduction of disease, and its sometimes disastrous effects, happened early in contact history in the Central Arctic. Even though contacts with whites continued on a low level throughout the contact-traditional phase of history, they were sufficient to bring about a number of epidemics. The HBC records for the post at Bathurst Inlet for 1928 reveal the effects of an epidemic of undiagnosed disease: "June 13, Qaniak's wife died ... June 23, Nakanyak's wife died, also Morphayak ... July 13, Haugak and Umiligoitok died, many sick ... July 20, Talgnaluk died, other deaths ... [And for early August] ... much sickness reported among natives. Annie, Wiznik's wife died ... August 18, everyone sick ... August 22, Heak died (ill long), Paneguik had died also ... August 30, Anrowiuk died, Nethin's wife died ... [for early September] ... Tamahungnak and boy report that Kalhook and Nalugak had died."[77] In 1928 an influenza epidemic "killed half the population of Bernard Harbour."[78] At Coppermine tuberculosis was reported in epidemic proportions for the district in the period 1930–31, followed in 1935 by a measles epidemic; later, a number of other epidemics plagued the Copper Eskimo regions.[79] A report from the HBC manager at the King William Island post for 1927 indicates a problem that continued to occur in the Central Arctic. The rival Canalaska schooner *Nigalik* was in port from the 28th to the 30th of September. By 11 October the manager reported "natives all afflicted with colds and influenza."[80] Indeed the yearly visits of supply ships often brought minor, and in some cases major, sicknesses. For the east Central Arctic a formidable series of epidemics included spinal meningitis, high incidences of venereal disease and tuberculosis, and, later, polio. It was reported that between 1941 and 1944, 304 deaths occurred due to epidemics in the Eastern Arctic.[81]

One effect of the epidemics was the tendency of the Inuit to cluster together, most often at the points of trade, when illnesses struck. Also as early as 1936 concern was expressed about natives who were employed at settlements being exposed to infection of every kind. It was felt that even the small number of people who lived at the settlements at this time "would be better off in their own camps ... living their own life ... [they] would not be so apt to get infection as when they are employed around a post."[82] Thus scattered settlement gained support from arguments concerning health.

Much of the care for the sick had to be carried out by the local whites of the small settlements. The RCMP in particular, on their frequent patrols to the camps, had to serve in a medical capacity. One report from the Cumberland Gulf detachment for 30 April 1928 gives some indication of the state of health and treatment in the outlying areas. "There are always sick at every camp and we do what we can for them. Undoubtedly we often give at least relief."[83] Hudson's Bay Company managers also had to serve as lay medics, as did local missionaries. The two major churches provided the most important medical care. Both the Catholics (1925) and the Anglicans (1926) had built hospitals at Aklavik, and for many years the only other hospitals in Arctic Canada were at Pangnirtung, founded by the Anglicans (1930), and at Chesterfield by the Catholics (1929). Government involvement included the brief experience of Dr R.D. Martin in Coppermine in 1929–30.[84] His departure and the failure to continue operations there appears to have been a direct response to the austerity policies of the Depression era. As well, the yearly visits of the Eastern Arctic Patrol vessels beginning in 1922 carried at least one physician.[85] They could treat certain diseases during the short stops made in each port, and organize transport of patients to hospitals in southern Canada. All in all, no serious response to the health conditions of Canada's Inuit came until the very end of World War II.

The chief effect on settlement resulting from this dearth of medical facilities in the Arctic was that a significant number of family members were moved to hospitals in the south, and those families whose heads were absent tended to cluster as welfare cases around posts. Indeed, such people, together with other destitutes, formed the nucleus of residents around posts and constituted a slow beginning to the process of centralization. At the two places in the Central Arctic with hospitals this sort of community was more highly developed. A medical report from Pangnirtung stated: "This institution like that operated at Chesterfield ... is serving a very useful purpose as it enables the natives who are able to hunt and trap to carry on their normal occupations without being handicapped in looking after their aged, sick or crippled relatives who are cared for in the home."[86] In the long run these arrangements related to health problems did not in themselves affect overall dispersal of populations.

A factor that in later years provided an incentive for in-gathering was housing. For many years the choices of habitation were snowhouses, tents, sod and canvas shelters, and, at places where wood could be obtained, scrap lumber "shacks." One of the common beliefs of administrators at this time was that traditional native dwellings, especially snowhouses, were superior to these latter shelters in terms of cleanliness, health, and comfort. Actually support for the Policy of Dispersal underlay this position: "All these people, were they in their own camps living their own life, would not be so apt to get infection as when they are employed around a post."[87]

Correspondence in 1942–43 between Deputy Commissioner Gibson and H.V. Chesshire, manager of the HBC's fur trade department, clearly states the position of the government in this period regarding housing and its relationship to settlement practices. In response to an unconfirmed report that the HBC was supplying wooden houses at Cape Dorset, Gibson wrote: "As you know it has been our policy to keep the natives in their natural environment in so far as it is possible to do so. However, this cannot be done if immobile buildings are provided for their use. Experience has shown elsewhere in the Territories ... that Eskimos confined to fixed positions soon lose their initiative. Their health likewise deteriorates, because the matter of heating and sanitation in wooden houses is not understood."[88] This statement contains two misconceptions current at the time. First, Inuit settlement was still being characterized as "nomadic," whereas the semi-permanent hunting-trapping base camp had long been the typical residential situation. The statement also assumed that the native housing in the outlying camps was well heated and free from the filth with which disease is associated. Anyone who has lived in such camps, and knows the actual conditions that existed, could dispute these positive associations. Such attitudes are another example of the philosophy of preservationism that was an important element in the Policy of Dispersal.

At the time of this correspondence Chesshire disclaimed any HBC involvement in the matter of importing wooden houses, blaming their appearance at Dorset on the opposition, the Baffin Trading Company. In internal correspondence of 1946 he expressed a different view: "We cannot do other than expect that the Eskimos as they become prosperous will want to live in wooden houses."[89] It is possible that the HBC saw economic advantage in eventually supplying material for the houses. However, the company was to have little involvement in the construction programs of the 1960s, and never did they carry any large inventory of building materials for their northern posts.

Another fear of those who favoured dispersal of settlement was that building schools in the various centres would encourage clustering of populations. Conception of the educational needs of Inuit youth was poorly developed before 1950. By 1944 there was only one day school in the Central Arctic, at Pangnirtung, and otherwise classes were casually arranged by the missions "during such times as the natives were within the settlements."[90] The nature of population dispersal, of course, conspired against any serious attempts at education in the Central Arctic. There was yet in the 1940s no plan for movement of people from scattered settlement sites in order to make education more available to the youth. Residential schools were still only on the horizon. As with health care, education was largely left to the churches. It was in 1947 that the government took over control of education on a formal level and three years after that before school construction was begun.

The most important step made to enhance the welfare of the Inuit before the 1950s was the implementation of the Family Allowances Act of 1944 in the Canadian Arctic. I shall deal with the particulars of the act as it applied to the Central Arctic in a later chapter, but with respect to the conditions of settlement as they existed in the 1940s, reference to the discussion of allowances in the minutes of the 187th meeting of the Northwest Territories Council, held 20 January 1949, is appropriate: "In the past, some few families at various settlements have been inclined to rely to too great an extent upon the credits available – remaining in the vicinity of the post rather than proceeding to the hunting and trapping ground during the winter months. Such, however, have been minimal in number and it is likely that this problem will be overcome now that the Royal Canadian Mounted Police have been given unequivocal authority to deal with this."[91] This statement was to be prophetic for the coming decade, for the pressures to disperse settlement continued for the most part, not only from the RCMP, but also from other governmental representatives and the HBC throughout the 1950s. Special circumstances in some locales did begin to work against this policy. As will be shown in later chapters, the iron hand by which the allowances were controlled played an important role in maintaining dispersed settlement. Meanwhile, an evolution of policy was taking place in Ottawa that was to eventually spell the demise of the Policy of Dispersal.

SHIFTING POLICIES IN THE 1950S

Late in 1949 James Cantley was appointed member of the Arctic Service Section of Northern Administration.[92] He had been just previously with the Baffin Trading Company, but before that had also worked for the HBC, a connection that was to influence his role in policy-making in the Arctic. Gibson was instrumental in this appointment just before his retirement, and the close relationship that Gibson had had with the HBC would have been expanded considerably if some of Cantley's recommendations had been followed.

Indications of Cantley's position came early in 1950, when in examining depressed conditions at Aklavik he recommended that the operations of independent traders in the region be shut down and trade concentrated in the hands of the HBC.[93] There is no indication that senior administrators ever seriously considered this possibility, but they did refer to a lengthy report that Cantley submitted in 1950 entitled "Survey of Economic Conditions Among the Eskimos of the Canadian Arctic." In this report, he reviewed something of Eskimo history and compared conditions in Alaska and Greenland with those in Canada. The chief recommendation that he made was that a closer relationship should be developed between the government and the Hudson's Bay Company. He submitted that such a relationship would be all to the advantage of the government as an alternative to any government-run trading industry. In keeping with this position, he recommended that the administration of family allowances and other forms of welfare should be taken from the RCMP and given to the company.[94] His views of the Inuit were clear: "the actual needs as opposed to the desires – of the average Eskimo are small, generally as long as he can obtain a minimum of food, clothing and shelter without exertion on his part he will be satisfied. It is therefore easy for him to adapt himself to a relief economy and beg rather than work for a bare subsistence."[95] Regarding the Policy of Dispersal, "Concluding this report, I wish to note that I am of the firm conviction that Eskimos should be kept out on the land away from settlements, as they are primarily hunters and not workers."[96]

Excerpts of this report were circulated among various government departments and elicited some negative responses. Col. Craig, in charge of family allowances for the Arctic, objected to the idea of shifting this administration from the RCMP to the HBC.[97] Representing the RCMP, Inspector H.A. Larsen, Officer Commanding "G" (or Arctic) Division, painted a grim picture of contemporary conditions among the Inuit as based on an inspection trip. He outlined what he described as appalling conditions of destitution and filth, confusion about government aims, poor clothing and habitation, lack of adequate and local health treatments, the dominance of the fur trade over subsistence hunting, and undesirable concentrations of people around settlements. He made several recommendations, among them appointment of an independent commission "to travel into the country and visit the camps at different times of the years ... and see at first hand how the Eskimos exist."[98] He also recommended that a crown corporation replace private trading firms. Finally, he urged a meeting of persons having experience in the north and in Eskimo administration to discuss the whole problem. Of course, his view on trading opposed that of Cantley's. His advocacy of a government-run trading organization echoed Cory in 1924, as well as Gibson in 1946.

Cantley's response made it clear he regarded most of Larsen's comments as exaggerations of existing conditions, and while agreeing with Larsen about the desirability of dispersing the population, one by one he dismissed the other suggestions as impractical.[99] An exception was the meeting of Arctic administrators and others, which he regarded as "most practical, and I would strongly recommend that it should be done as early as possible."

A proposal sent to the deputy minister eventually resulted in the formation of the Eskimo Affairs Committee, the significance of which was characterized by James P. Clancy: "During the 1950s, a decade of socioeconomic turbulence in the Arctic seas in Canada, the Eskimo Affairs Committee played a significant role in shaping a new set of policy initiatives that Ottawa was framing toward Eskimos. In bringing together representatives of the major Arctic field organizations, both public and private, the committee served as a corporatist device for overcoming the limitations of a colonial and underdeveloped state."[100] Notwithstanding the eventual role of the committee, some idea of the conservative and paternalistic stance that governmental representatives would bring to it can be gleaned from correspondence from Deputy Commissioner F.J.G. Cunningham to the Northwest Territories commissioner that "the fullest possible exploitation of hunting and trapping as a means of livelihood for the Eskimo should be allowed until some means is devised of regulating the use by Eskimos of his whole income, that is the cash income from the sale of furs, in addition to their income from relief and family allowance."[101] The paternalistic attitude was consistent with the substance of the draft invitation to the organizational meeting of the Eskimo Affairs Committee, which was sent out a month later by Cunningham and which included the following: "The basic issue seems to be this, are we to regard the Eskimo as a fully privileged, economically responsible citizen with the right to spend his income as he pleases, or are we to regard the Eskimo as backward people who need special guidance in the use of their income? ... I personally feel that if we are realistic we must consider the Eskimo to be in the second category."[102] Among the responses to the invitation was submitted correspondence between Inspector Larsen and the commissioner of the RCMP. Larsen deplored the practice of monthly payment of family allowances and suggested that it would be better to pay the allowance once a year in order to avoid the problem of too frequent concentration of people around the trading posts.[103] Another response came from Chesshire of the HBC, who complained that the HBC had realized only $2\frac{1}{2}$ per cent profit in the past year and that it had suffered a loss of 2 per cent over the preceding four years. On the other side of the equation, he remarked that, with rising prices, the slump in the fur market, coupled with a loss of income from the trade, had imposed a great burden on the Inuit.[104]

The organizational meeting of the nascent Eskimo Affairs Committee convened 19–20 May 1952. Some of the statements brought forth continued to espouse the hunting-trapping economy and its associated scattered settlement. An example was the statement issued in the report of the meeting that "Eskimos should be encouraged and helped to live off the land and to follow their traditional way of life. Surveys had shown that where natives subsisted on the produce of the land they were less subject to disease."[105] At the same meeting it was noted that medical attention and facilities were inadequate and schooling poorly developed, that relief payments were rising, and that fluctuations in fur prices and supply of fox were beyond control. This latter condition brought forth the proposal that a floor on fur prices should be established. Other concerns and suggestions reveal some cognizance of acute and changing conditions in the Arctic, such as the comment that concentration of settlement had resulted in rapid depletion of resources in some adjacent locales. There was also the feeling that some Inuit had lost their desire to seek game while depending on governmental support. At this stage, however, some of these concerns were exaggerated. While there was some appreciation for realistic problems, there was no clear recognition of the conflict between maintaining the hunting-trapping economy in scattered settlement while resolving some of the basic problems of health, education, and welfare.

When news of this meeting was publicized a query reached Cunningham asking why no Inuit had been invited to attend. He responded that "[t]he only reason Eskimos were not invited to the meeting was, apart from difficulties of transportation and language that it was felt that few, if any, of them have yet reached the stage where they could take a responsible part in such discussion."[106] This attitude perhaps had some truth to it, in view of the low level of education available to the Inuit at this time, but the quotation also reveals the overall paternalistic view that still prevailed within the administration of Arctic matters in Ottawa.

The official first meeting of the Eskimo Affairs Committee was held in October 1952, with Cantley acting as secretary.[107] A number of matters that were discussed followed upon issues raised in the organizational meeting. Most important were matters that called for action and that were part of a second report by Cantley. This report, issued a few days after the meeting and entitled "Immediate Steps That May Be Taken to Improve Eskimo Economy and Welfare," contained more optimistic and progressive recommendations than had his earlier submission. Among the recommendations was "transfer of Natives from overpopulated areas to places where they can more readily make a living and be self-supporting."[108] Also recommended were the utilization of a loan fund, organization and improvement of hunting techniques, including fuller use of walrus resources, greater use of nets for catching sea mammals, and enhancement of whale hunting. At the same time, Cantley again advocated a wider distribution of population during winter months for trapping and hunting. All these recommendations implied a greater and more efficient use of game resources. He also recommended development of handicrafts and other local industries. So, while Cantley has been given credit for providing impetus for developing the sealskin market, as well as the eventual creation of Inuit cooperatives, he still insisted on the continued prominence of the hunting and trapping economy, and the dispersed settlement pattern it implied at that time.

The third meeting of the committee, held on 20 October 1953, reflected growing concern with matters of health, education, and welfare.[109] The concern with possible concentration of settlement was less vocally expressed, although not laid to rest. Subsequently, meetings in the year 1954 proved to be something of a watershed between the preservationist stance and a more active role for the government. In summarizing the results of the meeting held in 1953, B.G. Sivertz, chief of the Arctic Division, wrote to Graham Rowley, secretary of the Advisory Committee on Northern Development, that "rapidly changing conditions throughout the North have made necessary new approaches to the problem of the Eskimo people."[110] Sivertz also wrote: "It is clearly necessary to provide more medical, educational and welfare services which in time will mean extra staff and scope for the department concerned. It would appear, however, that this is the time for a vigorous program which will enable the Eskimo to pursue self-sufficient participation in the life of the country. They are at present a liability which is tending to become heavier. A successful program of development could transform these people into an asset to Canada."[111] The shift in attitude influencing policy had begun to gain momentum. In 1954 Inspector Larsen submitted a report based on an inspection flight made during that March and April. This report was conveyed from the commissioner of the RCMP to Cunningham, now promoted to commissioner of the Northwest Territories, in August of that year. Larsen proposed that "small Eskimo villages" should be set up at such localities as Chesterfield Inlet, Fort Chimo, and Frobisher Bay, being "places where the Eskimos are already in the habit of congregating," that buildings should be erected to house the people, and that cold storage facilities should be supplied. These accommodations would serve the families of hunters who would meanwhile range away from the villages under more carefully directed hunts, so that "hunters would be unburdened by families in their pursuits and the results of the hunts carefully preserved in the villages."[112]

Cunningham's reply expressed agreement with Larsen's proposal and stated that the first steps had been taken toward his objectives, citing the newly established Northern Service officer program that would come into effect in the near future.[113] Larsen's report was remarkable in two respects. First, it appears to reverse his statement of two years earlier regarding the dispersal of Inuit populations. It also presents the effects of population concentration in a more favourable light, that is, endorsing the possibility of combining hunting-trapping economy with the advantages of settlement living. Concentration of settlement was no longer viewed by Larsen as being responsible for breaking down the existing economy for overdependence on social legislation funds.

Two meetings of the committee held in 1954 brought other matters to the fore. For the Mackenzie Delta region, family allowances were now being paid in cheques rather than goods.[114] The Northern Service officer program was established at several points in the Arctic, and the x-ray survey was now expanded to cover the entire Central Arctic, rather than being restricted to the range of the Eastern Arctic Patrol ship.[115] It was also proposed that where "Eskimos were doing skilled or semi-skilled work comparable to that done by imported labour they should be paid at the same rate."[116]

With regard to the in-gathering of Inuit near posts, a memorandum from Rowley to Sivertz reveals another shift. "Until fur trade conditions are good enough for trapping to provide a chance of raising the Eskimo's standard of living appreciably, it is hard to justify any attempt to coerce them to go out and trap. I would therefore reconsider that where the Eskimos hang around the post chronically it is an indication that a school should be provided. In this way there would be some chance of a long-run solution."[117]

Despite the more positive and progressive tone of his second report, Cantley was obviously annoyed by some of the policies being proposed or supported by the Eskimo Affairs Committee in 1954. Early in the next year he wrote in frustration to the deputy minister of the newly formed Department of Northern Affairs that he was disappointed in the role that the committee was playing, that Northern Service officers would aggravate problems in the north, and, further, that: "[w]e should never delude ourselves into believing the Eskimos are just waiting to be shown a better way of life, their present way suits them very well so long as they can be assured of the necessities and a few small luxuries."[118] Cantley wrote that some means of control should be exerted over how the natives spent their income, and he repeated his assertion that greater use should be made of the Hudson's Bay Company and, rather surprisingly, the RCMP, in administering the Arctic and preventing the natives from "being entirely dependent."

This memorandum was sent to Rowley for comment and the latter felt that it did "not offer any constructive suggestions."[119] Cantley's memorandum was something in the way of a letter of resignation, for shortly after he was replaced as secretary of the committee by Alexander Stevenson, though Cantley did remain with the government until sometime in 1956. Consistent with one of the recommendations he had made, Cantley was a key player in the relocation of Inuit from Quebec and Pond Inlet to the Arctic Islands, discussed later in this study.

In the late 1950s a number of incidents of starvation prompted relocation schemes and a general increased awareness in Ottawa of some of the problems confronting the Inuit. Regardless of relocations, and other measures designed to improve the lot of the Inuit, aggregations at posts were still discouraged, even while the inevitability of centralization was slowly, if sometimes reluctantly, beginning to be recognized. In 1958 representatives of various branches concerned with Arctic administration met to discuss the establishment of "camp units,"[120] a transitional project to serve those still living in outlying settlements. This plan set out the idea of small insulated plywood or styrofoam structures to serve camps in a twenty- to thirty-mile radius with emergency supplies and equipment. Each station would be manned by a native man and equipped with a radio, in order to prevent tragedies such as had occurred recently in the Keewatin.

Commissioner Nicholson of the RCMP, a late advocate of dispersed settlement, addressed a January 1959 meeting of the Northwest Territories Council. He praised the relocation projects at Grise Fiord and Resolute but felt that if the resources of the country were more efficiently exploited, "as they should be, more small permanent settlements are indicated, settlements of a dozen or so families ... Eskimos who continue an old-fashioned nomadic existence must accept to a very great extent primitive health standards and ... substandard housing of an igloo and skin tent society with the mortality rate that goes with them ... This brings me to the most important suggestion that I have to make. It is that we should take steps if necessary, firm steps, to keep these people from clustering about white centers of population and housing ... I think most seriously that the administration should have the authority to bar the Eskimo from the area where defense installations, mines and the like are central to keep a distance of 20 miles or more." He also stated that where employment was available it should not be discouraged, that relief should be discouraged, but that "these things should be tackled with all possible attention to the Eskimos own wishes. He must not be looked upon as curiosity but as a man and as a Canadian."[121]

There was, of course, a basic contradiction between his proposal of an empty zone around white installations and this last condition of volition on the part of the Inuit. A memorandum from Sivertz responded that more rapid change should be promoted, and he also expressed his opposition to the twenty-mile zone proposed by Nicholson as violating the individual freedom of the Inuit.[122] However, as future references will indicate, members of the RCMP and other government personnel in the Arctic were actually taking measures to enforce the isolation of Inuit from DEWline stations. But in southern Canada, the highly conservative, if not reactionary, stance Nicholson represented did not reflect the spirit of the final days of the 1950s. In 1959, after seven years of meetings of the Eskimo Affairs Committee, Inuit were invited to attend, and they joined actively in discussions. Some of the problems brought up by the Inuit representatives had decidedly local importance – for instance, the need for a larger boat for hunting at Rankin Inlet, and concern about the possibility of closing the mine there. Dichotomous views were expressed about drinking alcoholic beverages: one Inuit representative deplored the drinking that took place in Churchill, while another argued for upholding the right to drink to be the same for Inuit as for whites. There were also suggestions of condescending behaviour toward Inuit by whites.[123] The question of establishing hospitals in the north, raised by Inuit representatives who were concerned with separation of families, was shot down by the representative of Indian and Northern Health Department, Dr Proctor.[124]

The concentration of Inuit settlement was again raised at this 1959 meeting. Bishop Marsh of the Church of England, in the context of a lengthy discussion of housing needs for the Inuit, stated "that new housing tended to collect Eskimos around trading posts when they should be out hunting and trapping." The chairman, R.G. Robertson, asserted that there were good prospects for developing an economy based on combining revenue from the land and from wage employment. This view was seconded by Rowley, who thought permanent housing and hunting could be combined. Inspector Larsen reiterated his earlier proposition that "men could travel farther and search for game, up to the radius of 100 miles," while their families remained in comfort in the settlements. One Inuit representative agreed in part that housing could be established at outposts, but proposed that they should have schools as well, so that the children would not be separated from their parents. This suggestion ignored the impracticality of spreading school facilities so widely. Other Inuit representatives stated that the old way of life was passing. It was too difficult to make a living on the land, since the caribou were disappearing.

While some of the suggestions and remarks of the Inuit representatives bore a parochial flavour, others were pithy. They expressed their positive impression of the marvels of the outside world and wished that such benefits and comforts could be theirs as well, but they also showed resistence to the notion that they wished to be wards of the state. When H.W. Sutherland of the HBC commented on the movement of people from small settlements to Frobisher Bay without any real prospect of full employment, one Inuit representative replied that the people did not seek handouts and asked whether it was intended to make idlers out of Inuit people or to make them productive citizens.

The real significance of the meeting, and the several remaining meetings of the committee to which Inuit representatives were invited, was that, after three and a half decades of assuming administrators knew what was best for the Inuit, there was finally some response from representatives of the Inuit and a clearer idea of what their needs were.

The other significant development of 1959 came from the HBC in Winnipeg. While the fur trade was not at an end, and continued to provide substantial support for a large number of Inuit for some years to come, a decided shift had come in the marketing practices and policies of the company. H.W. Sutherland, who at this time was general manager of the company's Fur Trade Department, described thus change as it affected his department: "The Fur Trade in the last decade was going through a transformation due to large scale developments in the Canadian North and unorganized territory. In this period the traditional trade in wild fur has been largely replaced by increasing merchandise sales which today represent more than 90% of the business and consequently, its name has been changed to Northern Stores Department."[125]

This statement is extreme when applied specifically to the Central Arctic regions considered here. There were wide variations within which the fur trade flourished from place to place in the next decade, and the balance between returns from furs and other sources of income for the Inuit also fluctuated widely from year to year at any one of the places of Central Eskimo habitation. It is true, however, that social legislation funds became an increasing source of income for the Inuit during these latter years as the philosophy of preservationism and the Policy of Dispersal weakened. Another factor that altered Inuit relations with the outside world was the relinquishment of administrative functions by the HBC during the 1950s as the Northern Service officer program developed. The slow policy changes of Ottawa and Winnipeg were being driven by events taking place in the Arctic, events to which I now turn.

CHAPTER THREE

Settlement in the 1950s – I

While policies regarding the Inuit were undergoing gradual change during the 1950s in Ottawa, the Policy of Dispersal continued to be implemented to a large extent in the Arctic during that decade. One aspect of dispersal was relocation. During the 1950s a relocation program for the High Arctic regions saw the movement of people from the east coast of Hudson Bay and from northern Baffin Island to Ellesmere and Cornwallis Islands.

THE HIGH ARCTIC RELOCATION

The resettlement of Inuit to Ellesmere Island and Cornwallis Island in 1953 was the subject of much debate and criticism, and several reports, especially during the 1990s. While I cannot treat all aspects of the controversial relocation here, the history of the two colonies is appropriate within the context of my focus on changing Central Arctic settlement patterns.

While Canadian sovereignty over the Arctic Archipelago was a concern before and after 1953, it is not at all clear that the relocation strengthened Canada's claims to the islands. In fact, the moves were made primarily for economic reasons that were consistent with the Policy of Dispersal then in force,[1] which endorsed moving people from perceived areas of overpopulation, in terms of game resources, to underpopulated regions of good resource potential. The resettlement project of 1953 differed from earlier relocations, however, in that the Hudson's Bay Company, earlier the major player, showed no interest in the moves. In a memorandum to J.G. Wright, then chief of the Arctic Division (Northern Administration and Lands Branch), on 12 February 1951, before plans for the High Arctic Relocation scheme took shape, James Cantley wrote of the HBC's possible involvement in relocation projects, although "from the business standpoint they probably consider their investment in the north is already heavy enough."[2] Eastern Arctic Patrol reports from Cantley and Stevenson, who supervised sections of the patrol in 1952, encouraged the moves of 1953. Indeed, both sites of emigration were chosen in the autumn of 1952, and shortly after, so were the sites of the new colonies.[3] While the ostensible motive for establishing the colonies was to relieve overpopulation and over-reliance on relief in the Port Harrison region, the Pond Inlet people were drawn into the project so that they might help the Port Harrison people adapt to High Arctic conditions.[4]

Although the people and conditions of the Quebec–Labrador Peninsula are not part of this study, since the resettlement project occurred in what has been designated here as the Central Arctic, and included Central Arctic Inuit (the Pond Inlet people), it is necessary to consider conditions at Port Harrison at the time of the resettlement. Willmott, who studied the community of Port Harrison and its environs in 1958, estimated that in 1953 only about 60 to 70[5] of the total of about 500[6] in the trading area at that time lived in the centre itself. Thus, in-gathering, a focus of the Policy of Dispersal, was not a major factor in this case. Instead, the argument of overpopulation was more persistently enlisted. It is true that caribou had virtually disappeared from the region, and that fur production was particularly poor just prior to 1952. However, in that year 1,500 pelts were traded, a substantial income from carving realized, and successful sea-mammal hunting reported.[7] It is therefore ironic that plans had already been set in motion for the removal of people when the community appeared to be in a condition of recovery, or at least temporarily improved conditions. On the other hand, it could be argued that, since another removal of people took place in 1955, to Great Whale River,[8] there was long-term justification for the perception of overpopulation in the region. With the movements of people, the total population of Port Harrison was reduced from about 500 in 1953 to 337 in 1958.[9]

Approval of the plans for relocation came from the deputy minister of National Resources and Development in early 1953,[10] and planning proceeded through the spring and early summer. Finally, after some adventures, due largely to ice conditions, colonies were established from the Eastern Arctic Patrolship *C.D. Howe* (with the help of the ice breaker *d'Iberville*) at Lindstrom Peninsula on the southern coast of Ellesmere Island and at Resolute Bay on Cornwallis Island, in August and September of 1953.

Ottawa's chief source of information about the Ellesmere colony was the RCMP detachment at nearby Craig Harbour (moved to Grise Fiord in 1956). The year-end report for 1953 stated "the native camp was in very good condition,"[11] setting the tone for the generally optimistic reports that followed. Constable A.C. Fryer of the Craig Harbour detachment submitted an article in February 1954 to the RCMP *Quarterly*, which reported that the Port Harrison people were adapting well to the unfamiliar conditions of the High Arctic.[12] Caribou and walrus hunts had been successful and government relief support was bridging the gap until they could bring in items to trade. All natives except one "old Fogey" had expressed their desire to remain.[13] Subsequent reports for 1954,[14] 1955,[15] 1956,[16] and 1957[17] indicated that the Pond Inlet family and the majority Port Harrison Inuit were living in harmony, that morale was good, and hunting successful. Contentment with the prospect of remaining was repeatedly reported. However, young men from the Pond Inlet contingent sought wives, and indeed in 1957 one left to seek a wife, and another came from Pond Inlet with a wife.[18]

The 1958 report indicated additions to the community of three families, one each from Resolute, Port Harrison, and Arctic Bay, to bring the total Inuit population of the colony to eleven families of forty-three persons. The community's total income of $12,133 for that year was derived from carvings, family allowances, and fur, and meant that "the majority have accumulated substantial credit which if properly used should see them through the non trapping season."[19]

Morale slumped in 1958, however, after two children drowned and supplies in the local store were exhausted. With the arrival of the supply ship in summer, morale was reported as having improved, and "the men who had mentioned their wish to move from this area had now changed their minds."[20]

The decade ended with the yearly report, issued 13 January 1960,[21] which described a divided colony: sixteen Pond Inlet people were at Grise Fiord, and eight families (twenty-four persons) of Port Harrison Inuit were at another camp three miles away. There were also two families at the Craig Harbour detachment site, and one family had been moved to the new detachment at Alexandra Fiord.

The reports of the RCMP for the period 1953 through 1959 had painted a rosy picture. The colony had been established intentionally some distance from the detachment in order that the Inuit would lead as close to a "traditional" (actually contact-traditional) life as possible. The police appear to have kept a close watch on the little colony and undoubtedly provided assistance of various kinds. Indeed, from an economic point of view the experiment was proving successful, with hunting providing the basis of diet. Trapping, carving, and family allowances together prevented the large-scale issuances of relief that were anathema to the policy and philosophy of dispersal. On the basis of the police reports there had been no great desire on the part of the Port Harrison people to return, while some of the Pond Inlet Inuit moved between the colony and the north Baffin Island locale. The significance of the colony's division at the end of the fifties does not seem to have been clearly understood by the local RCMP detachment, and the move suggests that the reported harmony may not have been altogether achieved.

The second colony, at Resolute Bay, consisted of one Pond Inlet family (five persons) and three families (fourteen persons) from Port Harrison. The RCMP officer assigned to the group had been stationed previously at Port Harrison and was known to that element of the colony.[22] Given good communication with and transportation from Ottawa, available through the Department of Transport station and the RCAF base, a number of officials visited the colony during the fifties. The first of these was C.J. Marshall of the Advisory Committee on Northern Development. His report of 9 November 1953 emphasized hurried planning and the inadequacy of the supplies and equipment that had arrived with the ship that brought the colonists to Resolute.[23] The deputy commissioner of the Northwest Territories, then F.J.G. Cunningham, tried to counter Marshall's complaints, and elicited comments from the RCMP officer at Resolute,[24] which were, however, qualified in this regard. The officer felt that more careful planning could have been made, but "with no reflection being cast on any department or the person who made up the store lists."[25]

A March 1954 report indicated that the natives had had to work hard for subsistence during the winter because of their late arrival, but that "probably more natives should come to the area as it is felt that there is plenty of game."[26] A year later the Inuit were reported as being "content to remain" but anxious for their relatives to join them.[27] Indeed, beginning in 1955, a number of requests for transferral to the new colony reached Ottawa from the Port Harrison region. These requests stressed the superior hunting conditions reported by friends and relatives at Resolute. A few people went north in 1955.[28]

Building material was sent to Resolute in 1956, but this shipment proved superfluous since the colonists had constructed substantial dwellings (probably superior to those in the two donor regions) from scrap lumber obtained at the RCAF base.[29]

In a report of November 1956, the resident officer indicated that some of the Port Harrison people wished to return for one-year visits, and he expressed the view that the people had been promised the option to return "after a given time."[30] He also recommended that a rotation system should be instituted to accommodate such visits. Further reports during the fifties were generally optimistic. By 1958 all of the colonists were living in wooden houses equipped with electricity furnished by the base. Morale was reported as being high except among those men whose wives were away in hospitals in the south.[31] The then resident RCMP officer indicated that "all Eskimos have advised the writer at one time or another that they are very happy at Resolute Bay and under no circumstances would they consider returning to their original homes."[32] It was also reported for 1958 that by that time the people had accumulated approximately $9,000, excluding family allowances.

With a rise in population by 1958 to seventy, due both to additional immigration and natural increase, the officer in charge stated that this number "should not be increased to any extent."[33] There was also concern that the Port Harrison region was being depleted of good hunters.[34] However, at about the same time, a lengthy report was submitted listing a number of Port Harrison people who wanted to move to the colonies in the High Arctic: "[They] have been given enthusiastic reports of life there. At the same time they are discouraged by the economic possibilities of the Port Harrison and Pouungnituk areas."[35] Ottawa allowed that people should be granted the choice of moving to the two outposts, but decided that they would have to pay for their own transportation.[36] Meanwhile, the previously optimistic reports of conditions at Resolute were modified somewhat in the final RCMP report of the 1950s: "There is only one factor of morale that could develop – jealousy between Port Harrison and Pond Inlet people. Openly they get along together well but as a person such as the writer visits with individuals of both groups, the dislike, jealousy, or whatever it might be called is plainly present."[37] Thus, the division between the two groups, which was mainly unrecognized by the local RCMP at Grise Fiord, even though it manifested in spatial separation, was, by the end of the 1950s, being recognized at Resolute.

I have relied largely on police reports and related correspondence in depicting conditions at the two colonies for the period of the fifties. I shall later consider other perceptions as they came to light in following years, but at this point it is well to summarize certain features of the High Arctic relocation that relate to considerations of settlement changes. Clearly this project falls within the realm of relocation as the term is being used here, rather than migration. In reading the available documents it is not clear as to the degree of volition as opposed to compulsion that was involved in the selection of emigrees. In contrast to earlier relocations, the HBC was not involved. While the relocation fit the Policy of Dispersal's aim to maximize economic potentials, it also moved people from conditions of scattered settlement to compacted, if small, communities. The two colonies were economic successes in terms of subsistence pursuits and avoidance of massive relief support.[38] However, no provisions were made for the Port Harrison people to return. Although morale was reported as good for the most part in both colonies, there was also, in the case of Resolute at least, the beginnings of a perception that relocating people from widely diverse regions could result in internal friction.

Establishing the two northern colonies took people great distances from their home regions. This movement involved only a small portion of the total Inuit population, and the largest number of people involved in this relocation actually came from regions outside the scope of this study; the majority of the Inuit of the Central Arctic, as defined here, remained closer to their traditional ranges. For convenience it is useful to consider the Central Arctic as consisting of two major divisions. The first stretches from Victoria Island and opposing mainland regions along the Northwest Passage eastward to King William Island and the Boothia and Melville Peninsulas, and includes Baffin Island. I am designating this division as the Arctic Coast–Arctic Islands area (even though adjacent inland regions were also inhabited at times). The second division of the Central Arctic will be designated as the Keewatin, and it includes the western and northwesterly parts of Hudson Bay and the interior west of the great Bay. This chapter focuses on the first of these major divisions, and the next chapter the second.

Studded throughout the Arctic Coast–Arctic Islands region were the points of trade that served the Inuit. By the 1950s some of these points were beginning to be loci of aggregations of populations. Others became so in the following decade. My procedure will be a case-by-case examination of these points of trade and their adjacent districts in terms of the impact of government policy on the distribution of Inuit populations through the 1950s. I begin this survey in the southeastern part of this range of Inuit habitation.

SOUTH BAFFIN ISLAND AND FROBISHER BAY

By the end of the 1950s, a rapid in-gathering of people at Frobisher Bay had created a large community of mixed ethnic composition. Part of the eventual Inuit population that concentrated there came from the Bay region itself, but a large number also moved there from elsewhere, especially from the south coast of Baffin Island. The Baffin Island coast had, according to Higgins, no fewer than thirty-four sites of habitation along this coast for the period up to 1938.[39] These sites were divided into three trading districts, Lake Harbour in the east,

Cape Dorset to the west, and Amadjuak in the centre. In 1938 the post at Amadjuak closed and the Inuit from that region began to trade at Dorset. Most of the camps remained in operation up to 1950.[40]

C.E.B. Sinclair, director of the Northern Administration Branch, wrote to A.H. Chesshire of the HBC on 15 January 1951 to express his concern over the contraction of population around Cape Dorset.[41] Only fourteen of seventy families who traded there lived more than 100 miles away and thirty of the families were within 50 miles of the post. Chesshire attributed this contraction to declined economic circumstances, especially a drop in fur prices, as well as to too easy access to family allowances. Confirmation of depressed conditions came in May 1951 in an RCMP report that stated that "Family Allowances and relief issuances have been the mainstay in the prevention of widespread starvation during the past winter."[42] Both this report and the letter from Sinclair suggested the possibility of relocations to better hunting areas. It will be recalled that this region was one of the original places for a relocation scheme of the 1930s.

Nonetheless, by 1957, of 104 people who had moved to Frobisher Bay from the south coast of Baffin Island, only eleven had come from Dorset.[43] There was evident opposition to moves to Frobisher on the part of James Houston, the Northern Service officer (NSO) stationed at Dorset. He wrote to Ottawa that he was discouraging such moves, since he felt that there would be little prospect of work for more emigrees.[44] The employment from the carving and handicraft industries introduced by Houston was judged by the RCMP in 1952 as having "improved conditions of many camps."[45] In addition, the NSO outlined a number of construction projects that could be initiated at Dorset. Indeed, by 1956 construction employment had expanded to the extent that the welfare teacher thought that hunting was being ignored.[46] There was a famine in the winter of 1956–57, which brought on the death of many dogs,[47] but after that, hunting improved in the area, and by the end of the fifties an abrupt rise in fur prices helped improve the local economy.

Whether because of fluctuating game conditions or, more likely, expanded employment opportunities, the centralization process gathered force at Cape Dorset during the later years of the fifties. In 1958 five camps were abandoned,[48] and after two more were closed in 1959,[49] only seven remained of the twenty whose members had traded into the post in 1951. Meanwhile, contraction continued, ostensibly to reduce the distance that had to be traveled to trade.

While the chief change in settlement for the Dorset trading district during the fifties was concentration in, or contraction around, the post, in the Lake Harbour region migration to Frobisher was the most prominent settlement change. The anthropologist Graburn provides a detailed account of the migration of Lake Harbour people to Frobisher.[50] This movement appears, with very few exceptions, to have begun in 1956. According to Graburn the annual totals of families who moved were: in 1956–57, 18; 1957–58, 14; 1958–59, 9; and 1959–60, 2.[51] From an estimated 250–300 before 1956, the population had declined to 117 by 1960. Thirty-four families, or 22.5 per cent, lived in the Lake Harbour settlement,[52] while the remainder were in three camps.

Graburn lists among the motives for the movement to Frobisher the following: the demand for wage employment; relative material advantages, especially improved housing; relative ease in purchasing essential equipment; and, initially at least, better hunting and trapping opportunities.[53] These latter motives were influenced by a poor hunt in 1956–57, and poor trapping returns in the following years around Lake Harbour.[54] The flow of migration was also sustained for a time by the attraction of the expanding programs of the Department of Northern Affairs, which had increased employment possibilities at Frobisher Bay, while another factor was the presence of friends and relatives who had moved there already.[55] Eventually, 150 people had moved from Lake Harbour to Frobisher.[56] However, by the end of 1959 "the Eskimo migration ... [appeared] to have stopped."[57] Indeed, not only had it ceased, but return migration had begun. Graburn cites several reasons for this. As the settlement at Frobisher became more crowded, wage labour opportunities shrank, expectations of housing provision went unmet, and social and emotional conflict arose in such situations as dogs being shot by police, seduction of women under the influence of alcohol, and greatly reduced hunting and trapping conditions.[58] As well, conditions at Lake Harbour were perceived as having improved with the reduced populations. A summer school program had been installed and the fear that the Hudson's Bay Company would cease operation was dispelled. While actual centralization at the post was not pronounced at the end of the 1950s, contraction had occurred. According to Graburn, outlying districts that had been abandoned were "those of relatively simple coastlines, less suitable for seal hunting," whereas the region around the post was more favourable for this hunt.[59]

For Frobisher Bay, even though game conditions were reported as being good in the early 1950s,[60] in-gathering had begun around the air base by the end of 1951. Three modes of residence developed.[61] The first was a small minority of the families of permanently employed men. The second and largest group comprised those families who lived around the base during the summer months and returned to "the native way of life" during the winter. The third group, said to be the smallest, was made up of "those who prefer to follow the native mode the whole year." The annual 1952 RCMP report gave an estimate of seventy-five families or about 300 people in the entire Frobisher Bay area and listed fourteen permanent employees at the base, who were provided with wooden houses and allowed one day a week for hunting.[62]

By 1956 there were, in addition to those at the air base, two other Inuit population segments.[63] These were a temporary tent encampment near the government establishment, and a still substantial population scattered in camps around the bay. Indeed, a 1956 RCMP report stated that thirty-nine of the seventy-six families (estimated at 383 people in total) lived in the camps during the winter months, being employed during the summer unloading supplies.[64] Caribou hunting was reported as being good during 1956–57, and conditions in general must have been favourable since only $189 was issued in relief during 1956.[65] The annual autumn movement back to the camps slackened in the fall of 1956, for in January 1957 only nineteen families were living away from the main settlement.[66] At that time, there were forty-two at the air base and seventeen at the new government townsite. By the summer of 1957 the influx from Lake Harbour had increased the population of Inuit to 489,[67] and by January 1956 there were 650 Inuit in the Frobisher Bay region.[68] By May 1960 there was a white population of 590. The Inuit then numbered 800, and almost all lived in the settlement itself.[69]

In southern and southeastern Baffin Island variations on the process of centralization prevailed. In Cape Dorset, efforts were made to develop small-scale industries as well as construction projects, which in time accelerated the drift to the settlement. Though some people still lived in camps they were increasingly compressed near the post. At Lake Harbour, a wholesale migration to Frobisher had drained much of the Inuit population by the end of the fifties, even though a number of people had returned. Compression of camps around the village occurred in Lake Harbour as at Dorset, but in the case of Lake Harbour, more favourable hunting conditions were said to exist nearer to the community. Large-scale centralization, as such, had not occurred before 1960.

In Frobisher, employment attracted a large number of people, and the size and composition of that settlement was unique for the Central Arctic at the end of the fifties. The large number of whites in the community, together with the high degree of concentration of the total population, brought on a series of social and economic problems that presaged those that would occur more generally in the Canadian Arctic as centralization advanced. Among these were unsanitary conditions, the danger of loose dogs, undesirable fraternization with white personnel, poor communication because of differences in language, problems of inadequate housing, and large-scale unemployment.

BAFFIN ISLAND: THE EAST COAST

The trading area of the post at Pangnirtung included Cumberland Sound and, before the founding of the post at Broughton Island in 1960, the north shore and environs of Cumberland Peninsula as well.[70] Settlement in this entire area during the 1950s remained largely dispersed, as it had been formerly. A census in 1951 indicated that 461 Inuit were living around the Sound itself[71] and in the entire trading area there was a total population of 618.[72] Only seventy-five people were at the main village of Pangnirtung,[73] while sixteen camps were scattered along the coasts of the Sound, together with several others to the north.[74] Nevertheless, Pangnirtung did have an unusually large population for Arctic communities of the 1950s. To what extent this degree of in-gathering was due to the presence of the Anglican mission with its hospital, one of the only two in the entire Central Arctic, is not clear. What is clear, however, is that considerable effort was being exerted to keep the population dispersed, and away from the main settlement: the RCMP report for the year of 1952 indicated that "the natives do not loiter in the settlement. They are not tolerated unless circumstances warrant their staying."[75] In 1956 another police report stated that, while "the majority of natives remain in their camps during the summer months following their normal way of life, ... loitering around the settlement is not permitted ... Some of the poorer types of Eskimo have been trying to move into Pangnirtung and loiter away the summer months, but all the natives have been told they can not live in Pangnirtung unless they are employed by one of the White Concerns."[76]

By the end of 1957 the RCMP report indicated that the problem of loitering had been resolved.[77] Later, in 1959, hunting conditions were reported as being poor due to deep snows hampering hunting and travel,[78] but a summer patrol that visited seven of the camps reported generally improved conditions, as well as a successful whale hunt.[79] By the end of that year hunting was assessed as successful (one of the men of one camp killed forty caribou), with "the women preparing skins for the market."[80] In general, hunting in the Pangnirtung trading district was successful during the 1950s.

The effectiveness of the Policy of Dispersal as enforced in the Cumberland Sound region can be judged from the figures on population distribution. By 1961 the population of the Sound had increased from

461 in 1951 to 559.[81] Even though Pangnirtung had grown (from seventy-five to ninety-six Inuit), this growth represents only a small percentage increase – from 16 per cent to 17 per cent – of the total Sound population during that period.

While centralization was being controlled around the main settlement, it was causing concern elsewhere in the trading area. The building of DEWline radar sites, beginning in 1955, provided some employment for Inuit, but after this phase was completed, there was a tendency for people to remain at or near the sites. In one case, while fifteen men had been employed during construction at a site, only three worked there afterwards. However, a group of sixty-one people had settled about a half mile away. Since hunting had been curtailed in favour of trying to live off the offerings of the radar station, the result was a near famine that required food to be flown in.[82] While this did not happen at every one of the sites along the north shore of Cumberland Peninsula where the DEWline was strung, it was widespread enough to stimulate action by March of 1957. Concern reached Winnipeg and Ottawa. Fitzsimmons wrote to Sivertz that the local NSO "should make the people move away from sites."[83] Sivertz agreed,[84] and further correspondence ensued between the DEWline projects officer in New Jersey and the Federal Electric Company, which operated the radar chain.[85] On the basis of cooperation between governmental representatives and DEWline administration and personnel, considerable pressure was exerted on the Inuit of the area. Consequently, the problem of in-gathering near the sites was all but eliminated by the end of the decade.

For the next trading region to the north, that of Clyde River and environs, Wenzel gives a population of 120–40 for 1951, and adds that "only five or six nuclear households, perhaps twenty-five to thirty-six people lived at the post. Most still maintained fixed winter residences in six villages."[86] An August 1953 RCMP census reported a population of 147 natives in the district, with only two men employed by the Department of Transport at Clyde, and one man and a woman working for the HBC; "the others depend on hunting."[87] Summer gatherings at the post led the local police to contact headquarters in Ottawa with the complaint that the company manager held people at the settlement in order to await the arrival of the annual supply ship.[88] It should be noted, however, that this ship also brought the annual x-ray party. The officer also later observed the tendency for Inuit to gather around the post at other times as well, and to depend on "odd jobs" for support. "As soon as this condition was apparent and the tendency 'to loiter' noticed, the writer took steps to see that the natives concerned were moved to suitable camps and were encouraged to hunt and generally improve their economic status."[89] The police also reported in 1954 that there were too many white personnel, including those at the U.S. Coast Guard station at Cape Christian, ten miles away from Clyde, and at the Department of Transport facility in Clyde.[90] These men were charged with giving away food, clothing, fuel, etc., which caused the Inuit to visit these places "at slightest pretense."[91] The officer in charge of the local RCMP detachment (also at Cape Christian) thought that there were sufficient resources to support the Inuit population in the area, but that the hunters were poorly supplied with hunting equipment, dogs, and boats. He also felt that "loitering" around the settlement was "one of the most vital problems that has faced the writer."[92]

By mid 1956 the perceived problem of in-gathering at the post appears to have been largely overcome by the efforts of the police.[93] It was also reported that "the situation was greatly improved," with only three families at the settlement at Clyde, all of whom were on relief, with a total of $1,889.20 being paid out during 1956. An increase in fur prices was, however, a help in the economy and morale was reported as being good, "as long as there was a little tobacco and sufficient food." However, in June of 1957 there was "a marked decline in economy," despite the "various camps in the district "being" well distributed and located in the best game and trapping areas."[94] A census of June 1958 gave twenty-seven families living in camps and five others at the settlement at Clyde.[95] There were 189 Inuit and 30 whites (including 22 at the U.S. Coast Guard station) in the district.

The annual report for 1959 indicated that $3,526.75 was being paid in relief and that "procuring of food represents increasing hardship during the passing of each year." In keeping with the policy enforced throughout the decade, the report stated that "loitering around settlement [was] not tolerated at Cape Christian or Clyde, and since the natives are generally anxious to get back to their camps no problems have been encountered in this matter."[96]

During the 1950s a great deal of fluidity existed in outlying camps, whose composition was unstable. There was also compression of settlement around Clyde into camps that were within easy communication with that centre. On the other hand, actual concentration in Clyde was to be a phenomenon of a later period.

In summary, during the 1950s, in the regions from Cumberland Sound northward to Clyde, the presence of substantial numbers of installations and white personnel tended to draw Inuit, but the population remained largely scattered into a number of camps. This dispersal was endorsed and enforced by the RCMP with the approval and encouragement of administrators on Baffin Island. Even though the stringent policy of preservationism and austerity began to be liberalized in Ottawa during the fifties, there is no indication of any directives from there that would lead to relaxation of the Policy of Dispersal, and indeed there are some indications that it was still being supported in the capitol.

NORTH BAFFIN ISLAND AND THE IGLULIK REGION

With the advent of the trade in arctic fox, the people of the Melville Peninsula and North Baffin came to focus around the points of trade established in the area. These were at Pond Inlet and, after 1938, Arctic Bay in the north and Repulse Bay in the south.[97] For the northern Melville Peninsula and surrounding regions, the HBC established a post at Igloolik in 1939. The post was closed between 1943 and 1947,[98] during which time long trips had to be made to these other points, but after 1947 operations of the company were continuous at Igloolik. RCMP patrols emanating from the Pond Inlet detachment reached Admiralty Inlet and Igloolik throughout the period leading up to 1960, and in the case of Igloolik, into the sixties.

Pond Inlet had been a locale of long-term contact with whalers and explorers that included some trade, but not of the regular nature of the contact-traditional period. In 1951 the trading area comprised 182 people, with the largest gathering at the post where forty-six were living, and outlying camps ranging from four individuals to twenty-six.[99] There are two counts for 1956. One census gives a total of 203 people in the trading community, with forty living at the post,[100] and the other counted 211 people distributed in seven camps, and thirty-two people at the Pond Inlet settlement.[101] The spectre of population concentration, accompanied by the associated perceived idleness, was a concern for the RCMP detachment at Pond Inlet throughout the fifties and beyond. On the basis of their reports it is clear that the police exerted pressure on the population to remain as dispersed as possible. A 1952 report indicated that "loitering" was "nonexistent" at Pond Inlet but that a constant watch was being kept there,[102] and concern was also expressed over in-gathering at Clyde River, Arctic Bay, and, especially, at Igloolik, where people were seen as aggregating around the mission.

A 1955 report indicated again that there was "no loitering" at Pond Inlet and that there had been "a big improvement" in this regard at Arctic Bay.[103] The departure of nineteen people from Arctic Bay for the colony at Resolute had eased the perceived congestion during the year. In the Admiralty Inlet region, where the post at the subsidiary inlet of Arctic Bay was the centre of trade, a 1956 census indicated that only twenty-eight of the total of 132 people in the trading area lived at the post, with the remainder being distributed into five camps.[104]

These camps ranged in size from fifteen to twenty-seven persons.[105] However, another report showed that only twenty-two lived at Arctic Bay itself.[106] There was, in addition to whatever pressures being exerted by the police, another factor that discouraged residence at the post at Arctic Bay: the Inuit of the region had found that the southern part of Admiralty Inlet was "a relatively rich resource area" as contrasted to the less favourable one in the immediate region of the Arctic Bay Post.[107] As late as 1961 there were still five camps in operation in the trading district.[108]

As at Arctic Bay, the in-gathering process continued to be thwarted at Pond Inlet. In 1958, of the total 170 people, eleven families or 19.62 per cent were living at the post,[109] or a lower percentage than at the beginning of the decade. At the end of the decade, there were still "six permanent camps" in the trading district.[110] The continued emphasis on camp living, to a great degree enforced by the RCMP, left settlement basically unchanged during the 1950s.

A different situation was developing around Igloolik. To gain some appreciation of this growth it is necessary to review briefly events of the 1930s and 1940s. During this period the population of northern Melville Peninsula and adjacent parts of Baffin Island had doubled, largely because of immigration, especially from the Repulse Bay region.[111] A number of these people created a large, at least seasonal, settlement at Qarmat Point on the mainland to the south of Iglulik Island.[112] In June of 1949 there were eighty-three people at that place, about 60 per cent of whom were immigrants. Another large group of sixty-eight people was located at Iglulik Point,[113] a place of seasonal aggregation reported as long ago as the visit of Parry and Lyon in 1822–23. Such large aggregations were atypical for the Central Arctic during contact-traditional times and may be related to superior marine mammal resources in the area. On the other hand, the expanded population was for the most part absorbed in multiple habitation sites. I have attributed this tendency to the independence that extended family units could achieve through the use of the whaleboats that entered the area around 1930.[114] Returning to the 1949 census, it is interesting to note that the settlement in Turton Bay, locally known as Ikpiakjuk, and from the time of the establishment of the post as Igloolik, was one of the smaller sites, with only nineteen Inuit individuals.[115] During the fifties, congregation moved rapidly and by 1956 seventy-seven were in residence.[116] This accretion was largely made up of Catholics in the population who had previously lived to the west on the mainland.[117] In 1949, they moved to Iglulik Point, and it could be granted that the presence of the mission had an effect on the concentration of people there. At the same time, this element of the population had hunted

nearby throughout most of their traceable history. While Turton Bay
was regarded as a poor hunting locale, with the use of dogsleds in winter and increasingly motorized boats in summer, good sea-mammal
hunting was within daily reach of the village that grew there. Indeed,
the police patrol of 1959 reported that a large number of people
"were in the settlement" but were actively engaged in hunting from
the centre.[118]

Another source of concern to the police and eventually to administrators in Ottawa was the construction of a main DEWline station forty-
eight miles south of Igloolik in 1957.[119] In contrast to the situation of
Baffin Island, there was no great tendency for in-gathering around the
station, but two traditionally located settlements had easy access to it,
and a small colony was growing near the nursing station that was established close to the site in 1957. The residents there included employees at both the hospital and the station. Rather than clustering their
habitation around these facilities, the main interest of the Iglulingmiut
was visiting the dump near the station. Especially valued was plywood,
which brought on a building boom that had no relation to the government housing programs that later followed. As late as 1956 an RCMP
report noted that there were "many snowhouses" in the Iglulik region
with the "odd family in sod" structures.[120] By 1960, when I visited the
region, nearly all of the outlying camps (of which there were thirteen
plus several seasonal sites) were supplied with plywood houses, some of
which were insulated with sod. The snowhouse was restricted mainly to
temporary hunting camps and for use in travel. The wooden shelters
certainly made conditions more livable in the outlying habitation sites
that were occupied for the major part of each year.

While centralization was to proceed apace in the next decade, certain factors were working against this inevitability. The centrifugal
forces of the subsistence requirements of the region as a whole provided practical motivation for continued habitation of the camps. The
Catholic mission may have been a factor in the centralization that had
by then taken place, but the HBC trader and the newly arrived area administrator, a former RCMP officer, favoured the dispersal of people in
the trading area.

THE NETSILIK AREA

The regions that stretch north and west from Pelly Bay to include
Boothia Peninsula, the lower Back River and Chantrey Inlet, King William Island, and the shores and adjoining interior of Queen Maud Gulf
as far west as Perry River were the traditional ranges of the Netsilik Es-

kimo. As noted earlier, some of this tribe moved to northwestern Hudson Bay as early as the 1860s, and people from Baffin Island came to the area in the 1930s.[121] These latter people, as well as some Netsiliks, were served by the HBC post at Fort Ross during the 1940s. When Fort Ross closed in 1948[122] some of the people on Somerset Island moved south, and all who had formerly traded at Fort Ross used Spence Bay, founded in 1949, to barter their furs. The RCMP established a detachment at Spence Bay as well in 1949,[123] and patrols went out regularly to keep watch on conditions in the camps of the area. In addition to the post at Spence Bay, other trading locales were at Gjoa Haven on King William Island and the mission on the shore of Pelly Bay. As well as dogsled patrols of the RCMP, a number of government-sponsored flights emanated from Cambridge Bay beginning in 1949, and brought in supplies in reported cases of famine.[124] Such attention to conditions in outlying camps helped sustain dispersed settlement.

The lack of integration between the indigenous Netsiliks and the immigrant Baffin Islanders manifested in two major ways during the fifties. First, there were few marriages between members of the two groups.[125] Second, elements of each group tended to occupy separate locales due to contrasting subsistence emphases. Immigrants from the Cape Dorset region were in particular said to be unfamiliar with breathing-hole sealing methods and showed little interest in fishing.[126] These occupations were the mainstay of Netsilik economy. In consequence, the Dorset people chose sites where floe edge sealing was possible.

As early as 1951 the police had expressed concern about the degree of in-gathering at Spence Bay and queried headquarters in Ottawa about what policy to pursue.[127] One of the arguments against the clustering of people was that it could cause spread of disease. Accordingly, meetings were held with the Inuit at both Spence Bay and Gjoa Haven in 1951. To what extent these meetings were instrumental in the continued dispersal that was largely maintained during the fifties in the area is difficult to judge. The problem of aggregation at the posts continued and in 1951 the officer in charge of the Spence Bay detachment reported: "When this detachment was built there were only three families living locally and these were here before the white man. Now there are about ten families, some of which are destitute, but some of which are not. If they do not voluntarily move soon they will be 'shooed out.' "[128]

Another problem relating to settlement practices in the area at this time concerned health. Tuberculosis was widespread and the x-ray surveys had not yet been introduced in these regions. The police suggested that if the surveys were to be carried out, they should be scheduled for the end of trapping season (or Easter), for the Christmas–New Year holiday season, or at ship time, since the population was "otherwise scattered."[129] Of course, following any of these options would contribute to the continued dispersal of people for the balance of the year.

Patrols each year brought information on the distribution of populations.[130] For example, the patrol of the winter of 1952–53 reported that only three families lived at the post at Gjoa Haven and that much of that trading area population was dispersed into camps of five, seven, two, five, four, and five families. These numbers represent camp populations that were typical throughout the contact-traditional period for much of the Central Arctic. However, here as elsewhere, there were cases of larger gatherings. For instance, in the lower Back River–Chantrey Inlet region aggregations of up to fifteen families[131] occurred during the 1950s at favourite fishing sites. Another large but probably more temporary gathering was noted for the east side of Boothia Peninsula: "All the Eskimos from the outlying camps of Thom Bay, Lord Mayor Bay, Spence Bay and Netchilik Lake, when short of food in the winter gather at Cape North Hendon to do their hunting."[132] The police were concerned that such a concentration of people might be too great for effective trapping. In this case the Inuit were following a time-honoured perception that breathing-hole sealing was adapted to clustering of a significant number of hunters.[133]

The process of centralization proceeded slowly during the fifties at both Gjoa Haven and Spence Bay. It was reported that during the first half of 1955 only five families lived at Spence Bay,[134] as compared to ten in 1951.[135] At Gjoa Haven, there were in 1955 still only three families. By mid 1957 there were again ten families at Spence Bay,[136] but this increase was due to the temporary abandonment of a camp on the west side of Boothia Peninsula because of famine conditions. However, these people did not impose a burden, as they were able to build up caches at Spence Bay and Lord Mayor Bay, at which latter place they hunted out from the centre.[137]

It appears that health concerns had an impact on efforts to keep the population dispersed in the region in that, as described in a 1957 RCMP report: "It has been found at the Spence Bay settlement from which so many Eskimos have been evacuated to hospital, that the relatives do not want to camp any great distance from the settlement. This is understandable, of course, but in a bad hunting year things would be very grim for them around the Spence Bay locality."[138]

In 1957 the Gjoa Haven community showed a slight increase, with six families in residence – still, however, only a small part of the total population of the trading area. Indeed, the large camp at the Back River comprised fourteen families during the winter, which split into smaller units in spring and summer for caribou hunting.[139]

In 1958, twelve families lived at Spence Bay with only two having employed members, though no hardships were contingent upon this increase and good hunting was reported largely through expeditions from that base.[140] At Gjoa Haven the preceding year saw an increase from six to eight families, even though the police thought "this settlement should never have more than six or so permanent residents."[141] The people at Back River and Chantrey Inlet experienced hard times and split into small groups, but this did not prevent starvation that took the lives of six people. This tragedy did not result in immediate abandonment of that region, since in January 1960 ten families of "about 40 people" were living there, concentrated again into one camp.[142] With regard to the concentration of population for 1958–59 at Spence Bay, there was an average of eleven families during the winter months, with only three having employed members. The remainder made the settlement "a sort of head-quarters in between their hunting and trapping activities."[143]

Shortly after DEWline stations were stretched across the Netsilik area, concern was shown regarding the possible effects of the sites on the Inuit.[144] However, as it turned out, at sites in the western part of the Netsilik area, relations between the Inuit and DEWline personnel appear to have been favourable. For example, at one site seven Spence Bay men were employed, but had apparently worked out an equitable arrangement with the DEWline people.[145] At that place men were building houses for their families from scrap lumber obtained from the site, and were planning to put up caches in the summer to return to work at the station in the fall. At the site built three miles from the mission at Pelly Bay, certain difficulties developed between the local missionary and officials in Ottawa. While the priest did not object to natives visiting the site and bringing materials for house construction, he discouraged them from seeking employment there.[146] R.A.J. Phillips, then chief of the Arctic Division of the Department of Northern Affairs, objected to this policy: "We have worked hard to find these opportunities for jobs with good return, and have now supported a training program so that good and capable workers can improve their qualifications and earn yet more money for their families."[147]

Meanwhile, centralization was proceeding among the Pelly Bay Inuit. Steenhoven[148] depicts a gathering of most of the population in a snowhouse village for the Christmas of 1956, but this had been a customary occurrence for some years. In 1957, most of the twenty-seven families lived in one large camp that shifted among three sites during the course of the year.[149] Shortly, however, such an aggregation was to be permanent for much of the year, with only two small winter camps still in operation. The mission was obviously a factor in this degree of centralization, but the population concentration occurred a quarter of a century after its establishment at Pelly Bay. Balikci cites several factors for the in-gathering near the mission. While the presence of the mission as a trading centre and access to a "heated room" provided some motivation, he also notes, "Additional factors were operative in this process, such as the lack of suitable fur clothing making travelling by whole families back and forth to the ice-edge and the mission difficult; technological changes and increased individual mobility producing a decrease in ecological pressures and allowing the hunter to settle at great distance from his hunting ground, repeated epidemics and general fear of sickness causing people to rely frequently on the missionary's medical kit."[150] While a high degree of centralization had developed at Pelly Bay by the end of the fifties, the community continued as a mainly subsistence hunting economy.

While in-gathering had been limited at Gjoa Haven and Spence Bay through the 1950s, an April 1960 report presaged a condition that would develop in the next decade: "There appears to be a definite trend by the Eskimos to congregate in larger communities than in the past, and with the establishment of the Federal Day School at Spence Bay, it seems that this settlement will increase as time goes by on."[151]

The effects of the Policy of Dispersal were clearly evident during the 1950s in the Netsilik area. One position taken in Ottawa, which had some effect on settlement practices here, as in other parts of the Central Arctic, did not exactly fit that policy: when wage employment was available the Inuit were encouraged to take advantage of it. In this area, such opportunities occurred at DEWline sites.

Aside from the circumstances described for Pelly Bay, population remained dispersed in the Netsilik area at the end of the fifties. Periodic famines were experienced, but their effects were ameliorated through emergency flights or in temporary relief offered in residence at the centres of Spence Bay and Gjoa Haven. Apart from the efforts exerted by the police (and by administrators operating out of Cambridge Bay) to prevent in-gathering, the attractions of settlement living during the 1950s were not such as to inspire movement to them on a large scale. With the lack of alternative employment, the hunting-trapping economy from dispersed bases was the most practical and desirable choice of occupations and settlement.

THE CAMBRIDGE BAY AREA

The eastern elements of the aboriginal Copper Eskimo populated the regions on the mainland from about Cape Barrow eastward to Perry River, southern Victoria Island, as well as regions of the sea ice during the winter months. By the end of the 1930s trading was focused at HBC posts at the mouth of Perry River, in Bathurst Inlet, and at Cambridge Bay. Later, Cambridge Bay became the administrative centre for the entire eastern Copper Eskimo area.

As noted in chapter 1, by 1925 the pattern of inland winter habitation had been established for those who lived on the mainland. Those Inuit in the eastern part of Copper Eskimo country who continued to spend much of each year on Victoria Island crossed to Kent Peninsula for autumn caribou hunts after animals ceased to cross northward over Dease Strait sometime in the early 1920s. On the mainland, winter camps existed as far to the southwest as Contwoyto Lake and as far as Beechey and MacDougall Lakes on the Back River system to the southeast. Descent to the sea could begin as early as February or, more commonly, in April at the end of the trapping season, depending on the success of winter hunts. Normally, throughout the period before the 1950s, the regions to the south of Queen Maud and Coronation Gulfs were well supplied with caribou, especially during the migration seasons. To gain some appreciation of the importance of that animal in the area, one can cite records of caribou hide purchases at the Bathurst post. In the years 1949–50 through 1954–55 an annual average of 1,258 were traded.[152] It must not be supposed that this average represents any approach to the total animals killed in the trading district. Skins were saved mainly from the summer months when they were suitable for clothing, and also represent surpluses after local needs were met. In the years 1955–56 through 1959–60 the average traded dropped to 281.[153] It is thus clear that a decline in the total kill characterized the later years of the fifties. Other indications of this change can be gleaned from the records of the Catholic mission at Bathurst.[154] From 1936 through 1953 both spring and fall migrations occurred in significant numbers almost yearly. In 1953 both migrations were described as comprising "very few" caribou. After that, while spring migrations continued, although in decreased numbers, the only fall migration during the rest of the decade was in 1957, and that again with the notation "very few."[155]

The reduction in numbers of caribou paralleled a movement of Inuit who traded at Bathurst away from winter habitation of the interior during the second half of the 1950s. Indeed, there was a general shift in economy from primary dependence on caribou for much of each year to greater emphasis on sealing and fishing at coastal sites for all or most of the year. That this re-adaptation was not entirely successful can be seen in the need to bring in food to some of the camps. In January 1955, 1,000 pounds of buffalo meat had to be dropped at a camp at Gordon Bay.[156] While most of the people deserted the interior during this period, a few remained around Contwoyto Lake. Hard times there required that in April 1956, 400 pounds of buffalo meat and 800 pounds of "offal" (presumably dog feed) had to be left.[157]

Beginning in 1955 a further dislocation of people from the mainland as well as from southeastern Victoria Island took place due to the construction of radar stations along the southern coast of the island and to the eastward on islands in Queen Maud Gulf. After the construction phase some of the men who had been employed returned to their former regions, but a number remained in the vicinity of the sites, especially around the CAM Main Station at Cambridge Bay. Some idea of the effects of the attraction of employment at Cambridge Bay can be derived from Hudson's Bay Company records at Bathurst Inlet. Between 1952 and 1955 the trading population varied between 158 and 170, including a small number in hospitals in the south.[158] After migration northward for employment at Cambridge Bay, the 1956 figure dropped to 126.

The shortage of caribou seems to have hit the Perry River region at about the same time as it did the Bathurst trading district, for in January 1954 destitution was reported and buffalo meat had to be flown in.[159] Further relief was necessary in March after the local Inuit made their customary move to the sea ice from their camps or from the post at Perry Island. Sealing was reported as a failure, and the buffalo meat had been exhausted.[160] There followed some controversy regarding the actual need of the people.[161] The officer in charge of the district at Cambridge Bay expressed the view that "unless absolutely necessary no more assistance be given, as these natives might soon begin to like a soft life with government assistance."[162] On the other hand, Chesshire of the HBC who visited the Perry River region at this time found it necessary to leave a ton of dog feed behind.[163]

The view of the RCMP officer demonstrates the continued application of a policy that had been in force before the 1950s. One manifestation of this position had been the withholding of family allowances except in cases perceived as being those of actual need. For example, a 1948 RCMP report from Cambridge Bay stated that no relief had been granted, and while allowances had been given to several families, "no more were anticipated until after the ship comes."[164] An example of how this policy extended into the following decade can be cited for Contwoyto Lake. A trapper who had been given the job of handling government issuances there reported in 1955: "Eskimos told they would receive no more Family Allowances until spring."[165] Population figures for Perry River for 1955 reveal that "25 families, of approximately 96 people" were trading there.[166] By the end of January 1959 there were fifteen families in residence in the district.[167] It is evident that a number of people had moved either to Cambridge Bay itself or to other radar sites. Contrary to the situation around Bathurst, the Perry River people continued to live inland during winter months, with one coastal camp and only one extended family (two or three nuclear families) residing at the post.[168]

The greatest concentration of people was taking place at Cambridge Bay, which had long been a gathering place of Inuit. As early as Collinson's wintering there in 1852–53 it was a place of assemblage,[169] especially in the fall when caribou gathered to cross Dease Strait as it froze over. Jenness also indicates Cambridge Bay as one of the "cache sites and gathering places on the coast."[170] In addition to the HBC trading post, there were the Anglican and Catholic missions and an RCMP detachment, all established before the 1950s. A Loran station was also stationed there in 1946–47. This station employed about twenty Inuit during construction and it is estimated that about 100 people lived at Cambridge at that time.[171] Later, most dispersed, except for "three or four families." However, even in 1948 there was concern about the tendency for in-gathering at Cambridge by the local RCMP detachment: "In view of this, it has been found necessary to keep the natives working and not let them gather in the settlement too often, or too long a time."[172]

In 1951 the Loran station was replaced by the Department of Transport facility employing two men.[173] But it was not until the CAM Main radar site was being constructed in 1955 that significant in-gathering of a more permanent nature began. Using scrap lumber from the dump at the site, three distinct neighbourhoods grew up, representing immigrants from Bathurst Inlet, Perry River, and outlying camps on Victoria Island respectively.[174] At the peak of construction, there were about 200 Inuit at Cambridge Bay, and in the summer of 1956 there were still 114 Inuit living there, with twenty-two men working in wage employment.[175] In the preceding year the Department of Northern Affairs had brought in a Northern Service officer, and in March 1956 a nursing station was established.[176] The RCMP deplored the perceived work habits of some of the Inuit men: "Some work permanently at the DEWline. Some work for a period, quit, and live on their earnings and return again to work." The RCMP were making an effort to have in residence only a few as permanent workers and the remainder were encouraged to continue hunting and trapping.[177]

Local problems that were to be common in the new centralized communities of the Central Arctic began to make their appearance. The making of home brew was widespread and there were seventy-one prosecutions for liquor offences in 1958.[178] Much of the material in the RCMP reports centred on situations at DEWline sites. The problem of "loitering" around the stations provoked the officer in charge at Cambridge to suggest in 1958 that Inuit not be allowed within ten miles of sites.[179] The suggestion was passed to RCMP headquarters in Ottawa and eventually to Sivertz, who responded, "On the question of prohibiting their residence within this distance I am not so certain. As you know it is not our policy to prohibit Eskimos doing anything that is within the law, although we try to guide them in their own best interests."[180] Paternalism is implicit in this statement, and it seems clear that the Policy of Dispersal was still in effect, even in 1958, for he continued, "an attempt should be made to try to discourage persons at the sites from giving handouts" as, if denied, Inuit might move back to their hunting grounds more readily.

The 1958 year-end RCMP report indicated that no actual "loitering" was in evidence at Cambridge Bay since trapping and hunting were being carried out from that base. "For some of the Eskimos it is necessary for them to live in the settlement if they want to be with their children who are attending school."[181] Further, with fox prices having risen to $25, twenty-seven people employed on the DEWline on a full-time basis, and summer employment available to most men in the immediate proximity to Cambridge Bay, few could be considered to be "loitering."

At the end of the fifties, of the total eastern Copper Eskimo population of about 500, 300 still lived in outlying hunting-trapping camps, while at Cambridge Bay a school and a nursing station served educational and health needs.[182] Housing was still mainly restricted to scrap lumber "shacks." In the camps, shelters were mainly snowhouses and skin or canvas tents.

Two chief factors brought on departures from contact-traditional locations and practices in the eastern Copper Eskimo regions during the 1950s. In the Bathurst Inlet region, the failure of caribou to arrive in usual numbers was clearly responsible for movement of people from winter sites of habitation in the interior to the coast. While this trend was not as pronounced in the Perry River district, there was considerable contraction around the post in order to be close to emergency aid when the caribou situation worsened. The centralization at Cambridge Bay was mainly due to employment possibilities there. Some Inuit were transferred by air to outlying DEWline sites, but the main movements in the entire area were by means of native transport, and there is no evidence for coercion being applied in any of these migrations.

COPPERMINE

The trading district of Coppermine included the mainland regions westward from about Cape Barrow on the coast, with adjoining inland areas as far south as Contwoyto Lake, to Dolphin and Union Strait. By the 1950s the settlement near the mouth of the Coppermine River consisted of an HBC post, both Anglican and Catholic missions, a small hospital operated by the Anglican mission, an RCMP detachment, a school, and a radio and meteorological station.[183] From 1932, annual police patrols reported, for the most part, satisfactory game conditions.[184] In June 1949, however, an RCMP report pointed to "a very bad year," with no fish, no caribou, poor sealing, and "nothing to trade."[185] However, earlier that year there had been the largest gathering at Coppermine during the Easter holiday "since 1932,"[186] an occasion attributed to caribou appearing near the post. This situation was to recur during the next few years and have profound effects upon the settlement practices of the area.

The contact-traditional settlement pattern had been, as in the Bathurst region, that of inland caribou hunting and habitation in the winter, with a return to the sea for sealing when winter supplies ran low. Some families spent the entire year in the interior. During the early fifties caribou populations in the interior began to drop, while in the district within easy reach of Coppermine they remained good. While the large aggregations of Inuit for sealing in late winter and early spring continued, the distribution of caribou created a temptation to cluster at Coppermine. The welfare teacher had assumed some administrative duties, before the institution of the Northern Service officer. In 1952 the teacher proposed that caribou skins available at the HBC could be distributed as family allowance issuances to Inuit for winter clothing.[187] The RCMP officer in charge disagreed, since he felt that this would discourage dispersal of people to hunt. The debate reached Ottawa, where Cantley, following his established stance regarding population distribution, wrote to the teacher's superior that "[w]e are very much concerned by the apparent desire among the natives to gather around a settlement. It seems to us it would be very difficult for 109 people to obtain a living in this limited area for any length of time. ... where the natives are encouraged to live around the posts they quickly lose the inclination to go back to their nomadic fishing and hunting ways and come to depend more and more on what they can beg from the white man."[188] Indeed, there was considerable concern among the white agents in the village about the degree of in-gathering occurring at Coppermine. This concern led to a general meeting shortly after Christmas 1952. An unusually large number of Inuit had been drawn to the centre not only because of the holiday but also because of the presence of caribou nearby and their absence in the deep interior. The rationale for the meeting was stated by the teacher as: "it would be better to advise them why they could not remain at the Post and to ask them to leave rather than use force."[189] At the meeting, the nurse asserted that a contagious disease could come and kill all or most of them and that they should, accordingly, spread into smaller camps. The RCMP officer also told the Inuit that it was necessary for them to leave. The people did, indeed, leave shortly afterwards.[190] Return to the village a month later brought lament from the teacher: "It is hoped that the caribou herd will move off soon as it is not good for the Eskimos to have so easy a supply of food. Too much is as harmful as too little as the natives have a tendency to become lazy and give up the pursuit of other game like seal and fish which are more difficult to secure."[191] In April of 1953 many people left for their annual seal camp on the sea ice,[192] but others were attracted by the income that could be earned from carving and preferred to remain in the village. The teacher, who appears to have had considerable control over the lives of the Inuit in the area, refused "to accept Handicraft items ... until they could show me that they had got some seals."[193] After the sealing season of 1953 most of the Inuit camped a few miles from the village occupied with fishing. There was no migration of caribou that fall. The teacher seemed relieved by that resource failure: "The natives will have to work harder for a living this winter. That will be a good thing as the settlement will not be overcrowded as it was last year and there will be less trouble in the way of epidemics and sickness. It will be better for the natives' morale to be on the hunt rather than sitting idle."[194] But the natives were less enthusiastic about the absence of caribou, and by November dogsleds laden with food had to be sent inland to alleviate famine. Those people who came to Coppermine from the interior quickly moved out on the sea ice, and the sealing season began two or three months earlier that winter.[195]

A herd did appear near the village in December of 1953 but weather conditions interfered with the hunt.[196] The winter of 1953–54 saw considerable controversy regarding local conditions, which involved HBC headquarters in Winnipeg as well as officials in Ottawa.[197] In a report to Winnipeg the local trader at Coppermine cited what he saw as "improvidence" on the part of the Inuit, and he recommended eliminating the monthly issuances of family allowances, the peddling of handicraft objects in heavy quantities, and the monthly issuances of relief and old age pensions. He proposed, among other recommendations, consolidation of income and issuances to be made in "installments" at no less than four-month intervals. Such measures would in his view accomplish the "main objective to reinhabit the country."[198]

When this letter from the Coppermine trader was forwarded to Ottawa an exchange followed between Sivertz and Cantley. Consistent with his by then established stance regarding in-gathering, Cantley supported the position of the trader and opined that the trouble in the community stemmed from failure of the RCMP officer to follow the advice of the HBC representative, but he did feel that some of the suggestions would imply "return to the old debt system."[199] Sivertz agreed that family allowances should not be paid on a monthly basis, but thought that the trader's recommendations were "highly dictatorial" and seemed to be founded on the idea "that Eskimos are improvident and childish and can never develop."[200] The rather mixed reaction to the trader's letter reflected the uneven but also changing character of policy-making in the 1950s in Ottawa. A June 1954 RCMP report indicated that the main occurrence of caribou was near the Rae River, only thirty-five miles from Coppermine, and that inlanders were again moving to the coast because of the dearth of animals in the interior regions.[201]

The problems of the Coppermine community were compounded in the spring of 1954, when it was hit by an influenza epidemic that was probably brought by members of the annual x-ray team. The epidemic supported the notion of the advantages of dispersal that had been raised in the December 1952 meeting with the Inuit.

After recovery from this epidemic and resumption of the normal period of hunting on the sea ice and later fishing, signs of caribou again appeared near the village in December 1954 and January 1955.[203] The same conditions prevailed in the winter of the following year (1955–56),[204] when people left the sealing camp to hunt caribou in the Rae River region. The new welfare teacher made an optimistic report in February 1956: "With average catch of seals and occasional good kills of caribou plus wages from DEWline employment, the general welfare of the community has been very good, also there have been unusually high earnings from handicrafts."[205] This optimism, and that of later reports, can perhaps to a large extent be attributed to the appointment of new welfare teachers. The picture given by the RCMP officer in May 1956 was less bright when he indicated that people had moved from inland locations and settled at Coppermine, a condition that "will have an undesirable effect upon them economically and socially."[206] In order to encourage people to return inland, they were given supplies and a number did indeed return. This move proved to be successful, for those who returned from the interior to trade in November quickly left again for their inland camps.[207]

During the winter of 1956–57, while a chicken pox epidemic hit the community, nearby caribou hunting was again productive. There were 200 people at the centre at the annual Easter gathering in 1957, but by the end of May "almost the whole settlement's native population moved away from Coppermine for the annual seal hunt."[208] The winter of 1957–58 was indifferent in terms of hunting, and another epidemic struck, but by the autumn of 1958 the hunting around Contwoyto Lake was so successful that concern was being expressed about conservation of the caribou at that place. Indeed, a fishing program was introduced to create another source of food, especially for dogs.[209] Centralization was meanwhile advancing at Coppermine, and little is written in the reports about sending people away from the village at this time. As well, nothing in the correspondence from Ottawa suggests pressures toward dispersal of populations in this area. By 1958–59 the people who had spent the year at the village of Coppermine comprised about half of the total population of the trading area.[210] As before, there continued to be annual migrations to the ice for seal hunting. In 1959 there came reports of people camping in the vicinity of DEWline sites where no employment was available.[211] However, here, as in other regions, the RCMP appear to have been successful in discouraging the practice. The winter of 1959–60 saw a pronounced increase in caribou kills, with no fewer than 2,000 animals being taken around Coppermine, and another 1,500 in the Contwoyto Lake region.[212] Thus, an upswing in the procural of caribou coincided with a period when centralization was quite advanced at Coppermine.

The special circumstances that brought on tendencies toward ingathering at Coppermine included the availability of game nearby, but the location of the growing centre itself was also a factor. Jenness noted that the immediate vicinity was one of "cache sites, and gathering places on the coast" of Copper Eskimo country.[213] As well, nearby Bloody Falls was a locale where, from the visit of Hearne in 1772 onward,[214] explorers nearly always met with people. Later, when Rasmussen traveled through the area, he reported that "88 caribou hunters" were camped there in January–February 1924.[215] The next chapter provides examples of situations similar to that at Coppermine, where inlanders dependent on the caribou for subsistence moved or were moved to coastal locales. What is unusual here is the proximity of the centre to the animals,[216] which drew people or helped maintain people there at a time of growing centralization. Given these conditions it is perhaps remarkable that complete centralization was delayed at

Coppermine throughout much of the 1950s, and it seems clear that there had been strenuous application of the Policy of Dispersal by local whites. Likewise, when such application was relaxed, and not reinforced from Ottawa, the in-gathering increased apace.

SUMMARY

The 1950s saw a wide range of settlement situations in the Arctic Coast–Arctic Islands regions. There was only one relocation project in that area during this time, that which brought people to Ellesmere and Cornwallis Islands. In this case the ostensible motive for moving people was to bring them from a region perceived to have been overpopulated to places of superior game resources. While this objective appears to have been achieved, the hoped-for integration of people from two distinct geographical regions and diverse economic adaptations made for difficulties.

Almost all movements of people during the fifties for the Arctic Coast–Arctic Island area were those of migration. Wage labour opportunities drew Inuit to some locales. At Frobisher Bay, military and, later, governmental installations provided such opportunities. However, after the initial expansion of work during construction phases, a large unemployed population remained, and problems of housing, education, and sanitation developed, as elsewhere where large-scale centralization advanced. At Frobisher, in particular, there were, already during the fifties, the problems contingent upon relations between elements of two diverse ethnic populations in close contact with one another. Other wage opportunities during the 1950s came in connection with the building of radar stations across the Central Arctic. One large community grew around the main DEWline site at Cambridge Bay. Significant numbers of men were employed in the building there, as well as the minor sites for which Cambridge was a distribution centre. People were drawn not only from the immediate trading area but also from the mainland regions to the south. After building ended, a large aggregation of people remained, bringing on some of the problems described above for Frobisher. All across the chain of sites, clustering of smaller groups was deplored by both local and central government administrators, and especially by the RCMP, who took measures to disperse these gatherings. These efforts were largely successful.

In-gathering also occurred at Igloolik and Pelly Bay, where aggregations formed in proximity to Catholic missions. The clustering of people could not be wholly attributed to the presence of the missionaries, however, since in both places the missions had been in existence for many years.

A decline in caribou numbers also affected movement. South of Coronation Gulf, where an inland orientation, based largely on the caribou, had been established, the decline brought people to the coastal regions. Around Bathurst Inlet this meant a much greater dependency on sea mammals the year round. Coppermine's situation with regard to the distribution of caribou in relation to the process of centralization was virtually unique: while the interior was increasingly stripped of winter occupation, the presence of herds nearer to the village fostered gatherings there. In regions to the east, caribou migrations onto the islands and peninsulas had ceased some years before, and, again, there was increased emphasis on sea-mammal hunting. For Baffin Island, in particular, caribou numbers had been unstable during the periods preceding the fifties. For most of the Arctic Coast–Arctic Island regions the shortages of caribou skins for clothing was a persistent problem, and this shortage was one component of the complex of the factors leading toward centralization at Pelly Bay. It is not clear as to what degree the shortage brought people to other trading centres, since in most places the pressures to disperse remained strong throughout most of the 1950s.

While in Ottawa policies that would affect Inuit settlement were beginning to shift, there was little departure from the implementation of the Policy of Dispersal of Inuit settlement in most of the regions considered in this chapter. The RCMP and other local representatives of the government applied pressure to discourage aggregations at the customary points of trade, with at least implicit and sometimes explicit endorsement from Ottawa. During the 1950s the process of centralization began to gather force in the regions of the Arctic Coast and Islands, but in much of this area the dispersal of populations was being maintained, and a large portion of the populations still lived in the all-native hunting-trapping camps of the contact-traditional settlement orientation.

CHAPTER FOUR

Settlement in the 1950s – II

THE KEEWATIN REGION

The Keewatin District, along with the District of Mackenzie and the District of Franklin, was one of the former three main divisions of the Northwest Territories. It extended northward from the northern boundary of the province of Manitoba to the Arctic coast and eastward from the eastern boundary of the District of Mackenzie to the western coast of Hudson Bay, including all the islands in the bay. Reference to such an extensive area is not useful here, since it includes much of the Netsilik area, which has been treated already in this study. As well, some islands in Hudson Bay fall within the Quebec–Labrador cultural and geographical region.

A more useful designation for the purposes of this study is one used by Brack and McIntosh, who delineate a Keewatin Region.[1] This region includes areas of Inuit habitation in the interior that reach from the upper Back River in the north, and in the west to Beverly and Dubawnt Lakes. It extends to Ennadai and Nueltin Lakes in the southwest and south, and eastward across to the coast just above the Manitoba border. The region also includes the west coast of Hudson Bay and Southampton and Coats Islands. To the northeast it extends to Repulse Bay and Lyon Inlet. By the 1950s it encompassed the total range of the Caribou Eskimo, elements of Iglulik (Aiviliks) and Netsilik groups, and some immigrants from Baffin Island and the Quebec–Labrador Peninsula. This Keewatin Region can be divided conveniently into three subregions: (1) Northwestern Hudson Bay, (2) the Northern Interior, and (3) the Southern Interior and Coast.

NORTHWESTERN HUDSON BAY

By the beginning of the 1950s the fur trade in this subregion had been concentrated into three loci: Coral Harbour on Southampton Island,

and posts at Repulse Bay and Chesterfield Inlet.[2] For the most part three separate communities had developed around these posts. It has been noted that a certain degree of centralization, as well as contraction of settlement, around Coral Harbour took place during World War II. These processes continued into the 1950s. Bird visited Southampton Island in 1951 and gave a census of 238 Eskimos and "half-breeds living as Eskimos." Of these, seventy-two lived at Coral Harbour and thirty-two close by in two small camps. Bird also noted that "in all 143 natives, three fifths [of the population] were living within one days journey from the post."[3] There were also one camp of forty-four people at the extreme southeast point of the island and another of thirty-two at its northern end.[4] The contraction that had by then taken place occurred despite the poor hunting area in the immediate vicinity of Coral Harbour. By this time, the acquisition of large Peterhead boats had made possible a wider range of hunting during the summer, the most productive sea-mammal hunting months.

A further contraction and concentration of population had taken place by the summer of 1959, when VanStone visited the island. Only three camps remained, apart from the centre at Coral Harbour, the most distant of which was only eight miles from that centre. Of the total population of the island of 215 (now decreased through emigration), ninety-two or 43 per cent lived at Coral Harbour as compared to about 30 per cent at the time of Bird's visit eight years earlier.[5] There appears to have been some degree of separation between those living at Coral Harbour, who were for the most part born either on the island or on the Keewatin Mainland,[6] and the people in the camps, who were mainly from southern Baffin Island or the northern Quebec–Labrador Peninsula.[7] While major subsistence and some of the trade in furs came from the hunting-trapping economy, men (at times with their families) moved back and forth to DEWline sites beginning in 1957 and brought an important source of cash into the community.[8] There had also been emigration of a more permanent nature: two families that had sought employment at Churchill, and "twenty seven individuals, representing six families and two single men" who had "moved to Rankin Inlet."[9]

The area around Repulse Bay had been populated jointly by Netsiliks and the indigenous Aivilingmiut since whaling times, and though elements of these groups often hunted together and shared localities of habitation, intermarriage was slow to develop.[10] The outside agencies were minimal, with only an HBC post and a Catholic mission. RCMP contact came through patrols from the detachment at Chesterfield. One of these patrols, made in spring of 1948, gives a false impression of the degree of in-gathering.[11] While it was reported that "all but four families" had gathered at the Repulse Bay post, it is clear that this represented the annual Easter gathering rather than any actual tendency toward centralization of settlement. In the later fifties, however, a more accurate depiction of settlement in the area was made. The 1958 patrol reported: "The natives in the Repulse Bay area do not remain in the settlement, with the exception of a few – they do gather at the Post three or four times a year and enjoy their dances, etc. on these occasions."[12] The RCMP reports for the 1950s basically agree with my information gathered in the field in 1967, that the 1950s was a period of general continuity of contact-traditional economy and settlement practices, which included largely scattered settlement based on hunting and trapping, with aggregation at ship time and at Christmas and Easter (or the end of trapping season).

As at Repulse Bay, the population of the Chesterfield district was made up of Netsiliks and Aivilingmiut, but a number of Caribou Eskimo also shared the general area. Concern with in-gathering was evidenced as early as 1947, when the newly arrived sergeant in charge of the RCMP detachment lamented that a large number of natives had congregated at the village. He attributed this situation to encouragement by the resident Catholic mission.[13] According to his report, the Inuit claimed that they did not have sufficient dogs, canoes, or other boats to adequately hunt outlying areas. However, the sergeant observed the presence of these aids to the hunt and wrote: "I made it known that I would not pay out Family Allowances to anyone who did not try to do anything for themselves."[14] While some of the men moved out, it was for distances of only twenty or thirty miles, from where they visited Chesterfield frequently. A further report issued in January 1952[15] recommended building a hostel for the school, which had been established the previous year.[16] At the same time the sergeant also feared that with the school in operation, parents would tend to congregate around the village.[17] This report brought forth comment by Henry Larsen. He wrote to G.E.B. Sinclair of Northern Administration that "our policy has been to keep as many people out of the settlement as possible."[18] By March 1952, the officer in charge of Chesterfield reported success in getting people out of the centre.[19] In April, a further report noted the role of the mission in organizing such community events as dances and "many religious meetings which tend to keep them briefly occupied and perhaps an incentive to keep them dwelling at or near the Post."[20]

The year-end 1952 RCMP report described a local population of 278 Inuit, of which 135 lived outside of Chesterfield.[21] This distribution of people would indicate that the police had had some success in keeping the population dispersed. In 1953, a number of the Chesterfield people moved to Rankin Inlet, where employment was available for a time for members of twelve families.[22] By then only sixty-six people were living in the camps that traded into Chesterfield, but even this reduced number tended to cluster close to the village, despite continued efforts to get them to be more widely distributed. At the end of 1954 only twelve of the total of fifty-six families in the area lived outside the centre, while "the remainder" were "either at Chesterfield or within a days traveling distance."[23] These conditions brought on considerable government involvement in the community. The Northern Service officer stationed in Churchill, W.G. Kerr, visited Chesterfield in early 1955, and when he wrote to B.G. Sivertz, then chief of the Arctic Division, he put much of the blame for the in-gathering on the mission.[24] In July 1955, Sivertz reported to the NSO that Bishop LeCroix had met with him in Ottawa. The cleric had suggested that in order to induce the people to move out of the village they should be given sufficient supplies of ammunition and at least two months' rations, as well as advice as to where they should hunt.[25] Meanwhile, the constable in charge expressed his confusion over administrative policy. He indicated that while the Inuit themselves would prefer to cluster at the post, "members of this detachment seem to be the only ones who try to encourage the Eskimos to live on the land."[26] In a letter to Sivertz,[27] Larsen lent his support to this latter policy and for the time, the various departments of northern administration were in agreement.[28] The upshot of correspondence was a meeting held at Chesterfield on 30 August 1955, attended by Kerr and the local representatives of the Church and of the RCMP. They agreed on a number of points. These included sending out all people not permanently employed to at least fifteen miles from the settlement. They were to be equipped with supplies, including ammunition, to last until the beginning of the trapping season in November. After that they would be expected to provide for themselves. Anyone staying in the settlement who was unemployed would not be provided with rations or dog feed.[29]

The meeting was significant in that the representative of the mission, the agency held largely responsible for the in-gathering, was in accord with the moves toward dispersing the population. The plan met with initial success, for as late as 25 November no relief had to be issued.[30] By the end of the year, however, all except a half-dozen families lived at no great distance while "the others are into the post at least once a week" and "most of the better hunting and sealing grounds are sparsely inhabited."[31] Indeed, in spite of the brief respite from relief issuances reported for the autumn of 1955, the year-end RCMP report stated that $13,682.98 had to be issued in relief during the year, in addition to $10,715.86 in family allowances.[32] Employment possibilities at Rankin Inlet in 1956 resulted in significant emigration for that purpose, but fur-

ther attempts at dispersing the remaining population were hampered by
a series of epidemics, including influenza, measles, and pneumonia,
which together resulted in nine deaths.[33] The epidemics drew people to
the hospital facility at Chesterfield. A lack of fur clothing and low morale led to "the tendency to loiter around the settlement."[34]

Hunting improved in the summer of 1956,[35] and in the next twelve
months, 600 hundred caribou were reported killed, providing skin
clothing as well as meat. Success in sealing was also reported, and 1957
was a better year for the Chesterfield people than the previous years of
the decade. Employment was by then expanding as well, with permanent jobs offered by the Department of Transport, the mission, the
RCMP, and the HBC.[36] In addition, the mission initiated a housing
project, and by the end of 1957 all but one family lived in a house.[37] By
the end of 1958 it would appear that the process of centralization was
all but complete,[38] and the final report of the decade indicated that
"game resources were not taxed too much in 1959."[39] Chesterfield natives (presumably mainly the men) were "all steadily employed," and
with only two families on relief.

This situation at the close of the fifties appears to have resulted from
several factors. First, it seems evident that the Policy of Dispersal,
which earlier had been so strenuously applied, was gradually relaxed.
Emigration to Rankin Inlet reduced the population of the Chesterfield
community, while growing wage labour possibilities absorbed most of
the remaining families. The existence of comfortable housing no
doubt also made the village more attractive, and several epidemics
made proximity to the hospital highly desirable, if not imperative. But
emigration to Rankin was the chief factor that left Chesterfield a relatively minor centre in the Keewatin as the new decade began, even
though the camp system in the area had collapsed, and the remaining
people were drawn to the village itself.

THE NORTHERN INTERIOR

The northern interior of the Keewatin is dominated geographically by
Baker Lake and the several rivers with their connecting lakes that flow
into it. This area is inhabited by several groups of Caribou Eskimo.[40]
There is also the upper Back River, including the chain of Pelly,
Garry, and MacDougall Lakes, occupied by people of mixed regional
derivation.[41]

After trading posts were established around Baker Lake in the
1920s, 1930s, and 1940s,[42] an inland version of contact-traditional settlement was established, being based largely on caribou hunting with
fishing a secondary occupation. As noted earlier, in this area trapping

was usually focused around winter cache sites, rather than being routes of any length. The fate of the population rested on that of the caribou. In the years leading up to the 1950s there was no steady or pronounced general diminution in the numbers of that animal, though shortages did occur.[43] These shortages in some years affected the entire subregion, but more often certain districts within suffered while others appeared to prosper. Conditions in camps also varied by season. Autumn migrations of caribou were expected to allow accumulation of sufficient meat caches to provide basic subsistence throughout winter until the spring migrations began. In some years, caches would be exhausted as spring approached, and conditions of hardship often prevailed at such times. RCMP sled patrols, earlier from Chesterfield[44] and from 1930 onward from the detachment then established at Baker Lake,[45] were vital: they provided information on conditions in camps and also emergency aid, especially food.

Events of 1949 portended declining conditions and the measures that would seek to alleviate them during the 1950s. In March the missionary who had been living at Garry Lake was brought out by airplane, and he reported that people there were short of food and that 75 per cent of the dogs had died from disease.[46] Shortly thereafter relief supplies were flown in.[47] As far as I have been able to determine, this was the first use of aircraft for emergency flights in this subregion of the Keewatin.

At the beginning of the 1950s, there was a tendency for in-gathering around the post at Baker Lake, where both Anglican and Catholic missions had been established, at Christian holidays. For instance, for Christmas 1951 it is reported that 100 families had gathered at the village, but the RCMP reported that otherwise "they do not loiter in the settlement."[48] Occasional and local food shortages continued to exist in the early fifties as before. In the winter of 1950–51, people in the Kazan River area reported shortage of food and were advised to come to the Baker Lake centre if there was danger of starvation.[49] It does not appear that such a movement actually occurred, and 1951, in general, was judged to be a good year for both caribou and fox. The year-end report again stated "the people do not loiter in the settlement."[50] By the end of 1952, however, both subsistence prey and trapping had declined.[51] A period of economic decline in the subregion appeared to begin in the winter of 1952–53, for it was reported in April 1953 that no fewer than four patrols had been made and that "[t]he reason for this is the extreme scarcity of country food, there being no Caribou in the area, and foxes are practically non-existent, also there has been a very poor run of fish this winter and the natives are forced to spend most of their time fishing."[52] However, no deaths were reported for this lean period.

A reprieve from the dismal conditions came for much of the trading area during 1954.[53] This was especially true in the vicinity of the centre at Baker Lake, where herds of caribou came very close. At year's end seventy-five people lived there, so significant centralization had taken place, but it was also reported that "the majority are employed," with "only 4 relief issues being made," and again, "little tendency to loiter."[54] Elsewhere in the trading district, good hunting and fur returns were reported, except for the Garry Lake–Back River district where "a number died from starvation or sickness."[55] This began a period of yearly severe hardship in that district, which received considerable attention in the archival record, as well as in published material.[56] These events require some detailed treatment here.

The Catholic mission at Garry Lake became a locus for apparently seasonal aggregations.[57] An airstrip had been built ten miles away at Pelly Lake by Spartan Airways that was to have a role in events to follow.[58] In March 1954 an RCAF plane left 400 pounds of food.[59] In 1955 the missionary radioed that conditions required another drop, and again in March another load of 500 pounds was left.[60] However, the RCMP officer involved wrote that the missionary had exaggerated the plight of the people and that, "with the food and ammunition now left with them, as well as the caribou recently obtained, no difficulties should be experienced."[61] That may have been the case for the next few months, but in March 1956, another 1,100 pounds of "food, ammunition, fish nets and supplies" were flown in and left with the priest "for redistribution in camps nearby."[62] Still another load of food and other supplies was dropped in May of that year.[63]

In the following spring, April of 1957, a flight was made to recover the body of the priest, who had died in a blizzard in the previous autumn, and it brought further news of conditions in the Garry–Pelly Lakes region.[64] At that time the natives thought that they had enough food on hand to last until winter,[65] but another drop had to be made, of 800 pounds in August.[66] A short time later conditions appeared to have improved as "all camps were obtaining caribou and fish."[67] The cycle of privation, however, continued, and on 4 December 1957, still another $900 worth of food and ammunition were left.[68] Although optimism was expressed, the winter of 1957–58 proved disastrous for the Garry–Pelly Lakes district, bringing on the deaths by starvation of seventeen people. The bare facts of the case appear in a report by the Northern Service officer at Baker Lake as follows: (1) Failure of caribou to appear in large numbers in the fall and winter of 1957–58; (2) Destruction of relief food kept in the area by fire; (3) Lack of guidance for the Eskimos in a difficult situation.[69]

In my view, such a tragedy as occurred can be said to have been al-most inevitable in the Garry–Pelly Lakes district, as perhaps anywhere in the Keewatin interior, especially during the decade of the 1950s. Given the fickle nature of the occurrences and habits of the caribou in the best of times, existence on the barrens of the Keewatin was always precarious. These tragedies occurred at the time of the year when fam-ine had been common throughout the history of the area, but the years of the later fifties, in particular, saw especially depleted caribou populations. I have summarized the high number of flights made to this district and it should be noted that under Arctic flying conditions, with severe temperatures and often darkness, it is not always possible to make flights, or to land, at will. The large loads that were left would have been impossible to transport by dogsled in the best of traveling conditions. Relief under these conditions was an almost insurmount-able task as long as the population remained dispersed to the degree it was throughout the northern interior at this period.[70]

Meanwhile, the remainder of the subregion continued to experi-ence fluctuations in game supply, but with an essentially downward trend. While 1955 was a good year for caribou,[71] conditions declined in 1956, with very few hides being traded at the post. The Inuit popula-tion contracted to within three or four days' journey from the Baker Lake centre, a condition that "reflects the caribou situation."[72] In-gathering was also advancing. In an effort to regain some of the dis-persal of people, a project camp was set up for hunting south of the lake,[73] but the next winter, 1957–58, brought famine around Aber-deen Lake and rations and other supplies had to be flown in, in Febru-ary 1958.[74] The winter of 1958–59 saw uneven conditions in the subregions from place to place. While people in the village itself were securing a fair number of caribou, others had to be evacuated from camps. Supplies were sent to other locales.[75] It was reported that 3,000 pounds of third grade beef was flown in to camps.[76] Reflecting the conditions that winter, only four camps were located outside a radius of fifty miles from the village of Baker Lake.[77]

To the end of the decade, local variations in the supply of caribou continued. While some relief had to be issued at some camps, else-where the autumn of 1959 saw improvement.[78] For instance, in the re-gion to the north of Baker Lake and east of the Thelon River where twenty families continued to live, "most hunters had forty to sixty caches."[79] As well, people who had been returned to the Schultz Lake region in September were "in high spirits" and had killed ninety cari-bou in a little over two weeks.[80] A fishing project that had been estab-lished southwest of the post produced 8,000 fish.[81]

But while in some locales an upswing in economic success was apparent, the general in-gathering continued, so that by the end of 1959 forty-two families were living at the Baker Lake village. Forty-one still lived in the outlying camps, some as far away as 80 to 100 miles, but most were much closer.[82] At the decade's end, winter habitation was distributed fifty/fifty between camps and the Baker Lake centre.

The regional administrator from Churchill, apparently conceding the inevitability of centralization because of chronically depressed local circumstances, recommended that most people should probably move to the post. He thought that some could remain on the land, but that they should be assisted by the administration by supplying dogs, building permafrost cellars, and assisting in fishing projects.[83]

The settlement situation in the northern interior during the 1950s was a complex of policy decisions interacting with movements of people. There was no evident application of such draconian measures to disperse people as, for instance, were being applied at Coppermine and Chesterfield during the same decade. On the other hand, frequent supplying of camps by aircraft was consistent with the Policy of Dispersal. Some flights brought people to the centre at Baker Lake for reasons of illness or famine, or even survival, others returned people to the camps, and much movement back and forth between camps and village was made on the ground and initiated by the Inuit themselves. Both relocation and migration were thus evident. In addition, a general contraction was also apparent, both voluntarily and under direction of the RCMP or administrators. Relocations outside the subregion to coastal sites in the Keewatin as the decade ended will be discussed later in this chapter.

All in all, governmental policy as applied to the northern interior of the Keewatin during the 1950s was flexible in the face of recognition of an uncertain economic base. Regional, seasonal, and year-to-year fluctuations in the availability of the caribou had each played a role in the area's history. There is much evidence to indicate that the 1950s were also a time of unusual shortage of caribou in the subregion and, as will be argued, in the Keewatin Region as a whole.

THE SOUTHERN INTERIOR AND COAST

The southern interior of the Keewatin was inhabited by elements of the Caribou Eskimo, including the Padlirmiut (or Patlirmiut), who lived on the upper Kazan River below Yathkyed Lake, west to Dubwant Lake and southeast along the lower Maguse River, and the Ahiarmiut, who lived to the southwest.[84] The Ahiarmiut traded at several posts

that operated in the Nueltin Lake region from the mid 1920s until
1950, when the last one was closed. Other trading posts – those at Maguse Lake (1925–26), Tavani (1928?–51), Maguse River (1938–60),
Padlei (1926–60), and Eskimo Point (1921–present) – served the Padlirmiut,[85] some of whom descended to the coast seasonally for sea-
mammal hunting.

Patrols from Baker Lake that reached the southern interior and
coast give some indications of conditions in the subregion.[86] After
1937, when a detachment was established at Eskimo Point, the record
is more complete.[87] While yearly and local fluctuations in game supply
were experienced, as in the northern interior, it appears that hardship
conditions occurred more regularly before the 1950s than was the case
in the north. In the period from 1937 through the early 1940s hardship was common,[88] and in 1947 starvation took the lives of some Inuit.[89] Supplies had to be flown into the upper Kazan River region in
1948. A report noted that caribou were abundant near the coast in
1949, but not in the interior, where dogs had starved to death and
fourteen families were receiving destitute rations.[90]

As the next decade began, there was no mention in the reports of
any large-scale in-gathering at Eskimo Point, but contraction was already beginning. A January 1951 RCMP report noted that "[s]ince the
last report was submitted ... on 4 February 1950, a definite change has
taken place amongst the Eskimo Point Eskimo. The Eskimos have all
left their old trapping ground and have moved closer to the settlement
of Eskimo Point. They are not trapping as in other years. The writer
has tried to find out just why they are doing these things but they only
give the following reason. They have no Caribou Caches put up and
therefore cannot trap also their dogs have starved and they have no
means of traveling."[91] A shortage of ammunition, which made it difficult to hunt, was also noted. The lack of adequate caches existed in
spite of the fact that thousands of caribou had been sighted in August
of 1950.[92] The removal of the last trading post from the deep interior
in 1950[93] was probably equal in importance to any game failure with
regard to contraction around Eskimo Point.

1951 was a year of hardship. The year-end RCMP report noted that
caribou had failed to reach the subregion and that forty families were
being issued relief. Of forty-three deaths in the detachment area for
the year, an alarming seventeen were attributed to "starvation exposure, and freezing."[94] At the same time it is clear that efforts were being made to keep people dispersed, and the report stated that there
was "no loitering around the post this winter."

The next year, 1952, saw improved fortunes for the Inuit of the
southern Keewatin, for the "majority" of people were reported as be-

ing "fairly prosperous with a good supply of fox and plentiful caribou"; "the Eskimos do not seem inclined to hang around the settlement when the trapping season is open or when there is caribou to be had inland."[95] A 1953 report stated "conditions fairly good," that 1,500 fox pelts were traded, and, again, that there was "no tendency to loiter around the settlement."[96] Gatherings at Eskimo Point occurred only at Christmas, Easter, and at ship time in summer. Another good year followed in 1954, with caribou again plentiful, and their procural being aided by considerable amounts of ammunition issued on relief.[97] 1955 was regarded as showing "marked improvement in economy over previous years." The price of fox furs, which had reached a low of $3.50 in 1949, rose to $6.50 in 1950, $8 in 1953, and $10.50 in 1954. The absence of "loitering" was once again noted and apparently there was no marked increase in in-gathering.[98]

There is little information in the reports of 1956 and 1957 concerning game conditions, since the reports were preoccupied with illnesses in camps and with the plight of the Ennadai Lake people. RCMP and other government reports and correspondence, and several publications both popular and scholarly have been devoted to the account at the Ennadai people,[99] yet only fifty-five people, or about one-tenth of the total number of Caribou Eskimo in the southern subregion,[100] were involved. It is possible, then, that this story has distorted the total picture of centralization in the subregion, especially in terms of the roles of migration and relocation in the process. Nevertheless, relocation did figure in this process, though in a secondary role.[101]

It is necessary to go back in time in order to encompass the full scope of the events that led to the tragedy of the winter of 1957–58. In 1941 the Red River post at which the Ennadai people had been trading was closed.[102] This closure eventually necessitated relief flights in 1948 and 1949. Concern with the lack of trading facilities for the Ennadai people led to a transferral of forty-seven people to Nueltin Lake, where free traders promised to provide such facilities, but this arrangement did not last and after less than a year, by Christmas 1950, the people had drifted back to Ennadai. Aid was possible from food and supplies stored at the weather station at Ennadai Lake, but the two harsh winters of 1955–56 and 1956–57 lent impetus to the eventual resettlement project of 1957. During these winters 2,000 pounds of buffalo meat had been stored at the weather station. This drop was not enough to prevent starvation deaths of the dogs.

Although the autumn 1956 caribou hunt was successful, by the end of January 1957 supplies were running low and flights with food had to be made. The expense of these flights to the deep interior, which had been going on for some time, must have figured among the motives for transferring the people from the Ennadai Lake area. This transferral was considered as early as April of 1956, and plans went ahead to move the people that summer. However, these plans fell through because of the unavailability of suitable aircraft.

The lean winter of 1956–57 brought matters to a head, and the move was made in four flights on 10 and 11 May 1957 to Henik Lake. The new location was forty-five miles from the trading post at Padlei, a distance that was thought reasonable to travel for trade. In executing this move, the regional administrator proclaimed that "the decision of the Eskimos was reached by themselves and no coercion or threat made to get these Eskimos to move to the present location and they willingly agreed to go when the benefits of the move was explained to them."[103] On the other hand, Graham Rowley wrote in January 1958 that "it is, of course, comparatively easy to get a temporary acquiescence from the Eskimos to any suggestion put to them."[104] This appraisal of Inuit personality could well be applied to other examples of relocation discussed in this study. Indeed, later discussions with the original Ennadai people cast doubt on the degree of understanding of the consequences of the move.

At the time of the relocation, fish nets, ammunition, tents, and other equipment, as well as a month's supply of food were provided. For a period during August and September a young man from the trader's family at Padlei was left to supervise the colony, which had early split into two camps. Unfortunately, there was no large migration of caribou in the fall, and the winter of 1957–58 at Henik Lake was marked by a series of disturbing events, including robbery of a miner's cabin, murder, starvation, and disease, which together accounted for the loss of seven lives. Later in 1958 the remaining forty-four people were moved, first to Padlei, and then to Eskimo Point.

In assessing the failure of this experiment in relocation, it can be seen that the project reflects the Policy of Dispersal. Rather than moving the Ennadai people to Eskimo Point[105] or to Churchill, they were put down instead at a place where they were expected to subsist on hunting and fishing, activities that were at this time associated with dispersed settlement. The risks involved in the experiment can be appreciated when it is noted that caribou shortages were acute at that time throughout both the southern and northern subregions of the Keewatin. With the removal of the Ennadai people to Eskimo Point, by the end of 1958 only twenty-nine people remained around Padlei and another thirty-nine at Yathkyed Lake of those who had lived in the deep interior of the southern Keewatin.[106]

Returning to the question of the relationship of the supply of caribou to the growing contraction of settlement around Eskimo Point, a

June 1958 game report drew a grim picture of the area: "During the winter of 1957/58 there were no caribou reported within the district and during the spring of 1958 a very few reports have been received of scattered caribou in the district, but the total caribou population at present is estimated at less than five hundred."[107] Fox were also rare, but considerable success was reported in sea-mammal hunting for those Inuit who lived on, or visited, the Hudson Bay coast.

Thus, as in the northern interior, the game situation in the southern Keewatin appears to have reached its nadir in 1958. 1959 showed a definite upswing. A June 1959 RCMP game report stated that "the spring migration in progress," "with the majority of Eskimos obtaining enough game for their needs."[108] This recovery was especially evident at Padlei, where a herd estimated at 40,000 was reported as passing close to the post, and the HBC manager indicated that his warehouse was full of hides.[109] It is uncertain what long-term effects these improved conditions might have had in terms of settlement patterns had they continued, since the concentration of people around Eskimo Point had developed to the extent that it is probably unlikely that repopulation of the deep interior was possible.

The anthropologists VanStone and Oswalt spent the summer of 1959 at Eskimo Point. In their view, the progress in centralization was in part due to the abundance of fox along the coast, and, they continued, "[t]hen too in recent years the people have failed to intercept the migrating caribou and faced starvation. They know that at Eskimo Point where there is a store, the police and the mission, they will not starve. This has been an additional attraction to the village in times of stress. All of these factors contributed to the growing concentration of people in the community and the abandonment of their aboriginal way of life."[110] To these factors could be added the cessation of radar site construction in October 1955, which had drawn a number of men who, with the lay-offs, "were very reluctant to return to a life of hunting and trapping after the apparent security and high earnings of the construction work."[111] Oswalt and VanStone reported three clearly defined population segments in Eskimo Point: 160–5 were the resident population of Caribou Eskimos, thirty came from other places around Hudson Bay, and thirteen were of European descent. Of the Caribou Eskimo population, 100 were year-round residents in the village in 1959, and another sixty spent at least part of the year in the centre. In addition, "approximately 120 Caribou Eskimo live year round on the Barren grounds."[112] The anthropologists also noted that "at least one hundred had moved to Rankin Inlet in 1957,"[113] though it is unclear how many of these people came from inland locations. For those who spent winters inland, the yearly cycle adhered closely to a long-established cycle of economy and settlement. These people moved to the coast about 15 April (corresponding to the end of the trapping season) to hunt seals at the floe edge. In late August they returned inland for the next few months to hunt caribou, before returning again to the coast for further sea-mammal hunting. Later, they again moved inland for the winter's hunting and trapping. Those who lived year round at the village made trips for caribou of "only a few days duration, while others were being engaged in hunting in the sea as a chief occupation. In addition, there were a number of people who subsisted primarily, on relief or quasi-relief from the Anglican or Roman Catholic missions."[114]

In referring to year-round residents of the inland areas, VanStone and Oswalt wrote, "they too will be drawn to the coast during the next few years."[115] This prediction was to be realized in the next year when the post at Padlei was closed. The group that had traded there was flown out, and they, together with the Ennadai–Henik Lake people, can be considered relocatees, but it is apparent that the bulk of the people who had moved from the interior had moved of their own volition. In this regard Burch wrote, "To a considerable extent centralization of the Caribou Eskimo was voluntary. Conditions on the land had been desperately difficult for two generations. Between 1956 and 1960 most came in on their own. A few diehards were brought in later by force."[116]

RANKIN INLET: ARCTIC BOOM TOWN

The centralization that took place at Rankin Inlet was, contrary to most other cases, based on industrial development. In 1928 a prospector discovered deposits of nickel in the locale, but it was only in 1953 that a permanent mining camp was established by the Rankin Inlet Mines Company (later renamed North Rankin Nickel Mines Limited).[117] Few Inuit lived in the area on a permanent basis, though some spent part of each year there.[118] After a series of correspondences with various branches of the government by the mining company, it was agreed that mining could go ahead, and, indeed, that a contribution of $20,000 would be made from Ottawa.[119]

In 1955 equipment arrived and the first ore was shipped out later that year.[120] In the preceding year some Inuit were briefly employed, but it was 1956 before serious planning of more extensive employment began. An RCMP report[121] was passed to B.G. Sivertz regarding proposed expanded Inuit employment, and he responded with enthusiasm: "because of poor conditions in the Chesterfield area generally, everything should be done to take advantage of any employment opportunities that are offered, whether they be of a casual or continuing nature."[122] He cautioned that care should be taken in the planning, and suggested that relocatees "could hunt during the summer to obtain meat." He also recommended, with a decidedly paternalistic attitude, that "part of Eskimo's earnings will be best set aside for future use ... it is necessary to exercise some control over all Eskimo spending in order to ensure that at the outset, at least, their earnings are used to purchase only essential goods." Northern Service officer W.G. Kerr, stationed in Churchill, reaffirmed Sivertz's view of control of Inuit earnings, but was concerned about the possibilities of the temporary nature of employment, and stressed that hunting and trapping opportunities should also be considered.[123] A little later Kerr visited Rankin and praised the emerging employment possibilities.[124] In November 1956 he indicated that fourteen Inuit men were employed, that their living conditions were favourable, with good food in the mess hall, and that there was available time for hunting and the beginning of housing construction.[125]

In early 1957 there was some concern in Ottawa about the length of time that the mine would operate, but the view that a school should be built there was also expressed.[126] In March of that year Kerr wrote to Sivertz that 130 native people lived at Rankin, and he requested immediate assistance in providing educational and medical services.[127] In the same month Donald Snowden of the Arctic Division visited Rankin and produced a report that included information from the mining company officials that the mine could operate for five to eight years.[128] Indeed, the vice president of the company, Dr W.W. Weber, wrote to the deputy minister of the Department of Northern Affairs and National Resources, Gordon Robertson, in this regard.[129] A few days later, however, C.E. de Capelin, chief of the Mining and Lands Division, threw cold water on the optimistic planning that was developing. He wrote that a geophysical survey conducted at Rankin "determined that the ore was too low grade to mine profitably" and that "unless further reserves are located the mine will not continue to operate after five years." Further, de Capelin asserted that before plans for a school or other construction got underway, considerations for the short term operation should be taken into account.[130] This warning was ignored in the eagerness to facilitate one of the rare employment possibilities offered the Inuit, and plans went ahead to build a school and to expand the existing airstrip.[131] Attempts made to have a hospital and physician at Rankin were blocked by Indian and Northern Health Services,[132] and instead a male nurse was to be installed and the physician from Chesterfield was to visit Rankin every two months.[133] Although the mining company had previously suggested that they would pay for a doctor's salary and supply heat, lights, water, and sewage disposal, they later withdrew these offers and thought that the government should pay for both a physician and a school.[134]

Negotiations between Kerr, who was now stationed in Rankin, and the mining company resulted in plans to train Inuit so that they would become the chief working force and replace a number of outsiders that had been employed.[135] Indeed, by 20 November 1957 seventy-three Inuit (fifty-three from Chesterfield and twenty from Eskimo Point) were employed at the mine and only one family was on relief.[136] Kerr, now compliant with the notion that wage employment was the only solution to local economic conditions, favoured centralization, in direct contrast to his earlier position about Chesterfield.

While Kerr's reports were in general optimistic, the welfare teacher at Rankin offered another picture of conditions.[137] He complained that hunting was limited, saw special difficulties in the adult education program, and felt that white employees at the mine regarded the Inuit as rivals, and he had heard rumours that the company was not in good financial condition. He did report favourably on such recreational events as two films a week and square dancing.

The year 1957 had seen truly remarkable development of the community at Rankin Inlet. Mining operations at the outset of the year had employed a small minority of Inuit employees, and the year ended with over seventy. Two missions had been founded, an HBC store opened, a school began operations, arrangements had been made for visits of a physician, recreation activities were encouraged, and the Inuit population had increased to over 200.[138] The mining company had been active in encouraging these developments, and, in general, common purpose and cordiality prevailed in their relations with the government in Ottawa, as well as with its local representatives. Early in January 1958, following upon the mining company's participation in planning, Dr Weber submitted to Deputy Minister Robertson a list of recommendations for the community that included establishing a resident physician, an RCMP detachment, a postal station, a voting district with voting privileges for the Inuit, as well as expanding the airstrip and dredging the harbour.[139] These recommendations met with a qualified reaction from Ottawa. Voting districts and privileges could not be implemented in the Northwest Territories, Indian and Northern Health would not support placing a physician at Rankin, and it was asserted that the mining company should supply medical equipment and drugs, use of which should be extended to non-employees. Weber was instructed to consult with the National Harbour Board, and was pointed to the Postal Service regarding mailing and the Department of Transport regarding the airstrip. As for the RCMP, their presence was required elsewhere.[140]

Weber's plans were being frustrated by bureaucratic inertia and division of responsibilities. Some of the proposed improvements were instituted over time, but much delay was experienced.

Information for the year 1958 comes in the report of the Daileys, anthropologists who spent June, July, and August of that year in the community.[141] The Daileys found three separate neighbourhoods. The first was the white or Western settlement, which consisted of the Department of Northern Affairs buildings and those of the HBC, the school, the two missions, and the quarters of the mining company personnel (exclusive of Inuit employees). The second neighbourhood, designated as the New Eskimo Settlement, consisted of fourteen houses built for Inuit employees of the company. The Old Eskimo Settlement was made up of about fifty dwellings, either tent frames or scrap lumber "shacks." People in the "Old" neighbourhood who worked at the mine earned lower wages than those who lived in the "New" neighbourhood.[142] By the summer of 1958 there were 332 Inuit at Rankin, two-thirds of whom were from Chesterfield, and the others from other places in the Keewatin. In addition, thirty people considered to be residents were absent, either in hospitals or in technical schools.[143]

One of the anxieties about centralization was the prospect of abandoning hunting and trapping. In Rankin Inlet, where employment possibilities were substantial at this time, some of "the men continued to hunt and fish to provide food for their families and food for those dog teams that are left."[144] However, much of this activity was seasonal. 5,000 pounds of beef were flown in during January and 3,200 pounds consumed by summer, after which sales fell off.[145] This indicates that subsistence hunting was not a prominent part of the winter and early spring periods. The Daileys also reported that only about 100 fox were traded during the preceding trapping season.[146]

The Daileys were not sanguine about Inuit-white relations. In criticizing Farley Mowat's praise of the contributions of the mining company in his popular book *The Desperate People*,[147] the anthropologists pointed to some significant problems. For one thing, the adjustment to an industrially based economy was far from complete, in that "the Eskimo does not as yet conceive of himself as a necessary part of the enterprise, nor does he recognize the need for regimentation."[148] Medical problems were not being met by existing facilities. The caste system separating natives and whites was seen as the most serious problem,[149] and it was aggravated by the language barrier. Workers ate in separate mess halls, and motion pictures were shown on alternate nights for whites and natives. The Daileys proposed a number of recommendations, including greater involvement of Inuit in community life, improvement of health facilities, education in public health, close supervision of wages and hours of work, education in the use of money, and more specific goals in the education program. "[L]astly there is a great need for the development of a more realistic expression of policy objectives which can be interpreted intelligently and decisively on the local level."[150] The Daileys were indeed presaging some of the problems that would face the new Arctic communities created by centralization.

As the fifties drew to a close, the new area administrator, formerly referred to as the Northern Service Officer, foresaw the end of productive mining as "the stocks of high grade ore were approaching exhaustion."[151] He saw that "we will be faced with the problem of re-establishing the people of the community." Since the now 434 Inuit were used to wages of about $200 a month, one way to preserve "wage employment ... would be the development of Rankin as a Regional Office." He submitted some suggestions for such a plan, but his report ended on a definite note of pessimism: "quite honestly, in my opinion some of the people might have been better off in the long run had they never entered the field of wage employment."[152] This remark is not surprising, considering the impulsive leap into industrialization as a solution to local problems that had characterized the Rankin Inlet project.

The plans of North Rankin Mining Limited for the new community had displayed concern for the well-being of the native people, and the company was more active in much of the planning than were the various governmental agencies involved. However, the company's overly optimistic prognosis about the longevity of the mine, too readily seized upon by these agencies, had led to an unsustainable centralization. It is puzzling that government bodies accepted this prognosis in the face of objections from de Capelin. I noted in an earlier chapter that an Inuit representative on the Committee for Eskimo Affairs had raised the question of possible termination of mining operations at Rankin, and had been brushed off. Their failure to heed these concerns would haunt the planners in Ottawa during the next decade, as de Capelin's estimate of the life of the mine proved prophetic. There would be no turning back to previous conditions of population dispersal.

The centralization that took place at Rankin Inlet in the second half of the 1950s was a combination of migration and relocation. Most or all of the people from Chesterfield who made up the majority of the immigrants moved themselves to Rankin. Movement had taken place between these two locales before the mining operation was established and was thus extended along a familiar route. Because of the distance involved, those from Eskimo Point and Baker Lake had to seek transport by plane or ship. Some of the immigrants came from conditions of scattered settlement, while others, such as those who had come from Chesterfield, Eskimo Point, or Baker Lake before the end of the fifties, came from situations where centralization was already advancing.

THE KEEWATIN RE-ESTABLISHMENT PROJECT

It was undoubtedly largely due to the tragedies at Garry Lake and Henik Lake, and the publicity that these events received in southern Canada, that hurried steps were taken to relocate the survivors of these disasters and other people to points on the west coast of Hudson Bay in the period 1958–60. A memorandum dated 9 May 1958 from the minister of Northern Affairs and Northern Development to the federal Cabinet first referred to the "Keewatin Reestablishment Project,"[153] and specified setting up a community for the rehabilitation of Keewatin Inuit that would entail an estimated cost of $150,000. A short time later, a Keewatin Committee was formed with representatives of the following sections of the Arctic Division: Projects, Development, Welfare, and the Traffic Development Committee. During the course of meetings held between 23 May and 28 July 1958, other persons from various governmental agencies, as well as P.A.C. Nichols of the Hudson's Bay Company, attended.[154]

At the first meeting there were preliminary discussions as to the choice of a site for the new settlement, with Tavani emerging as the first possibility.[155] Before the second meeting, a session of the Committee on Eskimo Affairs entertained the question of the new community.[156] The members of the clergy attending were especially concerned about the difficulty of inlanders adapting to a coastal situation.[157] Others pointed to the apparent decline of the caribou and suggested that, even though a recovery might be made, the interior would have to be abandoned in any event. B.G. Sivertz stressed "the importance of bringing these people together in communities sufficiently large to permit the administration to supervise and help them."[158] This is one of the very first clear-cut espousals of a definite shift in policy regarding Inuit settlement, and it was, of course, in direct contrast to the Policy of Dispersal that was still being maintained in much of the Canadian Arctic. The Henik and Garry Lake tragedies were viewed by R.A.J. Phillips as representative of circumstances becoming general in the Arctic,[159] and the eventual inclusion of other Inuit in the plans that were to materialize reflected Ottawa's endorsement of this view. In the second meeting of the Keewatin Committee, the opinion was expressed that, even though the caribou might return, "a more stable economy must be planned for the future."[160]

At the third meeting, some debate ensued over whether "an independent Eskimo Community" with minimal participation from outsiders should be entertained,[161] or whether energetic supervision should be planned. More sites were also discussed. Some practical considerations were raised at the fourth meeting, including incorporation of a larger group than the Henik and Garry Lake people.[162] At the fifth meeting, F.J. Neville of the Welfare Section was chosen as community development officer.[163] At this point Tavani was still considered the prime candidate for the new community, and accordingly, Neville led a small party to that place. He judged it to be unsuitable, largely because of an inadequate harbour for large ships, but Whale Cove fifteen miles to the north gave a more favourable impression.[164] Although the harbour appeared to be better than at Tavani, Neville expressed some concern about the limited area for the construction that would be required for houses for the expected Inuit population. However, since there was only a little more than two weeks from the time of this final meeting of the committee to the target date of 15 August, plans had to go ahead, and Whale Cove was selected as the site for the new colony.[165] One of the limitations brought on by these time pressures was the lack of a wildlife survey, but there was the general impression that Whale Cove and its surrounding district was good game country.[166]

In his report delivered at the 28 July meeting, Neville addressed the problem that was to be a bone of contention in later debates regarding Arctic relocation schemes in general, that of the willingness of the people involved to be moved. He had interviewed members of the white community at Baker Lake regarding the proposed transferral of Inuit. While this was a dubious approach, he also attempted to elicit responses from the Inuit, but with a rather ambiguous result: "They said that they would move because they did not have enough to eat, nor was there sufficient game where they were living at present. However, he was not sure of what they really wished to do."[167] It seems that here, as in other relocation schemes, communication with the Inuit left much to be desired. Also, the uncertainty of what would await the Inuit surely must have contributed to the apparent confusion.

(Vallee reported similar on responses of the Garry Lake people, who had been moved to the village at Baker Lake and camps nearby: "After a few weeks there the hapless *emigrees* were asked if they would like to relocate at the Keewatin Rehabilitation centre at Rankin Inlet, on the west coast of Hudson Bay. Most of them chose to do so, not so much from attraction to Rankin Inlet, but because the move offered at least some hope for rehabilitation."[168])

The composition of the immigrant group was also discussed at this final meeting of the committee. People were to come from most of the

Keewatin subregions. Eventually it was envisioned that a community of from twenty-five to fifty families would comprise the total population at the new site.[169]

Tester and Kulchyski describe the chaotic set of circumstances that surrounded the two attempts at founding the community at Whale Cove in August and September 1958 as being due to hurried and ineffective planning.[170] For instance, when the harbour was examined during the first attempt, it was found that it was strewn with boulders that had to be removed, and in the meantime, the ship left to unload supplies at Eskimo Point before returning. On the second attempt, after a channel had been cleared, stormy weather left supplies and equipment scattered on the beach.

Robert Williamson, who was to become area administrator at Rankin, also attributes these failures to inadequate planning, but adds that it was "lack of experience, rather than lack of dedication" that was involved.[171] Another view was that of Alexander Stevenson, who wrote: "Because of inclement weather, and an inexperienced (in northern navigation) ship's Captain, we could not offload our supplies at Whale Cove. Our Keewatin Community cargo was landed at Churchill, then shipped to the closest suitable place with favourable harbouring facilities near Whale Cove, Rankin Inlet."[172] This version can be interpreted as an attempt to absolve the planners of their part in the failed attempts to establish the colony, but it also points to factors that could not be easily avoided. While the planning was hurried, and no doubt plagued the project, the Arctic climate can be expected to interfere with any project at any time.

The initial colony split into two groups. Sixteen people moved to the Wilson River, which empties into Whale Cove a short distance from the planned site. Another group of thirty-seven people were moved to a location about a mile south of the centre at Rankin Inlet. This colony, called Itivia,[173] grew steadily during the autumn of 1958 and winter of 1958–59 as further relocations were instituted. A memorandum from C.M. Bolger, administrator of the Arctic, describing his visit to Itivia of 11–16 February 1959, summarizes the developments that had taken place. These included the building of fourteen houses and further buildings for a school, a workshop, a store, a warehouse, and a small power plant.[174] Bolger credited this progress to the work of Peter Murdoch, who had supervised the construction at Itivia. His report also included a list of people at the site: thirty-nine from Henik Lake (via Eskimo Point), ten from Chesterfield, five from Rankin, twenty from Baker Lake, and, without explanation in the context of the Keewatin-oriented project, twelve from Povungnituk across Hudson Bay. Women were reported as busy with handicraft work, while men hunted.

While at Itivia, Bolger held a meeting with Murdoch, the NSOs, Kennedy and Grant, W. Rudnicki of the Welfare Section, and D.G. Symington of the Project Section, as well as Neville.[175] Again, as in previous meetings of the Keewatin Committee, there was disagreement regarding the nature of the relocated community. In the end, the majority (with Murdoch and Grant abstaining) voted that the people at Itivia should remain there for at least another year, and those who then wished to return would be assisted in doing so in the summer of 1960.[176] There was no consultation with the Inuit, and during the summer of 1959 many began to drift back to the site of the original Whale Cove adventure; by early October a colony of eighty-two people had been re-established at the Cove.[177] The eagerness with which the people from Itivia resumed residence at the Cove has been attributed to the "caste system" at Rankin Inlet, both in terms of white-Inuit interaction[178] and in terms of interaction with the Inuit in the mining village, who held them in low esteem.[179] However, there is also evidence to support the view that they were eager to exploit the game resources of the Whale Cove district.

While this relocation project, like that of the High Arctic, has been subjected to criticism,[180] the criticism has been directed mainly toward the circumstances of the initial attempts to found the colony in 1958, which led to the designation as a "planning disaster."[181] In my view the success or failure of these relocation schemes must be judged on the basis of later developments. By the autumn of 1959 there was already some indication that things were going well. An RCMP report for 7 October indicated that the hunters at Whale Cove had been "very successful in obtaining large quantities of seal and whale meat,"[182] and that ten houses had been built. Work on house construction, however, had hampered caribou hunting, as had the shortage of dogs. There was a reported plan for some people to move to nearby fishing lakes to supply Rankin people during the winter,[183] and indeed a later report based on patrols to the locale described considerable subsistence activity, with some men sealing at the floe edge, several men fishing at the lakes, and two men hunting caribou.[184]

As the 1950s ended, the new community at Whale Cove was faced with problems that also typified other centralization situations. The possible lack of social integration of groups from diverse regions and possessing different dialects and economic orientations was among these. This was, as in the case of the High Arctic relocations, and especially that of Grise Fiord, an experiment in centralized but subsistence-based settlement. The degree of outside participation also had to be resolved. Since the Whale Cove project began as a clear case of relocation, it is easy to underrate the importance of migration in this case.

People were first moved to the site and later, when the 1958 plans fell through, some were again moved to the vicinity of Rankin. However, the return in 1959 was clearly self-directed and actually ran counter to the delay that had been decided upon by the white administrators.

SUMMARY

During the 1950s centralization in the Keewatin Region proceeded unevenly from one locality to another, and, while considerable in-gathering was experienced in the area as a whole, by the end of that decade the process still had some way to go.

For Southampton Island a process of contraction on the south coast of the island had begun during World War II, due largely to the presence of an American air base. This process continued during the 1950s, with the focal point at Coral Harbour where missions, school, and trading post drew the population inward. Such compaction of population into and near that centre was possible in part because of the use of large boats that enabled the hunters of sea mammals to expand their hunting areas. In addition to in-gathering, Southampton also saw considerable emigration during the 1950s, for shorter periods in connection with DEWline employment, and for longer periods, or permanently, to Churchill and Rankin Inlet.

The tendency toward concentration of population at Chesterfield Inlet has been attributed in part to encouragement by the Catholic Church, which maintained headquarters there, including hospital facilities and, later, a school, both of which served the entire east Central Arctic. An apparent shortage of game, especially caribou, was also cited as a cause. The most evident espousal of the Policy of Dispersal in the Keewatin Region came at Chesterfield, where representatives of local agencies united in attempts to restore dispersal of settlement. These attempts met with indifferent results, but during the later years of the fifties significant changes in settlement did occur at Chesterfield. Employment possibilities at Rankin Inlet drew a large number of people southward, and centralization of the remaining population was achieved through expansion of employment and by the attraction of a church-sponsored housing project. While the people of the Chesterfield trading area hunted caribou, their primary subsistence came from sea-mammal hunting, and fluctuations in the number of caribou were less crucial to survival than for the Inuit of the northern interior.

In the northern interior, with only fishing providing an alternate subsistence activity, fluctuations in availability of caribou led to widely varying conditions of economic success. Beginning in the late 1940s and continuing through the 1950s, a series of emergency air drops were necessary to avoid privation, and even starvation, among the scattered camps. The contraction around, and concentration in, Baker Lake was clearly related to the uncertainty of caribou, the chief resource of the area. The Garry Lake tragedy led to the removal of people first from the Back River country and later to the west coast of Hudson Bay, and also to the removal of other people from the northern interior. This move was predicated on a perception of the caribou being an unreliable source of existence. Nevertheless, as the 1950s ended, half of the population of the northern interior still lived in outlying camps, trying to subsist largely on a caribou-based economy. However, contraction around Baker Lake continued, and emergency flights were still necessary at times when local resources failed.

In the southern interior, movement of people from the far inland districts was probably as much a result of the closing of trading posts as of the hardships of living on the one-crop economy of caribou hunting. However, the subregion had long experienced shortages and famine. For those who remained in the deep interior, frequent relief flights were necessary to maintain them, and finally they were relocated to what was assumed to be a better game region around Henik Lake. With the failure of this plan and consequent removal of the Ennadai–Henik Lake people, only a few Inuit remained more than about 100 miles from Eskimo Point. There, both in-gathering and contraction of population took place. Those who moved to the centre had access to sea-mammal hunting as well as to the security provided by the missions and the governmental representatives. Even as the 1950s ended, a substantial portion of the total population of the subregion spent either significant parts of each year or the entire year's cycle scattered in camps, relying on caribou hunting for their livelihood.

The community that grew during the late fifties at Rankin Inlet was created because of local industry. Inuit were drawn from all subregions and trading centres in the Keewatin Region. With people from Repulse Bay, Southampton Island, and both northern and southern subregions, together with the majority from Chesterfield Inlet, a quasi-urban situation developed. At the end of the fifties there was already concern that the employment that had created this community had an uncertain future. Based on a different economic orientation, but equally centralized, was the community that appeared in the last year of the 1950s at Whale Cove. Here a subsistence-based community had been planned, and there were encouraging signs that this objective would be achieved.

It can be seen that the settlement changes that took place during the 1950s in the Keewatin had varying referents. These ranged from employment possibilities, which drew people to centres, and at times outside their normal districts of habitation, to movements of people nearer to trading facilities. Also, at Whale Cove, there was a shift to a region of superior resources while maintaining a subsistence economy under conditions of centralization. Both migration and relocation were involved in these population shifts. A persistent perception of a definite decline in a chief resource, the caribou, was also clearly involved in these movements and in the policies of planners.

In 1949 A.W.F. Banfield of the Canadian Wildlife Service reported that the large mainland herds "exist in numbers comparable to primitive times."[185] But by 1954 he estimated that a decline of 62 per cent in mainland herds had occurred since 1900.[186] Concern with an apparent decline in caribou numbers led to the formation of a Caribou Conservation Committee in early 1956.[187] The results of a series of aerial surveys overseen by this committee supported the view of a decrease of caribou from about 600,000 animals in 1949 to 200,000 in 1957 in the mainland herds between the Mackenzie River and Hudson Bay.[188] The chief reason given for this decline was a succession of poor calf crops, which had dropped from the normal range of 20–25 per cent to 10 per cent.[189] It was estimated that human utilization alone had been greater than the increment from calving. These conclusions resulted in conservation education as well as legislation. Already, the use of .22 calibre rifles and the feeding of dogs with caribou meat had been prohibited in the Northwest Territories Game Ordinance.[190] Further measures were introduced, including establishing a closed season on females from January to June and on calves at all seasons. Use of alternate food sources, especially fish, were encouraged and a predator control program instituted.

It became an accepted fact among administrators that the apparent decline in caribou populations was irreversible, and this view influenced policies toward Inuit settlement during the fifties. Other views of caribou demography were espoused. C.H.D. Clarke examined Hudson's Bay Company records and concluded that a cycle of thirty-five years existed in the rise and fall of caribou populations.[191] If one accepts a general decline during the fifties, this periodicity would appear to apply, counting from a period of extreme famine among the Caribou Eskimo in 1915–25. However, the case for a slump in the 1950s has also been challenged. James Clancy wrote of the "making of the caribou crisis," attributing the apparent decline to inadequate survey methods.[192] There were, indeed, some interregional and year-to-year fluctuations in supply of caribou, as in earlier decades, that made it difficult to judge the total picture. The increased concern of the government, improved communications, and relief measures may well have distorted perception of the game situation and its effect on the Inuit during the decade. All in all, however, it is well to note the conclusions of Ernest Burch in his examination of the caribou (*Rangifer tarandus*) as a human resource: "In sum, *Rangifer tarandus* is not the highly dependable continuously available resource it is usually pictured to be. On the contrary, wild populations of the species are extremely erratic in number and movements, present in vast quantity one season (or year or generation) and gone the next. Human populations dependent on this species must adapt to the seemingly capricious behaviour of their prey in order to survive."[193] It does seem that a nadir in Keewatin herds was reached in the winter of 1957–58. Signs of recovery were seen in the south in the spring of 1959 and in the north in the autumn of that year, but whether these signs pointed to a pronounced trend or merely one of the periodic increases of caribou populations remained to be seen.

The precariousness of an economy based on the caribou was illustrated by the tragedies of Henik Lake and Garry Lake. According to C.S. MacKinnon, "[t]he Henik Lake affair proved to be the catalyst for a reversal of policy on discouraging Inuit from clustering in the settlements. It showed vividly that life on the land could have tragic consequences."[194] The Policy of Dispersal was slowly abandoned across the Central Arctic, and new policies for the 1960s were introduced.

CHAPTER FIVE

The Welfare State Policy

The Policy of Dispersal had as its main ingredients a *laissez-faire* governmental philosophy, an austere economic stance, and the rationalization of preserving Inuit culture. We have seen that during the 1950s this policy was beginning to weaken in Ottawa. Later, the new philosophy and policy of the Welfare State dominated and produced profound effects on settlement patterns, as well as on other aspects of Inuit society and culture.

It has been noted that certain aspects of welfare, namely government relief and Hudson's Bay Company credit, have had long histories in the Canadian Arctic. I have indicated that these measures were minimal. During the caribou crisis of the 1950s, aid to the Inuit of the Keewatin, especially, was considerably expanded with the advent of airplane drops to outlying camps. Large amounts of food and other supplies sometimes totaling as much as 1,000 pounds were involved. Cooperation between the then recently formed Department of Northern Affairs and National Resources, with its rapidly expanding budget, the RCMP, and the RCAF expedited aid to the camps. These drops came at a time when policy changes were being considered, but also when sometimes desperate attempts were still being made to maintain dispersed populations. The poor communications associated with dispersed settlement ordained that hardship and famine would occur, despite strenuous efforts to avoid such conditions.

THE GROWTH OF SOCIAL LEGISLATION ASSISTANCE

The Family Allowance Act of 1944 brought a new source of aid to the people of the Territories, including the Inuit. The Northwest Territories Council approved that $6 would be paid monthly for each child under the age of ten and $8 for each child between the ages of ten and sixteen.[1] Due to the remoteness of many small communities in the north, and the consequent delays in registration for the allowances, full implementation of the plan took several years.[2] While, ideally, each family would be paid by cheque, "Eskimo children and a group of Indian children" were paid "in kind." Indeed "large quantities of powdered milk and other prepared foods are among commodities supplied."[3]

It was seen early that, given the sparse numbers of RCMP officers in the Arctic, traders would be drawn into administration of the family allowances. In this regard a lively correspondence grew between Roy A. Gibson, deputy commissioner of the Northwest Territories, and James Cantley,[4] who, during the early years of application of the act in the Arctic, represented the Baffin Trading Company. Cantley was concerned with whether the allowances could be paid in advance, from what date allowances would begin, what form of payment should take, and how frequently payment should be made. On 19 May 1946 J.G. Wright, superintendent of the Eastern Arctic, wrote to Col. Craig, who was handling the administration of the allowances for the Arctic, expressing a concern that these "extra benefits could impair the industry of the natives and develop a class of people who would spend their time in the vicinity of the trading post waiting for government aid."[5] He outlined policy regarding issuances in the Arctic as follows: "I might again emphasize that the Family Allowances are to improve the lot of the children. They are not to be used to reduce the cost of relief to infirm natives and widows by the Administration, or the cost of grub-staking hunters by the traders during periods of scarcity." In quoting Wright's letter to Craig, Gibson replied to one of Cantley's with: "In accordance with the policy no monthly issues will be made, issuances will only be made, as prevailing local conditions require."[6] This statement seems to run counter to the spirit, if not the letter, of the Allowances Act, but in fact represents the issuance policy as it was applied in the Arctic for some years to follow. The problem then became that of determining just how frequently issuances would be made. Other compromises to the act were made. The act specified that "[t]he Allowances shall cease to be payable if the child does not regularly attend school."[7] In the Territories at this time only Yellowknife was registered as a school district, and large areas of the NWT, especially areas occupied by the Inuit, were without schools. Consequently, this stricture had to be ignored if issuances were to be made. In the Yukon the concept of a "training equivalent" to school[8] was being employed to meet this measure, but under the circumstances of the Arctic regions of the NWT, even such modification of the act could not be applied.

Gibson was also obliged to answer queries by Chesshire of the HBC since representatives of the company were often responsible for distributing the allowances: "The policy has been explained before that it is not the intention to make Family Allowances a substitute for grubstaking or relief. They are to help raise the standard of living for the children and are particularly applicable when times are not so good. This prevents them from becoming a regular issue and, no doubt, their issuances will be regulated to a considerable extent by the fox cycle. The Hudson's Bay Company has long made a study of the cycle and it will be necessary to have supplies shipped in accordance so as not to create warehouse difficulties."[9] Chesshire could not help but see the fundamental contradictions in this statement, while at the same time appreciating that the HBC was being given a large measure of freedom in making the issuances.

The question of the appropriateness of items issued under the Allowances Act was highlighted in a report that a large Peterhead boat was being purchased with allowance aid,[10] though confirmation of this purchase seemed to have been lacking. In March 1947 a meeting was held by Wright and other persons concerned with the administration of family allowances for the Arctic. At this meeting Dr P.E. Moore of Indian Health Services objected to the withholding of allowances beyond the monthly periods specified by the act.[11] Wright responded to this in a memorandum to Gibson: "If the Eskimo were given the Family Allowances each month as it becomes due, they would rapidly come to depend upon it and would lose their initiative to help themselves. We find that Family Allowances should be reserved to help out the Eskimo children during periods when they and their parents may be on relief and when native food supplies are scarce."[12] Thus, even though Wright and other administrators of the Arctic denied that allowances should become substitutes for relief, statements such as the above directly contradict those assertions.

Another question concerned the interpretation of the principle that the issuances should be of benefit specifically to the children. While a list of the items eligible for distribution was provided, departures from this list soon took place. The principal rationale for expanding the list to include items for adult use was that such supplies were necessary to make possible the hunting-trapping economy that was vital to the survival of children, as well as adults. When a member of the RCMP queried about using the allowances to purchase a boat under the act, Gibson replied, "If the possession of a boat will enable an Eskimo to have access to better hunting areas, where he can secure needed seal and walrus meat and to tend whale and fish nets, his children will benefit by these added supplies of native food which, in the past have been found to produce a higher native health level than foods purchased from the trading post stores."[13] The Council of the Northwest Territories had previously concluded that "such things as rifles, fish nets, and other things which make it easier for the hunters to carry on his vocation and provide more abundantly for his children"[14] could be included. Clearly the items that could be so included were virtually without limit, and, indeed, it was left very much to the discretion of the local administrator of the allowances, whether RCMP officer, or trader, as to the handling of credits.

In the previous chapters dealing with settlement practices in the 1950s it has been shown that family allowance aid was withheld as an emergency source and provided a reservoir for sustaining dispersed settlement on the land. The withholding of issuances from monthly administration served to maintain such settlement conditions. It was clearly feared that if the monthly interval of issuance was observed then: (1) there would be more frequent visits to the trading posts, thus interrupting hunting and trapping activities in the camps, and (2) such visits could gradually lengthen into more permanent residence at the posts. It was only later, when the Policy of Dispersal gave way, that a more literal interpretation of the act was followed. As early as 1954 Sivertz had noted that allowances were being paid by cheque in the Mackenzie Delta region, and in 1961, at the twelfth meeting of the Committee on Eskimo Affairs, Chairman Robertson declared that it was "a step forward" that cheques rather than credit vouchers were being used in payment[15] (presumably throughout the Northwest Territories).

Meanwhile, although the total amount of the issuances made only a small contribution to families in the provinces, they had a significant effect on finances of such low income communities as those in the Canadian Arctic. Some reference to these finances will illustrate this fact. The economic underpinnings of the contact-traditional period with its dispersed settlement was the trade in arctic fox. While both supply of the pelts and the prices for them in the fur market fluctuated during the period 1931–32 through 1940–41, the fur purchases for a large sampling of HBC posts totalled $3,161,405, and for those posts, total sales were $3,027,820.[16] It is clear that the HBC made a definite effort to balance inventory with fur returns over the long run, even though this balance was not achieved on a yearly basis. For peak years of fur returns or when prices rose, the inventories would have fallen below demand for goods, while in poor fur years or when prices fell, credit was probably frequently extended beyond returns. During the years of World War II, and shortly afterwards, fur prices rose, with sales falling behind on the average due to inventories being depleted.

Table 5.1
Inuit income, Central Arctic 1950–52

Categories	1950–51	1951–52
Furs	$388,152	$162,619
Other produce, wages, & credit on account HBC	50,402	127,139
Other	59,010	63,062
Cash	18,397	23,276
Total Earned	515,961	376,096
Family Allowances	$199,845	$196,349
Old Age Allowances	2,441	3,216
Government Relief	27,053	58,885
HBC Relief	4,217	3,468
HBC Unpaid debt	3,971	11,759
Total Unearned	$237,527	273,677
Total Income	753,488	649,773

Source: NA, RG 85, Vol. 1234, File 251–1(2), Cantley to Wright, 24 December 1952, Comprehensive Analysis of Eskimo Income for 1950–51 and 1951–52. (Abstracted from Cantley's report with some alteration for presentation and to correct mathematical error in the original.

The period 1947–48 through 1949–50 saw an abrupt drop in the value of furs, while sales remained essentially equal to those of the preceding six years.[17] This was the period during which family allowances were introduced and gradually became universal in their distribution. As well, during these years the Old Age Assistance Act of 1927 was finally being honoured.[18]

As the 1950s began, family allowances had become a major source of income for the Inuit of the Central Arctic. A survey made by James Cantley for the years 1950–51 and 1951–52 reveals how great a part the allowances and other unearned income – including old age allowances, government relief, HBC credit, and unpaid HBC debt – played in an economy whose chief source of earned income still came from fur.

Table 5.1 shows that in both fiscal years, furs and family allowances were the two largest sources of income for the Inuit of the Central

Arctic, but the proportions of each of these two sources was reversed in the two years. In 1950–51, a good year for furs, returns from that source was nearly double the income from allowances. The decline in income from furs for 1951–52 can be seen to have been countered by such sources of unearned income as government relief and unpaid HBC debt. There was also an abrupt rise in "other produce" wages and unpaid credit on account with the HBC. That these measures and shortfalls did not achieve parity can be seen in the total income figures, which show a decline of over $100,000. It should be remembered that these years were a period of dispersed settlement, when few wage earning opportunities were available. Later, this latter source was to assume a prominent role in Central Arctic incomes.

For some years a small number of indigents had been gathering around the settlements. With the expansion of welfare benefits in the 1950s this number increased. We saw that larger aggregations formed in that decade at Frobisher, Rankin Inlet, and Cambridge Bay, where wage employment situations had appeared. Caribou shortages had brought people to several other locales where centralization was also expanding, but truly universal in-gathering belonged to the 1960s. Much more extensive government programs were then to become important ingredients in motives to move to the centres.

THE DIEFENBAKER "VISION"

Between the period of stringent application of the Policy of Dispersal and the wholesale embracing of the Welfare State Policy came the "Diefenbaker Years" of 1957–63 and a philosophy often referred to as the "vision."[19] This "vision" was to be the sequel to the westward expansion of the nation in the late nineteenth century with expansion northward. Alvin Hamilton, who became the deputy minister of the Department of Northern Affairs and National Resources, is credited with implementation of the "vision."[20] The new interest in Canada's north was mainly expressed as a dream of developing natural resources, especially mining and oil exploitation. As it turned out, the development that did occur was overwhelmingly restricted to the southern margins of the Northwest Territories and to the Yukon regions where gold and uranium had been found, and to the Mackenzie drainage region where oil discoveries were made.[21] These developments lay outside the regions of the Inuit considered here.

There was within the purview of this study the nickel mining operation at Rankin Inlet. The reader will recall that in 1957, during the first year of mining, concern had been expressed over the possible lack of longevity of the project. In 1959 Inuit representatives from Rankin

Table 5.2
Expenditures, Department of Northern Affairs and Natural Resources

Year	Expenditures
1954	$19,118,141
1955	20,155,118
1956	24,615,905
1957	36,970,235
1958	49,071,578
1959	65,176,832
1960	81,111,576
1961	74,205,902
1962	79,367,615
1963	81,563,579
1964	77,334,019
1965	127,306,147
1966	156,433,733
1967	197,415,393
1968	231,436,113
1969	266,992,760

Source: Canada Yearbook 1956, 1957–58, 1962, 1963–64, 1966, 1969, 1970–71.

Inlet voiced a similar concern at that year's meeting of the Eskimo Affairs Committee.[22] Their query was rebuffed with the prediction that other mines would be opened and provide further employment opportunities for Inuit. In 1962, when the mine was closed down, a quasi-urban environment was created that was characterized by unemployment and all its attendant ills.

While in terms of resource development the objectives of the "vision" can be judged as a failure for the regions concerned, its impetus did lead to some positive results. Primarily, there was an increased flow of monies into the Canadian north.

Table 5.2 indicates that for 1954, the first year of the existence of the Department of Northern Affairs and Natural Resources, its expenditures were only $19,118,141. There were some increases from that figure over the next two years but a larger increase came in 1957 that appears to have been an early manifestation of the "vision," implementation of which began in that year. Another large leap can be seen for 1958, the first full year of the "vision." Further significant increments came in 1959 and 1960, after which expenditures leveled off until

1965, when highly increased spending was evident again. In 1968 the DNANR was absorbed into the Department of Indian Affairs and Northern Development, with an even greater budget expansion.[23]

At the base of the increased expenditures, which contrasted so sharply with the austerity-conscious stance that underlay the Policy of Dispersal, was a fundamental change in fiscal policy that was appearing in Canada as a whole in the 1950s. K.J. Rea has characterized this change as follows: "With the growing appreciation during this period of the possibilities of deficit financing, it became less plausible to think of public intervention being limited by a certain amount of 'money' in the federal treasury."[24] While in some quarters expanded expenditures in the north were regarded as temporary relief measures, the trend of rising expenditures was to continue beyond such a preliminary phase. National pride was eventually to come to the fore when there was full appreciation of comparisons of Canadian administration of their Inuit with the policies of American and Danish approaches to their Inuit peoples. This appreciation was, however, slow in coming. In 1943 the United States military, which had built a base on Southampton Island, complained about the Canadian government's lack of concern for its Inuit. The complaints were brushed off as being based on "gossip and rumour."[25] Later, Cantley, in his oft-cited report of 1950, rationalized comparisons with American and Danish administrations as inappropriate.[26] In time, forces from within Canada were to promote greater humanitarian consideration on the part of northern administrators. Rea sees the emergence of this concern in the 1950s as affecting the Territories: "The level of economic development attained in the Territories before the 1950s could be justified in terms of the most conservative and business-like criteria. But during the 1950s an apparently emotional basis for the allocation of national resources for this purpose made its appearance."[27] In the case of Arctic Canada, these humanitarian values did not really take hold until the decade of the 1960s, but when they did, the new policy they encouraged had profound effects on the cultural and social changes among the Inuit, including those of settlement practices.

THE ESKIMO LOAN FUND

One of the forms of financial aid to the Inuit of Canada that had modest beginnings, and which later became a substantial part of a rapidly expanding budget for northern development, was the Eskimo Loan Fund. The fund began in connection with the High Arctic Relocation project. In 1953 $5,000 was allotted to four colonies, at Grise Fiord, Resolute Bay, Alexandra Fiord (or Cape Herschell), which was cancelled, and on Banks Island.[28] The funds were used to establish stores. While these stores were designated as "cooperatives," the term was a misnomer. The stores were operated by local RCMP detachments,[29] and at times poor accounting was applied. The profits were not distributed among the relocated Inuit, but rather returned to the Eskimo Loan Fund.[30] In 1953 a total of $50,000 was allotted to the fund and this amount was doubled in the next year.[31]

The fund was greatly expanded in the 1960s, in keeping with the general growth of budgets for the Arctic and sub-Arctic. In 1963 power was accorded the commissioner of the Northwest Territories to grant loans of up to $10,000 to individuals, $15,000 to groups of four Inuit, and $25,000 to groups of more than four, while cooperatives could ask for up to $50,000.[32] In the early years of the fund, 7.5 per cent compounding interest was charged, but this arrangement was later deemed to be too great a burden for the Inuit, and was changed to 5 per cent at simple interest.[33] The major categories of loans were the cooperatives, loans on boats and other equipment, and housing. Since the fund was planned as revolving or self-sustaining, with, indeed, growth potential through interest accrued, at first glance it would seem to diverge from the Welfare State Policy that evolved during the 1960s. This supposition is based on the expectation that loans would be repaid. By 1966–67 it became evident that repayments of loans were "very poor."[34] A memorandum by E.A. Cote, the deputy minister, on 14 April 1967, noted "Eskimos easily confuse loans with grants, even though the requirements for repayment have been well explained."[35] This attitude of the Inuit can be understood, considering the largesse of the government at this time in distributing various pensions, allotments, and relief. It would appear that in the eyes of the Inuit, such an apparently bottomless reservoir could be tapped without consideration for repayment. As the decade ended there appeared to be little prospect of the fund realizing its original purpose of being self-sustaining and revolving. The report for the fiscal year 1969–70 showed a total of $481,759.71 loaned out up to that time. The largest amount, $293,959.40, was loaned to cooperatives, as compared to $138,568.57 for housing and much smaller amounts for boat and equipment loans. In addition to these sums taken from the fund, another $98,300.26 had been charged in interest. By contrast, only $76,258.26 had been repaid.[36]

Boat and equipment loans could apply to both concentrated and dispersed settlement, while cooperatives were usually associated with already centralized situations. It was largely in the realm of housing that financing influenced settlement patterns toward centralization. I shall address the role of housing programs in the centralization process, but at this point it should be noted that the Welfare State Policy was being pushed forward in relation to the Eskimo Loan Fund. The resistance that the Inuit brought to the question of repaying loans, and the eventual acquiescence by involved administrators, came within the framework of that policy. This acquiescence was, however, not unopposed. In his memorandum of 14 April 1967 the deputy minister objected that failure to repay loans "distorted the revolving nature of the fund."[37] After that there is little evidence that repayment of loans was followed up, especially as they were applied to housing.

HEALTH CARE

Along with the general neglect of welfare during the years preceding and throughout most of World War II, the health care system remained poorly developed. While much of the illness that afflicted Inuit during those years was episodal or epidemic, tuberculosis was somewhat different, though at least equally distressing, as depicted by Grygier: "Isolation in their harsh climate preserved the Inuit from the ravages of southern diseases for thousands of years. But it also left them with no built in immunity and when Europeans began to arrive, inadvertently carrying the germs with them, epidemics of measles, influenza, poliomyelitis, and tuberculosis hit one community or area decimated the population, then retreated. But tuberculosis lingered, spread and became endemic."[38] Dr G.J. Wherratt of the Department of National Health and Welfare issued a report in 1945 that gives some idea of the extent of this disease in the Canadian Arctic. Compared to a 53 per 100,000 persons death rate for the rest of Canada from tuberculosis, the rate for Inuit was 314. What was even more distressing was that at that time 84 per cent of Inuit deaths "took place without a doctor or nurse being available."[39] While x-ray equipment was finally provided for the Eastern Arctic Patrol vessel in 1964,[40] it was some years after that before the death rate declined significantly and treatment for a variety of other diseases could be considered adequate.

The problem of distance from effective medical treatment became a concern for some administrators as well as a source of anguish to the Inuit whose relatives often spent several years in southern Canada hospitals. The lack of medical care in the Arctic had been a source of concern as early as 1930, when at a meeting of the Northwest Territories Council it was suggested that the number of physicians in the Eskimo area be increased from four to seven.[41] It turned out that not only was this increase not met but that Dr Martin, one of the four, who had been stationed at Coppermine, was recalled a year later.

The question of improved health services within the Arctic did not rest. In 1944 Bishop Flemming of the Church of England referred to his earlier request for a hospital at Lake Harbour made some years before.[42] This hospital had been, instead, built at Pangnirtung. He now renewed his request for a hospital at Lake Harbour. The bishop also suggested use of army doctors and of aircraft for flying patients out, suggestions that were actually beginning to be implemented at that time. In the meantime, the missions had taken up the brunt of health care in the Arctic. Internal correspondence in 1944 points to the rationale for this situation: "As you know it has been due to the need for strictest economy that the most unsatisfactory situation exists. No doubt had funds been available both the Anglican and Catholic Missions would have gone ahead with the construction of additional hospitals, industrial homes and schools."[43]

Early in 1945 J.G. Wright submitted a memorandum entitled "Considerations in Planning Medical Care of Eskimos," in which he proposed adding six hospitals to the Canadian Arctic.[44] He noted that with a then current population of 7,700 Inuit in Canada, only about 1,800 lived within a 300-mile radius of the four existing hospitals. With the addition of the proposed six, a total of 6,200 Inuit could be reached within such radia. He also proposed a flying medical service, citing the case of Australia, as well as more hospital ships. He recommended trips to camps by boat in summer and sled in winter, as "in no other way can all natives be reached over the greater part of the year."[45] The advantage of shipboard treatment was stressed in that surgery could be performed aboard. Patients could be returned to their homes, rather than having to be removed to hospitals in the south, bringing on painful separation of families. In the coming years the additional hospitals were not established, nor were additional ships brought in to serve medical purposes. However, flying services were instituted and did provide important health care functions.

The debates over the advisability of more hospitals in the north continued in correspondence and in discussions in the Committee for Eskimo Affairs well into the fifties. Bishop Marsh of the Church of England took up the cudgels in support of northern hospitals,[46] with members of the Indian and Northern Health Services opposed. Dr P.E. Moore argued that superior treatment was possible only in southern hospitals.[47] Grygier summarized the arguments against northern hospitals, particularly with regard to treatment of tuberculosis: "The arguments usually put forward for refusing to provide sanatoria treatment in the North were, first, that it was not possible to attract specialists to the region and that adequate modern treatment was therefore not possible, second, that the number of active TB cases was expected to

decline within five years, so extra beds in the North would be superfluous, and third, that the main purpose of hospitalization in the North
was not so much to give active treatment as to remove the infection
source from the community which could be done using the present facilities."[48] Ultimately, the most telling problem was that the Department of Northern Affairs and National Resources refused to meet the
gross salary for physicians of $31,414 proposed by the Northern
Health Services.[49]

Visits by doctors and nurses to outlying places of residence as suggested by Wright presupposed the continuation of dispersed settlement. For the period of the 1940s and 1950s when this possibility was
being entertained, it is questionable as to what extent expansion of
hospital service in the Arctic would have affected the treatment of disease. With the strenuous efforts being made during those years to
maintain scattered settlement, it is unlikely that large-scale clustering
in centres that contained hospitals would have been allowed. Cases in
point are Chesterfield and Pangnirtung, where there was some degree
of centralization, but settlement remained scattered for the most part
through the 1950s.

The expansion of hospitals in the Canadian Arctic did not materialize, but other facilities that improved health care began in the later
1940s and reached full development in the 1960s. Nursing stations
were established gradually throughout the north, beginning at Coppermine in 1947 (and also Port Harrison in that year), at Cape Dorset
and Lake Harbour in 1952, Frobisher Bay in 1955, in 1957 at Hall
Beach and Rankin Inlet, in 1962 at Coral Harbour, Eskimo Point, and
Spence Bay, and at Cambridge Bay in 1955.[50] In the sixties, nursing
stations were established at Pond Inlet and Igloolik and a hospital was
opened at Frobisher (replacing the one at Pangnirtung). In addition
to these stations based at the larger communities, during the 1960s a
string of "health stations" or quarters were developed for the itinerant
health survey parties that by that time had reached most Inuit in the
Canadian north. By the end of the 1960s virtually all Inuit were being
reached at one of these three levels of health care.[51]

A personal experience in the Perry River region in 1963 left me with
a mixed impression of how health care was being served in the north
at that time.[52] The district had a population in the spring of 1963 of
seventy-seven, of which only thirteen people lived at the post at Perry
Island, the remainder being dispersed in seven camps. Despite good
flying conditions it was not possible to bring the entire population to
the post because of unfavourable landing conditions in some of the
camps. Forty-six of the population of seventy-seven were flown in and
examined. While visits of the medical teams brought in were com-

monly referred to as the "x-ray survey," I noted that quite comprehensive physical examinations were carried out. The difficulties in reaching all people in such places as Perry River could be seen elsewhere. Commonly people had to be informed and encouraged to come to centres where provision for landing aircraft were installed. It was really only when centralization was well advanced that most or all people could be so served.

Closer surveillance of health brought a clearer appreciation of the magnitude of health problems in the north. In 1961 no fewer than ten communities in the Central Arctic suffered epidemics including influenza, measles, and strep throat.[53] Accidental deaths were another leading cause of mortality, and tuberculosis continued to be a chief problem, though important advances in treatment were introduced by the end of the sixties.[54]

The advantages of centralization for the health and especially treatment of Inuit can be appreciated, even when only nursing stations or access to outside facilities were available. Such arrangements are favourable compared to the problems of diagnosis and treatment under conditions of dispersed settlement. As well, problems of health became more and more identified with problems of inadequate housing during the 1960s. Accordingly, it is appropriate to examine this relationship at this juncture.

HOUSING

Anyone who visited Arctic communities from about 1970 onward and viewed the neat rows of multi-roomed dwellings might well have assumed that such housing had been an integral part of the villages from their very beginnings. This was far from the situation in most places, as the case-by-case examples in the succeeding chapters illustrate. As we have seen, at certain growing centres that were close to main DEWline sites or military installations, scrap lumber was used and "shanty towns" grew up. Inuit government employees were usually provided with more substantial housing. Elsewhere, as will be seen, the snowhouse and framed tent were in evidence until the building programs of the 1960s came into effect. Places that were easily reached by normal aircraft travel routes were the first to attract notice by officials from Ottawa on their visits to the Arctic. Consequently, these were the places that aroused alarm regarding housing conditions.

There was for some time a romanticized conception of such traditional structures as snowhouses. Anyone who has lived for any period in these structures, which are heated with animal oil lamps, is quickly disavowed of any notions of glamour. For example, take the difficulty of producing heated water for hygienic purposes. First, ice or hard-packed snow has to be melted over the lamp, and then the resultant water heats for another long period before it is usable for washing. Accordingly, charges of uncleanliness in the camps, or in the early stages of in-gathering where lamps continued to be used, were unwarranted.

I noted in chapter 2 how the relationship between housing type and health was cited in the early days of World War II. Later, the concern over this relationship became one of the primary driving forces in the housing revolution of the 1960s. The role inadequate housing played in Inuit health was highlighted in 1960 in the report "Eskimo Mortality and Housing."[55] This report focused on infant mortality and, while largely a pictorial study, had some pithy observations. For instance, "death of infants up the age of one year account for about half of Eskimo deaths. About half of Eskimo infant deaths occur within the first month of life."[56] These estimates were contrasted to a 10 per cent rate of death in Canada as a whole occurring within the first year of life. It was also noted that very few infant deaths came where professional medical attention was available.[57] The reasons given for these shocking facts were (1) exposure to a wide range of infections; (2) lack of continuous warmth and shelter and adequate nutrition; (3) aggravation of conditions of ill health by the environment; (4) lack of adequate medical care.[58] Some of the then existing Inuit housing was also illustrated in the report. Among the problems were lack of good wooden floors; the presence of dogs near tents, contributing to unsanitary conditions; sleeping platforms being too low; poor bedding; difficulty in heating dwellings, especially tents in late summer;[59] and garbage being strewn around camping sites. According to the report a dismal choice was presented: "For the Eskimo infant the choice is either gastro-enteritis in the shack or pneumonia in the tent."[60]

Experiments in developing alternate habitations were discussed in this early stage of concern about housing conditions in the north. At Cape Dorset and Igloolik styrofoam igloos were built that were said to provide cost-efficient accommodation, but their durability was as yet unknown. Another experimental structure was a styrofoam quonset hut that proved to be warm in winter. The RCMP also tried out double tents.[61] The first wood house was the so-called rigid frame dwelling. This was a house with sloping walls and overhanging eaves built with four feet by eight feet plywood panels and insulated with rock wool placed inside the space between the double walls. Floor dimensions were sixteen by sixteen feet. The house was introduced at Frobisher Bay in 1958–59 and was regarded as being so satisfactory that in 1960, 125 units were sent to fourteen settlements at a cost of $500 per unit.[62] These units were occupied for $15 a month, payments that were to be applied toward an eventual purchase by the occupant in seven to ten years.

It was seen early that the rigid frame dwelling would not meet minimum standards of sanitation and other health requirements set by Indian and Northern Health Services. Dr P.E. Moore at the twelfth meeting of the Committee on Eskimo Affairs in 1961[63] laid out these requirements: combined living room and kitchen, two bedrooms, stove properly guarded to prevent burning of children, a covered forty-gallon container with tap for melting ice, a two-gallon container with tap for drinking water, and a small sink with drain. None of the requirements were met in the rigid frame house.[64] Later two- and three-bedroom houses were offered for sale with Eskimo loan advances raised to $2,000 for each unit. However, by the mid 1960s, of 800 families that had been provided with new houses, 90 per cent had fallen behind in their payments and 50 per cent had made only one payment.[65] Clearly the concept of paying for housing, given the perceived wealth of the government, had not taken hold among most Inuit of Canada.

By the mid sixties, it had become apparent that the burden of house buying was too great to be borne by most Inuit. Accordingly, in 1965 a rental program was introduced that would charge rents according to the income of the inhabitants. The new houses consisted of a two-room (one-bedroom) structure with 250 square feet of living space and costing $4,000, as well as a three-room (two-bedroom) house of 500 square feet costing up to $7,500. There was also a plan for a four-room (three-bedroom) house of 700 square feet at $8,000. Three hundred dollars' worth of furniture was to be supplied. A four-year building project was proposed with expenditures estimated at $4,300,000 for the first year, $2,300,000 for the second and third years, and $3,000,000 for the fourth year.[66]

That the rents were to be based on ability to pay illustrates the extent to which the Welfare State Policy had been accepted by Ottawa by this time. The plan was that most renters would occupy the two- and three-bedroom houses supplied with the amenities outlined by Dr Moore, but single people and small families would continue to use one-room dwellings. As the rigid frame dwellings were replaced, they were to be resold to single people and small families or moved to outlying camps. The reselling price for the one-room dwellings would be on the order of $25 to $50, "when the Eskimos can afford it."[67]

The possibility of moving permanent houses to the camps had been brought up at the tenth meeting of the Committee on Eskimo Affairs in 1959 by one of the Inuit representatives[68] and also at the twelfth meeting held in 1961.[69] At the latter meeting, the difficulty of transporting such houses on the narrow sleds of the Inuit was raised. Indeed, very few of the rigid frame dwellings were in fact moved to the camps.

In the tenth meeting of the Committee, Bishop Marsh raised the recurrent question of dispersal versus concentration of population, with the view that the new housing "tends to collect Eskimos around trading posts when they should be out hunting and trapping."[70] The chairman, R.G. Robertson, expressed the view that "there were good prospects for developing an economy based on combined revenue from land and wage employment."[71] Others at the meeting concurred with this view, which was actually the one put forth by Henry Larsen back in 1954.

The building policies and construction programs that transpired during the 1960s have been criticized. Prominent among these critiques was the report of Thomas and Thompson, which appeared in 1971.[72] They stressed the need to observe Inuit values that are difficult to change. For example, they found a lack of facilities for butchering animals and repairing equipment and felt that, given the sleeping habits of the people, less space could have been devoted to separate bedrooms. However, Duffy argues that the Inuit were in general pleased with the housing that was provided.[73] I gained a similar impression in the field as these programs were being instituted.

The multiplicity of housing types and the shifts in means of payment and rental arrangements may seem to suggest a lack of foresight as well as inconsistent goals in housing policies during this period. But one should be aware that perceptions of what constituted adequate housing for the Inuit changed profoundly during that decade. These involved not only escalating considerations of health factors but also the growing conception that Inuit should not be disadvantaged in warmth, sanitation, and general comfort as compared with southern Canadians. While there were errors in planning, the evolution of thinking regarding housing in the north was rapid as the decade advanced. At the end of the 1960s almost all Inuit had comfortable houses with ample space for the occupants, fuel oil heating, and adequate furnishings, and which were served with garbage and sewage removal, water distribution, and in most cases electricity. The adoption of proper sanitation measures was taking time, but through education in public health, this was gradually being accepted by the Inuit.

The housing programs played important roles in the centralization of settlement in the Central Arctic, but the times of their advent varied from place to place. Consequently, housing was often inextricably interwoven with other factors in the in-gathering process, as later discussion of specific cases will show.

EDUCATION

The passive and apparently indifferent stance that the government took to education before and during much of World War II was threatened in 1944. That year Dr Andrew Moore, inspector of Secondary Schools for the Province of Manitoba, conducted a survey of existing schools in the Northwest Territories.[74] The survey was carried out during the months of July and August and a fifty-nine-page report was submitted in November. Copies were sent to Dr Charles Camsell, then deputy minister of the Department of Mines and Resources, to Gibson, and several others. Most of the survey was actually carried out in sub-Arctic communities, except for a visit to Aklavik where Inuit lived. The report is, however, relevant to this study since it contained recommendations that were to apply to the entire area of the Territories. There were no fewer than twenty recommendations, foremost of which was that the ultimate authority over matters of education should rest in a director of Education for the Territories and such a director should have a "very free hand" and "should reside in the Territories." The report also recommended that teachers should be members of the federal civil service and have a year of special training for northern work; separate schools should not be included in any public support; the curriculum should include occupational training; advice on health and hygiene should be given; summer school should be investigated; compulsory education should be enforced; and scholarships and bursaries provided to native students.[75]

Many of these recommendations were eventually adopted, but at the time reaction was stirred in Ottawa as well as among leaders of the two churches. The strongest opposition was then directed toward the recommendation of denominational schools being absorbed by the government. A.L. Cummings of the Bureau of Northwest Territories and Yukon Affairs proposed that this section be deleted, and amid general agreement,[76] it was.[77] The government was not yet ready to take over schools in the Arctic. This was, of course, an expression of the austerity policies of the previous years. While it was true that at this time the government was willing to let education be largely managed by the missions, the subsidies provided were minimal. In 1946 seven Roman Catholic and Anglican schools (two at Eskimo Point, two at Baker Lake, and one each at Chesterfield, Igloolik, and Frobisher Bay) were given grants of only $250 each per year.[78] Gibson described the nature of education in the mission schools in 1946: "Due to the nomadic life of the Eskimo there are only a few children available within the settlements. Consequently the majority only received training for the short periods their parents were in the settlements or immediate environs for purposes of trading, religious festivals, etc."[79] Here, again, the concept of nomadism is employed as representing typical Inuit settlement. It is true that the dispersed settlement that did exist brought about the conditions described by Gibson. In November 1946 Wright wrote to Gibson that there was "considerable difference of opinion ... as to how much education should be given the Eskimo and how it should be provided."[80] There was agreement that education should be met in the north, or the students "would become unfitted for the Native way of Life. This has been amply demonstrated in the case of children brought outside for hospitalization."[81]

Very little implementation of Dr Moore's recommendations was achieved before 1950, despite the formal declaration of federal control of education in the north. In 1947 Bishop Marsh of the Anglican Church met with various northern administrators. Marsh favoured day schools that would permit the Eskimo children to spend part of the year with their parents, thus keeping them "acculturated to their native environment."[82] He also felt that itinerant teachers should move to camps on a seasonal basis and "be provided with tents and boats." These and other points were largely supported by Gibson and the other administrators, except that it was pointed out that it would be difficult to get the teachers to give up their summer vacations by visiting camps.[83]

No immediate action was taken regarding Bishop Marsh's suggestions, but in 1949–50 federal schools were established at Coral Harbour, Lake Harbour, and Coppermine as well as two places in Arctic Quebec.[84] The duties of teachers were spelled out to include reports on community conditions, and thus the designation "welfare teachers" came into use.[85]

A survey of the region eastward as far as Spence Bay was undertaken by S.J. Bailey in April 1950 to ascertain responses to educational plans for the Arctic.[86] Some of the whites questioned the value of educating the Inuit, but these views were not shared by the latter people: "Amongst the natives with whom this subject was discussed, however, there was no difference of opinion – education is eagerly anticipated and actually pleaded for." There was agreement that education should be practical and that besides learning such activities as making fish nets, building and repair of small boats, use of tools should be taught. Girls should also have thorough training in the care of the home, cleanliness, and in particular proper diet.[87] There would be much further discussion in Ottawa regarding the curriculum, which became and persisted as a chief problem in education in the north. At this time there was also the problem of reconciling dispersal of settlement with the needs of education. The school at Coppermine revealed the essence of the problem, for there were only twelve students in attendance out of a school-age population of 120 in the trading area.[88]

One solution to the problem was to move school children to residential schools at Aklavik. In correspondence with J.G. Wright, then chief of the Northern Administration Branch, in 1952, Gibson noted that, given "nomadic habits," residential schools had to be continued for the time but that "when on the other hand a settlement mode of life became the rule and day schools can be established – the residential school should normally cease to function along ordinary lines."[89] While this statement showed recognition of the basic conflict between the resistence to in-gathering and the aims of education in the north, it also clearly showed a recognition of the inevitability of centralization that was rare in the early fifties. Two years later, in 1954, the doctrine of dispersal was again raised in the context of Inuit education by J.V. Jacobson, superintendent of Education for the Arctic: "We must take into account the nomadic character of the Eskimo who moves about in a pattern determined by the wildlife on which they depend. Eskimo children cannot follow the same fixed school term as white children and so do not observe standard schools hours. They cannot embark on standardized courses of studies leading up to and terminating in University education; unless they abandon the Eskimo way of life and this is not desired by anyone, least of all the Eskimo themselves."[90] This notion of preservationism, which implied scattered (rather than "nomadic") settlement, was very much alive in 1954. The statement presumed that such a pattern was a native preference, an assumption that belied the tendency of the Inuit to cluster at certain posts, which I have explored earlier and which had begun by the 1950s. In this same correspondence Jacobson also stressed that, besides learning arithmetic and English, the Inuit students should "learn how to keep healthy, to appreciate the need for conservation of wildlife resources." Further, he saw the aim in education "is not to make them fall into the pattern of the white man's way of life but to make them better Eskimos." The difficulty of defining just what elements of the native culture were to be retained and which were to be altered was not addressed.

By the early fifties there were two residential schools at Aklavik, one for Catholic and the other for Anglican children, which served part of the western Central Arctic. From 1951 there was also a Catholic residential school at Chesterfield for students from the eastern part of the area. But federal day schools were being built elsewhere: at Frobisher Bay in 1955, Broughton Island, Arctic Bay, and Resolute in 1959, Clyde River in 1960, Grise Fiord and Padloping in 1962, Lake Harbour in 1963, Igloolik in 1960, and Hall Beach in 1967 for the eastern part of the Central Arctic. Others were established at Spence Bay in 1958, Pelly Bay in 1962, Gjoa Haven in the same year and, earlier, at Cambridge Bay in 1958. For the Keewatin, besides the residential school at Chesterfield, there were established day schools at Eskimo Point (1959), Baker Lake (1957), Rankin Inlet (1957), and Whale Cove (1961).[91] A number of these schools were built before the in-gathering process was complete, and thus arose the problem of housing students if they were to attend schools while their parents still lived in outlying camps. There appears to have been two basic philosophies regarding hostels in the various branches of the administration. One was, even in the 1960s, based on the premise of continued dispersal of populations. This was clearly the view of the superintendent of Schools for the Territories and members of his staff based in Fort Smith, who proposed in 1963 that the then abandoned intermediate (or "I") sites on the DEWline could serve as locales for small school establishments by using existing buildings for hostels: "The use of these sites for educational purposes would bring the schools much nearer to the people and serve to counteract the present trend toward 'urbanization' without economic support which at present bedevils our northern operation."[92]

A lively exchange of correspondence ensued between Ottawa and Fort Smith regarding this proposal,[93] including a very optimistic report of prospects for such schools based on a visit to one of the "I" sites. These plans were eventually dismissed by administrators in Ottawa because the structures available at the sites would not allow enough space for even the small enrollments that were envisioned, and the costs of building and maintaining such small schools was estimated as being more expensive than larger centralized schools.[94]

The other view of hostel building in the north was put forward in 1964 by Alexander Stevenson, then administrator of the Arctic. His plan was to build large hostels at several major centres to draw children from extensive areas and other centres. He proposed a 100-bed hostel for Igloolik, a 200-bed pupil residence for Cambridge Bay, a 160-bed hostel for Fort Churchill, and a 100-bed hostel for Pangnirtung.[95] This proposal came with the expectation that all Inuit children would be enrolled in schools by 1968. While a number of smaller and local hostels were built, this program did not reach the proportions envisioned by Stevenson. In the end, many of the problems of the hostels were resolved through the expedient of centralization. A statement in a settlement description for Igloolik for 1969 illustrates this effect: "As most of the outlying camps have now been abandoned and the families concerned being now housed within the settlement, only a small number of children now make use of the hostel (only six children are in residence)."[96] Thus with the increased and, by the end of the 1960s, almost complete centralization of population, and with the construction of primary level schools in each centre, children then lived with their parents in the comfortable new houses provided by the government. However, for secondary and, in some cases, the higher grades of schooling, children were sent to Yellowknife and Churchill, where hostels of large size had to be built.

It can be seen that educational planning was closely linked with changing settlement patterns during the 1950s and 1960s. There was initial concern that building schools would encourage in-gathering of families. The problems of separating children from parents, which was much deplored by the Inuit, and of providing accommodations for the students during school terms were resolved, at least for those in the lower grades, with the later centralization of settlement.

COMMUNITY ORGANIZATION AND PLANNING

As the trend toward centralization began and slowly gathered force during the 1950s, some basic and far-reaching administrative changes began to take place. For a long time, the administration of the north on a local level was unevenly and rather haphazardly carried out. Much of the government involvement for many years rested in the hands of the RCMP. As we have seen, however, since the detachments were spread thinly, in many of the communities traders took on administrative responsibilities. Education and health care were handled predominately by the churches. With the founding of federal schools, teachers were given administrative responsibilities and thus became welfare teachers. Overarching local authority finally fell to the Northern Service officers beginning in the mid 1950s, and by 1958 they were stationed in "about 10 Eskimo communities."[97] After the Northern Administration Branch was recognized in early 1959, the Northern Service officers were designated as area administrators with the responsibility of coordinating departmental programs in their area.[98] The area administrators reported to regional administrators who operated out of Yellowknife, Churchill, and Frobisher Bay. The functions of the NSOs, or area administrators, were quite diverse for some time: "More and more time was spent on departmental paper work with a corresponding reduction in the amount of time available for close work with the Eskimo groups. This trend among NSOs continued as welfare, industrial, and engineering experts were assigned to the Eskimo communities."[99] The void was filled by specialists including project officers, social workers, teachers, and equipment mechanics. Finally, in 1964, a new position of office manager was instituted to handle paperwork, freeing the area administrator to revert to the earlier role of working with the people.[100] The number of area administrators grew slowly during the 1960s, only reaching the more remote communities at the end of the decade. Meanwhile, beginning in 1959 a series of Northern Administration Branch Policy Directives were issued. The first of these concerned establishing a fair wage structure for employed Inuit, and facing the problems of language communication in employment situations.[101] By the third directive, issued in 1960, the necessity of community planning was recognized and twenty-five communities were designated as most urgently in need of planning.[102] In 1961 a directive was issued that concerned family allowances.[103] While it was acknowledged that children should have the "maximum possible benefit" from the allowances, a reactionary note was also sounded in the midst of otherwise apparently humanitarian proclamations. With regard to parental involvement in the allowances program: "There are still a few people who have not yet learned to spend their money wisely. These people will not receive their Family Allowance in money."[104] More typical of the tenor of the directives is a statement by Sivertz later in 1961: "The Government's view on relations with Eskimo may be summarized as an anxiety on the one hand to prevent unfair social exploitation, and on the other, to avoid the suggestion that the government is imposing a situation of inferiority on the Eskimo people."[105]

By 1961, as well, directives were concerned with "community development and local organization." In this regard two critical factors were outlined: what decision-making could be assigned to the local group, and who was able to make decisions. A word of caution was interjected in the thirteenth directive in that "fundamental to Canadian political theory, responsibility must accompany authority." In that regard, "a local organization can only be advisory in character when it comes to the spending of others money."[106] It was proposed that "a southern model should be adopted," except that "we must recognize the principle that influence is always limited by the degree of financial responsibility."[107] Indeed, throughout the sixties this was a realistic dilemma, between the espousal of democratic and humanitarian principles on the one hand and the perceived responsibility to the taxpayers of southern Canada, whose contributions lay at the base of a growing welfare state situation, on the other. Branch Policy Directive No. 18 concerned movement of Inuit people. It stated: "The government will exert no pressures on Eskimos to stay where they are within the north or to go south. That no pressure, advice, or persuasion in the matter of movement or permanency of habitation should be made, that the decisions should be made by the people themselves, and, at the same time, any moves" should be advantageous, socially and economically, and the "drain on the public should not be out of proportion to the value expected."[108] This again attempts to balance an explicitly stated policy of Inuit exercising what was being posed as autonomy with certain perceived practical and monetary considerations.

Further branch directives were concerned with employment of southern Canadians in the Arctic, their selection, financial considerations such as rent, accommodations for the employees, and their families, etc. But in 1964, in Directive No. 32, a community development fund was established to provide local councils with a basic amount of $3,000, with grants of up to $1,000 for projects that "were of general benefit to the community." While earlier attempts had been made to organize Inuit in such councils, this is the first such direct action for their support by the government that I have been able to find. The directive continues on an optimistic note regarding the degree of autonomy sought and hoped for. While all members of the branch (presumably mainly the area administrators) "should become familiarized with the principles and techniques of community development," since "community development and self-determination are inseparable," leadership training was to be undertaken "through continued support of community councils and by initiative of regional councils."[109] It is not clear as to what these regional councils would be comprised of, since at this time there is no evidence for planning regarding organizations above the local community level.

In the meantime, other more tangible problems were being addressed. A Community Planning Group was formed in 1961, comprised largely of members of the Engineering Division, and its purpose was defined as follows: "To provide for the reasonable wants of an expanding population, low cost housing assistance ... mortgage money" for those "who could not afford the high cost of northern construction," including the need for fuel storage, and water and sewer programs, etc.[110] The plan was to give "local populations for the first time the advantage of modern urban life in the security of permanent land tenure and home ownership." Explicit here was the term "urban," suggesting clearly not only the assumed inevitability of the still nascent centralization but of the superiority of living conditions under such settlement arrangements. This is, of course, a far cry from the ideal of dispersed settlement, which was at this time only slowly dying. The obvious dichotomy between the living conditions of whites now living in the growing villages and the Inuit had to be addressed, and thus there was the "need to eliminate snob hill or 'separated shanty towns.'" "Intensive government activity" was bringing on the need for townsite planning. A number of engineering considerations were envisioned, including drainage, availability of water, construction of large buildings, airstrips, roads, and so on. Construction problems included those of contour, rocky outcroppings, availability of gravel for pads and roads, etc.[111]

During the early 1960s there was clearly considerable inconsistency and confusion regarding the effects of the centralization that was then beginning to advance. This was true especially on the matter of how much the Inuit would be expected, or allowed, to participate in community affairs. The involvement that Inuit representatives had been granted in the Eskimo Affairs Committee was not followed up after that committee was dissolved in 1962. It would be some time later before their voices would again be heard. Vallee and his associates put the situation squarely: "The considerable increase in the size of the settlements during the 1960s was accompanied by a growing need for local administration and control. There was a tendency in the late 1950s and early 1960s to vest control and administration in government-appointed officials with, in some cases, advisory councils with no legislative or executive powers. During the late 1960s the Northwest Territories government mounted a campaign to incorporate settlements as local legislative bodies, with varying degrees of authority ranging from settlement councils with quite limited power to village and town councils whose powers are comparable to those of the same kind of bodies elsewhere in Canada."[112] The level of autonomy that resided in such bodies was not significant during the period on which this study focuses. Part of the problem of stimulating native self-direction was related to certain personality and quasi-political characteristics of Inuit and their society, that is, the customary reticence in asserting one's views (this especially in the face of powerful outsiders) and the predominance of consensual over authoritarian decision-making. The other difficulty was the failure to appreciate an emerging capacity for leadership potential, which, indeed, at this time was only slowly developing and had to await the advent of a new generation of more educated youth.

The same humanitarian ideals that brought the growth of health and welfare, educational and housing programs by the 1960s were instrumental in developing more efficient government organization in community planning. Linked was the principle, if not explicitly expressed, that the Inuit of Canada should have facilities, if not equal to, at least approaching those available to southern Canadians in terms of comfort and convenience. Execution of planning had also to rely on the liberalization of subsidization by the tax base of southern Canada. This liberalization was possible only through a general shift in philosophy away from a preservationist stance to one based on humanitarian and democratic considerations. Intrinsic to these considerations, though not often overtly expressed, was the growing assumption that they were best actualized under conditions of concentrated settlement. Centralization was part and parcel of the Welfare State Policy.

CHAPTER SIX

Settlement in the 1960s – I

During the 1950s employment opportunities at places like Frobisher Bay, Rankin Inlet, and Cambridge Bay were clearly instrumental in the process of centralization. Elsewhere, the uncertain nature of the habits and occurrences of the caribou brought on in-gathering. In some cases the tendency for Inuit to move closer to, or into, the growing centres had less tangible reasons. I have cited documents that attest that the moves toward centralization during the fifties were in the nature of migration as well as relocation. Several cases combine the two processes, and in some cases migration clearly dominated in the formation of centres of population. One set of circumstances that was definitely that of relocation during the 1950s was the establishment of two colonies in the High Arctic. I shall take up the story of these colonies for the next decade here.

THE HIGH ARCTIC COLONIES IN THE 1960S

It will be recalled that people from scattered settlements along east Hudson Bay and from northern Baffin Island were drawn together into a compacted community some distance from the RCMP detachment on Ellesmere Island. Accounts of the founding and the early years of this colony suffer from considerable dichotomy. There are the consistently optimistic reports of the RCMP detachment at Craig Harbour (later Grise Fiord), which painted a rosy picture of the colony throughout the fifties.[1] Then there are the revisionist studies of the 1990s, which in general follow an approach that is highly critical of government policy and actions in their analyses.[2] Fortunately, there is a more balanced portrayal of the colony in the work of Milton Freeman.[3] He departs from the RCMP accounts of harmonious relations between the two elements of the Inuit population and concedes the difficulties of adjustment, especially for the Port Harrison people.[4] An important contrast between the accounts given by Freeman and those of some later writers is that the latter focus on the founding of the colony and reach into only the very earliest period afterward, while Freeman's time perspective extends to later developments. He argues for a more favourable subsistence environment than is sometimes accorded to the Grise Fiord region,[5] especially when it is compared to conditions in the Port Harrison region. He characterizes the area as follows: "Grise Fiord is an exceptionally rich hunting area, walrus, and ringed seal and bearded seal are available throughout the year, and beluga, narwhal, and harp seal are present throughout the open water season. Caribou, hare, char, ptarmigan, and polar bear provide some variety in a predominantly marine mammal diet."[6]

As the fifties ended and the new decade began, significant changes in living accommodations and settlement were on the horizon. By the end of 1959 the Department of Northern Affairs and National Resources had approved loans for new houses.[7] These were ordered and built in the two separate camps of the colonists. It was clear when plans for a school were being entertained in late 1961 that it would have to be built near the quarters of the RCMP detachment, and the Inuit agreed that, in order to be near their children, a move was indicated. The move was accomplished in May and June of 1962,[8] but the two elements of the population maintained their separation in distinct neighbourhoods. In 1964, however, "all the houses were moved into one row of dwellings east of the police and school buildings."[9] The first phase of housing proved inadequate, but by 1967 all families lived in new government-built houses.[10]

Despite continuing success in the hunt, a poor fur take in 1962 deprived the Inuit of the colony of an important source of income. The "majority of people" therefore required social assistance.[11] But this was an unusual circumstance in the decade of the sixties. Subsequent acquisition of motorized sleds benefitted both hunting and trapping.[12]

By the end of 1966 the RCMP were becoming aware of the effects of the division of the community along the lines of place of origin. It was reported at that time that three families wanted to return to their original homes, a situation attributed to intergroup tensions.[13] Despite this and other difficulties, RCMP reports consistently described morale as being high.[14]

In evaluating the results of the relocation to Grise Fiord, Freeman emphasized the improvement in health and in well-being, especially in terms of economic success. In this latter regard it was the Port Harrison people who had benefitted most.[15] Freeman praised the efforts of community participation (despite the factional division) in successfully petitioning the government for improved health facilities and more liberal application of game regulations in the period 1966–70. At the same time he stressed the difficulties of such relocated communities as Grise Fiord: "The long-term viability of a small artificial community such as Grise Fiord has always been in doubt. The inevitable in- and out-movement of people to any northern community would, due to the increasing urbanization and sophisticated tastes of the overall population, make small remote communities appear increasingly less attractive places to move to."[16]

By the end of the 1960s the colonists from Pond Inlet and Port Harrison had undergone a series of settlement changes, from scattered settlement in those regions in the early 1950s to a compacted, while divided, encampment at some distance from the sole white agency, the RCMP. Later, they split along the lines of diverse origins, and finally reunited at the site of the RCMP establishment.

The population had grown from the original thirty-six in 1953 to ninety in 1969 through both natural increase and immigration.[17] In some respects Grise Fiord had come to resemble, on a microcosmic scale, the condition of settlement that had become typical throughout the Central Arctic. However, it continued to display a greater emphasis on a subsistence economy than did most other centralized situations, and there was less institutional representation from the south and a smaller white population than was typical elsewhere.

Chief sources of information for the colony at Resolute for the 1960s are the reports of the RCMP detachment,[18] which usually provided a favourable picture, including yearly reports of high morale, and Bissett's study of 1967,[19] which gives a highly detailed and dispassionate account. While planning for the Ellesmere colony had been predicated in the dominance of a hunting and trapping economy, that of Resolute from the beginning envisioned a combined subsistence and wage employment situation, based on the existence of a Department of Transport weather station and an RCAF air base.[20] Indeed, a balance between hunting and wage work was quickly established, though by the sixties cash employment dominated. By the end of 1966 there was only one full-time hunter.[21] On the other hand, most of the employed men continued to hunt as a part-time activity.[22] The range of hunting was augmented by the replacement of dog team transport by motorized vehicles.[23] Trade in polar bear skins added to the income of the men, while trapping of fox was practiced less.[24]

The most important social development was the establishment of the cooperative store in 1961,[25] though in terms of economics it was far from a success. During the earlier years of the colony, the store was

run by the local RCMP officer, with profits being returned to the Eskimo Loan Fund.[26] After the store's operation was transferred to the
Inuit it was subject to significant losses. It was reported that individual
debts ran from $500 to $1,500 and the annual store debt ranged from
$19,000 to $33,000, due to "poor management" and lack of "supervision or proper accounting system."[27]

Population growth proceeded so that the original colony of twenty-
three had grown to 153 by the end of 1968.[28] This growth was partly
due to internal increase but also to immigration from such places as
Pond Inlet, Grise Fiord, Spence Bay, and elsewhere in the Central Arctic.[29] A certain amount of mobility was possible, including gratis trips
to the hospital in Edmonton to visit relatives.[30] Still lacking was the
provision of transportation for those Inuit who wished to travel
between Resolute and Port Harrison.[31] Social assistance was kept at a
minimum, due largely to wage labour opportunities. Bissett described
the employment possibilities in the colony in 1967: "The existing
labour force appears to be sufficient to meet existing employment
opportunities available at Resolute. In fact, the labour force is not pres-
ently fully exploiting the existing employment opportunities."[32] There
was some difficulty in keeping men employed on a permanent basis.
Termination was frequent, as was rehiring. The chief cause for termination was "excessive absences and drinking."[33] At Grise Fiord drinking was in the 1960s restricted to home brew, a practice discouraged
by the local RCMP detachment who, however, reported that there was
"really no liquor problem."[34] By contrast, Resolute had a bar at the air
base that was regularly supplied with beer and liquor from Frobisher,[35]
and some difficulties arose over alcohol abuse. Indeed, for a time, beginning in 1962, the Inuit lost the privilege to drink in the canteen at
the base because of domestic quarrels that drinking brought on "in returning home from the canteen."[36]

It is again unfortunate that, as with Grise Fiord, later critics of the relocations focused on the founding and earliest stages of the colonies,[37]
since major objectives were in time met. The colonies proved, on balance, to be economically viable. The colonists had comfortable housing, schools were established, and community projects organized. The
assessment of one of the RCMP officers stationed at Resolute indicates
some of the more tangible material benefits: "Compared with other
settlements in the Arctic, the Resolute Eskimo is fairly well off and continues to possess articles that are not owned by a good many other Eskimos in the North. There are washing machines, tape recorders,
record players, irons, sewing machines, transistor radios and 35mm
cameras."[38] Despite these material possessions and the general economic viability of the community, other aspects of the relocation of

people to Resolute were not so favourable. Among these was the failure to provide means for the Port Harrison people to visit or return to their original home. There were also social problems,[39] such as those connected with alcohol abuse.

SOUTH BAFFIN ISLAND AND FROBISHER BAY

Earlier I noted that the processes of contraction and centralization were well on their way in southern Baffin Island during the 1950s, and the abandonment of permanent camps continued throughout the 1960s. The decade would see the virtual disappearance of the hunting-trapping base camp of the contact-traditional orientation. The factors that had fostered this in-gathering during the fifties were augmented by others during the succeeding decade. This can be seen especially in the case of Cape Dorset. Higgins saw a transition from a trading to a "wage/marketing economy" during this period that related to the establishment of a cooperative in 1960.[40] However important the cooperative may have been, the effects of a cash economy with regard to centralization were already being felt. As early as 1949 a carving industry had been introduced, and construction projects had already aided in expanding cash flow before the 1960s. Together with social legislation contributions, there had been a shift in balance from trapping as the principal component of the total economy. Although the trade in furs and skins continued to play a role, hunting was still the basis of subsistence. Indeed, an RCMP report for 1961 estimated that 80 per cent of the population in the Cape Dorset trading area was supported by the "land" (presumably hunting) "indirectly," while 20 per cent lived "mostly" off the land.[41] The year-end 1962 report indicated that of 348 people in the area, 116 lived in the camps.[42] For the next year it was reported that "more and more of the camp Eskimos are moving into the settlement to live for reason of a more modern living and to enjoy the entertainment which settlement life provides."[43] This statement is one of the few references that I have found which cite the significance of recreation in the motives for in-gathering. This factor I found to be among those acknowledged by Inuit during my field research in the 1960s.

By the end of 1963 "about one third" (presumably of the men) had steady jobs in the centre.[44] The early sixties was also the period of a sharp rise in the price of sealskins, which gave the Inuit for a time an exceptionally fine source of income and which coordinated with subsistence hunting. It was estimated that approximately 6,000 sealskins were traded in 1963.[45] By the end of 1965 it was reported that a number of people were "making a fair living" from "carving, drawing, etching."[46]

Table 6.1
Sources of income, South coast Baffin Island

Community	Years	Hunting & trapping	Handicrafts	Wage labour	Unearned	Total
Cape Dorset	1962–63	$22,000	$38,000	$29,000	$22,000	$111,000
Cape Dorset	1966–67	38,000	158,000	153,000	43,000	392,000
Lake Harbour	1959–60	10,500	11,760	8,900	5,500	26,600
Lake Harbour	1966–67	21,000	12,400	28,000	13,000	74,400

Sources: For Cape Dorset, Higgins, *South Coast-Baffin Island*, 110; for Lake Harbour 1959–60, Graburn, *Lake Harbour*, 9; Lake Harbour 1966–67, Higgins, 133.

These occupations were seen as compensating for the loss of income due to the fall in the price of sealskins that had begun in the spring of 1965. Changes in dwelling types had a profound effect on the centralization process at Dorset. Earlier, Dorset had been supplied with low-cost government housing,[47] but a new phase of building began in 1966: "The new housing has of course attracted more families who were previously living on the land." In 1965, there had been 25 families of 155 individuals in 5 camps. At the end of 1966 there were "7 families or 55 people in 3 camps." A further 24 Eskimo houses "are to be erected next year leaving very little purpose for an Eskimo family to live in camp unless it is a particularly strong and independent one."[48] With more construction the next year, still more people moved to the centre, and at the end of 1967, of 505 Inuit in the area, only forty-one lived in camps.[49] 1967 also saw a revolution in transportation, and by the end of the following year there were only fifteen dog teams as compared to seventy-five tracked vehicles. There were, as well, sixty-eight freighter canoes.[50] The effects of improved transportation on settlement can be seen in the following: "This acquisition makes it possible for settlement residents to operate at much greater distances with greater economy in time and expense while trapping and hunting than was hitherto possible from such locations. The obvious advantages of basing in the settlement were not lost on the Eskimos because ... permanent camps are becoming fewer with each passing year."[51] By the end of 1968, only two camps, with twenty-five and eleven persons respectively, remained.[52] While it can be said that the hunting-trapping base camp was all but finished by that time, the hunting-trapping economy was far from being so.

Table 6.1 shows the shifting balances of the Cape Dorset economy as the sixties advanced. It is remarkable that the proceeds from hunting and trapping showed a marked increase between 1962–63 and 1966–67, given the drop in the price of sealskins in 1965. It is to be noted from the table that this source of income, though increased, was swamped by income from arts and crafts and wage labour during the 1960s. Arts and crafts income was expanded due to the advent and development of the West Baffin Eskimo Cooperative.[53] Wage labour expansion resulted from extensive construction. House-building contributed to a great extent to in-gathering at Cape Dorset, and this construction, together with construction as government agencies expanded, also became a leading source of support for the people of the growing village. These sources of income would be expected to diminish the importance of hunting. It must be noted, however, that animal produce continued to play a crucial role in the diet of the Inuit of Cape Dorset. Higgins estimated that for 1966–67, 224,318 pounds of meat, edible internal organs, and blubber were obtained from the hunt.[54]

Graburn described the settlement situation at Lake Harbour in 1963: "From November or earlier all except three families, whose heads are permanently employed, live in camps."[55] Further, Graburn stated, "there are no post parasites." There were then five camps, four in close proximity to the centre at Lake Harbour and the fifth about 100 miles away.[56] There was gathering at the post for temporary employment at the time of the visit of the supply ship in summer, as well as at the customary Christmas and Easter occasions. At the end of 1961, of the total population in the trading area, only thirty-four lived at the post.[57] By the end of 1963, the population had grown to 150, due in large part to return migration from Frobisher Bay.[58] With the rise in the price of sealskins to $20 in 1963, that trade dominated over trapping that year, with only seven fox being traded in the trapping season of 1962–63 despite the increase in the price of pelts from an average of previous years of $11 to $30.[59] Even though a school had begun operation on a full-time basis in the autumn of 1963, with no accommodations in the settlement, only eleven students from the camps attended.[60] There was no significant movement to the centre that year.

While some movement to the centre was evident by the end of 1966, there were still three camps in existence, and almost half the population lived in them.[61] There were only five dog teams by then, and most men owned skidoos.[62] By 1966, as well, all but one family lived in one-room houses supplied by a government construction program.[63] During the following year, ten three-bedroom houses were built. This latter construction supplied all families at the Lake Harbour village, with the exception of three, with government housing.[64]

It would appear that, as at Cape Dorset, by the end of 1968 the camp orientation had all but ceased, as two of the three camps were abandoned that year.[65] The remaining camp was in very close proximity to the centre. The people who moved in bought one-room houses from those who then occupied the more commodious dwellings. By this time, the price of sealskins had dropped to $7, reducing income from that source.[66] Table 6.1 shows that some recovery had taken place by 1966–67 in this category. The table also shows that the products of hunting and trapping had been overtaken by other categories of income. Handicrafts had expanded, though not to the degree attained in Cape Dorset. Wage labour income had quadrupled since the beginning of the sixties, largely due to construction programs. As at Cape Dorset, total income tripled during the same period.

In examining the likely causes for the culmination of centralization on the south coast of Baffin Island, the powerful forces that followed the adoption of the Policy of the Welfare State dominated. The attraction of good housing, the employment that came with building such houses, as well as with other construction, including the school and structures for other government agencies, and the ready availability of welfare, all stemmed from that policy. One possible exception might be the arts and crafts industry, which had particularly dramatic growth at Cape Dorset. Improved transportation, which increased the range of hunting and trapping, helped keep alive those pursuits despite the centralization of settlement.

One of the major concerns of those who espoused the Policy of Dispersal had been that the Inuit would become wards of the state. This concern was not entirely without foundation in the cases of the two South Baffin communities. The large increase in the "unearned" column in table 6.1 is evidence of a significant degree of dependency on governmental funds, even with the expansion of income sources, including wage labour.

In writing of centralization, I am referring to basic habitation centres, and not to seasonal camps, which continued to exist in this region as well as elsewhere in the Central Arctic. Such an encampment is described for the Dorset region: "Most of the Eskimos being out in Spring Camp, the annual holiday period where for over a month and a half the majority of the residents move out on the land east of Cape Dorset approximately 65 or 70 miles and live in tents, pursuing hunting and other leisure activities."[67]

Turning to the near urban situation that had developed at Frobisher Bay, by the spring of 1960 there remained only one camp of "two tents" situated thirty miles from the settlement of Frobisher Bay.[68] By the end of 1961 three distinct neighbourhoods had formed in the settlements.[69] These were (1) the airport site, with eight Inuit families living in modern apartments together with the majority of whites; (2) Ikhaluit, the Eskimo village, where 60 per cent of the Inuit lived

together with a few whites; and (3) Apex Hill where nearly 40 per cent
of the native people lived together with a few whites. At this time
"about 50 male Eskimos" were "gainfully employed," with the largest
number working for the Department of Northern Affairs.[70] This department also operated a rehabilitation centre, which accounted for
"approximately 80 men, women, and children."[71] According to the
RCMP report of 1961, the two ethnic populations lived apart "both
physically and socially," the main problem in interethnic relations being the language barrier. The 1961 report also stated that morale was
characterized by "a great sense of frustration," and that the "insecure,
confused, demoralized" condition of the Inuit population accounted
for the "liquor problems."[72] These problems are constantly referred to
in the annual RCMP reports. There were only eight full-time hunters
and the employment possibilities were thought to be inadequate to
support the native population. As well, by the end of 1961 "there were
no Eskimos in any outlying parts of the Frobisher Bay Detachment
area."[73] By the end of the next year the population of Frobisher Bay
was 913 Inuit and 689 whites.[74] During 1962 a number of layoffs were
reported, while "8 to 12 families" were making their living from
hunting, being especially aided in caribou hunting by autoboggans (or
skidoos).[75]

A detailed picture of life in Frobisher Bay for 1963 is available from
John J. and Irma Honigmann, anthropologists who spent six months
there. The Honigmanns describe a community that had already undergone considerable change, with a number of facilities available, government housing (though some "shacks" were also in use), and an
elaborate recreational culture. They estimated that "about one third"
of the men were steadily employed, though "a considerably large number of men held jobs during our visit and still more had held and lost
jobs during the previous year, some losing them in the autumn of 1962
after onset of the 'austerity program.' "[76] I shall return to the problem
of these lay-offs below. The Honigmanns found neither social disorganization nor lawlessness,[77] as they had been led to believe before visiting the community. They discussed the consumption of alcohol at
some length[78] but did not attach the almost wholly negative associations to the practice that the RCMP reports did. A final section of the
book deals with Inuit personality, depicting both a normative "social
personality" as well as several dominant types.[79] These depictions
present a picture familiar to observers of Inuit in the field, as well as
some interesting interpretations. While detailed descriptions of centralized communities of the scale of Frobisher cannot be attempted
here, the Honigmanns' report does articulate changes in settlement
patterns. For instance, a sample of seventy-nine households showed

the Lake Harbour region as predominating among the various points of origin for immigrants.[80] Also, interviews revealed some of the difficulties of eliciting motives for migration that apply as well to other places of in-gathering in the Central Arctic. The Honigmanns had assumed on the basis of their research that movement to Frobisher had been in order to take advantage of economic opportunities: "Nevertheless, we must honestly say the very few informants whom we interviewed specifically gave greater economic security or physical comfort as a goal they had in mind when they settled in town. Many people who replied to this question simply said they had accompanied other relatives or came to join a sibling or grown child who had already chosen Frobisher Bay as home. Many respondents gave no satisfactory explanation at all for coming."[81] While the Honigmanns attribute such responses, or the lack of response, to characteristics of Inuit personality, it should be noted that the pull of kinship played an important role in the migration to Frobisher. My own observations in other communities in the 1960s concur with this view.

Despite the fact that the Honigmanns lived in Frobisher Bay during the period of austerity mentioned above, they drew a favourable picture of the economy: "Eskimos in Frobisher Bay reveal few signs of poverty."[82] Quite a different picture emerges from the RCMP reports from the same period. The year-end RCMP report for 1963 indicates that "approximately 50% have turned to the native way of living."[83] The revival of hunting was seen as threatening the resources of the area. Certainly, with the massive influx of people, total reliance on subsistence may well have produced such stress, but employment, though reduced, still maintained a number of families. There was some movement from the centre related to the cut-backs in the labour force. For instance, a camp of twenty people was established at Ward Inlet, sixty miles away.[84] However, for the main part the increased hunting took place from the centre at Frobisher, where fifty skidoos were owned (though only thirty were said to have been operational in 1965) and used for hunting.[85]

The employment situation appears to have improved by the end of 1966 and the following survey was reported. About 25 per cent of the families were living from hunting supplemented by carving, about 50 per cent were supported by employment, and most of the remaining 25 per cent survived on welfare together with income from carving, while a "few live entirely from carving."[86] The percentage of steadily employed climbed to 60 per cent the following year, though "the majority" hunted on a part-time basis.

A community description issued in November 1968 gives a graphic picture of the community at Frobisher, attesting to the great degree of development that had been attained by that time. Four distinct neighbourhoods had developed. Two of these housed white employees and their families, one of which included an apartment complex that housed 450 people. A third neighbourhood was home to 550 Inuit, and a fourth was "a planned settlement" with "418 Eskimos and 75 non-Eskimos." This was the site of DNA operations that employed 131 people, including sixty-three Inuit. The Department of Transport operated the airport that serviced twice-weekly flights from Montreal. The community had two missions, the HBC store, and a five-man RCMP detachment. Health services included a twenty-eight-bed hospital, which had been re-established from Pangnirtung, and a traveling dentist. There were two banks, a 300-pupil school, and a radio telephone service. At this time, as well, there were two oil companies, a liquor store, a power plant that supplied electricity to Inuit as well as whites, water distribution and sewage, and garbage collection.[87] Even with this high development of urbanization some traditional scenes still existed: "The same Eskimo who drives a bulldozer may be hunting walrus tomorrow or building their own house ... sled dogs sleep beside trucks, sealskins are drying on lines stretched between hydro poles ... In summary, the sighting of seals in the bay still bring men, women, and children running to the shore to launch their boats."[88]

EAST BAFFIN ISLAND

The bulk of the population in the Cumberland Sound–Cumberland Peninsula regions remained dispersed at the beginning of the sixties. RCMP concern was at that time focused on "loitering" around posts,[89] a situation that had been previously avoided both at the long-standing post at Pangnirtung and at Broughton Island, where a new post had been established in 1960.[90] Anders et al list ninety-six people living at Pangnirtung in 1961,[91] and another census for 1961 gives 564 people for the trading area, divided into twelve camps, in addition to the main centre.[92] 191 people were said to trade at the new post at Broughton Island,[93] though there is little information on the dispersal of the population into camps. It is clear from the low rate of year-long employment that considerable hunting was being carried out from the centres.[94] However, considerable summer construction employment was taking place at Pangnirtung, as $20,000 was paid out in wages during 1961. The trade in sealskins also flourished, even though the price for the skins was still low.[95]

The events of 1962 in the Cumberland Sound region were dramatic and almost unique in terms of the process of in-gathering that was occurring throughout much of the Canadian Arctic during the 1960s. Responding to reports of dog disease, Peter Murdoch of the Department of Northern Affairs visited seven camps in Cumberland Sound from 11 to 14 February, and reported deaths of dogs in each camp.[96] Indeed, the disease was found to have spread to all places of habitation in the Sound within a few days of having started in one of the camps. By March 1962, the dog population of the Sound of 800 to 900 had declined to only 273. Men were reported as having to walk to the floe edge for their sealing.[97] After some discussion among local whites, the suggestion of taking food to the people in camps was rejected in favour of moving them to Pangnirtung as the only practical solution.[98] However, "[i]t was agreed by all involved that this would be a temporary programme to see the Eskimo people through this difficult time. Every encouragement would be made to have them resume their normal activities once the situation permitted."[99] The Policy of Dispersal still dominated the plans of the local Europeans at this time.

A police aircraft arrived on 3 March, and from then and through the 5th, eighty-eight people were moved by plane from the camps to Pangnirtung. Many more moved or were moved by sled or motorized vehicles, with the people of Pangnirtung assisting.[100] By early May the dog disease appears to have run its course, but by then only eighty-three people remained in three camps, out of the total Sound population of 556.[101] A number of projects were organized. Men hunted at the floe edge in rotation, with the catch being shared throughout the village. Thirty men were engaged in carving and another sixty were occupied "in other projects."[102] Relief issuances of camping equipment and other supplies were made. Temporary shelters of wooden frames and sealskin or canvas cover were constructed, with 20,000 running feet of wood being ordered for this purpose.[103]

Meanwhile, by mid May the disease was ascertained to be hepatitis, "a virulent pathogen transmitted by dog-to-dog contact,"[104] and plans were set in motion to innoculate 8,000 dogs throughout the Canadian Arctic. To recover the dog population, efforts were made to import dogs from various places in the north, but with indifferent results. Of eighty-nine dogs flown in, only forty-seven survived,[105] the others having died en route or shortly after arrival at Pangnirtung. In the end, a dog breeding program was successful.

A report to the regional administrator at Frobisher dated 16 January 1963[106] summarized the events following upon the epidemic among the dogs. At that time seventy people from the camps were remaining in Pangnirtung for the winter because of the continued shortage of dogs. Otherwise, all of the camps were occupied. It was estimated that sixty more dogs were needed to make the Cumberland Sound people self-sufficient. Meanwhile, men grouped together their remaining dogs to form teams.[107]

The developments of 1962 in the Cumberland Sound region were remarkable in several respects. The high degree of cooperation and the successful execution of planning in the face of disaster were unusual in the history of the administration of the Canadian Arctic. These measures included movement of people from the camps, provisions for their comfort in new quarters, as well as providing employment. The return of most of the people to their camps by the following winter is a rare reversal of what was by then a definite trend toward centralization. In view of the stated intent by local whites, including administrators, that this would be a temporary disruption of settlement, we might infer that some pressure was exerted on the Inuit to return to the camps. There is, however, nothing to support this supposition in the record. There is also no suggestion that the return to the camps was resisted by the people themselves.

After the resettlement, again we are told that "loitering was nonexistent" as men of the outlying camps came to trade about once a month and returned quickly to their camps, of which eleven remained in 1963 in Cumberland Sound.[108] By the end of that year there had been a 50 per cent increase in the dog population and conditions of relative prosperity were at hand in both trading districts. The sharp rise in the price of sealskins increased incomes: a total of 9,000 skins were traded at Pangnirtung, realizing an income of $114,000 from that source for the year.[109]

In 1964 there were again twelve camps in the Sound and, in the north, two main settlements at Padloping and at Broughton Island. The dog population had been fully recovered from the episode of 1962.[110] Centralization appears to have moved faster on the north shore of Cumberland Peninsula than in the Sound, for in 1964 fifty-one people were reported as living at Padloping and 187 at Broughton Island, numbers that appear to represent the total population of that coast.[111]

Government construction started in earnest in 1965 with eight new houses erected in Pangnirtung, making a total of fifteen. Twenty-one welfare houses were built at Broughton Island and nine at Padloping.[112] The RCMP officer in charge at Pangnirtung reported: "Although many of the Eskimos rely solely on hunting for a living, many are tending to move into the larger settlement at Pangnirtung where modern facilities are available to them, some are reluctant to return to their camps."[113] By the end of 1965, motorized sleds were being adopted even though the dog population had recovered.[114] By the end of 1966 it was evident that the in-gathering process had gained considerable force, since only eight camps remained and most of the local people lived at Pangnirtung. The settlement now had thirty government houses, of which fifteen were of the three-bedroom type, and a further twenty-three were planned for 1967.[115] However, at the end of 1966 about thirty families still lived in tents in Pangnirtung.[116] Housing advanced to even a greater degree to the north: there were now forty-six government houses at Broughton Island, twenty-five of the three-bedroom type, and at Padloping sixteen new houses had been built.[117] The RCMP officer in charge at Pangnirtung deplored the ingathering, which he attributed to welfare being too easy to come by, as well as to the availability of houses with fuel oil heating and electricity. He predicted that "an almost complete welfare state" was "in sight,"[118] despite the fact that income from carving had taken up the slack from the drop in sealskin prices. The snowmobile revolution was taking place by the end of 1966, with about fifty in evidence at Pangnirtung and thirty for the Padloping–Broughton Island region, paralleling a drop now in the number of dogs.[119]

As was the case in the same year at Lake Harbour and Cape Dorset, 1968 saw the demise of the hunting-trapping base camp. By the end of that year 571 people lived at Pangnirtung and only two camps, of sixteen and nineteen people respectively, still existed in the Sound. Padloping had been abandoned and 317 people were living at Broughton Island.[120] The abandonment of the camps in the Cumberland Sound–Cumberland Peninsula regions took place as the effects of the Welfare State Policy came to bear. The final stage of centralization came with the housing programs of the second half of the sixties, but ingathering had begun before then. While motivations are in part intangible, there had already existed substantial summer employment, even though there were still few full-time jobs as the decade drew to a close. Other sources of income, such as carving and crafts, continued. As in other examples of centralization, rapid adoption of motorized sleds made it possible to sustain a high level of game exploitation from the central bases.

Further north, the trading region of Clyde River was also undergoing changes in settlement during the 1960s. In the first year of the decade a school was opened.[121] At first this establishment did not seriously affect settlement, for the RCMP report for the year stated that the parents left shortly after leaving children at the school.[122] Clyde was one of the places where overt pressure was put on the people to disperse settlement or to keep settlement dispersed. In 1961 the officer in charge (actually at the detachment headquarters at Cape Christian) met with the "camp bosses" regarding redistributing people in the various camps. It would appear that the school may have had an effect on the contraction (rather than concentration) of people since "this detachment is being faced with the fact that the school at Clyde River is tending to move the Eskimos closer to the settlement."[123] In 1962 people from southern camps moved closer to the post at Clyde. Again the police appeared to have intervened: "members have cautiously helped guide them ... purposely to prevent any over population in relation to resources of each camp."[124] In 1962 the population of the trading district was forty-four families who resided in eight camps.[125] At Clyde in 1963 there were still only seven resident families, all of which had employed members, working either for the Department of Transport, the HBC, or the Anglican mission, in addition to family members whose heads were in hospitals in the south.[126] The rise in sealskin prices in 1963 revived an economy that had sagged during the previous year. In 1962 only 469 skins had been traded, but the number increased to 1,881 the following year.[127]

During 1963 "some loitering" was reported at Clyde, since people who had come for the summer remained until November.[128] There was only a slight increase to eight families at the post in 1964, but in the following year that number doubled, while only five had employed members. Another nine "depend on hunting and some part time work."[129] In 1965 the boom in price of sealskins was over, but a residual effect was apparent, for 2,031 skins were traded.[130]

In 1966, for the first time, employment became the highest source of income, even though 3,000 sealskins were traded. Families at Clyde now counted twenty, with support coming from handicrafts and hunting, "along with part-time employment."[131] Twenty-four families lived in the camps and only six Inuit were employed at the centre at Clyde. The 1967 year-end RCMP report indicated the pull of housing: "with the DIAND housing program last year erecting 7 new dwellings it is expected that still more families will move in this year."[132] At this point the government decided to move the village across the bay facing the original village site. At the end of 1968 only fifty-two of the population of 266 lived in camps, but only eight Inuit were employed in the centre.[133] The chief means of support came from hunting, despite the concentration of population. A large part of the community still lived in "shacks," even though eleven houses were being constructed at the new village site. In 1968, as well, the balance of transport fell to motorized vehicles, with twenty-one in evidence as compared to fourteen dog teams.[134]

According to Wenzel, only two camps remained apart from the settlement at Clyde in 1968.[135] One of these folded in 1969. He describes the compatibility between centralized living and a hunting economy: "Motorized snowmobile and canoe travel provided Clyde Inuit with both winter (over ice) and summer (open water) access to areas remote to the settlement, white allowing a relative ease of return as cir-

Table 6.2
Sources of income, East coast Baffin Island

Community	Year	Hunting & trapping	Handicrafts	Wage labour	Unearned	Total
Pangnirtung (Cumberland Sound)	1965–66	$66,042	$5,000	$100,725	$74,593	$246,360
Broughton Island	1965–66	19,298	3,000	73,440	17,115	112,853
Padloping	1965–66	8,819	–	6,000	5,988	20,807
Clyde River	1965–66	13,316	2,760	34,412	17,286	67,774

Source: Anders et al., *Baffin Island–East Coast*, 181.

cumstances dictated."[136] It is possible that in the later years of the decade of the sixties the presence of the school may have encouraged in-gathering at Clyde, as it had the contraction that took place in the early 1960s. While the final stages of centralization were, as in other places in the Central Arctic, closely linked to housing construction, significant movement to the centre had already occurred before that construction was well advanced. Certain intangible factors were at work. However, it does seem clear from the record that the overt efforts of the police to keep people dispersed were relaxed as the 1960s advanced. Here, perhaps as much as anywhere else in the east Central Arctic, hunting, together with the trade in sealskins, remained the dominant subsistence economy, even though centralization culminated by the end of the sixties. As elsewhere, hunting could be sustained from a central base by using motorized transport.

Table 6.2 outlines the sources of income for 1965–66, a year of increasing centralization in eastern Baffin Island, though the process still had some way to go, especially at Pangnirtung and Clyde. The table shows that income from hunting and trapping was still significant, due largely to sale of sealskins. On the other hand, wage labour had become the chief source of income except at Padloping. This labour was largely devoted to construction activities. There was also income derived from DEWline employment. Anders and his associates, who compiled the above figures, were pessimistic about these sources continuing: "should present trends continue and no new industrial development or community and regional construction projects be started, it is predicted that the regional economy will steadily revert to the pre–1956 structure whereby the sale of native products will be the single most important income source."[137] In 1965–66, however, the predicted decline in sealskin prices did not bode well for income from that source. It is also to be noted from the table that development of handicrafts for this region lagged far behind that of other communities so far treated in this chapter.

NORTHERN BAFFIN ISLAND AND THE IGLULIK REGION

At the beginning of the 1960s there were 248 Inuit living in the Pond Inlet trading area and 177 for Arctic Bay–Admiralty Inlet.[138] There were, as well, 501 in the Iglulik region. This entire area was patrolled by the Pond Inlet RCMP detachment. As noted in chapter 3 there had been concern with in-gathering and associated "loitering" during the 1950s, but the RCMP reports indicate success in enforcing dispersal. By 1960 there was again concern about in-gathering.[139] The local police officer proposed in 1961 that people on relief at Arctic Bay should establish a camp for better hunting.[140] It is interesting to note that the strategy for bringing about this dispersal lacked an authoritarian tone: "The fact was stressed that they were not being told to move but that this was only a suggestion for their benefit." By the end of 1962, "loitering" at the post at Arctic Bay was reported as a concern. "When the HBC manager came in 1958, [there were] only a few employees or old people, now [there are] 10 families of which only two are employed."[141] By 1961 it was recognized that contraction was occurring around Arctic Bay: "first they move to Kurkasak Island, then to a point three miles from the settlement and finally right to the post."[142] While other members of the European community at Arctic Bay did not feel that they should compel the Inuit to disperse, the RCMP constable from the Pond Inlet detachment lamented, "the writer feels that a firmer stand should be taken in this regard. Perhaps Headquarters could offer a suggestion in regard to this situation."[143] Correspondence did indeed ensue between J.T. Parsons, officer in charge of "G" Division, and C.M. Bolger, administrator of the Arctic.[144] Bolger wrote to Parsons that the problems of in-gathering and associated "loitering" were general in the Canadian Arctic. He asserted that the problem was being aggravated by separation of parents from their children as schools were established in the centres. On the other hand, Bolger commented that medical conditions were at times interpreted as "laziness." He also remarked that "[c]ertainly, as Constable Pilot has noted, we cannot tell an Eskimo where he should live, but should instead explain and emphasize the advantages of camp life in comparison to living in a settlement."[145]

Bolger's statements had implications throughout the changing conditions in the Central Arctic during the 1960s. Certainly, what some

Table 6.3
Sources of income, North Baffin Island

Community	Year	Hunting & trapping	Handicrafts	Wage labour	Unearned	Total
Pond Inlet	1966–67	$20,139	$1,341	$76,131	$28,148	$125,759
Arctic Bay	1966–67	23,982	6,000	40,000–45,000	19,450	89,432–94,432

Source: Bissett, Northern Baffin Island, 169, 199.

RCMP officers termed as "laziness" masked other factors, including medical conditions. However, by espousing the notion that life conditions in the outlying camps were desirable, Bolger was endorsing one of the arguments intrinsic to the Policy of Dispersal and ignoring the attractions of the growing centres. Some of these, including possibilities of wage employment, the pull of kinship, ready access to welfare, and recreational possibilities, were already being recognized by local administrators at this time.

In commenting to the officer in charge at Frobisher Bay regarding Bolger's remarks, Parsons wrote: "We are not in complete agreement at all, nevertheless we do not feel it would be prudent or otherwise to take an issue with the Department."[146]

By 1963 the Department of Northern Affairs had representatives in both North Baffin communities. By the end of that year there had been an increase both in total population and in settlement sizes. At Pond Inlet seventy-nine Inuit lived at the centre, with seven camps dividing the remainder of the population.[147] At Arctic Bay the settlement situation remained about the same as in 1962, with forty-eight at the post and six camps in operation.[148] The changes were more pronounced by 1965, with over half (155 of 298) of the Pond Inlet people now concentrated at the post. In 1965, as well, housing construction at Pond Inlet gained force with fourteen more prefabricated houses "being imported" and thirteen of them "built and occupied."[149] In 1966, twenty more new houses arrived at Pond Inlet and eleven at Arctic Bay, to accelerate the process of centralization at both places.[150] Despite the degree of in-gathering, hunting and trapping continued from the centres, and the balance of sources of income also gradually replaced the yield from furs, as table 6.3 reveals.

Table 6.3 shows that hunting and trapping continued to provide some income on North Baffin Island. The extent to which game continued to be a major source of food can be inferred from a report by Bissett that estimated that consumption of animal products averaged 555.4 pounds per person in the area for 1966–67.[151] Table 6.3 indicates that, as at other communities treated here, wage labour had become the largest source of income, and as elsewhere in the Central Arctic during the 1960s, the largest part of such labour was in construction. In 1967 further house construction was noted.[152] With the building of three hostels in the previous year, the number of children attending school increased markedly. By 1968 full-time employment had expanded, especially with the Department of Northern Affairs.[153] The table does show that the adoption of handicrafts as a source of income was not highly developed. Notwithstanding this lack, some idea of the growth of the economies in the North Baffin region can be seen in the following comparisons. Pond Inlet's total estimated income for 1959 was $30,000.[154] Table 6.3 shows that this amount was more than quadrupled in 1966–67. The total estimated for Arctic Bay in 1959 had nearly tripled by the later date.

Bissett's study of 1967 gives much valuable information on the locations, histories, and economies of the camps of North Baffin. Most germane here is his analysis of the factors that featured in the decline in the number and occupancy of camps. He includes the following: (1) growth of government administration and schools: with the failure of the hostel system in the area, parents tended to cluster closer to and into the settlements; (2) the housing program of 1963–65 (although attempts were made to preserve camp life by building houses in camps); (3) the drop in sealskin prices after the rise in the early sixties, which left a gap in sources of income; this gap was subsequently compensated for by wage labour sources due to construction in the centres; (4) the establishment of a nursing station at Pond Inlet in 1966 following an epidemic in some camps, which impressed the importance of not being too distant from medical help; (6) a decline in availability of caribou skins for clothing, which made mobility between camp and centre more difficult; and, finally (7) the attraction for women of the ease of visiting offered by the growing centralized communities.[155]

These factors have been and will be cited for other communities in the Central Arctic. One other factor that must be stressed, which applies in the North Baffin examples, is the relaxation of pressures for the Inuit to remain dispersed. The gradual lessening of reference to this concern in the reports of the RCMP officers for the region as the 1960s advanced attests to this shift in policy applied locally.

When I arrived at the settlement on Turton Bay on Iglulik Island in August 1960 there were two distinct neighbourhoods, which I have termed the Catholic village and the Anglican village.[156] I indicated in chapter 3 that the Catholic village had its origin during 1950s. The Anglican village began with the arrival of immigrants from the Repulse Bay region, and its numbers increased when the native pastor came down from Pond Inlet with his three sons and their families in 1959. The total population of the centre had grown only slightly since 1956, from seventy-seven to eighty-seven, largely due to the arrival of this family.[157] In addition to this concentration at Turton Bay, my census for 1960–61 indicated thirteen camps, ranging in size from five to sixty-four persons. Thus, of 514 in the total population, 83 per cent still lived in a condition of dispersal. One of the places of settlement, where nineteen Inuit lived in 1960, was at the nursing station that had been built in close proximity to the Fox main DEWline site at Hall Beach, about forty-eight miles south of Igloolik.[158]

In the main centre of Igloolik, government buildings recently constructed consisted of a school and residences for the teachers, the Northern Service officer and his wife, a mechanic, and a janitor who would work for the Department of Northern Affairs. The NSO and teachers arrived in September. The school did not foster in-gathering during its first year of operation, in 1960–61.[159] A few students came from outlying camps, but they boarded with relatives, and their parents did not join them in residence in the centre. The NSO shared with the HBC manager a common resistance to any large-scale centralization at Igloolik. Concern with problems of in-gathering was voiced by the RCMP officer who patrolled the region in 1962, when he wrote, "a large number of people hanging around the settlement claiming to be transients, but informed stay around a month or two living off employed Eskimos."[160] The same report noted that only five people were permanently employed at that time.

A 1963 census showed an overall population in the Igloolik region of 580, with an increase to 130 in the centre at Turton Bay and an increase to 70 for the camp at the nursing station of Hall Beach.[161] As late as 1965 certain members of the force still felt ill at ease with the growing centralization that was taking place at Igloolik. The resident corporal wrote in his year-end report, "I feel it would be a very serious mistake to encourage the camp people to move into Igloolik. Igloolik is over crowded now and the resources around Igloolik will not support the present population. If the long ranged plan is to provide every Eskimo family with a house, they should be built in the camps where this is applicable."[162] This officer thought that the Inuit should be required to work for relief. He also questioned the aims of education as it was being pursued.

Hunting continued to be the major occupation in the mid sixties, despite growing centralization. Dog teams dominated as the means of transport until 1968, when it was observed that "powered toboggans" were now "used as much as dogs," even though there were still 400 dogs in the region.[163]

Meanwhile, the total population of the region grew, as did the populations of the main centres, accompanied by the decline in camps both in numbers and in populations. Between 1965 and 1967 the number of inhabited places in the region declined from fifteen to eight.[164] By the end of 1968, only three permanent camps were in operation, with a total of only thirty-eight people, compared to 733 in the entire region.[165] This acceleration of in-gathering can be closely linked to the massive housing programs, which advanced rapidly during the decade. In 1966, a nursing station and twenty-four new three-room houses were being built at the centre at Turton Bay, and fourteen houses were under construction at Hall Beach.[166] By 1968 all settlement residents were living in government houses at those two places. Crowe writes of this revolution: "The rental housing scheme has brought most of the Iglulingmiut quickly from the domestic environment of tiny dwellings of sod, canvas, and paper, of seal oil lamps and communal sleeping platforms to one of separate rooms, electrical outlets, tables and chairs."[167] The change in dwellings was accompanied by the growth of village living. The population of Igloolik grew from 77 in 1956 to 130 in 1963,[168] but after substantial government building was instituted, the expansion was more rapid and by 1967 the population of the centre on Turton Bay reached 357 and at Hall Beach 237.[169] The total income from all sources also grew dramatically. A June 1959 RCMP report indicated a total income of $59,143, with the largest sums coming from furs, ivory, and other animal products.[170] By the end of 1966 the total was $191,025, with wages growing from $16,000 in 1959–60 to $99,000 in 1969.[171] While this comparison in wages may seem impressive, Vestey qualified such a conclusion: "This increase is far from representing a satisfactory employment situation, as all employment is involved with serving the village itself, and is largely supported by the government. Without subsidies the economy would collapse. Secondly, it is not sufficient to provide an acceptable income to even a fraction of the families at Igloolik."[172] Of course, these were to be general problems throughout much of the Canadian Arctic as centralization proceeded.

Vestey provides a camp-by-camp, and even individual-by-individual, analysis of reasons for moving to Igloolik and Hall Beach.[173] This information, which is seldom available from elsewhere in the Central Arctic, reveals more of the complexities and interaction of the various attractions of the quasi-urban situation. Among the motivations that Vestey derived from her interviews were especially relevant to Hall

Beach, where the nursing station had been long established, but also, later, to Igloolik when such a station was built there. When elderly family heads moved to the vicinity of such facilities, extended families tended to be broken up and, eventually, more junior members gradually drifted to the two centres.[174] Some employment was also available, but as Vestey has pointed out above, this was limited in nature. She also mentions one case where the Inuk head of the Housing Committee applied pressure to people living in outlying camps to move to Igloolik.[175] There may well have been other similar situations, here as elsewhere in the Central Arctic near the end of the 1960s, but it is also clear that movement to Igloolik and Hall Beach was by and large voluntary.

THE NETSILIK AREA

As the 1960s opened there were eight camps in the Spence Bay trading district, the heart of Netsilik country.[176] As noted in chapter 3, the typical number of families living at that post during the fifties was ten or eleven. However, during 1960 a total of sixteen families gathered there.[177] This aggregation was attributed to an influenza epidemic in April that had prevented the afflicted people from returning to their camps. Ironically, this disease was said to have been introduced by the x-ray party that had visited the community at that time. Official correspondence from this period was frequently concerned with health problems,[178] and there were requests for bringing a nursing station to Spence Bay, as well as stationing an airplane there for evacuating patients.[179]

At Gjoa Haven, which centre served the western part of Netsilik country, "about six families" lived at the post during 1960,[180] and there were also five camps in the trading area. At Pelly Bay, in the eastern part of the area, over twenty families spent 1960 in the immediate vicinity of the mission.[181] Bad times prevailed in the Spence Bay region as the decade opened. The shortage of caribou skins for clothing and bedding made winter travel, hunting, and trapping difficult and probably contributed to some of the sickness that was common at this time.[182] Indeed, caribou had been scarce throughout Netsilik country for some years, and skins had had to be shipped in by the HBC. Early in 1961 pneumonia struck one camp and the inhabitants had to be visited several times by airplanes bringing in penicillin and food.[183] Poor health and old age were given as reasons for a number of people living at the post; such people "could not exist off the land" and "relied heavily on government assistance."[184] The officer who thus conceded that certain people were compelled to live at Spence Bay expressed concern regarding the in-gathering tendencies in the region: "While the trend toward the settlement is slow and many [of them] include the less self reliant individuals, it seems reasonable to expect that this pace may be quickened as a result of pending government expansion here. Should this prove to be the case we will have a predominantly welfare society at Spence Bay unless steps are taken to counteract such a transition."[185] In 1962 an area administrator arrived and took over the administration of welfare, and a nursing station was also established. In that year, as well, it was reported that there was "a considerable increase in wage employment" at Spence Bay due to construction.[186] This construction appears to have concerned mainly government buildings, since most of the Inuit were still living in snowhouses and tents. At Pelly Bay proximity to a DEWline site made possible building of "shacks" from scrap lumber.[187] A dog team patrol to Pelly Bay reported that "this is the first year [1963–64] that all the native population is living in the settlement." Also, at that place there was practically no relief, as sufficient meat caches were available.[188]

While a number of people spent the winter of 1962–63 at Spence Bay, they scattered when spring came. However, by the end of 1963 the constable in charge of the detachment lamented that "no amount of encouragement seems to make these people want to return to the land."[189]

The first mention of housing construction for the Inuit comes in 1964, when in September "several welfare houses were built in Spence Bay and Pelly Bay."[190] Throughout the early sixties the RCMP reports indicate a lack of caribou skins, which made hunting and trapping in the winter difficult, but in April 1965 a large shipment of caribou and reindeer skins arrived at the HBC store. But, by the end of that year, the annual report stated: "Trail clothing is becoming less important each year in Spence Bay itself since so few men were moving out to hunt or trap anymore. The Hudson's Bay Company has an ample supply of skins for use."[191] While this statement may have been true for the centre itself, such a supply was still quite meaningful for people still living on the land, as I was able to witness during my stay in the area in that year.

I arrived at Gjoa Haven in early March 1965 and found 107 of the 175 people in the trading area living at the post, with the remainder in six other places on the mainland opposite King William Island.[192] Undoubtably the construction of dwellings had had much to do with this degree of in-gathering. The priest from the Catholic mission had engaged in two building phases. He had first constructed circular cement dwellings, which had been superceded by more conventional wooden houses. There were also two flat-topped welfare houses, but no concerted government building programs had yet been undertaken.[193] The priest's attitude toward in-gathering was influenced by his humane view that he would not encourage men to brave the winter cold on the trail. Indeed, I was able to sympathize when, accompanying a hunting expedition, I observed how ill equipped the men were, especially in lacking warm clothing and bedding. In keeping with these considerations, and his lack of opposition to in-gathering, the missionary had established a system employing the lay brother of the mission with hauling fish from a camp in Chantrey Inlet. The camp was maintained by an Inuit family and the fish sold to the Gjoa Haven people for 15¢ a pound. It comprised a substantial part of the diet of the community, especially during the winter months.[194]

Arriving at Spence Bay in late April, I found a large number of deserted snowhouses on the ice of the bay. I was told that, while some of these were temporary dwellings of people visiting during the winter, others were used by the village people. The housing situation was in a state of flux that early spring. There were a number of rather dilapidated scrap lumber dwellings and a few welfare houses, but the actual construction program began with warmer weather in 1965.[195] At the year's end the constable in charge of the detachment reported on the effects of this construction as follows: "increasing trend toward loitering in the settlement where welfare is available – this trend can be expected to increase where welfare benefits are close at hand. This together with the housing programs now undertaken will mean that settlement living will become increasingly attractive."[196] Earlier in 1965, when I visited the area, there were still five camps in existence with a total of 138 people, as compared to 188 living at Spence Bay.[197] The largest outlying camp was at Thom Bay, where sixty-three people lived at the time of my visiting them in May and early June.[198]

In the spring of 1967 there were thirty-two low-cost houses at Spence Bay, thirteen at Gjoa Haven, and twenty-one at Pelly Bay, and forty-four more houses were due to arrive in the area in the following summer.[199] But, while there was to be much summer employment associated with this construction, full-time jobs continued to be scarce.

Pelly Bay in 1967 was described as being a "very industrious and successful" community[200] with an active cooperative organization and an economy thriving with hunting, trapping, and handicraft production. At the other two main centres, however, the people were described as "losing the desire to live on the land ... It is understandable that a person living in a settlement and supplied with a house complete with oil heating plus ready availability of welfare is reluctant to spend his time out on the land trapping while living in a snowhouse with a primus stove for heat."[201] Yet, in 1968, when the geographer Villiers entered the area, there was still a total of five camps with a population of seventy-six people living away from Spence Bay, although this number had dropped from the previous year from ninety-three.[202] By the end of 1968 most people in the three centres had been provided with government housing. The in-gathering process in the Spence Bay trading district became virtually complete later in 1968 when the largest camp, at Thom Bay, was reduced to one family. The death of the senior male precipitated the migration[203] in a pattern seen elsewhere in the Central Arctic: with the removal of native leaders from camps because of illness, infirmities of old age, or, in this case, because of death, camps collapsed.

Treude's study of 1970–71 treats the question of processes of the 1950s and 1960s that led to centralization in the Netsilik area.[204] He cites the factors of the availability of family allowances and old age pensions, and the desire for education of children, religious instruction, and medical assistance as having "provoked a gradual abandonment of the isolated camp."[205] Indeed, his survey showed that of the 814 people in the total Netsilik area, only 5 per cent still lived in the camps at the time of his visit.[206] Important as he saw these factors, Treude especially stressed that of welfare: "It can certainly not be disputed that a real situation of economic need had existed in innumerable cases, yet it should not be overlooked that the readiness and the extent to which this assistance was accorded produced a negative effect on the intensity with which the availability of natural resources were utilized."[207] Indeed, I gained the impression from conversation with the area administrator who had managed welfare at Spence Bay in 1962–63 that he had been reluctant to encourage men to go out and endure the rigours of winter weather and, by extension, camp life.[208] While individual cases varied from place to place in the Central Arctic, it was my general impression that with the shifting of welfare responsibility to the Northern Service officers or area administrators welfare was liberalized. The NSOs became purveyors of the Welfare State Policy on the scene.

To the factors cited by Treude as responsible for the centralization process in the Netsilik area can be added the previously noted shortage of proper clothing and bedding, but in the final stages, as in many other places in the north, it was the massive housing programs that were the most visible motives for in-gathering. In describing conditions in the centralized communities of the area, Treude describes the related services of the water supply, electricity and heating fuel, and of garbage and sewage collection, which were entailing considerable expense. He estimated that these services amounted to an annual expense of about $250,000 a year for the three communities of Gjoa

Table 6.4
Sources of income, Netsilik area

Community	Year	Hunting & trapping	Handicrafts	Wage labour	Unearned	Total
Spence Bay & camps	1967	$25,727	$978	$92,265	$47,879	$166,849
Gjoa Haven	1967	10,595	4,026	61,559	29,542	105,722
Pelly Bay	1697	2,454	1,940	44,597	16,179	65,170

Source: Villiers, *The Central Arctic*, 150, 158, 167.

Haven, Spence Bay, and Pelly Bay.[209] Such estimates attest to the degree that the Welfare State Policy had been adopted by the end of the 1960s and beginning of the 1970s.

While hunting, fishing, and trapping were still being carried out, this support alone did not supply an adequate economic base. Treude felt that "success depends largely upon ... intensification of the use of natural resources of the area and/or introduction of new branches of the economy."[210] Table 6.4 indicates that in these three communities wage labour was once again the dominant source of income. In the Spence Bay trading district the trade in arctic fox fur continued to be important, especially for people living in the camps. Only at Gjoa Haven was income from handicrafts significant, attesting to the mission's encouragement in this activity. In all three communities unearned income from government sources was important, contributing about 28 per cent of the total income at Spence Bay and Gjoa Haven, and nearly one third at Pelly Bay.

The description and analysis of conditions of change under centralization in the Netsilik area apply to many other situations in the Central Arctic, but the dominance of missionaries at Pelly Bay and Gjoa Haven was more rare during the sixties. The missions did not discourage in-gathering during this period, and may have actually encouraged the process directly or indirectly. At the same time they were instrumental in developing local industries and cooperatives before the government took an active role.

THE COPPER ESKIMO AREA

By 1960 the Copper Eskimo area had been divided administratively into two districts. The eastern part of the area was focused at Cambridge Bay, with satellite trading posts at Perry Island and in Bathurst Inlet, where the post was at the mouth of the Burnside River. In the west, Coppermine was the main centre, with trading posts as well at Read Island and Holman. It was noted in chapter 3 that two major population movements took place in the 1950s in the eastern area. First, there was movement from the interior south of Coronation Gulf and Bathurst Inlet that was clearly related to the slump in caribou populations. Second, substantial numbers of people moved to Cambridge Bay for the employment opportunities during the building of DEWline sites. By 1960 about 150 Inuit had concentrated at Cambridge.[211] A number of outlying camps remained, not only around Perry River and Bathurst Inlet but also on southeastern Victoria Island. The year-end 1960 RCMP report from the Cambridge detachment indicated that the majority of people were "still living in makeshift shacks."[212] These were undoubtably constructed from materials taken from the nearby CAM Main radar site dump. About twenty men were employed at DEWline sites, either at CAM Main or at those sites that were administered from there. Another ten people worked for other agencies in Cambridge itself.[213] Aside from these full-time workers, there was also considerable summer employment and "very little loitering," according to the police. Trapping in winter was still important, especially in the 1959–60 season, with a high price of fur at $19.00.[214]

The Perry River region had at this time a total of twenty-five families. While it is reported that seven of these families lived at the post, it is likely that this number represented temporary gathering, perhaps as the trapping season was ending for annual trading.[215] Despite some contradictory information, there appears to have been a general shortage of caribou both around Perry River and Bathurst Inlet, continuing from the late 1950s.[216] It will be recalled that Bathurst in particular had been a place from which caribou skins were exported. One of the camps in that region had to be supplied with food in March 1961 since "people are quite hungry and with improper fur clothing as they were unable to get seal, caribou or fish."[217]

While the game report for 1961–62 for Bathurst showed an estimated 1,000 caribou had been taken, this report covered only the period through 30 June.[218] When I arrived at the post at Bathurst in September only fifty skins had been traded and there was no migration that fall.[219] This situation had been true during six of the preceding seven autumns.[220] My November census of the Bathurst region counted ninety-three people in the trading district, with an additional five children out at school. Eighteen people lived at the post, the remainder being scattered in six other sites around the inlet.[221]

Arriving in the Perry River region in February 1963, I found only two nuclear families at the post on Perry Island and the rest of the total population of seventy-seven in the trading district distributed among five camps, four of which were located in the interior.[222] This was in marked contrast to the settlement situation around Bathurst Inlet, where only one interior site was occupied and this for only part of the winter.[223] After an Easter gathering by a large part of the Perry River people at the post and another gathering, as described in chapter 5, for the x-ray party in April, the people dispersed on the ice of Queen Maud Gulf for the sealing season.[224] This pattern of seasonal movement had been established for several decades.

Upon landing at Cambridge Bay in May of 1963, I compared conditions there with what I had witnessed in the camps of the two mainland regions. While housing was still in a "shanty town" condition for most of the Inuit, I observed the benefits for the village dwellers: "What the local whites fail to see is that relief rations, together with wooden houses, have given these people a higher standard of living than some of those living in camps. I have seen how the Bathurst and Perry River people live in unheated snowhouses with poor bedding, sometimes with little game food, and how the allotment monies can extend, with the proceeds from a few foxes, over most of the few things which can be considered survival items."[225] Meanwhile, in-gathering had continued at Cambridge Bay with, in 1963, a total of 198 people living there, an increase of about 25 per cent from 1960. However, fifty-one people still lived in camps on southeastern Victoria Island.[226] In reports dating from 1963 the corporal in charge of the Cambridge Bay detachment argued that the immediate district was poor game country and efforts should be made for some degree of dispersal.[227] In his 1964 report, after recommending that "fresh meat and fish ... should be made available" in outlying camps, "my other suggestion is to attempt to reverse the trend of movement into the settlement by surveying areas of potential wildlife resources." The following year he recommended "air transportation to promising areas and assistance in getting started."[228]

Indeed, in 1967 three men moved to Hadley Bay on the northern part of Victoria Island and found hunting there good.[229] Although expeditions across the island continued,[230] especially after motorized sleds came in general use, the attractions of the new quasi-urban community rapidly made hopes of reviving greater dispersal unrealistic. Specifically, here as elsewhere in the Central Arctic, the housing program ordained continued and virtually complete in-gathering by the end of the sixties.

After an eighteen months' absence from Cambridge Bay, I was very impressed by the visual changes that had taken place by March 1965. A neat row of new government-built houses had replaced the homemade structures I had seen during my earlier visit.[231] By the end of 1967 all families in the community "were living in houses provided by DIAND with fuel and electricity being supplied, and the smaller one room houses were being replaced by three bedroom dwellings."[232]

Meanwhile, while the people of Perry River and Bathurst Inlet did not benefit from the housing revolution, they had begun to experience better hunting conditions. When I returned to the Bathurst region in August 1963 I learned that a herd of 500 caribou had come right up to the post.[233] I also visited a camp where large amounts of drying caribou meat could be seen.[234] But these indications were minor as compared to what followed. In 1963 a herd estimated at 5,000 was sighted near the mouth of the Ellice River,[235] and in 1966–67 the Bathurst people killed 2,000 caribou when, for the first time in decades, the Barren Ground Caribou reached eastern Victoria Island, presumably from a herd of 12,000 seen on Kent Peninsula.[236] Good takes of the animal continued to be recorded, with 2,500 for 1967–68,[237] 2,800 in the following year,[238] and 4,000 in 1969–70.[239] A herd estimated at 165,000 was sighted from the air, near the Ellice River that same winter.

I have cited these estimated figures for caribou since it is clear that the continued occupancy of the Bathurst Inlet region is to be attributed to the recovery of the herds after the dismal years of the fifties and the beginning of the sixties. By March 1968 the human population around Bathurst Inlet had increased to 108 from the 93 I had counted in 1963.[240] At that time dispersal into eight camps was maintained, with only twenty-two people living at the new post at Baychimo Harbour. Even though this post was closed in 1970, as late as 1974, 131 Inuit still lived in the Bathurst region.[241]

For the western part of Copper Eskimo country, I noted earlier that by the end of the 1950s considerable centralization had taken place at Coppermine, despite strenuous efforts to keep the population dispersed. As the decade ended, about half the people in the trading district lived in the village. The tendency for people to gather around DEWline sites had been, however, effectively discouraged. One of the locales that continued to be populated in the interior was around Contwoyto Lake, where two camps remained into the 1960s.[242]

The pace of concentration of population at Coppermine gathered force in the early 1960s so that, by the end of 1962, of a total of 623 Inuit in the western Copper Eskimo regions, 297 lived at Coppermine and another 124 at Holman,[243] a post that was also becoming a centre of settlement. The remainder were distributed into fourteen camps ranging in size from five to forty-five people. In 1962 the post at Read Island was closed, and the Inuit who had traded there began using the Coppermine and Holman posts.[244]

A survey of housing in Coppermine in 1962 revealed that the majority of dwellings were made of scrap lumber. This type of housing also characterized camp living, and it was asserted that "the need for better housing is essential."[245] Indeed, prompt action must have been taken, for by the end of 1963, twenty-eight low cost and twenty-seven welfare houses had been installed of the total of eighty-nine dwellings in the village.[246] The recovery of the caribou herds in the area did not seem to affect the rate of in-gathering as the decade advanced. Abrahamson et al write of the caribou situation around the Coppermine trading region at this period as follows: "The number of caribou taken in the area may vary widely from year to year. As many as 4,000 animals have been killed in a good year and as few as 150 in poor years. In recent years the caribou take has averaged between 1,500 and 2,000 animals."[247] They also commented that "caribou are seldom hunted far from camps or settlements."[248] It would seem that their estimate for the early sixties, while not signifying wide-ranging hunting activity, does indicate considerable success for effort expended.

Centralization continued apace, and by the end of 1965, 450 Inuit lived at Coppermine and 164 at Holman.[249] During that year forty-three new houses were built[250] and by the end of 1966 it was reported that all Inuit at Coppermine lived in government-supplied housing.[251] By the end of the 1967, of 700 Inuit in the western Copper Eskimo area, 500 lived in the village at Coppermine and 165 at Holman,[252] so the centralization process can be said to have been completed by that time for all intents and purposes. At the same time, seasonal camp living still persisted. In the absence of year-long dispersal of the population, the RCMP detachment took the following position: "The theme for this detachment will again be to encourage the hunters and trappers to leave the Coppermine settlement for extended periods in order to make certain that the considerable game is harvested."[253] This statement of 1966 was repeated in reports of 1967 and 1968.[254] In 1968, there were ninety-three occupied dwellings in the native part of the settlement, twenty of the three-bedroom type, and all were provided with garbage and sewage collection. It had been a poor year for trapping and there were "no jobs in the settlement at the present time." Dog traction was being gradually replaced by tracked vehicles, but there were still 350 dogs as compared to 60 motorized sleds at Coppermine, and at Holman, 250 and 15 respectively. The "only real source of income" was from carving, and unearned income increased correspondingly.[255] Another problem was that of alcohol abuse: "most natives have difficulty in handling their liquor."[256] But in 1968 a marked decrease in the use of liquor was observed, due to a lack of cash for purchasing it.[257]

Table 6.5
Sources of income, Copper Eskimo area

Community	Year	Hunting & trapping	Handicrafts	Wage labour	Unearned	Total
Cambridge Bay	1962–63	$17,650	–	$123,375	$29,300	$170,325
Perry River	1962–63	5,262	–	1,848	9,827	16,937
Bathurst Inlet	1962–63	5,247	2,060	2,134	8,288	17,729
Coppermine	1962–63	17,458	9,329	60,964	48,779	136,530
Holman	1962–63	19,369	4,106	2,626	16,460	42,561

Source: Abrahamson et al., *The Copper Eskimos*, 57, 87, 100, 114, 133.

At both Cambridge Bay and Coppermine, a considerable amount of centralization had taken place by the beginning of the sixties, for reasons discussed in chapter 3. In both places, considerable in-gathering was apparent before government housing programs took hold. After that, the process became complete for surrounding regions, with few exceptions. With a shift in emphasis from the fur trade as the dominant source of income, together with increased emphasis on general merchandising by the HBC, posts were closed at Read Island (1962), Perry Island (1967), and Bathurst (1970, moved to Baychimo Harbour in 1964).[258] The trading centre at Holman, on the other hand, became a growing site of centralization during the sixties.

As the emphasis on the fur trade was thus declining, other sources of income grew in the Copper Eskimo area. Table 6.5 shows the figures available for 1962–63 for each of the then existing trading centres. It can be seen that in the smaller posts of Perry River, Bathurst, and Holman, income from wages was very low and that "Unearned" sources were much higher in each of these places. The principal contrast came in the hunting and trapping category, where Holman exceeds all of the other posts in the table. Bathurst and Perry River were showing the effects of a slump in caribou populations; Holman, on the other hand, had always been a prominent trapping centre. Wage labour dominated the incomes in the two larger communities, but the DEWline employment at Cambridge Bay far outshone income possibilities from that source at Coppermine, where a much larger unearned income had to take up the slack.

By the late 1960s the Inuit living in these centres were well served in a number of respects, with access to good housing and associated services, health facilities at nursing stations, schooling for the children, and the ever-present safety nets of various welfare and other social legislation arrangements. Nevertheless, economic and social problems remained. While hunting and trapping were carried out to some extent from the centralized communities, and seasonal employment was widespread, the desire to expand into a wage economy on a regular basis was thwarted by extensive unemployment. Alcohol-related problems were evident, and native autonomy or leadership was seriously underdeveloped. During the 1950s changes in settlement in the interior of Copper Eskimo country had been linked to failure of caribou to enter the region. During the 1960s a resurgence of herds made possible the retention of a largely subsistence-based economy and associated scattered settlement pattern in the Bathurst Inlet region. This situation was virtually unique in the Central Arctic as the sixties drew to a close.

CHAPTER SEVEN

Settlement in the 1960s – II

THE CULMINATION OF CENTRALIZATION
IN THE KEEWATIN

The Keewatin had experienced a high degree of centralization during the 1950s, especially in the final years of that decade. There were, however, still a significant number of Inuit who spent much of each year in the interior, away from the growing centres on the coast and the centre at Baker Lake.

For the southern Keewatin some in-gathering had taken place at Eskimo Point by the end of the fifties. We saw that when VanStone and Oswalt visited that community in the summer of 1959 there were about as many Caribou Eskimo living on the land through most of the year as there were in the village at Eskimo Point year round.[1] Eskimo Point also had a number of Inuit from outside the Keewatin, as well as a growing white population.[2] The balance between inland dwellers and those at the village was to be drastically altered in the next decade.

When the post at Padlei was closed in early 1960 the people who had traded there were flown to Eskimo Point, but many of them were moved to Maguse Lake in September, together with some supplies.[3] It is ironic that while the Padlei district had shown an increase in caribou shortly before the post closed,[4] a far different situation awaited the relocated people in the new location at Maguse Lake. A "moderately successful" fall caribou hunt was reported, but by December hardship conditions prevailed.[5] An air patrol visited the camps on 28–31 December and reported the abandonment of some of the camps and movement of people to Eskimo Point because of starvation conditions.[6] Conditions improved later in the winter and a report of 15 February 1961 indicated that fourteen families still remained on the land and were "in good shape."[7] Apparently Inuit repopulated the southern interior in the latter part of 1961, for Brack and McIntosh reported thirty families trading into Eskimo Point for that year, in addition to the sixty families living at the centre.[8] It is not clear whether these latter people were only summer residents, but there is some evidence for further habitation, either seasonal or more permanent, during the next few years.

Reports from the autumn of 1960, the summer of 1961, and June 1963 indicate significant numbers of caribou.[9] For instance, in June 1963 a herd estimated at 30,000 was seen eighty-five miles northwest of Eskimo Point and about 3,000 were killed in the Eskimo Point trading area that year.[10] Reports from later years in the 1960s continued to support an argument that caribou populations had, indeed, increased.[11]

It is difficult to specify the year in which the in-gathering at Eskimo Point could be said to have been completed. One factor that discouraged rehabitation of the interior, despite the resurgence of the caribou herds, was the growth of government housing at the centre. The annual RCMP report at the end of 1962 stressed inadequate housing, describing only seven one-room welfare houses while 75 per cent of the people "lived in tents heated by primus stoves."[12] The next year it was reported that poor housing affected the health of the people. Dwellings were described as being mostly "scrap lumber shacks."[13] By the end of 1964 responses to these concerns had brought on a revolution in housing: by then every family was living in either a government-supplied house or one built by the Catholic mission. At this stage almost all welfare houses were the one-bedroom type, fifty-one having been erected since 1961.[14] The relationship between housing and settlement is also noted in the same report: "The only drawback in providing all the Eskimo with housing is that it tends to keep them in the settlement more rather than trapping. Only ten families are living inland this winter in two separate camps on Maguse Lake." This 1964 mention of wintertime dwellers in the interior is the last definite one that I have been able to find in the records.[15]

The one-room welfare houses were declared unsuitable shortly afterwards. The association between adequate housing and health was quickly extended to these structures, as it had with the native-built shelters. In 1966, sixty-four people were evacuated for health reasons, principally tuberculosis.[16] The district housing coordinator cited the lack of adequate housing and outlined plans to erect sixty-three three-bedroom houses "over the next two years."[17] Indeed, a 1968 report indicated that sixty of this type had been erected and were "wired, with oil furnaces."[18] Eskimo Point is one settlement where housing programs followed large-scale centralization, whereas in a number of other cases cited here, housing was the chief discernable reason for centralization to occur.

Returning to the question of the degree of permanent in-gathering in relation to possible inland habitation, Welland wrote of conditions up to 1974 that, as far as I have been able to determine, had been established in the mid 1960s. His report indicated that while some out-lying cabins were used in trapping in the winter, residence in the interior was primarily in the spring, when some hunting camps were occupied; otherwise "the settlement is now the permanent winter home of all the residents."[19]

The northern interior of the Keewatin during the 1960s provides a prototypical example of the conflict between the Policy of Dispersal and the Policy of the Welfare State – of the struggle to balance a subsis-tence economy with one requiring massive support from the federal government. At the end of the fifties, administrators for the area were smarting from the criticism they had received for the starvation deaths at Garry Lake. The close surveillance now accorded the outlying camps can to a large extent be attributed to reaction to that tragedy. The early 1960s was a period of intense activity for the RCMP detachment at Baker Lake. No fewer that twenty-three flights were made to camps in the period of January to March 1960.[20] In some cases supplies were flown in, as it was reported that "the majority of camps" did not have meat caches. In response to conditions in the Baker Lake district, a meeting was held in Churchill on 14 February 1960 with a group of government representatives and the corporal in charge at Baker Lake. The corporal made a number of recommendations to relieve condi-tions, including bringing people who required "continuous assistance" to the settlement "where their children of school age could attend school." He thought a general in-gathering was not practical because of a shortage of good housing. Rather, he felt that most people should be rendered assistance on the land. He left the meeting in a state of frustration since his suggestions were not "met with total agreement" even though, in his words, "no other suitable suggestions were put forth at this time."[21] Upon returning to Baker Lake he registered a de-spairing comment in his next report: "Are we to encourage them to re-main on the land? Is the policy the writer has adopted for years regarding encouraging the people to remain on the land wrong? If so would you please advise?"[22] There appears to have been no response to this plea, and a large number of people continued to live in the camps.

With increased success in the hunt, thirty-seven families remained in the camps at the end of 1960. As part of the emphasis on surveillance, a comprehensive survey of the sixteen existing camps was made by air in December 1960 and January 1961.[23] This survey reported generally good conditions, with a large number of caches of meat evident in most camps from successful autumn hunts. However, at the end of February people were moving back to Baker Lake and it was admitted that the detachment had "overestimated the length of time that the number of caches would last each family."[24] Of course, relief issuances had to be increased with the influx of people from the camps. The local RCMP officer assessed this situation as follows: "As can naturally be deduced, from the figures, relief payments run high, but when one considers the high cost of chartering aircraft to ferry the necessary supplies to the camps, and the possibility that malnutrition may take its toll if supplies are not received on time, then this is surely the most economical, if not most sensible approach in affecting such conditions."[25] There was some success in the caribou hunts of the summer of 1961,[26] but results were poor in the fall and there was already a heavy influx of people into the community at Baker Lake.[27] During the winter of 1961–62, the number of camps was reduced from the sixteen of the previous year to nine. The increased settlement population meant an other increase in relief payments, which exceeded $7,000 for the month of January 1962.[28] Game conditions improved modestly during 1962, but at year's end it was reported that 80 per cent of the population of 467 were living in the settlement.[29] Housing was still inadequate, with only a few sales of government houses reported. 1963 saw an abrupt upswing in caribou with a reported 75 per cent increase in kills over 1962,[30] and the good hunting of the year made it possible for a large number of people to remain in outlying camps for the winter. At year's end, thirty-four families or 178 people were living on the land,[31] which represents a return to numbers at the beginning of the decade. However, despite the increased number of caribou in the area, the hunting efforts of men from the centre itself were hampered by the lack of dogs to carry them to the hunt.

Hunting conditions continued to improve during the next several years. For instance, in the summer of 1964, a herd estimated by the Canadian Wildlife Service at 150,000 crossed the Thelon district, and another dense herd "about six miles long and three miles wide" was reported for the Kazan River region.[32] These improved conditions drew a large number of people from the settlement in the summer and fall of 1964, when there were as many as 201 people in camps, but 174 moved back to Baker Lake by the end of the year.[33] While this movement was attributed to the lack of caches, there is another factor that must have been at least as important. That is, thirty-five new houses were built, including the first of the three-bedroom dwellings.[34] In order to stem the threat of widespread unemployment and large relief issuances, government industrial programs had made their appearance, with fifty people "receiving fairly substantial income from D.N.A.

carving and craft projects."[35] There were also twenty-one employed on a full-time wage-earning basis, and relief issuances leveled off at about $3,000 month, despite the increase in population in the centre.

Sightings of numbers of caribou were reported for the spring and summer of 1965, including estimates of herds of 175,000 and 200,000.[36] These improved hunting conditions helped to continue dispersal in camps that year. The year-end RCMP report indicated that there had been 97 persons in camps "for the majority of the year." More houses were built in 1965 and the craft industry continued to flourish with about 100 persons employed full time, even though only "about 50 received an adequate living from craft work alone."[37] However, only eight people were on permanent relief, a circumstance that must attest to success in combining various sources of income and subsistence.

1966 appears to have represented a plateau in the improvement of conditions at Baker Lake. While the caribou were plentiful, they did not follow the usual migration routes and were missed by the local people.[38] The government had tried to encourage trapping but with little success. During the winter of 1966–67 only four families lived in camps, together with five men who left their families in the settlement. Welfare also increased, with thirty-five families on relief for part of the year. The housing program was said to be "at a standstill."[39]

This dismal picture improved during 1967 with twelve more houses being built, and by year's end there were "no people left living in igloos." The craft program now employed 113 men and 39 women.[40] A report issued in January 1969 noted that only one man lived out of the village at Baker Lake,[41] so the in-gathering process can be said to have been complete. Employment had expanded to accommodate most of the people in residence, with thirty-three people engaged in full-time wage work and 180 working in craft production. However, only twenty or thirty of the latter group were judged to be self-supporting on the basis of crafts alone. Consequently, relief payments now averaged $4,400 a month in spite of this improvement in employment.[42] The housing situation also reached culmination in 1968 with eighty new houses,[43] most of which were two- and three-bedroom dwellings, and all of the people at Baker Lake were now supplied with government housing. From the RCMP reports as the decade ended, it would seem that the hunting-trapping economy was at an end. However, Welland, writing of the period up to 1974, paints another picture. He indicates that while settlement was indeed centralized at Baker Lake, camps were set up for caribou hunting, fishing, and trapping seasonally. "The camps may be as far as 200 miles from the settlement, for the concentration of people at Baker Lake makes it necessary for hunters to range widely."[44] Welland indicates that snowmobiles made access to this wide range of hunting and trapping activities possible.

In reviewing the events and processes that transpired in the northern interior of the Keewatin during the 1960s some chief factors can be cited as centralization advanced at Baker Lake. The original ingathering, which began in the 1950s, can be traced to a slump in caribou numbers and the attendant hardships of living in the outlying districts. A recovery of the caribou beginning in the early sixties made possible continued occupancy of camps by a significant number of Inuit. Usually, however, many of the camps were abandoned in the winter as stores from the summer and autumn hunts ran low. As in the past, the period preceding the spring migrations of caribou was the time of greatest economic stress. It is clear, then, that the primary factor influencing the settlement/camp population distributions up to the middle of the decade was the degree of success in the caribou hunts. After the middle of the decade other factors became paramount. Earlier, strenuous efforts had been made to keep people dispersed by taking supplies out to the camps by aircraft. Later, the efforts to keep people on the land were relaxed as housing became available at Baker Lake. Settlement living was made more attractive and was no longer resisted by local administrators (including the RCMP). With the development of services offered in the centre, a full expression of the Welfare State Policy came about and camp life became a seasonal orientation, despite continuing favourable game occurrences. In order to combat unemployment, local industries were created to absorb much of the workforce.

SOME CENTRALIZED COMMUNITIES OF THE KEEWATIN

As indicated earlier, a large proportion of the people of the Keewatin had been gathered into a few centres by the 1960s. These centralized communities varied in size and acculturative development. I had the opportunity to live in one of the smaller villages, Repulse Bay, in the late summer, autumn, and early winter of 1967.[45] The local trader had spent the period 1933–40 around Repulse Bay as a Hudson's Bay Company clerk. Upon returning as a manager in 1960 he noted some significant changes. First, occurrence both of sea mammals, especially narwhal and white whale, and of caribou, had increased. He also found that most of the people in the trading district were living at the post, housed in structures built from wood and sod. The wood stemmed from the earlier presence of DEWline operations, since Repulse had served as a staging site for establishing more permanent sites in the Melville Peninsula region. During DEWline operations in 1955–56 employment was possible, and doubtlessly had contributed to the in-gathering that had taken place by 1960. After that, of those who traded at the post, only a small group at Wager Bay lived away from the post.[46] By the time of my arrival in 1967 everyone lived at the centre and most now had government housing. These houses stemmed mainly from the second phase of housing programs, being wooden, insulated structures heated by oil stoves, with a separate bedroom. The presence of outside establishments was minimal, with only the trader and his wife and two Catholic priests. Government duties were in the hands of the trader, who acted as Northern Service officer even though at this time he was not paid for his duties of administering government issuances. These included pensions, family allowances, and relief. Consistent with the policies of his commercial employer, he kept what appeared to be a ju-dicious but firm hand on relief issuances. His policy ensured that most of the men engaged in hunting, which was based mainly on excursions from the central base. Only in summer were outlying camps of tempo-rary nature used.

The Catholic mission's sphere of influence included not only the spiritual but also the social and part of the economic realm. The then new mission building, which included the missionary quarters, was the site of religious services, informal socializing, and meetings of a newly formed cooperative association and the equally new village council.

As far as I was able to discern, neither the priests nor the trader ap-peared to participate actively in the elections or the operation of the village council. The youth of the organization, however, meant that re-alization of any functions was still in very rudimentary stage. Meetings were carried out in the Inuit language, as consistent with the wholly native composition of the body.

With respect to the cooperative, the mission took a more active role in the management of the carving industry, including arrangements for marketing in the south. In a community of fewer than 200 native residents there were sixty-five carvers, ranging in age from twelve to over seventy, including members of both sexes. The industry provided an income of about $2,000 a month for the community.[47] Carvings were made from soapstone, ivory, coming mainly from narwhal tusks, and whalebone taken from a nearby Thule site. Social legislation funds and some income during the brief period of the sea lift in September rounded out sources of cash, but subsistence still came from hunting and fishing.

I was able to piece together a picture of the year's subsistence cycle for the period of the 1960s from my own observations of August to De-cember 1967, supplemented by statements of the Inuit, the trader, and the missionaries. During August and September, the open water season, most activity was devoted to sea-mammal hunting from boats. White whales and narwhal entered the inner bay near the community frequently and appeared to be more important quarries than seals at that season. From the beginning of October until about mid November most of the men of the village made dogsled journeys into the interior and as far west as Committee Bay. During these trips, which lasted up to and beyond ten days each, nets were set in lakes and considerable time was spent in caribou hunting, which was often quite successful both at this season and later. Women and children fished at a lake that was within walking distance from the village. During the latter part of November and through most of December a number of visits were made to caches of sea-mammal meat that had been made in the summer around Repulse Bay itself. According to the trader, these caches supplied needed dog feed right through the winter and at least as late as May. While sealing was carried out throughout the winter, both from the floe edge and at breathing holes (usually with set guns), caribou hunting also continued and apparently provided the chief source of meat for human consumption. In the late spring, camps were set up around the bay where fish were caught and caribou shot whenever they came close to the coast (though they were hunted less intensely than in October when sled travel was possible). As the open water season began again, there was a return to sea-mammal hunting.

Repulse Bay in 1967 closely approached the ideal settlement arrangement as envisioned by Henry Larsen in 1954. Women and children were comfortably housed in the central community with certain amenities and services while men ranged widely in their hunts and some trapping. In this case, as well, the community had minimal outside personnel, as in contact-traditional times, with only the trader and missionaries. Hunting and fishing formed the basis of the economy as they had in that earlier orientation, though carving had also assumed a role. The trader controlled the economic destiny of the people to a large extent. Despite the general firmness he applied to issuances, his close watchfulness of local conditions assured the people of Repulse Bay that he would provide aid in emergencies.

It will be recalled that centralization at Chesterfield was complete by the later years of the fifties, and that the population was greatly decreased by the wholesale emigration to Rankin Inlet. Indeed, Brack and McIntosh estimated that the total of between 220 and 246 Inuit for the period just prior to this exodus had been reduced to only seventy-two at the time of their 1962 study.[48] However, these permanent residents, assumed to be Chesterfield people, did not comprise the total population, since there were also 117 children from various places in the eastern Central Arctic attending the Catholic school. In addition, at this time, mission personnel was twenty-one, including priests, brothers, and sisters of the Oblate order. These latter people served in a number of capacities, including teaching school, maintaining the hostels, nursing at the hospital, and various community services.[49]

With the small indigenous population and the various jobs available, including construction, there was primary emphasis on wage earnings. Relief issuances and proceeds from trapping were far less at this time.[50] Indeed, very little hunting or trapping was being carried out from the centre. Fishing was a more prominent activity, with a project organized by the mission accounting for 3,000 to 4,000 pounds a year being taken. Much of this catch was used to feed the children in hostels. Some of the Inuit men also caught significant quantities of fish at season from nearby lakes.[51]

In addition to the school and the twenty-four-bed hospital, installations included a Department of Transport meteorological station some distance from the main part of the village.[52] The HBC had moved to Rankin, but the mission operated a small store. Housing in 1962 was mixed, with only four houses from the Department of Northern Affairs and an equal number built by the mission, the remainder being an assortment of shacks and tents.[53]

A number of changes had taken place by the time of my arrival in the community in July 1968.[54] Return migration from Rankin after the mine closure, together with natural increase, had augmented the native population somewhat. The RCMP detachment had moved to Rankin and an HBC store had been in operation for several years. Housing had expanded considerably. The mission had built several more houses, not all of which were occupied, since an extensive government building project in 1967–68 now accommodated most families with twenty-five new houses. Construction continued during the period of my stay, from July through September 1968, so that most of the able-bodied men were continuously employed. This employment situation brought to light one of the chief problems regarding extensive housing projects in the Arctic. Because the men worked fifty hours a week, there was little time for hunting or fishing. To make matters worse, the HBC store had run out of most of its inventory sometime in June, which meant that, although men were earning as much as $195 a week, there was little to spend it on until the arrival of the annual supply ship in early September. When weather was favourable, men hunted on Sundays, their day off. A few caribou were taken during my stay, as well as some seal and white whales, and a couple of polar bears. A steadier subsistence pursuit was tending nets along the shore to catch char during their annual period in the sea. Older men, women, and girls tended the nets and the fish caught provided the chief, but inadequate, source of food for the village. In talking with the construction foreman I learned that he felt that the men displayed a very low level of energy, a circumstance he attributed to the general shortage of both game and store-bought food. This condition prevailed, especially during July and August before the arrival of the supply ship. In my notes I described Chesterfield as "a hungry town."[55]

Administratively, the community was in a state of transition. An area administrator had arrived in the spring of 1967, and certain functions that had been performed by the mission were being gradually taken over by government. For instance, one of the brothers of the mission had been in charge of mechanical and construction projects, as well as such public services as garbage disposal and supplying water in the village. Now, Inuit men were being hired by the government and were gradually assuming these duties. The area administrator was regarded as a diplomat by representatives of the Church, and the transition appeared to be moving smoothly.

The chief social problems related to alcohol abuse. Domestic quarrels could frequently be overheard. These problems brought on the formation of a "peace keeping" group that included the HBC manager, the area administrator, and several Inuit. Members of this committee actually entered houses in order to quell disturbances. Despite the disturbances, the supply of alcohol was somewhat limited. The supply ship brought beer once a year. Liquor could be ordered from Churchill, but with only twice-monthly flights, fewer in summer, obtaining a steady supply was difficult. I was told, however, with the advent of skidoo travel in November, some men made trips to Rankin for beer.[56]

Though being one of the smaller Keewatin communities, especially when only permanent residents were counted, Chesterfield presented a number of contrasts with Repulse Bay. The two settlements shared a lack of recreational facilities, but good housing had been established in both villages at the times of my visits. Of course, as the headquarters of the Church for the east Arctic, together with having a school and hostel facilities and one of the two hospitals in the area, Chesterfield stood out among most communities. While the mission was also prominent in Repulse Bay, it did not have similar resources, and there was neither a school nor a nursing station at Repulse in 1967. The area administrator at Chesterfield had been there only a year, but he was already making an impact; at Repulse the trader had taken on extra duties as sole representative of the government. Probably the most prominent contrast was in their economies: Repulse's was predominately subsistence based, complemented by active carving, whereas at Chesterfield wage labour occupied much time and was the chief source of income, with subsistence activities relatively marginal. Alcohol had not entered the scene at Repulse, but was the chief source of social problems at Chesterfield.

Most of the contrast was due to the relative degrees of isolation between the two communities. Air service to Chesterfield northward was not as regular as was desired, but for Repulse Bay there was nothing resembling scheduled services. Pilots were reluctant to cover the long uninhabited stretch from Chesterfield and weather conditions were often too severe to attempt flights. This was true in the autumn and early winter of 1967, when several months passed without flights arriving.[57] Of course, the expanded religious, educational, health, and administrative installations at Chesterfield called for more frequent communication with the outside.

The founding of the community at Whale Cove, described in chapter 4, was beset with difficulties, including an ill-fated attempt in 1958 to establish relocated people. In the next year, however, most who had left had moved back, and changes accelerated rapidly from 1959 onward. An area economic survey of 1962 provides us with a largely favourable picture of the new community.[58] By that time the population had grown from eighty-two in the fall of 1959 to 150, and a total of twenty-one government-designed houses had been built, leaving thirteen families living in tents or "shacks." There were two missions and a school. Other buildings were a large warehouse, a cooperative store, and a power plant.[59]

Sources of income included both casual and regular wage work and much more active trapping than was reported for either Repulse Bay or Chesterfield.[60] The main activities of the men were hunting and fishing. Hunting appears to have been balanced between sea mammals and caribou. Sealing was carried out at all seasons, from boats in summer and at the floe edge at other seasons. January and February were slack months in game production, sealing was poor, and "caribou hunts required searches over wide areas inland."[61] Fishing, sealing, and whaling were the main activities in summer, as was caribou hunting, along with some fishing, in the fall.[62] The area survey report opined that "the choice of Whale Cove as a location central to resources has been vindicated."[63] The integration of people from several regions seemed to be facilitated by the cooperative store: "the social implications of this (the store) are encouraging as it indicates a willingness on the part of the various Eskimo groups to work together for the common good."[64] One of the rewards contingent in organizing the cooperative was the sharing of resources across the community, with surpluses from successful hunters aiding those who were less able to subsist on their own resources. This resource sharing was also conceived of as a benefit of centralized settlement over previous patterns of dispersal: "Previously, when Eskimos were encouraged to move away from the post, farther into the land, this was done largely in accordance with the theory that if they were spread out, more of each resource would be available to the individual camps. The reasoning was, on the face of it, sound, but failed completely (and understandably perhaps) to envisage chains of events and general lack of resources which could lead to disasters like Garry Lake and Henik Lake."[65] The favourable picture of a centralized community subsisting largely from hunting, which this report gives for the early 1960s, is augmented by Welland's report.[66] His description emphasized the continued importance of hunting and trapping throughout that period. He also described caribou meat as the "mainstay of the diet."[67] It seems clear that the general recovery of caribou herds in the Keewatin that took place during the sixties brought the importance of that animal to the fore again at Whale Cove and elsewhere in the Keewatin.

One reservation of some of the planners had been the practicality of trying to make sea-mammal hunters out of inlanders moved to the coast. The increase in caribou within the range of Whale Cove appears to have relieved that problem to some extent. On the other hand the hunting activities of the former inlanders at Whale Cove expanded: "Seals provide an important source of food and income. They are hunted primarily by people who had formerly lived along the coast. However, former inland residents also hunt seals now at the floe edge and have acquired a taste for seal meat, though they may still prefer caribou."[68] All in all, then, despite forebodings by some planners and later criticisms of the project, the Whale Cove experiment was proving to be a success in economic terms and, there is reason to believe, in social terms.[69]

The communities so far considered in this section were small, compared to some in the Central Arctic during the 1960s. Among the larger villages that grew in the Keewatin was Rankin Inlet, which had grown to 500 people during the operation of the nickel mine. After the mine closed, a decline in population was but one of the changes, for a period of slump followed. In their 1962 study Brack and McIntosh reported that "[t]he situation at Rankin is in a state of extreme uncertainty, and change. A few men are hunting and trapping and about a dozen are engaged in regular employment. By November there were 40 able-bodied heads of families on public assistance who will remain so unless there is a massive emigration movement or unless projects are established to enable them to be more self-sustaining."[70] In fact, both of these possibilities followed. Significant emigration did occur shortly, not only to such places of origin like Chesterfield but also to other mining locales in the Northwest Territories, and by 1965 Rankin was down to 287 Inuit.[71] After that the community recovered as energetic projects were instituted. These included the widespread carving industry, which was growing up in many places in the Central Arctic, and also handicraft production of sealskin boots, coats, and purses. Pottery was also manufactured. A fish canning industry established in 1964 at Daly Bay north of Chesterfield did not enjoy success and was transferred to Rankin in 1966, where it employed fifteen to twenty-five men.[72] Fish camps were set up in season to supply the cannery, employing more men.[73] Other employment came in the service occupations of garbage collection and water provision (in winter in the form of freshwater ice). More skilled occupations were also filled: "In addition to the expanded bureaucracy required to handle new government projects, increased sophistication and specialization of agency duties provided more direct employment opportunities for the Eskimo. Maintenance, handy-man, trade, custodial, construction, clerical and equipment operation positions became available to the Eskimo population."[74] Indeed, employment possibilities had expanded so much that one observer in 1971 indicated that "social assistance" was "largely limited to widows, the elderly and the infirm." By May 1970 the population had almost resumed the peak population of the mining days,[75] as the men and their families who had left for other mining occupations returned.[76]

Most of the innovations had taken place by the time of my visit in the autumn of 1968.[77] The RCMP detachment had been moved from Chesterfield and a large HBC store established. There were also a school, fire department, laundry, and two missions, and an area administrator was in residence. The white population had swelled due to government expansion, and their personnel made up the single largest element of the outsiders, replacing the mining people in this regard. As Jansen wrote a few years later, "Over the past ten years Rankin has changed from a mining town to 'being a government town.'"[78] The housing programs were well advanced and had replaced a neighbourhood of structures originally built by the mining company. To me Rankin appeared to be a hive of activity of both employment and social events. The large community hall was the site of social, recreational, and business meetings, which seemed to occupy every night of the week with the exception of Sunday.

The community council meetings were chaired by the resident area administrator, rather than being run solely by the Inuit as I had observed at Repulse Bay. Meetings were conducted in English and, I suppose partly because of language usage but also perhaps because of a more aggressive nature of personality, the white members of the community appeared to be dominant in discussions. These meetings also seemed to provide the administration with information on conditions in the community that otherwise would have been difficult to obtain.

I observed little hunting activity, beyond some sealing from boats and wild fowl shooting. This was, however, from late September to the end of October, a season of transition in that there was not yet sufficient snow for the skidoo hunting of caribou, which was becoming an important subsistence activity. Indeed, a later report indicated that along with the increase in that animal's availability, caribou meat was becoming an important food item.[79] Trapping was also carried out by a number of men well into the 1970s. For most of the men these activities were part time, or seasonal.

In the short time that I lived in Rankin it was not possible to determine the degree of integration among the various people from different sites of origin. Robert Williamson, however, noted that between 1957 and 1965, of twenty-six marriages in the community, only one was between members of different dialect groups.[80] There was one marriage at the time of my visit, between a young HBC clerk and an Inuit woman, and I observed some socializing between white men and Inuit women.

The chief cause of social disruption came in the form of alcohol abuse. Each adult was rationed to twenty-four cans of beer each week. Some hard liquor was also flown in from Churchill on order, but the main source was the weekly beer ration. I remember men stopping by my tent, to leave shortly in the fear that a wife might be attacked by some drunken recipient of the week's supply. I also attended an invited social drinking event in a native's house where a violent domestic scene took place. I think that such scenes were not uncommon. At Rankin and other places that I visited in the Central Arctic during the 1960s, I noted a great deal of ambivalence regarding use of alcohol. It was recognized that use of alcohol could result in relaxed and happy socialization, but also in some disruptive outbursts. One young man, while acknowledging possible harmful effects, complained that he thought the ration of twenty-four cans a week was too little.

The course of change at Rankin Inlet during the 1960s was rapid and comprehensive. With the closing of the mine it changed from an industrially based community to one with an unemployed population from diverse regions. By the end of the decade it had grown to an apparently thriving village with cottage industries flourishing. Few arctic communities at that time showed such a vigorous series of projects with the degree of success realized at Rankin. The outcome resulted from governmental agencies playing a very active role. On the surface it might appear that such success would run counter to the image of a welfare state community. However, it has been reported that by 1969 97 per cent of the "Eskimo community income was in some way related to both Territorial and Federal government sources."[81] This emphasis extended into the next decade and beyond.

At the end of the sixties, the Keewatin communities discussed in this chapter showed a range in size from around 200 at Chesterfield, Whale Cove, and Repulse Bay, to 500 at Eskimo Point and Baker Lake.[82] At the beginning of the decade the degree of centralization had also ranged widely, but by its end the communities shared a common virtual completion of the process of in-gathering. There was, as well, a range in economic adjustments. At one extreme was Whale Cove, where, in accordance with the original plan, a high degree of subsistence exploitation dominated. At the larger communities of Baker Lake and Rankin Inlet, extensive craft programs and related industries helped in keeping down relief issuances. Even though the degree of game resource exploitation differed, everywhere some subsistence activities could be observed. These were, by and large, carried out from the centralized communities, though seasonal camps were temporary bases for such activities. Trapping was also apparent in most places during season, though in general at a reduced level and, as ever, strongly influenced by the vagaries of the market and the supply of fur bearers. One reason that hunting was still carried out and was in some locales an important source of food was the recovery of the caribou during the sixties in the Keewatin.

Table 7.1 compares the economies of several Keewatin communities for the 1960s. At the village of Chesterfield Inlet for 1961–62, wages were the predominant source of income.[83] The Catholic mission was the chief employer. Indeed, with the heavy emigration to Rankin Inlet, most of the employable men who remained had jobs. This high degree of employment accounts, in large part, for the small returns from the land, since time for hunting and trapping was limited.

Whale Cove was, like Chesterfield, completely centralized in 1961–62,[84] at least in terms of family residence, while the men ranged widely in their hunting trips. These latter excursions account for the importance of activities on the land (largely trapping) among the income sources. The significant wage labour income listed in the table is rather misleading. Most food came from hunting, and employment was mainly temporary, for example unloading the annual supply ship and maintaining the airstrip. The bulk of income in the "unearned" category came from pensions and family allowances, with only $1,797 representing welfare.[85] This low rate attests to the success of the hunting-trapping economy that had been the basis of planning for the community.

Table 7.1
Sources of income, Keewatin region

Community	Years	Hunting & trapping	Handicrafts	Wage labour	Unearned	Total
Chesterfield Inlet	1961–62	$3,729	–	$22,800	$6,125	$32,654
Whale Cove	1961–62	14,320	$1,362	19,567	6,117	41,366
Baker Lake	1961–62	4,531	5,136	75,991	79,828	165,486
Eskimo Point	1961–62	21,350	–	42,150	30,075	93,575
Eskimo Point	1965–66	8,715	9,575	40,256	71,857	130,403
Rankin Inlet	1960	5,100	–	201,330	9,856	216,286
Rankin Inlet	1969	2,659	60,026 Profits $40,003	275,400	13,150	391,238

Sources: Brack and McIntosh, *Keewatin Mainland Area Survey and Regional Appraisal*: for Chesterfield, 72, for Whale Cove, 79, for Baker Lake, 96–7, for Eskimo Point 1961–62, 72; for Eskimo Point 1965–66, NA RG85 Acc 85–86/220, File A1000/153, Eskimo Point Settlement and Area. For Rankin Inlet, Foster, "Rankin Inlet," 40.

In the period of 1961–62, Baker Lake was undergoing a transition in settlement.[86] The previous twelve months had seen a resurgence of the caribou, which had encouraged camp living. Following this, hunting conditions became less favourable and people began moving from the land in mid 1961. By mid winter 1961–62 there was a predominance of village living at Baker Lake. This swelling of the local population brought on heavy reliance on government sources of income. Indeed, two-thirds of the amount in the "unearned" category, which was in itself the largest income source, came from welfare payments. I indicated earlier that in January 1961, relief payments peaked at $7,000 for the month.[87] The large amount in the "wages" category in the table does not signify any real boom in the economy, but rather the proliferation of places of employment. These included the Department of Northern Affairs, the Department of Transport, Indian and Northern Health Services, two missions, and the Hudson's Bay Company.[88] The small returns from hunting and trapping were attributed to the concentration of population and the depletion of fox from the adjacent district. Handicrafts were just beginning to be developed, and, as discussed earlier, would be more actively pursued. As the decade advanced, handicrafts and construction became the two chief sources of income.

In 1961–62, about one-third of the Inuit trading into Eskimo Point were still spending much time in the interior.[89] This emphasis can be seen in the large income from hunting and trapping.[90] The clustering of population in the centre brought significant reliance on government support, but the income from wages was the largest source, even though opportunities for employment were fewer than at Baker Lake. Conditions worsened with centralization, which was virtually complete by 1965–66.[91] At that time over half of the income came from government pensions, family allowances, and welfare, with the latter category totalling over $40,000 for the period.[92] Construction, especially of native houses, had earlier provided temporary employment. It can be seen from the table that income from wages had actually declined from four years earlier. Neither the development of handicrafts nor income from the land – then falling off – could fill this gap.

The figures in table 7.1 for Rankin Inlet are especially interesting since they represent large wage earnings from separate sources.[93] For 1960, the major source of income was from mining operations, with 78 per cent of the wages coming from that source. Unearned income comprised only about 4.5 per cent of the total, attesting to the near full employment situation in the community. The decade-end figures are associated with a transformed economy. After a severe economic slump following the closure of the mine in 1962, recovery began in 1965,[94] due in part to the development of local industries and to profits from local industries like the cannery, and a cooperative organization (listed as "profits" in the table). But even more significant as a source of income were wages. This expanded employment was occasioned by the growth of Rankin Inlet as an administrative centre, for fully 95 per cent of wages came from government jobs.[95]

It can be seen that local economies in the Keewatin showed considerable variation during the 1960s. Variations were both temporal and subregional. It had been a central concern of those who favoured dispersal of Inuit population that concentrated populations would result in heavy reliance on welfare, but the case for this tendency was ambiguous for the Keewatin as the process of in-gathering neared culmination. The extent of relief or welfare depended largely on the relative development of local industries and the proliferation of governmental agencies and their functions.

Another concern about in-gathering was the potential for the spread of disease. Indeed, examples have been given in earlier chapters. In the Keewatin, Eskimo Point was one of the communities most heavily hit by disease, both epidemic and endemic, and I have indicated how health considerations in this community in particular lent impetus to the housing programs there in the 1960s. Indeed, it was reported that in six months in 1963, eighty-two new cases of tuberculosis had broken out at Eskimo Point.[96] As the decade advanced, however, new diagnostic and treatment methods were developed,[97] and home treatment procedures were instituted to reduce the time that patients had to spend in hospitals in the south. This arrangement alleviated the painful separation of families.

In the Keewatin, as elsewhere in the Central Arctic, the advantages of centralized living were appreciated by the Inuit. There were, however, certain disadvantages. Social disunity could be expected, given the conglomerate composition of several of the communities. The creation of community councils and cooperatives promised to counteract disunity in this regard, though alcohol-related problems appeared to have a considerably disruptive effect in some of the centres.

SUMMARY: SETTLEMENT IN THE 1960S

While a significant degree of centralization had occurred during the later years of the 1950s, for the Central Arctic as a whole, the process had a long way to go as the new decade began. It would take the thorough demise of the Policy of Dispersal for the process to accelerate. Whatever intangible motives the Inuit of the Central Arctic may have had, it was clearly the rise of the new Welfare State Policy that had the greatest impact on population concentration during the 1960s. The related loosening of the purse-strings of the government made it possible for humanitarian considerations to supercede the austerity that had dominated the Policy of Dispersal.

During the early years of the sixties local representatives of the Canadian government and of the Hudson's Bay Company continued to resist in-gathering at many places in the Central Arctic, despite earlier policy changes in Ottawa and Winnipeg. Gradually, a new set of considerations replaced the stern imposition of preservationism on the local level in the north. One of the shortcomings of enforcing dispersed settlement was the expense, inconvenience, and dangers of maintaining aircraft contact with outlying camps. This was especially true in the Keewatin, but was also apparent elsewhere. With the expansion of the Northern Service officer program, control over issuances was concentrated in their hands and also, in many cases, liberalized. However, these officials also tried to encourage other means of income and in some cases promoted measures to aid the exploitation of natural resources.

Motives for in-gathering during the early years of the sixties were not always clearly visible, and often considerable pressures continued to be put on the Inuit to disperse. The tendency for periodic gatherings at ship time, at Easter, and at Christmas had long been in evidence, but by this time these gatherings often extended into much longer periods, and in some cases into permanent residence in the centres. Establishment of schools was, in some places, the forerunner of further government construction and expansion of installations. Schools brought a certain degree of contraction around the villages but less often actual concentration. Building hostels made it possible for children to attend school, but parents were not encouraged to join their children.

In addition to the continued local application of the Policy of Dispersal, the slow pace of centralization that characterized the early 1960s can be in part attributed to the lack of employment possibilities. This was true at places where few such opportunities had existed, but it was also true for a time at Frobisher and Rankin Inlet, where employment had been possible. Both places, beginning in about 1962, saw lay-offs of workers. At Frobisher there was a renewed emphasis on hunting around the bay, with some camps being re-established. Mainly, however, the revival of hunting was based on excursions from the village itself. At Rankin there was an immediate rise in welfare payments, followed by extensive emigration, both to other mining locales and to previous sites of habitation. At Frobisher and Rankin, only vigorous and extensive government programs made a return to significant employment possible.

The concentration of populations that began in the fifties in the Keewatin can be attributed largely to game failure, except at the mining centre of Rankin Inlet. A slump in prices of fox fur at the end of the 1940s appeared at that time to be dictating an end to the trade in arctic fox. This did not actually occur, even though by the 1960s in most places trapping did not provide the most important source of income or trade wherewithal. Fluctuations in prices and supply of fur continued to influence the energy devoted to trapping but even in the sixties the trade continued to play a varied, reduced, but not insignificant role in local economies. A rise in the price of polar bear hide made for an added source of income in several communities. Likewise, a rise in sealskin prices brought on a boom in their sale for several years in the early 1960s, before the actions of environmentalist groups caused the prices to decline precipitously by the mid 1960s.

The caribou crisis of the 1950s, which in some places extended into the early sixties, did not spell an end to the hunt of that animal, as afterwards the caribou population generally increased. This was true not only in the Keewatin but also at a number of other places in the Central Arctic. Further, the hunt did not cease when centralization advanced. Both from temporary or seasonal camps, and from the centres themselves, the animal was sought and often provided an important item of diet. The hunt did not, however, result in a wholesale return to camp living, for by the time recovery became evident, forces other than game supply that led to settlement concentration had over-whelmed subsistence considerations.

At first slow, and later accelerating, the process of in-gathering was nearly universal in the 1960s, but there were also temporary returns to, or sustaining of, camp life, such as the temporary re-establishment of camps around Frobisher Bay. A notable case was that around Cum-berland Sound to the north. In 1962, spread of hepatitis among dogs caused the local administration to relocate most of the camp dwellers to Pangnirtung, where provision was made for their comfort and liveli-hood. A return to camps was made within a year. Most of the people re-mained in the camps for several years until an extensive building program made life at Pangnirtung highly attractive, and centralization was all but complete by the end of the 1960s.

Another example of temporary return to life on the land took place in the northern Keewatin interior. With the increase in caribou in the region, a large number of people moved back to the camps in the late sixties for a couple of summers and autumns. However, most of the In-uit concerned moved back to Baker Lake during the winters of those years. A more remarkable case in this decade of generalized concen-tration of populations occurred at Bathurst Inlet and was also related to the resurgence of caribou herds. Here, rather than joining the large-scale migrations to Cambridge Bay, which were reaching culmi-nation, a number of Inuit remained in the region, where the principal support continued to be from hunting, fishing, and trapping, rather than from the wage labour and social legislation of the centres. In ad-dition to these examples of temporary and, in the last case, more per-manent return to the land, there continued to be seasonal camps in which significant numbers of people from the new villages moved away to favourite hunting or fishing places.

The early sixties saw slow in-gathering and, with the few exceptions noted, continued efforts to keep the populations of Inuit dispersed. The events of the later years of the decade were usually more visible, and were related to the shifts in overall government policy and the programs that they stimulated. Health considerations were among the factors forcing these policy changes. These considerations began much earlier than the 1960s but did not develop fully until that decade. Small numbers of the dependents of people who were in hos-pitals outside the Arctic tended to gather around trading post commu-nities as indigents, and they formed the nucleus of what were to become centres of in-gathering. The hospitals at Pangnirtung and

Chesterfield also developed clusters of such people, together with the patients who were being treated. Later, nursing stations also spawned colonies of Inuit. In the final stages of centralization, as elderly or ailing extended family heads moved to the nursing stations, families were split. Eventually, younger members of such units joined their elders and added to the in-gathering process.

The housing programs of the 1960s were definitely linked to health considerations. It is clear that with improved communication to the north, housing and health conditions became more visible to visiting government officials. In places where significant centralization was present prior to extensive housing construction, conditions of life became of special concern to visiting medical officials. The usually unsanitary conditions, especially when associated with the occurrence of both endemic and epidemic disease, drew matters to a head. While the first wave of government housing – the single-room, rigid frame structure – was an improvement over previous dwellings, it was quickly perceived that it did not meet minimum standards of sanitation and comfort. Subsequently, multi-room houses were provided to most people by the end of the sixties.

The new housing, together with the services that were installed along with them, brought previously unknown levels of comfort, sanitation, and convenience to the life of the village-dwelling Inuit. House construction, as well as extensive construction of other buildings, provided some employment but did not fill the employment and income needs of most new centres. Craft and art projects were considered crucial ingredients in achieving viable communities. When successful, these projects strived to stave off overdependency on relief issuances. It will be recalled that early advocates of the Policy of Dispersal considered that such dependency would be the inevitable accompaniment of centralization.

There was, in certain branches or departments of the government, considerable interest in exploring improved subsistence possibilities. Most prominent among the advocates of expanding this sector of Inuit economy were members of the Industrial Division of the Department of Northern Affairs and National Resources. This group conducted a number of area economic surveys in various parts of Arctic and sub-Arctic Canada. In a programmatic statement contained in the report of one of these surveys, the chief of the Division, Donald Snowden, noted: "One of the most disturbing aspects of the Arctic today is that many employable persons have no opportunity for regular productive work, yet renewable resource research carried out so far points to the fact that a significantly larger proportion of the Arctic's population can gain a livelihood from its resources than are doing so."[98] Indeed, Snowden felt that "this is true even of the Keewatin which can be considered to be deficient in such renewable resources." This theme was often reasserted as the surveys were carried out during the 1960s. In terms of the researchers of these surveys, underexploitation of resources could be probably argued for a number of regions in the Central Arctic. As well, considerable hunting, and in some regions trapping, did continue to be carried out despite increasing and eventually complete centralization. It should be noted, however, that employment and social and recreational activities in the new centres restricted the time of many Inuit for hunting and trapping. The reports of the area surveys did not advocate return to dispersed populations, but there was, as the sixties wound down, a move to maintain the degree of dispersal that did exist at that time.

This was a plan considered by the Study Committee on Eskimo Hunting Camps.[99] Plans were set in motion in August 1966 to form this committee and its formation took place in January 1967. It was made up of six representatives of various divisions of the Department of Northern Affairs. Over the next year and a half a great deal of discussion and debate ensued within the committee. The information from the Arctic that formed the basis for discussion and debate came largely from Northern Service officers on the scene, as well as from visits by other governmental representatives. The plan that evolved concerned the feasibility of maintaining the camp orientation, which was estimated for 1967 to include "about 1/5 of all Canadian Eskimos."[100]

Much information was gathered on the population distributions and local resources of several Canadian Arctic regions. Various regions were considered before the Spence Bay trading district was finally selected as the site for this experiment in settlement patterning. It was proposed to move government-designed houses to existing camps in the region, to improve transportation facilities from Spence Bay itself, to encourage cottage industries and establish small food depots, and to build hostels at the centre at Spence Bay for camp children for schooling.[101] The committee also recommended that resource studies should be made for the region. Indeed, an area economic survey did materialize in the spring and summer of 1968. By that time, however, the plans had been dropped. It was eventually agreed within the committee that all hunting camps in the area, with the exception of the one at Thom Bay, were likely to disappear, due largely to the house building project that was developing at Spence Bay.[102] This prediction came to pass, for within a year or two all of the camps (including that at Thom Bay) were abandoned.

Thus ended an eleventh hour attempt to preserve a degree of scattered settlement in the form of the hunting-trapping base camp. While considerable data had been collected on local conditions in the Arctic, the plan did not take into account, until the very end, the strength of the attraction to the centres experienced by the Inuit of this period. This was especially true, here and throughout the Central Arctic, with regard to the pull of housing programs.

CHAPTER EIGHT

Reflections and Retrospect

THE PATH TO CENTRALIZATION

From archaeological times through the period of first contact, the fur trade era, and past the middle of the twentieth century, the Inuit of the Central Arctic have undergone a series of shifts in their settlement practices. The Thule ancestors of the modern Central Eskimo lived in permanent dwellings for significant parts of each year. Small clusters of people usually built their houses at sites of important sea mammal occurrences or caribou migrations, though they were also probably more mobile at some periods of their yearly hunting cycle. Their descendents lived a more nomadic existence for the most part. In the more mobile periods of yearly cycles, they usually dispersed into small groups, but aggregations of larger size also occurred at certain seasons. Economic factors often related to such settlement practices. Advantage in winter sealing, or cooperation at caribou drives and at fishing weirs were examples. In most places there were shorter or longer periods during which people tended to aggregate at places of cached meat. Also, certain social purposes were served by the fusion and fission of local populations. The periodic aggregations served to create and reinforce social ties, while the dispersals helped to resolve conflicts.

For parts of the Baffin Island coasts, and in northwestern Hudson Bay, patterns of settlement were altered by the presence of whalers during the nineteenth and early twentieth centuries. Gatherings at whaling stations or around overwintering whaling ships produced new sorts of aggregations as well as movements of people from traditional ranges of habitation. Trade with whalers brought on a technological revolution that in turn affected settlement practices during and after the end of the whaling period. Firearms, steel traps, other metal implements, and wooden boats were the most obvious innovations.

During the late eighteenth and early nineteenth centuries, year-round habitation of the interior west of Hudson Bay replaced earlier seasonal forays. Contact-inspired conditions appear to be largely responsible for this movement. As much of the interior was abandoned or depopulated due to epidemics among the Chipewyan, use of firearms, and trade in the skins of animals hunted, interior habitation became attractive to the Inuit. New patterns of seasonal movement emerged along with economic readaption. The largest aggregations occurred yearly at sites of caribou kills, and some groups also moved to the coast where other large gatherings took place. Long journeys to trade at Churchill were undertaken until late in the nineteenth century, when the Hudson's Bay Company expanded its trade northward with watercraft.

While these changes in settlement were taking place in the eastern and southern extremities of the Central Arctic, in the regions to the north and west little change in aboriginal patterns of cyclical aggregation and dispersal occurred until well into the twentieth century. On Melville Peninsula superior marine resources made possible long periods of living from stores. This economic enhancement was usually accompanied by substantial aggregations of people at habitual sites of periodic gathering. For the regions to the west along the Northwest Passage such periods of living from cached food were less extended and the times of greatest congregation took place during the season of winter sealing. Dispersal occurred during the late spring, summer, and early autumn. These seasons were devoted to hunting land game, fowling, and fishing, occupations that normally favoured scattering of people into small groups.

The next set of changes in settlement came in conjunction with the full establishment of the trade in arctic fox. Some trade in this fur, as well as that of other animals, had taken place during the whaling era. As trading posts were established throughout the Central Arctic, the regulated fur trade came into force. This was accomplished by the middle of the 1920s, when only a few of the Inuit of the more remote regions were required to make long trips to trade. For much of the Central Arctic it was this regularized trade that brought about important changes in settlement practices. Firearms had reached much of the major area earlier, but now that a steady supply of ammunition was available from the trading posts, guns became an important element in subsistence. Their use correlated with the locations and movements of people. In those regions where a strong marine emphasis had been long established, it became more firmly fixed as wooden boats, available from the traders, and firearms were used. Elsewhere, where the warmer months had been devoted to inland wanderings, some Inuit, now provided with wooden boats, spent summers hunting seals in open water. The hunting of caribou was especially enhanced with use of rifles, and elements of groups hunted inland at the same seasons, and in some cases well into the winter months. In the regions south of Queen Maud and Coronation Gulfs, inland habitation for significant parts of the year was made possible through this increased procural of caribou and accumulation of meat. These Inuit also used fishnets, another important item involved in the trade in arctic fox.

Some general, but I think largely valid, statements can be made regarding the economy and distributions of Inuit for the fur trade-dominated, or contact-traditional period in the Central Arctic. With improved technology, game resources were more efficiently exploitated. This does not mean that a high degree of security was universal. Failure of game in some years, adverse weather conditions that limited hunting opportunities, epidemics, and the uncertainties of the fur industry all limited what could be called an unqualified improvement in economy. Nevertheless, almost everywhere in normal years, longer periods of subsistence from stored food were possible to a greater degree than had been the case earlier. These conditions also led to a more stable, less nomadic life. To a large extent the need for frequent shifts in residence for entire families was eliminated, together with the attendant hardships that these moves had entailed. Whereas periodic large aggregations had earlier been based on certain economic pursuits, or for periods of living on stores, they now coincided with visits of supply ships, and, at Christian holidays, at points of trade. The sizes of the all-native hunting and trapping basecamps, which were now the chief settlements, resembled most closely the more dispersed settlement phases of the aboriginal seasonal cycles. The composition of these groups, usually an extended family, also showed continuity from former times. This unit, composed of the father and mature sons and their spouses and progeny, formed the basic building block in most of the Central Arctic. Voluntary relationships also played a role, being especially important to integration in the Copper Eskimo area. During most of each year these camps had a great deal of autonomy. At times of aggregation at the small centres of trade and worship, missionaries and traders brought religious and economic influences to bear upon the Inuit. The RCMP also enforced certain laws during these visits and on their patrols to the camps.

In the east Central Arctic the HBC relocated people to better hunting and trapping regions. By the early 1930s Ottawa had become involved in these movements and was exerting greater control over the trading companies, including the opening and closing of posts. These openings and closings to some extent influenced the locations of Inuit. The final phase of change in Central Eskimo settlement came with the concentration of people into quasi-urban centres or villages. A core of native residents at trading centres began with some Inuit being employed by traders and police. They, together with a small number of indigents, were the main native elements at points of trade throughout the period before and during World War II. Some clustering of people also occurred during that war close to American military bases. At Frobisher Bay a military base made possible the temporary employment of men, bringing on seasonal in-gatherings. On Southampton Island clustering around an air base was discouraged, but a general contraction around the trading centre at Coral Harbour did occur. Elsewhere, little change in settlement patterns took place during World War II. The Policy of Dispersal endorsed by the traders and by the government prevented any large-scale clustering in most places during this period. The traders favoured dispersal since it supported the trapping economy that was the basis of their trade. The RCMP, the representatives of the federal government in the north, also enforced this policy. Dispersal was supported in Ottawa for reasons of economy and a commitment to a philosophy of preservationism.

During the late 1940s large influxes of money came to the Inuit in the form of the family allowances. Concern was raised that settlement would concentrate at places where issuances were to be made. However, continued application of the Policy of Dispersal resisted such a development in most of the Central Arctic. There is some evidence that the Catholic Church encouraged clustering around some of their missions, though overt opposition to the trader-government policy is not evident. In 1953 the government launched a relocation project that involved moving Inuit from east Hudson Bay and north Baffin Island to High Arctic locations. These moves involved very small numbers of Inuit as compared to the populations that moved to form the villages of mixed ethnic composition.

The construction of a chain of radar stations in the mid 1950s brought employment opportunities for a number of Inuit, and therefore migration. A case in point was the large influx of people to Cambridge Bay where a major, or Main, site was established. After the construction phase, however, employment possibilities fell off, leaving a large underemployed population. The RCMP, with government backing, strenuously resisted the gathering of unemployed men and their families around the stations, during the 1950s and beyond.

Also in the 1950s, a large centre of population grew at Rankin Inlet, where a nickel mining operation employed Inuit. After five years the mine closed, leaving a large indigent population drawn from several regions. In the southern Keewatin withdrawal of trading posts from the interior brought on contraction of Inuit settlement around Eskimo Point. With the failure of the caribou as the chief resource in the interior, in-gathering at Eskimo Point was virtually complete by the early 1960s. Famine in both the southern and northern interiors of the Keewatin led to relocations of people to Eskimo Point, Baker Lake, and Rankin Inlet, as well as to the new colony at Whale Cove.

While a certain degree of centralization was underway during the 1950s, as the decade ended large numbers of the Inuit of the Central Arctic remained dispersed in the hunting-trapping base camps. At the same time, the HBC began to reorient its northern trade, and preservationism began to fall out of favour in Ottawa. Austerity measures were replaced by humanitarian considerations, particularly concern for the health of the Inuit, and as the efforts to keep Inuit scattered were relaxed, centralization gathered momentum. Indeed, concentration of settlement in the Central Arctic was not so much a considered policy (and its inevitability was for a long time only reluctantly recognized) as it was a largely unintended consequence of the new Welfare State Policy.

The Welfare State Policy was implemented in programs that promoted better health conditions, education, and comfort for the Inuit of Canada. In particular, poor health was thought to be related to inadequate housing, and the government embarked on a series of housing programs in the centres of settlement. Motives for in-gathering in the early stages of the process were diverse and are not easily isolated. It is likely that, as the process accelerated, the "gradual acquisition of urban preferences by Native people" cited by Vallee et al entered into the picture. However, by the latter part of the 1960s the high development of the housing programs, accompanied by related services, brought on the final stages of centralization. My own view coincides with that of Duffy, who, after considering the various other forces at play in the Central Arctic, noted: "These developments set in motion a slow but perceptible flow of Inuit families toward more or less permanent residence in the settlements. Later, as the pace of building and provision of services accelerated, the flow toward the settlement became a riptide."[1]

DIVERSE PERCEPTIONS

To return to the basic concepts of relocation and migration introduced at the beginning of this study, for many years relocation was associated with the removal of Inuit from regions considered to be

overpopulated relative to resources to regions that were better endowed. From the standpoint of the Hudson's Bay Company, considerations of the fur trade were paramount. For the government, the
expressed concerns in granting permission for such HBC-inspired
moves were those of subsistence. In the case of the High Arctic relocation, where the HBC was not involved, these subsistence considerations were cited, together with the need to ease dependency upon
relief measures in the main donor region. There has been also some
debate as to whether the desire to affirm sovereignty in the High Arctic played a role. The concept of relocation as I have used it in this
study does not include the application of coercion or compulsion by
the agencies that planned the various relocation schemes,[2] and my
usage is also consistent with that favoured in much of the correspondence within and between governmental agencies involved in
northern administration.[3] The term came to be widely used by administrators who insisted that transfers were arranged with the consent of
the Inuit involved.

Relocation played a role in several instances of concentration of Inuit populations into centres during the 1950s and 1960s. Since there
has been some disagreement on the matter, it is necessary to assess the
prominence of migration as opposed to relocation in the centralization process. Tester and Kulchyski take the position that relocation was
at least as important when they state that "in the 40s and 50s settlements were developed by state planners, Inuit were moved, as often as
not, rather than moving themselves."[4] Of course, as described in this
study, the major concentration of settlement actually took place during the 1950s and 1960s. Also, much of the centralization took place
in advance of, or in spite of, state planning. It is not surprising that
these authors emphasize relocation in the creation of settlements,
since they have focused on such cases as those of the Ennadai–Henik
Lake people and the Garry Lake people, as well as the Keewatin Re-
establishment Project. The Ennadai Lake people were clearly repeatedly relocated. On the other hand, in the southern Keewatin interior
as a whole, the forty-four survivors of the Henik Lake tragedy and the
twenty-nine people who were relocated from Padlei, comprised only a
small portion of the 500 or so people who eventually settled at Eskimo
Point. Most of these Inuit, whose movements depleted the southern interior of population, were clearly migrants as defined here.

For the northern interior of the Keewatin and the village that grew
at Baker Lake, the picture is a complex combination of in- and out-
migration, temporary and permanent relocations, and cases of individuals being returned to camps by airplane. Inuit, including some of the
Garry Lake people in the Baker Lake trading area, were also relocated

to Rankin Inlet, and eventually to Whale Cove, to join Inuit from other regions. As well, there was re-relocation, or return migration, from Rankin Inlet to former homes in the interior. While Rankin became a community made up of people from every subregion of the Keewatin, the original core population consisted of migrants from Chesterfield.

For other centres in what has been here considered to be the Keewatin Region, mixed populations were evident. Thus, Coral Harbour on Southampton Island brought together people originally from the Repulse Bay region, comprising both relocatees and migrants, with people relocated from the eastern Arctic. However, both elements had been residents of the island for a long time and eventually gathered at Coral Harbour from neighbouring camps. While Repulse Bay had both Aivilik and Netsilik members, the latter were early migrants into the region. Again, both groups had long been members of that trading community before moving to the village itself. It is thus clear that for the Keewatin, relocation did play a very important role in the creation of the major centres of eventual settlement, but migration was at least as important in the process of in-gathering.

The quasi-urban community that grew at Frobisher Bay was made up originally of camp people drawn from the bay itself. Later, there was a large influx of migrants from Lake Harbour and elsewhere. Relocation played practically no role in the centralization at Frobisher. The same can be said for Coppermine, where in-gathering was for a long time fiercely resisted. On the basis of my exploration of archival and published material and my field enquiries, I conclude that the majority of centres that developed in the Arctic Coast and Arctic Islands regions (aside from Resolute and Grise Fiord) were built through the process of migration rather than relocation. Thus, Coppermine, Holman, Cambridge Bay, Gjoa Haven, Hall Beach, Igloolik, Pond Inlet, Pangnirtung, Lake Harbour, and Cape Dorset were all formed by people drawn through migration largely from their traditional habitation districts. Arctic Bay and Spence Bay, on the other hand, included people originally moved in from places from outside their trading districts, but they too had become local camp people before moving to the new villages. At Clyde, a small original population was swelled by relocations engineered by the Hudson's Bay Company in the period from 1920 to 1940, and by migrations from regions to the south and north, but all of these Inuit had become local people by the time of centralization.

Thus far I have regarded as relocated those Inuit who were bodily moved by outside agencies, and as migrants those who moved themselves. A third designation, which would lie at the margins of the category of migrants, is possible: those who under pressure of persuasion moved themselves into centres from within the trading community.

Such a position is taken by Brody: "Most observers feel that great pressure was put on Eskimos to move, that the Whites were anxious to draw people into settlements. The pressures were informal and diverse, both attractions (medical services, housing, proximity to store and church) and threats (no camp schools, illness in the camps)."[5] It is not clear to me who the "most observers" are, since Brody does not cite sources. In my view, the attractions cannot be considered pressures. Indeed, even after some of the services were installed, Inuit in a number of places were still being encouraged to remain dispersed in camps. With regard to threats, I have referred in this study to the fear of epidemics, as aggravated by in-gathering, as being instilled as an overt form of pressure to keep populations scattered. It has been noted, as well, and emphasized, that the withholding of family allowances beyond the specified monthly payments was a form of pressure designed to keep the populations dispersed.

Other views of the process of centralization have been advanced. For example, Mathiasson, who based his research in the Pond Inlet (Tununermiut) region, writes that he had at first accepted the view of an embittered Inuk youth that "the people had been forced to move by government pressure."[6] But, after reflection on the matter, he wrote, "I no longer think that the impetus for centralization was for the Tununermiut quite as contrived … but I do think that the Tununermiut who accepted centralization did so without full understanding of the implications."

Rasing lists a number of factors involved in in-gathering at Igloolik and Hall Beach, including declining fur prices, employment, improved health facilities, the new schools, etc., but states that "the provision of more houses was the dominant motive for moving into the settlements."[7] Rasing did believe that some pressures were exerted on the camp dwellers to move to the two centres. He cites an example,[8] as did Vestey[9] for the same region. While the date or period of Rasing's example is ambiguous, the case cited by Vestey indicates native-inspired pressures since the instigator was a member of the Inuit Housing Committee at Igloolik. This latter case highlights the temporal context within which such pressures were probably applied. In this vein, the cases cited by Brody where pressures were said to have taken place came in the last stages of centralization, and probably after the housing programs were well established.[10]

The forces behind in-gathering must be considered within a historical context. I have argued, on the basis of material presented here, that for a long time, pressures were brought to bear to keep Inuit populations scattered under what I have called the Policy of Dispersal. While weakening of that policy was evident in governmental circles by the end of the 1950s, local application continued in some places well into the sixties. These measures effectively slowed the process of centralization. Later, government programs, especially housing programs, sped the process. How widespread pressures to centralize may have been applied is not clear, but I submit that they did not occur to any great extent. When they did, it was not until the final stages of the in-gathering process.

One misconception that appears and reappears in writings that concern the period of in-gathering regards the nature of Inuit settlement in the period just preceding centralization. The term "nomadic" dominates much of this literature.[11] The designation fits much of the aboriginal period in the Central Arctic, but is less appropriate for the fur trade or contact-traditional period that preceded village living than is the anthropological designation *semi-nomadic*.[12] This mode of settlement was implied in the common practice of wintering at camps established at sites of meat caches for several months and shifting camps or traveling during other months, which was the widespread pattern in the Central Arctic during the fur trade period. Examples have been given for the regions south of Queen Maud and Coronation Gulfs, and for the Keewatin Region. The *semi-sedentary* settlement pattern, found in the Iglulik Eskimo area, and much of Baffin Island, is occupation of a single site for much of the year and moving to other locations for a shorter period of each year. A continuum from semi-nomadic to semi-sedentary was evident in the Central Arctic during the contact-traditional period, but there were fewer examples of a continuum from nomadic to semi-nomadic as the contact-traditional settlement practices became established.[13] I would argue that these distinctions are more than merely semantic. In understanding the processes that led to concentration of settlement in the Central Arctic, it is important to recognize that the changes were not so much from highly mobile settlement to fully sedentary conditions as from dispersed to highly aggregated circumstances.

Representatives of the Canadian government have received much criticism for their role in inhibiting positive changes in Canada's north. In response to such criticisms, Alexander Stevenson, who occupied a succession of positions in northern administration, stated, "With all fairness in looking back, governments and bureaucrats are not to blame for what we in the 1960s think was an apparent state of apathy of Canadian interests in the North for so many years ... in comparison with those in more accessible parts of the country which had to cope with growing pains in the early years of the century. Moreover, it also seems unfair to apply the social conscience of the 60s in respect to the 20s and 30s. It was not until the end of 1953 that in the creation of

the Department of Northern Affairs that the role and responsibility of
the federal administrators were clearly recognized. It was a big mile-
stone which ended the years of so-called indifference."[14] This statement would not mollify those critics of government policy who
compare developments in Canada's north with those of Danish or
American administrations. Nor will it satisfy those who cite humanitarian concerns. Stevenson's statement does highlight a fundamental evolution in the philosophy and policies of administration that had to
occur before the massive changes of the 1960s could take place. Advocates of a work ethic persuasion had to be replaced by those favouring
social benefits before changes could be made. That such changes in
administrative policy did eventually take place, beginning in the 1950s
and culminating in the 1960s, was due not only to changes in personnel in the decision-making agencies but perhaps more so to an evolution in the thinking of individuals such as Alexander Stevenson in
those agencies.[15]

EPILOGUE

One of the concerns of those who had espoused the Policy of Dispersal
had been that the Inuit of Canada would cease to be hunters and trappers and become instead virtual wards of the state if they abandoned
their camps for centres around trading posts and other installations.
Some degree of hunting, in particular, continued after centralization,
but there was, indeed, a less primary role in Inuit economies for produce from the land. An early example of this shift is found in Treude's
study of the Pond Inlet region in 1973–74.[16] The last camp was abandoned in 1971 and while the majority of men over the age of sixteen at
Pond Inlet continued to hunt, the intensity of the hunts declined dramatically. While the hunting range was maintained through the use of
motorized transport, greater time and energy were devoted to hunting
in close proximity of the village. Hunting had clearly become a part-
time activity and Treude estimated that less than 29 per cent of food
energy needs came from the hunt.[17]

In the 1980s, concern over the lack of appropriate exploitation of
resources led to a study that was published under the title *Keeping on
the Land*.[18] According to this study the chief problem was the expense
involved in keeping a hunting economy alive. It was estimated that as
much as $20,000 was needed for "a complete hunting, trapping and
fishing outfit," and "operating costs can run in thousands of dollars annually."[19] The report proposed a "Harvest Support Programme" with
an estimated cost of $10 million to $20 million for the entire Northwest Territories.[20] The report did not gain immediate endorsement,

but in 1994 a number of the recommendations were incorporated in the Nunavut Hunters Support Programme[21] as the new Territory of Nunavut began to achieve political prominence. The chief difficulty in accumulating enough funds to provide for hunting equipment and its maintenance without the financial aid of the support fund was, as always, fluctuation in the price and supply of fox furs. Added to that problem was the disappointing drop in the price of sealskins after a brief revival in the early eighties, with the boycott of the European Union in 1983 (renewed in 1985).[22] There was also the endemic unemployment situation that had assailed the area.

Hunting activity continued to decline throughout the Central Arctic in the later decades of the century, and especially among the youth. In a study based in the community at Holman, but which the authors posited "may be generalized to all of northern Canada,"[23] Condon et al concluded that "fewer and fewer young Inuit display the same degree of commitment to, or even interest in, subsistence hunting or fishing"[24] than was formerly the case. The following factors were listed as contributing to this situation: inadequate training in hunting techniques; lack of funds to purchase equipment; marginalization of hunting and trapping; limitations in time imposed by wage labour work schedules; and "addiction to organized sports such as basketball, hockey, and baseball."[25]

The decline of the hunting economy was but one of the many changes that took place in the later years of the century. It will not be possible to engage in a comprehensive survey of the entire scope of Central Arctic communities for these years. Rather, it might be more useful to compare a community as it was in the early stages of centralization with the same community a quarter of a century later. The village of Igloolik or, as known to the Inuit, Ikpiakjuk, was studied by Rasing in 1986–87.[26] At the time of my visit in 1960–61, there were two mission houses, the HBC buildings, and newly installed buildings of the Department of Northern Affairs, including a small school and quarters for employees.[27] Rasing depicted a village that had grown considerably. Among the buildings were the following: a large grade school as well as an adult education centre, a nursing station, a community hall, skating rink, coffee shop, and several stores, in addition to the HBC buildings. There were, as well, a hamlet office, a research centre, RCMP headquarters, a fisheries office, and three missions, all in addition to the numerous houses that were the living quarters of the Iglulingmiut.[28]

The population had also undergone dramatic growth. At the time of my study there were eighty-seven permanent Inuit residents.[29] The white population had increased from four to ten during the first month of my residence by the advent of the teachers (with one spouse), and the area administrator's wife and infant daughter.[30] At the time of Rasing's study there was a total of 806 Inuit,[31] a population increase due to both natural increase and the collapse of the camp system. With the addition of the white population, now totaling forty-eight,[32] growth of the village since 1960–61 was almost exactly tenfold.

A number of social changes had taken place in the intervening years. My survey of household composition had shown that the majority favoured extended family households: 78 of the total number of households in the trading area of 103 were of that composition type.[33] This compares to only 13 extended family households and 111 made up of nuclear families in the Igloolik village at the time of Rasing's study.[34] It would appear that the traditional preference for composite households had given way to a government view based on southern Canadian standards of avoidance of overcrowding.

Employment had expanded greatly. Upon my arrival in August 1960, three Inuit were employed by the HBC and two women, part time, at the Catholic mission. After the arrival of the teachers and the area administrator in September, the DNA hired (and housed) two men, and in the year that followed, a third.[35] In 1986–87 there were ninety-nine full-time jobs filled by Inuit men and women as well as eleven part-time jobs, with the greatest number being with the various government agencies.[36] Impressive though this growth in employment may seem, unemployment was rife, since Rasing estimated that the employable population was 359 as compared to the approximately 100 jobs actually occupied.[37] The concept of unemployment was absent from my data from 1960–61 since all men, except the extremely old or crippled, were assumed to be hunters. Most men devoted all their time to that occupation (as well as to trapping), and even the employed men hunted in their free time. Rasing appears to include hunters among the unemployed, but he notes the sharp drop in the number of full-time hunters, commenting: "The decreased significance of hunting in terms of survival was revealed by the decreasing number of full-time hunters and the appearance of part-time hunters … Apart from providing a major (supplementary) food resource for the majority of families, hunting gained importance as the means to express Igluling-miut identity."[38] In the case of my study, it was clear that at that time, rather than being a secondary source, game foods were the chief source of diet, especially given the meagre inventory of food carried by the HBC store.[39]

A horizontal segmentation of the Inuit society was apparent at the time of Rasing's study that had not existed earlier. Society was divided into older and more traditional Inuit, a middle-aged group who held most of the important committee positions, and "marginal youth," who were usually more educated young people whose "views and behaviour differed from the views and attitudes of their parents and became more and more in line with Euro-Canadian values and norms."[40] I had noted a religious split in the community twenty-five years before as being prominent both in terms of separation into two distinct neighbourhoods and also, in large degree, in various aspects of social interaction.[41] For a time after my study this split took on political significance, with election to various committees being affected. However, Rasing reported that "when the religious controversies ameliorated in the 1980s, the political factionalism lost the salience it had had in the 1960s and 1970s."[42]

The chief position of power in the village had shifted from the HBC manager to the area administrator upon the arrival of the latter in 1960.[43] The area administrator still held the paramount power at the time of Rasing's study, but a number of functions had been moved over to the social worker, the RCMP officer, the renewable resource officer, and the bylaw officer.[44] According to the account of Rasing, both the Anglican minister and the resident Catholic priest influenced secular matters to a greater degree than I had earlier observed.[45] Undoubtedly the most important development in the social organization of the village during the years that followed my study was the growth of community committees run by the natives themselves. Chief among these elected bodies were the Housing Association, the Hamlet Council, the Igloolik Cooperative, and the Alcohol Education Committee.[46] These groups were a necessary development in coping with a large compacted community among a people who had no traditional institutions equal to such situations. Their appearance also reflected a change in government policy and administration from the earlier paternalism.

The concepts of crime and criminality that feature so strongly in Rasing's account for 1986–87[47] were all but absent in the Igloolik village of 1960–61. I recall only one incident that could be called "criminal" behaviour, and its interdiction. This was related to the Iglulingmiut practice of leaving dogs run loose. There were always at least 100 of the animals in the centre, none of which were normally tied up. The area administrator at first tolerated this practice, but when his infant daughter was badly bitten, he became active in enforcing the Dog Ordinance of the Northwest Territories, and began to shoot loose dogs.[48]

By contrast to this isolated case, formal law enforcement had become one of the salient features of community life by the 1980s. Rasing cites no fewer than 333 charges being brought to local courts from 1980 to 1986. A number of these were referred to the Territorial

Court and two to the Supreme Court of Canada.[49] Of the total reported offences from 1982 to 1986, alcohol-related offences ranged from a low of 27.7 per cent in 1986 to a high of 47.5 per cent in 1983. However, Rasing also noted that much violent and otherwise antisocial behaviour went unreported.[50] Motivations for drinking were those of "relaxation and laughter."[51] However, "behavioural changes stimulated by alcohol included outbursts of violence": "drinking parties lead to fights due to lessened inhibitions or uncontrolled behaviour that follows from the use of alcohol."[52] Indeed, alcohol abuse led to several homicides during the 1980s.

Alcoholic beverages consisted of liquor flown in from Frobisher Bay, as well as home brew, at the time of Rasing's study.[53] These sources were not evident for the native population of Igloolik in 1960–61. The only regular drinker was the HBC manager, who imported a large quantity of various kinds of alcoholic beverages on the annual supply ship, as well as making his own beer. He shared some of his stock with the company clerk, and with white visitors.[54]

Also lacking in 1960–61 was the use of drugs reported for the 1980s. During the latter period hashish and marijuana use were widespread in the village. Rasing estimated 40 to 60 per cent of people between twelve and forty used them, and the estimates for the age group sixteen to thirty was 70 to 80 per cent.[55] Rasing reported that "no, or very few crimes were committed under the influence of soft drugs."[56] Rather, break-ins were associated with stealing solvents,[57] which were sniffed, especially by adolescents. Neither drug use nor such sniffing was in evidence at the time of my study at Igloolik.

Clearly, substantial physical, administrative, social structural, and behavioural changes took place in the community between the times of the two studies of Igloolik. Some of these features of changing Inuit culture and society had general application during the final decades of the twentieth century. It is possible to gain a conception of the nature of Central Eskimo society during this period from some statistics from 1996 for the territory that was emerging as Nunavut (see map 4). Due largely to improved medical conditions, the population had increased. It was estimated in a 1996 report that by 1 April 1999 there would be 27,213 people in Nunavut,[58] compared to somewhat over 5,000 for the same regions in 1951.[59] The sizes of communities had grown as well during these years, with 25.3 per cent having at least 2,000 people; the largest single local population was at Frobisher Bay, with 4,556 in 1996.[60] Unemployment for the whole district was reported at 29 per cent.[61] In keeping with this average rate, social assistance expenditures grew rapidly from 1985, with $6,524,071 reported, to 1995, when $21,551,190 was spent.[62] Some of the so-called vices of civilization

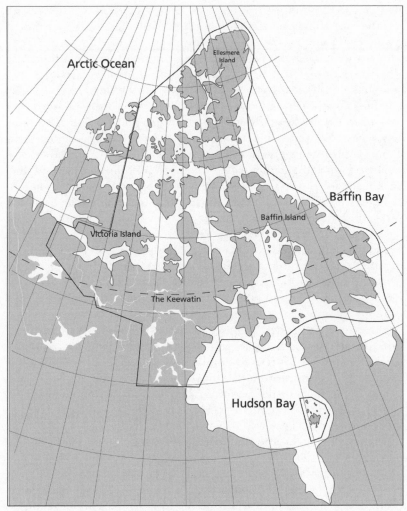

Map 4   The boundaries of Nunavut. Adapted from map of Nunavut, settlement areas, (Ottawa: Indian and Northern Affairs, n.d.)

were also prominent. For instance, the use of marijuana in Nunavut was set at 28 per cent of the population, as compared to 7 per cent for all of Canada.[63] An apparent graduation to hard drugs was apparent by 1996, for use of speed, cocaine, and heroin was reported at 5.5 per cent of this population, as compared to 1.5 per cent for all of Canada.[64] Sniffing of solvents also showed a higher estimated rate, 1 per cent for all of Canada and 21 per cent of the Nunavut population.[65]

Rather surprising to me on the basis of my experiences in the sixties was the rate of once-a-week consumption of alcohol, which was put at 35 per cent for all of Canada and only 17 per cent for Nunavut.[66] One wonders if the frequent use of homebrew is incorporated in this latter percentage. Probably the most vital index of social disorganization and personal conflict is the suicide rate. Between the beginning of 1985 and the end of 1994, there were 226 cases in the Northwest Territories as a whole. For Nunavut during that period there would have been 147 cases computed on a hypothetical population of 100,000. This compares to about a rate of two per 100,000 for all of Canada.[67]

These statistics, together with material from Rasing's study of Igloolik for 1986–87, give some indication of the problems of the culture change that followed from the centralization of settlement in Canada's Arctic. It should not be overlooked that there were substantial positive developments. General health conditions improved with the expansion of nursing stations, which were established in most of the centres, together with access by air to outside hospitals. Comfortable and more healthful housing and associated services were important features of the centralization of settlement. The establishment of schools in each of these communities gave many youth a headstart on a process that could extend to higher grades and beyond. From this increasingly well-educated youth, a new leadership type has emerged, and its representatives are in the forefront of the growing independence and assertiveness that is transforming Inuit society in Canada. For, while the 1950s and 1960s was the period of centralization of population, the later decades of the twentieth century saw political and legal development of the Inuit of Canada.

Already, during the 1960s, the first steps toward polity among the Inuit came in the shape of quite informal settlement councils, but beginning in the early 1970s more elaborate levels of political involvement grew rapidly. The Inuit Tapirisit (ITC), formed in 1971, became an overarching organization over a number of regional organizations.[68] Between 1965 and 1972 a small number of Inuit had been elected to the Northwest Territories Legislative Council, but the number rose sharply after the election of 1975.[69] In 1979 an Inuk was elected for federal office in Ottawa, representing the newly formed electoral district for Nunatsiaq, which included the regions of the Central Arctic.[70] Meanwhile, a still more expansive level of political participation by the Inuit of Canada came in the formation and first meeting of the Inuit Circumpolar Conference in 1977,[71] to be followed by more meetings every third year.

Each of the levels operated to achieve objectives that concerned their membership. On the local level, an example comes from the

Grise Fiord people. Beginning in the sixties they successfully petitioned the federal government for liberalization of game regulations,
as well as for establishing health care facilities for the community.[72]
More dramatic actions came on the levels of the regional organizations
and the ITC. One of these concerned the High Arctic relocations, and
involved the ITC, but mainly the Makivik Corporation of Quebec. This
latter organization had approached various ministers and deputy ministers concerning Inuit complaints regarding the moves of the 1950s.[73]
Requests by the colonists to return, especially to Port Harrison (now
renamed Inukjuak), were repeatedly turned down until 1988, when,
under pressure from Makivik, families were reimbursed for trips back
to Port Harrison that had been made, and other funds made available
for those who then wished to return.[74] In addition, houses were built
at Inukjuak for returnees and, indeed, in the next year twenty-two people took advantage of these concessions on the part of the federal government.[75] Reports were later submitted regarding the relocations,[76]
and in 1992 a Royal Commission on Aboriginal Peoples was formed
and began a series of hearings that extended into 1993. Their report
contained a number of recommendations, chief of which concerned
compensation for the colonists and an apology: the government
"should acknowledge the wrongs done the Inuit and apologize to the
relocatees."[77] While the relocatees were from the Quebec region, and
represented by the Makivik Corporation and their lawyers, the Tungavik Federation based in Frobisher Bay (now called Iqaluit) became involved in the publicity of the case. Eventually the final meetings that
led to a settlement were held in Iqaluit in March 1996.[78] The agreement specified that $10,000,000 would be paid to survivors of the relocations (now being termed "exiles" by the native organizations) or to
their descendents in cases of deceased relocatees. The terms were accepted with reluctance by the survivors because an apology was not
forthcoming from the government's representatives.[79]

Another example of the political effectiveness of regional organizations was shown in the emergence of Nunavut. As early as 1977,
and again in 1979, the ITC had proposed the separation of this Central Arctic area from the western part of the Northwest Territories.[80]
The Tungavik Federation, which had come to represent the budding
political district, was instrumental in achieving an agreement in
1992.[81] This agreement included providing the Inuit of Nunavut
with $1.148 billion to be allotted over a fourteen-year period and
confirmed title to 350,000 square kilometres of this land. The land
allotment included about 18 per cent of the region, together with
subsurface mineral rights.[82] The negotiations regarding the status of
Nunavut continued until 1 April 1999, when Nunavut was declared a

separate Territory.[83] The provisions included gave the Inuit of Nunavut rights of ownership, and use of land and participation in decision-making of various kinds. Harvesting rights were emphasized, with a Nunavut Wildlife Board being established, and a Hunter's and Trapper's organization was to be recognized. Inuit place names would replace English language names, and among other innovations, the Inuit Heritage Trust Fund would be established.[84] Indeed, several of the provisions indicated that ongoing financial aid from the government would be expected. This being the case, the agreement can be seen as an extension of the Welfare State Policy.

In the forefront of the negotiations has been an elite of young educated Inuit. Their participation alters the image of the Inuit from the apparently passive and largely withdrawn people of the hunter-trapper tradition of the fur trade era to the assertive, intelligent, articulate, and politically aware representatives of the people of the Canadian Arctic. Their actions have gained considerable unity and influence through a number of organizations, and especially with the emergence of Nunavut and its related agreement. The achievements that the Inuit have gained are especially remarkable in view of the extensive degree of subsidization that was required throughout the Northwest Territories, including that which helped support the Inuit. One view of this subsidization was expressed by an official of the Government of the Northwest Territories who pointed out that only $1 billion a year had been required from the national budget of $110 billion for the entire Territories for 1989.[85] Such high levels of subsidization continued through the late 1990s with the establishment of Nunavut. The 1999–2000 budgetary estimates for the new Territory included income of over 90 per cent of projected income as consisting of grants and transfer payments from Ottawa.[86] Both the processes that led to centralization in the Central Arctic and those that maintain the villages so created have been the legacy of the Welfare State Policy. This being the case, it would seem that the economy of the area would be subject to a fundamental vulnerability, with dependency on a liberal philosophy and fiscal policy. As the century ended there was no indication that deviation from this philosophy and policy was on the horizon.

Notes

1 I have used the designation *Inuit* rather than *Eskimo*, with two exceptions. First, in quoted materials the original designations are retained. Second, in the case of major groupings like Central Eskimo or Netsilik Eskimo, I have followed established usages in the anthropological literature. For a discussion of the limitations of "Inuit" and the origins of the term "Eskimo," see Damas and Goddard, "Introduction," 1–7.

2 I have used this designation beginning with Damas, "The Contact-Traditional Horizon," 116, in favour of the previously employed "village" in Damas, *Igluligmiut Kinship*, 66–97. The basis of the change was the small size of many contact-traditional era sites of habitation. "Camp," should not, however, be associated with impermanence. It follows a convention employed by most other writers dealing with such units (but *cf* Wenzel, review of *Living on the Land*, 152). Here "village" will be used to designate the large mixed ethnic communities that formed mainly in the 1950s and 1960s.

3 Vallee et al., "Contemporary Canadian Inuit," 664.

4 Lieber, "Conclusion: The Resettled Community," in *Exiles and Migrants in Oceania*, 342.

5 Rowley, "Population Movements in the Canadian Arctic," lists no fewer than twenty-seven migrations over a 200-year period.

6 Royal Commission on Aboriginal Peoples, *The High Arctic Relocation*; Tester and Kulchyski, *Tammarniit*; Marcus, *Relocating Eden*.

7 For more complete depictions of this approach, see Sturtevant, "Anthropology, History and Ethnohistory"; Hudson, "The Historical Approach in Anthropology." As applied to the Central Arctic regions, see Damas, "From Ethnography and History."

8 This area stretches from Dolphin and Union Strait and Western Victoria Island eastward along the Arctic Coast and adjacent mainland and insular

regions to include Baffin Island. It follows southward to include the District
of Keewatin and north to the Arctic Islands that have been inhabited by
Inuit peoples whom anthropologists have designated as Central Eskimo
(or Central Eskimos).

9 The boundaries of Nunavut are shown in map 4. Of the regions and communities discussed in this study, only Holman and environs are not part of
Nunavut.

10 The files of the RCMP (RG 18) have been especially important. Weissling,
"Inuit Redistribution and Development," also uses these files extensively
while addressing problems of centralization in the Arctic.

CHAPTER ONE

1 Among the archaeological sources for the Central Arctic are Mathiassen,
The Archaeology of the Central Eskimos; McGhee, *Canadian Arctic Prehistory*. Important ethnographies for the area include Boas, "The Central Eskimo";
Jenness, *The Life of the Copper Eskimos, Report of the Fifth Thule Expedition,
1921–24* (Vols 5, 6, 7, 8 and 9). For a comprehensive treatment of the archaeology, ethnology, linguistics, and physical anthropology for the entire
Eskimo area, see Damas, *Arctic, Handbook of North American Indians. Vol 5*.

2 Mathiassen, *The Archaeology of the Central Eskimos*, Part 1, 2.

3 McGhee, "Thule Prehistory of Canada," 371. Savelle and McCartney, "Geographical and Temporal Variation," 52, posit 80 per cent occupancy of
Thule winter houses at any one time. Park, "Thule Winter Site Demography," argues that winter village group size was no greater than fifty people,
essentially agreeing with McGhee's estimates. On the other hand, it has
been suggested that larger aggregations occurred in connection with
breathing-hole sealing: Savelle and McCartney, "Geographical and Temporal Variation," 50; Savelle, "Information Systems and Thule Eskimo Bowhead Whaling," 83. Regarding the economy of the Thule people, it has
been suggested that rather than hunting whales they made use of stranded
animals for construction of their winter houses: Freeman, "A Critical View
of Thule Culture."

4 Savelle and McCartney, "Geographical and Temporal Variation," 40.

5 The dates are those of McGhee, "Thule Prehistory of Canada," 373.

6 Mathiassen, *The Archaeology of the Central Eskimos*, 1: 306–11; McGhee,
Copper Eskimo Prehistory, 53.

7 Savelle and McCartney, "Geographical and Temporal Variation," 67.

8 McGhee, "Speculations on Climatic Change," posits a cooling period beginning in the thirteenth century when increased ice accumulation interfered with the movements of large whales. This would account for the
southward shift of the Thule peoples. As well, Savelle and McCartney,
"Geographical and Temporal Variation," 35–6, 67, propose that the same

cooling affected the populations and distribution of caribou, accounting for the abandonment of permanent villages in the coastal regions to the south.

9 Helm and Damas, "The Contact-Traditional All-Native Community," 10.

10 Stefansson, *The Three Voyages of Martin Frobisher*; Albert Markham, *The Voyages and Works of John Davis The Navigator*; Clement R. Markham, *The Voyages of William Baffin*.

11 Stefansson, *The Three Voyages of Martin Frobisher*, 86.

12 W.G. Ross, "Commercial Whaling and Eskimos in the Eastern Canadian Arctic," 249.

13 Ibid., 253.

14 Hall, *Life with the Esquimaux*, 235.

15 Boas, "The Central Eskimo," 451.

16 Ibid., 461.

17 McClintock, *The Voyage of the Fox in the Arctic Seas*, 108–10.

18 W.G. Ross, *Whaling and Eskimos*, 25.

19 Glover, "Introduction," xiiv.

20 Ibid., xiix.

21 Burch, "Muskox and Man," 140.

22 Birket-Smith, *The Caribou Eskimos*, Part 1, 9, while arguing for the unity of the Caribou Eskimo on grounds of homogeneous yet distant culture, notes that "the caribou is the pivot round which life turns. When it fails, the mechanism of culture comes to a stop and hunger and cold are the consequences for those tribes which, relying upon it, have created an almost incredibly one-sided culture." Five subgroupings of Caribou Eskimo are recognized as follows: the Qairnirmiut, the Hauniqtuurmiut, the Havaqtuurmiut, the Padlirmiut, and the Ahiarmiut (Arima, "Caribou Eskimo," 447).

23 Burch, "Muskox and Man." Another important treatment of the early history of the Caribou Eskimo is Csonka, *Les Ahiarmiut: A Lecart des Inuit Caribous*.

24 Lofthouse, *A Thousand Miles from a Post Office*, 107, 109.

25 W. G. Ross, *Whaling and Eskimos*, 60, 112, 113, 126, 129, 131.

26 Gilder, *Schwatka's Search*, 41.

27 J.W. Tyrrell, *Across the Sub-arctics of Canada*; J.B. Tyrrell, *Report on the Doobawnt, Kazan and Ferguson Rivers*, 126–36. This second source estimates the total population along his route as being "between 500 and 600" (126). However, this figure may be too high since J.B. Tyrrell reports sixteen camps on the Kazan River totalling forty-four tents, which would mean a large number of people for each tent.

28 Hanbury, *Sport and Travel in the Northland of Canada*, 65.

29 Burch, "Knud Rasmussen and the 'Original Inland Eskimos,'" 90, cites archival material for 1919 census figures and compares them with those of

Birket-Smith's, *The Caribou Eskimos*, Part 1, 67–8, for 1922–23 to indicate a drastic slump between these years, due largely to the Great Famine of 1919. For four of the five major-*miut* groupings named in n22, the decline was from 800 to 336. Birket-Smith does not provide a census of the fifth group, the Ahiarmiut. Gabus, *Vie et Coutumes des Esquimaux caribous*, is credited for first recognizing the Ahiarmiut (Arima, 447).

30 Birket-Smith, *The Caribou Eskimos*, Part 1, 70.
31 Ibid., 71.
32 Ibid., 72.
33 Ibid., 74.
34 Parry, *Journal of a Second Voyage*; Lyon, *The Private Journal of Captain G. F. Lyon*.
35 Mathiassen, *Material Culture of the Iglulik Eskimos*, 6(1):24–9.
36 Rae, *Narrative of an Expedition*, 39–40 .
37 Robinson, "The Influence of the American Whaling Industry," 133.
38 Nourse, *Narrative of the Second Arctic Expedition*, 255–6, 269.
39 W.G. Ross, *Whaling and Eskimos*, 128.
40 Parry, *Journal of a Second Voyage*, 388–9; Lyon, *The Private Journal of Captain G. F. Lyon*, 149–50.
41 Mathiassen, *Material Culture of the Iglulik Eskimos*, 6(1):29–30.
42 Ibid., 30.
43 John S. Ross, *Narrative of a Second Voyage*.
44 Amundsen, *The Northwest Passage*; Rasmussen, *The Netsilik Eskimos*.
45 Balikci, "Netsilik," 42.
46 Author's field notes, Netsilik area, 1965.
47 Exceptions are the expeditions of McClure (Osborne, *The Discovery of the Northwest Passage*) and Collinson (*Journal of H.M.S. Enterprise*), both of which wintered in Copper Eskimo country.
48 Stefansson, *My Life with the Eskimo*; Jenness, *The Life of the Copper Eskimos*, 120.
49 Stefansson, *My Life with the Eskimo*, 169–70.
50 Jenness, *The Life of the Copper Eskimos*, 120.
51 Ibid., 121–44.
52 Ibid., 110.
53 Ibid., flyleaf.
54 Rasmussen, *Intellectual Culture of the Copper Eskimos*, 78–85.
55 Jenness, *The Life of the Copper Eskimos*, 123–4.
56 Stefansson, *The Stefansson-Anderson Expedition*, 26.
57 Stefansson, *My Life with the Eskimo*, 290.
58 Damas, "Characteristics of Central Eskimo Band Structure," 122.
59 Wenzel, *Clyde Inuit Ecology and Adaptation*, 86–95.
60 Damas, *Igluligmiut Kinship*, 102–7.
61 Steenhoven, *Leadership and Law Among the Eskimos*; Balikci, *Development of Basic Socio-Economic Units*, 39–40, describes this unit as the "restricted ilagiit."

62 Arima, "Caribou Eskimo," 455.

63 Damas, "Characteristics of Central Eskimo Band Structure," 122–5.

64 Ibid., 123; Wenzel, *Clyde Inuit Ecology*, 122; Steenhoven, *Leadership and Law*, 52–7; Arima, "Caribou Eskimo," 455.

65 Damas, "Characteristics of Central Eskimo Band Structure," 129.

66 W.G. Ross, "Whaling, Inuit, and the Arctic Islands," 44. It is clear from the context that Ross is referring to World War II.

67 This designation was first applied to the Athaspaskans of the Mackenzie and the Igluligmiut by Helm and Damas in "The Contact-Traditional All-Native Community," 9–21. It was later applied to the Central Arctic in general in Damas, "The Contact-Traditional Horizon."

68 Apparently the first attempt to trade with Inuit along the west coast of Hudson Bay came with Kelsey in 1719. There were further trading trips in 1720, 1721, and 1722 (Holland, *Arctic Explorations and Development* 89); Robson, *An Account of Six Years' Residence*, 645, reported that there were yearly trading voyages to Whale Cove from 1738 to 1744.

69 Williams, *Andrew Graham's Observations*, 214.

70 Glover, "Introduction," liv.

71 W.G. Ross, *Whaling and Eskimos*, 109.

72 Ibid., 66–7.

73 Ibid., 98; HBCA B. 42/a/193, fol. 16.

74 Low, in *Report of the Dominion Government Expedition*, 151, described Inuit trapping at the beginning of the new century as follows: "At every stopping place traps are set for furs – single and spring steel – each native has two or three."

75 Robinson, "The Influence of the American Whaling Industry," 119.

76 W.G. Ross, *Whaling and Eskimos*, 66.

77 One example of a single post exceeding these totals is Cambridge Bay, where in the trapping season 1942–43, 12,025 white fox were traded. HBCA, RG 3/1/35/5.

78 Usher, *Fur Trade Posts*, 125.

79 Ibid.

80 Ibid., 127–30.

81 Ibid., 144.

82 Ibid.

83 Ibid., 145.

84 Ibid., 142.

85 Ibid., 145.

86 Ibid., 142–3.

87 Ibid., 139.

88 Jenness, *The Life of the Copper Eskimos*, 31.

89 Ibid., 38, 49.

90 Usher, *Fur Trade Posts*, 101.

91 Ibid., 111–16.
92 Ibid., 112.
93 Ibid., 114.
94 Ibid., 116.
95 Ibid., 115.
96 Ibid., 117.
97 NA, RG 85, Vol. 1069, File 251(1), Correspondence, Fitzgerald to Cory, 10 April 1925.
98 NA, RG 18, F1, Acc. 83–84/068; File G567–88(1), RCMP Patrol Report of the Pangnirtung Detachment, 1924.
99 Boas, "The Central Eskimo," 426.
100 HBCA, AG 3/26B/8, Annual Report, Pangnirtung Post, Outfit 269.
101 Freeman, *Inuit Land Use*, 3: map 117.
102 HBCA, AG 3/36/1, Annual Accounts, Frobisher Bay Post, Outfit 269; AG 3, 2B/6, Annual Report, Frobisher Bay Post, Outfit 269.
103 Accounts of these changes can be found in Damas, *Igluligmiut Kinship*; Rasing, *Too Many People*; Vestey, "Igloolik Eskimo Settlement."
104 Usher, *Fur Trade Posts*, 132.
105 Freeman, *Inuit Land Use*, 3: map 132.
106 Manning, "Notes on the Coastal District," 101–2.
107 Balikci, *Development of Basic Socio-Economic Units*, 44–59.
108 Ibid., 75–77.
109 Ibid., 52–60.
110 Ibid., 59.
111 Much of the material here on the Netsilik comes from data that I gathered in the field in 1965. Also see Brice-Bennett, "Inuit Land Use"; Freeman, *Inuit Land Use*, 1: 66–82 and 3: maps 49–66.
112 Author's field notes, Netsilik area, 1965.
113 Ibid.
114 Freeman, *Inuit Land Use*, 3: maps 61, 63.
115 Author's field notes, Netsilik area, 1965.
116 Hoare, *Report of Investigations Affecting Eskimo*; HBCA, B. 461/a/1, and Journal of Events, Perry River Post, 4 August 1926 to 1 May 1927; NA, RG 18, Acc. 83–84, File G567, Patrol Reports from the Coppermine Detachment, 1932–44; author's field notes, Copper Eskimos, 1962–63.
117 Farquharson, "Inuit Land Use in the West-Central Arctic," 1: 53.
118 Rasmussen, *Intellectual Culture of the Copper Eskimos*, 69. RCMP patrols continued to encounter sealing villages on the ice throughout Coronation Gulf into the 1950s (NA, RG 18, Acc. 83–84, File G567–146), as well as on the ice of Queen Maud Gulf into the 1960s (author's field notes, Perry River, 1963).
119 Farquharson, "Land Use in the West-Central Arctic," 52–3.

120 Ibid.

121 Freeman, *Inuit Land Use*, 3: map 24.

122 Ibid. For example, see 3: map 67.

123 Welland, "Inuit Land Use in Keewatin District," 1: 86. An ethnography of the Ahiarmiut of the contract-traditional period is found in Csonka, *Les Ahiarmiut.*

124 Freeman, *Inuit Land Use*, 3: map 87.

125 While information on local group or camp sizes is not abundant for the Keewatin during contact-traditional times, patrol reports of the Baker Lake Detachment give some indications. Some examples: a patrol report of 27 April 1932 to Eskimo Point, Chesterfield, and return to Baker Lake (NA, RG 18, 3661–G567–8) lists camps of thirty-five people, "3 families," and "14 natives"; another report for 2 December 1939 (ibid., 9 May 1941) for the Back River region, describes a camp of ten families or forty-nine people.

126 Records for the years 1941–50 for Baker Lake show a range from 947 to 3,844 white fox traded annually, with an average of 2,393. For Eskimo Point over the same time span, the range was from 576 to 2,626, with an average of 1,773 (HBCA, RG 3/35/5).

CHAPTER TWO

1 Usher, *Fur Trade Posts*, 16.

2 Royal Canadian Mounted Police, *Annual Report for Fiscal Year 1924–25.*

3 Zaslow, *The Northward Expansion of Canada*, 24.

4 Ibid., 9.

5 Department of the Interior, *Annual Report for the Fiscal Year Ending March 31, 1923.*

6 Department of the Interior, *Annual Report for the Fiscal Year Ending March 31, 1924.*

7 NA, RG 85, Vol. 1069, File 251(1).

8 Ibid., Cory to Fitzgerald, 16 October 1924.

9 Ibid., Burwash to Finnie, 30 October 1924.

10 Ibid., Report by Finnie, registered in File 251(2), 2 July 1925.

11 Ibid., Fitzgerald to Cory, 10 April 1925.

12 See Jenness, *Eskimo Administration*; Tester and Kulchyski, *Tammarniit*; Marcus, *Relocating Eden*; Royal Commission, *The High Arctic Relocation.* For a more complete treatment of this aspect as well as the general history of HBC-government relations see Damas, "Shifting Relations."

13 HBCA, RG 2/4/F87.

14 Wenzel, "Inuit Demographic and Ecological Relations," 37, indicates that "in all, some 8–10 [families] … were brought to Clyde by the HBC in the 1920s and 1930s."

15 HBCA, RG 2/4/F87: A. Brabant, Fur Trade Commissioner to Edward Fitzgerald, Deputy Chairman, Canadian Advisory Committee, 22 December 1921.

16 Ibid., Ralph Parsons to Fur Trade Commissioner, 8 January 1922.

17 HBCA, AG 3, B/461/a/i, Journal of Events, Perry River Post, 1926–27.

18 HBCA, AG 3, File B/427/a/2, Journal of Events, King William Island Post, 1927–28.

19 HBCA, AG 3, File B/394/a/1, Journal of Events, Fort Brabant Post, 1927–28.

20 Usher, *Fur Trade Posts*, 115–17.

21 HBCA, AG 3, File 74B/6, Journal of Events, Arctic Bay Post, 1941–42.

22 NA, RG 85, Vol. 1069, File 251(1): Finnie to Cory, 9 June 1925.

23 Ibid., Cory to Finnie, 10 June 1925.

24 Ibid., Finnie to Brabant, 13 June 1925.

25 Ibid., M. Conn for the Fur Trade Commissioner, HBC, Winnipeg, to Finnie, 5 September 1925. Conn wrote: "We cannot approve of the suggestion of prohibiting further posts in the Preserves or requiring permission of the Commissioner before establishing posts in the territories. These posts are, we believe, of decided advantage to the natives as well as a necessary factor in the pursuit of our trade." On 30 September 1925, apparently as a response to a message from Finnie regarding Conn's statement, Maxwell Graham, chief Wild Life Division, commented that the HBC response was premature in the absence of the fur trade commissioner, Brabant. Subsequently, on 17 October 1925, Finnie wrote Cory that "all our suggestions were turned down flat," and on 20 October, that Brabant had returned and agreed to a meeting in Ottawa (Memorandum for Mr Brabant respecting his conference with the Advisory Board on Wild Life Protection, held on 12th November, 1925).

26 Jenness, *Eskimo Administration*, 34–5.

27 PWNHC, Vol. 2, Northwest Territories Council Minutes, 5th Session, 23 June 1925. NA, RG 85, Vol. 1059, File 251–1(1). Memorandum to W.W. Cory, 17 October 1926 (with reference to resolution of 30 March 1925), stated the following: "the Departmental solicitor … says we have absolute power to forbid traders in the Northwest Territories to deal with the natives and that we might establish a government protectorate similar to that in Greenland, if we so desire."

28 Department of Northern Affairs, Arctic Correspondence. File 405–5–1, Vol. 1, "Trading posts operated by the Hudson's Bay Company." The uncertainty regarding the number of posts was due to the question of whether two posts, on Banks Island and on Cockburn Peninsula, Baffin Island, had been previously established.

29 Ibid.

30 Jenness, *Eskimo Administration*, 56.

31 Grant, *Sovereignty or Security?*, 27.

32 Jenness, *Eskimo Administration*, 59.

33 Royal Canadian Mounted Police, *Annual Reports for the Fiscal Years 1922, 1924, 1926.*

34 Department of the Interior, *Annual Report, For Fiscal Year, 1933*, 31.

35 Jenness, *Eskimo Administration*, R57.

36 Department of Northern Affairs, Arctic correspondence, File 405– 5–1, Vol. 4 notes that while two families were returned to Pangnirtung, "52 natives are being transported on the Nascopie to Arctic Bay on their own request, and 48 natives will be left at Dundas Harbour." Since only fifty-two people had made up the original party relocated from places in southern Baffin Island, it seems from these figures that a number of people must have moved to Devon Island from northern Baffin Island to hunt and trap, which would follow from the closing of the post at Arctic Bay in 1928.

37 HBCA, A/74/53, Annual Report from District Offices, Outfit 254, (1923– 24), St Lawrence–Labrador District, 387.

38 Department of Northern Affairs, Arctic Correspondence, File 405–5–1, Vol. 4.

39 Ibid., Vol. 3.

40 Ibid.

41 PWNHR, Vol. 416, Northwest Territories Council Minutes, approved at the 66th Session, 23 March 1937.

42 It is not clear from either the maps in Freeman, *Inuit Land Use* Vol. 3, or my enquiries in the area when this expansion took place.

43 HBCA, RG 7/1/1748, Transfer of Natives, Fort Ross to Dorset, 6 April 1943.

44 HBCA, RG 7/1/1750, Manager, Ungava Section to General Manager, Fur Trade Department, 28 November 1947; Closure of Fort Ross – Dorset natives.

45 Ibid., Manager, Ungava District to General Manager, 6 April 1943.

46 HBCA, RG 7/1/1750, Manager, Ungava Section to General Manager, Fur Trade Department, 28 November 1947; Closure of Fort Ross – Dorset Natives.

47 Ibid.

48 HBCA, RG 7/1/1748, Parsons to Gibson, 24 February 1940.

49 Wenzel, "Inuit Demographic and Ecological Relations," 35, writes, "The composition of the Piniraq camp between 1941 and 1943 appears to have included Inuit from Cumberland Sound and Kivituq, Cape Dorset and Lake Harbour; Inuit from the latter communities having been transported to the Clyde region by the HBC." Wenzel also indicated in a personal communication to me that those from the nearer sites, Kivituq and Cumberland Sound, moved themselves.

50 HBCA, RG 7/1/1748, Gibson to Parsons, 28 March 1940.

51 Ibid. There is a notation in the margin of the letter from Gibson as to whether this responsibility should be undertaken. Parsons replied, "as we are moving the Eskimos mainly in our own interests, we cannot refuse to be responsible for their maintenance" (17 April 1940).

52 HBCA, RG 7/1/1748, Manager, Ungava District to Manager, Fur Trade Department, 7 March 1943. There is no little irony in the expectation of good fur returns from the Clyde post. George Wenzel, who spent considerable time in the Clyde community, quotes an informant who described the early period of the fur trade there: "Inuit just did not pay very much attention to foxes." Wenzel continues, "the Clyde post log reinforces this idea. Traders' comments make it seem that Clyde Inuit invested far less effort in trapping than the Qallunaat (white men) felt they should, with more than one Inuit referred to as 'lazy' because his fox tally did not meet HBC expectations" (Wenzel, *Animal Rights, Human Rights*, 107–8).

53 HBCA, RG 7/1/1748, Manager, Ungava District to Manager, Fur Trade Department (ref. to letter of 12 February 1943).

54 Ibid.

55 Mathiassen, *Material Culture*, 28.

56 Manning, "Remarks on the Physiography,"25.

57 Ibid., 35.

58 Ibid.

59 HBCA, AG 3, 74B/14. Synopsis of Journal of Events, Southampton Island, Outfit 272 (1942–43).

60 Ibid.

61 Ibid., November 1942.

62 Ibid., January 1943.

63 NA, RG 18, Acc. 83–84/058, Vol. 24, File G567–66(5).

64 NA, RG 18, Acc. 83–84/068, Vol. 24, File G567–38.

65 Damas, "The Contact-Traditional Horizon."

66 NA, RG 18, Vol. 3661, File G567–8, Patrol Report, Baker Lake Detachment. Report for period 30 June – 31 December 1939.

67 HBCA, AG 3/26B/30, Annual Report, Lake Harbour, Outfit 270.

68 HBCA, AG 3/26B/31, Annual Report, Cape Dorset, Outfit 270.

69 HBCA, AG 3/2B/16, Annual Report, Arctic Bay, Outfit 270.

70 HBCA, AG 3/26B/21, Annual Report, Frobisher Bay, Outfit 270.

71 NA, RG 18, Vol. 3661, File G567–8: Patrol Report, Baker Lake Detachment. Re; Relief to Starving Eskimos, 16 May 1931.

72 Ibid., Report of Baker Lake Detachment for period 30 June to 31 December 1939.

73 Dominion Bureau of Statistics, *Canada Yearbook* (1929), 750.

74 Ibid. (1930), 738.

75 Ibid. (1940), 800.

76 Ibid. (1938), 781.

77 Records of the HBC post at Bathurst Inlet, 1928.

78 Usher, *Economic Basis and Resource Use*, 115.

79 Ibid.

80 HBCA, AG 3/B427/9/2, Journal of Events, King William Island Post, 1927.

81 J.L. Robinson, "Eskimo Population in the Canadian Eastern Arctic," 142.

82 NA, RG 85, Vol. 1871, File 550–1(1), Memorandum from Dr L.D. Livingston to M.J. Turner, 22 October 1936.

83 NA, RG 18, Acc. 83–84/048, Vol. 24, File G567–66(1), Cumberland Gulf Detachment, Patrol Report, Kivitoo and Padlei, 30 April 1928.

84 Dr Martin's trials at Coppermine have been described in several sources, including the NFB film "Coppermine," and Richard Finnie's popular book *The Lure of the North*. See also Grygier, *A Long Way From Home*, 56–8.

85 PWNHC, Stevenson Fonts, M–1991–023, File 38–2. Eastern Arctic Patrol General.

86 Duffy, *The Road to Nunavut*, 53.

87 NA, RG 85, File 550–1, Vol. 1, L.D. Livingstone to M. Lorne Turner, 22 October 1936.

88 HBCA, RG 7/1748, Gibson to Chesshire, 19 December 1942.

89 HBCA, RG 7/1/1749, Manager, Ungava District to General Manager, Fur Trade Department, 11 February 1946.

90 Duffy, *The Road to Nunavut*, 95.

91 PWNHC, File 1/16, Special Meeting of the Council of the Northwest Territories, 20 January 1949.

92 NA, RG 85, Vol. 1969, File 251–1(1a): Gibson to Wright, 2 November 1949.

93 Ibid., Cantley to Wright, 18 November 1950.

94 Library of Department of Indian and Northern Affairs: Cantley, "Survey of Economic Conditions Among the Eskimos of the Canadian Arctic," 48.

95 Ibid., 45.

96 Ibid., 51.

97 NA, RG 85, Vol. 1069, File 251–1(1a), Memorandum for Commissioner of the Northwest Territories from E.B. Sinclair, 22 March 1951.

98 PWNHC Stevenson Fonts, File 42–5, RCMP – 1949–1973: Larsen to Commissioner, RCMP, 30 October 1951.

99 Ibid., Cantley to Wright, 20 November 1951.

100 Clancy, "The Making of Eskimo Policy in Canada," 191.

101 NA, RG 85, Vol. 1069, File 251–1(1a): Cunningham to Commissioner, Northwest Territories, 16 January 1952, citing conversation with Alexander Stevenson.

102 Ibid., Draft Invitation to Conference (Eskimo Affairs Committee) by F.J. Cunningham, 18 February 1952.

103 NA, RG 85, Vol. 1234, File 251–1(2): to Commissioner, RCMP from H.A. Larsen, 29 February 1952.

104 Ibid., Chesshire to Young, 9 May 1952.

105 NA, RG 22, Vol. 234, File 251–1(2), Report on the Committee on Eskimo Affairs Meeting May 19–20, 21, 1952.

106 NA, RG 22, Vol. 254: File 40–8–1(3), Cunningham to Clyde Kennedy, 7 June 1952.

107 Ibid., File 40–8–1(1), Minutes of the First Meeting of the Special Committee on Eskimo Affairs held in Ottawa, 16 October 1952.

108 NA, RG 85, Vol. 1234, File 251–1(2), "Immediate Steps That May Be Taken To Improve Eskimo Economy and Welfare" (with covering letter to Mr Mielke), J. Cantley, 18 October 1952.

109 NA, RG 22, Vol. 254, File 40–8–1(4), Minutes of the Third Meeting of the Committee on Eskimo Affairs, 20 October 1953.

110 Sivertz to Rowley, 13 December 1954.

111 Ibid.

112 NA, RG 85, Vol. 1234, File 251–1(3): L.H. Nicholson, Commissioner, RCMP, to Cunningham: Regarding Report of Arctic Inspection Flight by H.A. Larsen, March–April 1954, 4 August 1954.

113 Ibid., Cunningham to Nicholson, 4 August 1954.

114 NA, RG 22, Vol. 298, File 40–8–1, Minutes of the Fifth Meeting of the Eskimo Affairs Committee, 29 November 1954.

115 Ibid.

116 Ibid.

117 NA, RG 22, Vol. 298, File 40–8–1: Rowley to Sivertz, 4 June 1954.

118 Ibid., Cantley to Deputy Minister, 13 January 1955.

119 Ibid., Rowley to Deputy Minister, 19 January 1955.

120 PWNHC, Stevenson Fonts, File 17–1 (Policy Inuit 1935–1959).

121 Council of the Northwest Territories, "The Problem of the People," Address to Members, January 1959.

122 PWNHC, Stevenson Fonts: File 17–7, Memorandum for File, Staff Information from B.G. Sivertz, 11 March 1959.

123 Ibid., File 13, Minutes of the Tenth Meeting of the Committee on Eskimo Affairs, 25 May 1959.

124 Ibid.

125 HBCA, RG 9, File 402.1.1, Hugh Sutherland, 11 March 1959.

CHAPTER THREE

1 The Royal Commission on Aboriginal Peoples, *The High Arctic Relocation*, "A Report on the 1953–55 Relocation," 133. After a careful study of the evidence for sovereignty as a crucial ingredient in the project, it was concluded: "As we have seen, economic and social concerns were primary. It is doubtful, therefore, that sovereignty was the primary consideration. The High Arctic Islands provided opportunities that were, in the eyes of the planners, consistent with the economic concerns."

2 PWNHC, Stevenson Fonts, File 17–7.

3 NA, RG 85, Vol. 1234, File 251–1, Cantley to Mielke, October 1952. In this communication, Cantley recommended transfer of ten families from Port Harrison to Ellesmere Island, and ten families from northern Quebec or Cape Dorset to Resolute Bay. The Cape Dorset and northern Quebec people were eventually not included in the move, but the two sites were, of course, occupied by the Port Harrison people.

4 PWNHC, Stevenson Fonts, File 24–10, Stevenson to Cantley, 8 November 1952. Bissett, *Northern Baffin Island*, 8–9, gives the following reasons for movement of Pond Inlet people to Resolute and Ellesmere Island: (1) the Craig Harbour region was known to Pond Inlet Eskimos who had served as special constables for the RCMP at that place and regarded it as a good sea mammal hunting area; (2) there had been poor fox takes in the Pond Inlet region during the early 1950s; (3) having hunted in the Somerset Island and the Lancaster Sound region (Bathurst, Cornwallis, and Devon Islands or the district where the Resolute people would be using), it was known to the Pond Inlet people to be a good hunting area.

5 Willmott, *The Eskimo Community*, 18 (fig. 2).

6 Ibid., 15 (table 2).

7 NA, RG 18, Acc. 85–86/048, File TA 8–1–13.

8 Willmott, *The Eskimo Community*, 12.

9 Ibid., 11.

10 Royal Commission on Aboriginal Peoples, *The High Arctic Relocation*, "A Report on the 1953–55 Relocation," 71.

11 NA, RG 18, Acc. 85–86/048, Vol. 53, File TA 50–8–1–5, Eskimo Conditions, Craig Harbour, Period Ending 31 December 1953.

12 Fryer, "Eskimo Rehabilitation Program," 139–42.

13 Ibid., 142; also NA, RG 18, Acc. 85–85/048: Eskimo Conditions, Year Ending 31 December 1953.

14 Ibid., Eskimo Conditions, Year Ending 31 December 1954.

15 Ibid., Eskimo Conditions, Year Ending 31 December 1955.

16 Ibid., Eskimo Conditions, Year Ending 31 December 1956.

17 Ibid., Eskimo Conditions, Year Ending 31 December 1957.

18 Ibid.

19 Ibid., Eskimo Conditions, Year Ending 31 December 1958.

20 Ibid.

21 Ibid., Eskimo Conditions, Year Ending December 31, 1959.

22 NA, RG 18, Acc. 85–86/048, Box 55, File TA 500–8–1–14, Eskimo Population, Resolute Bay, NWT, 15 September 1953.

23 NA, RG 22, Vol. 254, File 40–21(3): Eskimo Settlement at Resolute Bay, 9 November 1953, from C.J. Marshall, forwarded from G. Rowley to F.J.G. Cunningham, 12 November 1953.

24 Ibid., Cunningham to Marshall, 15 December 1953.

25 Ibid., Constable Gibson, Resolute Detachment, RCMP, Conditions Amongst Eskimos, Resolute Bay, 8 December 1953.

26 NA, RG 18, Acc. 85–86/048, Box 55, File TA 500–8–1–14: Conditions Amongst Eskimos, Resolute Bay, NWT, 26 March 1954.

27 Ibid., Conditions Amongst Eskimos, 22 March 1955.

28 Bissett, *Resolute*, 65, lists thirty-four immigrants joining the Resolute colony in 1955; about twenty more joined before the end of the fifties.

29 Dr P.E. Moore of the Northern and Indian Health Service requested pictures of these dwellings. Since he did not renew or follow up this request after viewing the prints, it appears that he was satisfied. NA, RG 18, Acc. 85–86, Box 55, File TA 500–8–1–14; Dr P.E. Moore to Henry Larsen, 6 August 1957; Moore to Larsen, 29 October 1957.

30 Ibid., Conditions Amongst Eskimos, 14 November 1956. I have been unable to find any response from northern administrators to this suggestion of providing transportation for return flights to Port Harrison, though such may exist.

31 NA, RG 18, Acc. 85–86/048, Conditions Amongst Eskimos, Report for Year Ending 31 December 1958.

32 Ibid.

33 Ibid.

34 NA, RG 85, Vol. 1970, File 251–4(4): Larsen to Sivertz, 16 April 1958.

35 Ibid., Sivertz to Deputy Minister, 6 June 1958.

36 NA, RG 85, Vol. 1382, File 1012–13(3), Sivertz to Larsen, 9 November 1958.

37 NA, RG 18, Acc. 85–86/048, Report for Period Ending 31 December 1959.

38 For Grise Fiord, the report that substantial amounts were accumulated by most of the families through trapping and carving has been mentioned. There is the notation (NA, RG 18, Acc. 85–86/048, Vol. 55, Conditions Amongst Eskimos, Year Ending 31 December 1957) that family allowances were being reduced. This seems to indicate that the allowances were being used as relief and that such measures were not necessary. The chief source of subsistence came from the ringed seal. Procural of that animal increased with the growing population. In 1954, 302 were killed, while in 1959–60 the number was 500, paralleling an increase in Inuit population from 36 to 58.

For the Resolute colony, seasonal access to wage labour was available at the base but hunting provided the chief subsistence at this time. Not only did the people succeed in meeting human demands, but the 105 dogs were reported as being "well fed and in good condition" (NA, RG 18, Acc. 85–85/048, Conditions Amongst Eskimos, Period Ending 31 December 1958).

39 Higgins, *South Coast–Baffin Island*, 95–6.

40 Ibid., p. 203–4.

41 NA, RG 18, Acc. 85/86, Vol. 55: Sinclair to Chesshire, 15 January 1951.

42 Ibid., Conditions Amongst Eskimos, Cape Dorset, Lake Harbour, NWT, 17 May 1951.

43 NA, RG 85, Vol. 1266, File 1000/67(4), Conditions Amongst Eskimos, Generally, Annual Report, Year Ending 31 December 1957; Annual Report, Year Ending 31 December 1957.

44 NA, RG 85, Vol. 1266, File 1000/67(4), D.O.T. Message from James Houston, 2 May 1957.

45 Ibid., Conditions Amongst Eskimos, Cape Dorset Area, 30 August 1952.

46 NA, RG 85, Vol. 1266, File 1000/167(3), Welfare Teacher's Report, September 1956.

47 NA, RG 85, Vol. 1266, File 1000/67(4), Radiogram from James Houston to Chief, Arctic Division, 18 April 1957.

48 Higgins, *South Coast–Baffin Island*, abstracted from table of camps, 203–4.

49 NA, RG 18, Acc. 85/86, Vol. 55, Patrol by Otter to camps, 24 October 1959.

50 Graburn, *Lake Harbour, Baffin Island*, 20–8.

51 Ibid., 23.

52 Ibid., 21.

53 Ibid., 23.

54 Ibid., 21.

55 Ibid., 23.

56 Ibid., 20.

57 NA, RG 85, Vol. 1951, File 1000/107(1), Conditions Amongst Eskimos, Generally, Annual Report, Year Ending 31 December 1959, Lake Harbour, NWT.

58 Graburn, *Lake Harbour, Baffin Island*, 24.

59 Ibid.

60 NA, RG 18, Acc. 83–84/068, File G567–38, Patrol to Native Camps, west side of Frobisher Bay, 18 to 22 December 1950. This report described "no needy circumstances." However, a patrol later that winter (Patrol Report to Native Camps, east side of Frobisher Bay, 15–21 March 1951) indicated poor sealing conditions related to lesser expanses of sea ice for a platform for hunting operations. The next year's report (Patrol to Native Camps in Frobisher Bay area, 4–6 December 1952) reported better hunting with plenty of seals being caught. Even as late as December 1954 (Patrol to Native Camps, 21 December 1954), it was stated that "as yet no real difficulty has been experienced at outlying native camps in obtaining food."

61 NA, RG 18, Acc. 85–86/048, Vol. 55: Frobisher Bay Annual Report year ending 31 December 1951.

62 Ibid., Annual Report, year ending 31 December 1952.

63 NA, RG 85, Vol. 1267, File 1000/169(8), Conditions Amongst Eskimos Generally, Annual Report, Year Ending 31 December 1956; NA RG 18, Acc. 85/86/048, Vol. 56.

64 Ibid.

65 NA, RG 18, Acc. 86–86/048 Vol. 55, Annual Report, Year Ending 31 December 1956.

66 NA, RG 85, Vol. 1267, File 1000/169, pt. 8: Welfare Report, Month of January 1957.

67 Ibid., Northern Service Officer's Report for June 1957.

68 NA, RG 85, Vol. 1951, File A1000/169(1), Correspondence: Sivertz to Administrator of the Arctic, 27 April 1960.

69 Ibid., Regional Administrator to Administrator of the Arctic, 12 May 1960.

70 Usher, *Fur Trade Posts*, 130.

71 Anders et al., *Baffin Island–East Coast*. There are minor discrepancies in this book, as for instance between table 22 (page 150) and table 29 (page 158). For consistency, I have elected to use only the former table.

72 Ibid., 150.

73 Anders et al., *Baffin Island–East Coast*, 150.

74 Ibid., 150. Also table 23, 24.

75 NA, RG 18, Acc. 85–86/048: File 500-8-11, Annual Report for Year Ending 31 December 1952.

76 Ibid., Annual Report for Year Ending 31 December 1956.

77 Ibid., Annual Report for Year Ending 31 December 1957.

78 Ibid., Re: Conditions Amongst Eskimos Pangnirtung area, 26 February 1959.

79 Ibid., Re: Conditions Amongst Eskimos Generally, Cumberland Sound area, Patrol 25 July to 30 July 1959.

80 Ibid., Annual Report for Year Ending 31 December 1959.

81 Anders et al., *Baffin Island–East Coast*, 150.

82 NA, RG 18, Acc. 85–86/048: Memo for Mr Farley from R.A.J. Phillips, Eskimo Families at DEWline sites, 10 May 1957.

83 Ibid., Fitzsimmons to Director, Northern Administration and Lands Branch, 3 May 1957.

84 Ibid., Sivertz to Fitzsimmons, 10 May 1957.

85 Ibid., T.A. Lawrence, Eastern Region Manager, Federal Electric Company to DEWline Projects Officer Federal Electric Company, Lodi, New Jersey, 6 April 1957.

86 Wenzel, *Animal Rights, Human Rights*, 140.

87 NA, RG 18, Acc. 85–86/048, Box 55, File TA 506-8-1-3: to "G" Division, Re: Native Conditions Clyde River Detachment, 11 August 1953.

88 Ibid., Officer Commanding "G" Division to Director, Northern Administration and Lands Branch, 16 September 1953.

89 Ibid., To Officer Commanding "G" Division from E.A. Marshall I/C Clyde Detachment, 22 December 1953.

90 Ibid., E.A. Marshall, Constable in Charge, Clyde Detachment to Officer Commanding "G" Division, 13 February 1954.

91 Ibid.

92 Ibid., Annual Report for Year Ending 31 December 1953, from 1 September 1953.

93 Ibid., Annual Report, Year Ending 30 June 1956.

94 Ibid., Annual Report, Year Ending 30 June 1957.

95 Ibid., Annual Report, Year Ending 30 June 1958.

96 Ibid., Annual Report, Year Ending 31 December 1959.

97 Usher, *Fur Trade Posts*, 131–3.

98 Ibid., 132.

99 Bissett, *Northern Baffin Island*, 1: 63.

100 Ibid.

101 NA, RG 18, Acc. 85–86/048, Box 55, File TA 500–2–2–12: Annual Report, Pond Inlet Detachment, Year Ending 30 June 1956.

102 Ibid., Annual Report for Year Ending 31 December 1952.

103 NA, RG 18, Acc. 85–86/048, Box 55, File TA 500–2–12: Annual Report for Year Ending 31 December 1955.

104 Bissett, *Northern Baffin Island*, 1: 78.

105 Ibid, 1: 175.

106 NA, RG 18, Acc. 85–86/048, Annual Report, Year Ending 30 June 1956.

107 Bissett, *Northern Baffin Island*, 1: 114.

108 NA, RG 18, Acc. 85–86/048: Conditions Amongst Eskimos, Arctic Bay WW II, 14 March 1961.

109 Ibid., Annual Report for Year Ending 31 December 1959, Pond Inlet Detachment.

110 Ibid.

111 Manning, "Notes on the Coastal District," 101–2. Manning attributed this movement to the exhaustion of walrus in the Repulse Bay region.

112 Damas, *Igluligmiut Kinship*, 67–8.

113 Ibid., 66–7.

114 Ibid., 27.

115 Ibid., 68 (fig. 14).

116 NA, RG 18, Acc. 85–86, Box 55, File TA 500–8–1–12, Annual Report for Year Ending 30 June 1956, Pond Inlet Detachment.

117 Vestey, "Igloolik Eskimo Settlement," 99, attributes the movement from the long-inhabited site on the mainland (Abadjaq) to the decline of local game resources.

118 NA, RG 18, Annual Report for Year Ending 30 June 1959, Pond Inlet Detachment.

119 NA, RG 18, Acc. 85–86, Report for the Year Ending 30 June 1957. Apparently the end of the fiscal year changed from 30 June to 31 December during 1959 for RCMP Arctic posts. This report includes correspondence from Inspector Larsen to the Director of Northern Administration and Lands Branch, 17 September 1957 stating that "regarding DEWline site near Igloolik, must discourage hanging around."

120 NA, RG 18, Acc. 85–86, Box 55, File TA 500–8–1–12, Annual Report for
      Year Ending 30 June 1956, Pond Inlet Detachment.

121 See chapter 1 for these movements.

122 Usher, *Fur Trade Posts*, 116.

123 NA, RG 18, Acc. 83–84/068, File G567–90: Spence Bay Patrol Reports.

124 Ibid., Vol. 2 Patrol Reports, Cambridge Bay Detachment. Airplane Patrols
      to Fort Ross, 1 February, 5–6 March, 18–25 May 1949; Patrol, Cambridge
      Bay to Sherman Peninsula, 28 December 1950; Patrol Report, Cam-
      bridge Bay to Perry River, Sherman Inlet, January to 7 February 1954.

125 Regarding intermarriage NA, RG 18, Acc. 85–86/048, Box 56, File TA
      500–8–1–32: Conditions Amongst Eskimos–Spence Bay. NWT to Fort
      Smith Subdistrict, Re: Conditions District of Spence Bay, 30 June 1951.

126 Ibid., Annual Report, Year Ending 31 December 1951.

127 Ibid., L.K. Capelin to Officer Commanding "G" Division, 5 September
      1951. In reference to 30 June 1951 report (Eskimo Conditions District of
      Spence Bay).

128 Ibid., Annual Report, Year Ending 31 December 1951.

129 Ibid.

130 NA, RG 18, Acc. 85–86/048, Box 56, File TA 500–8–1–32: Report of
      Patrol to Simpson Strait and Sherman Inlet, 31 March 1953; Also NA,
      RG 18, Acc. 83–84/048, File G567–90.

131 NA, RG 18, Acc. 85–86/048, Conditions Amongst Eskimos, Spence Bay
      Detachment to Fort Smith, 28 January 1956.

132 NA, RG 18, Acc. 85–86/048, Annual Report for Year Ending 31 Decem-
      ber 1956.

133 Balikci, *Development of Basic Socio-Economic Units*, 17; Damas, "Environ-
      ment, History, and Central Eskimo Society"; Damas, *Ecological Essays*, 51.
      More recently, I have modified this position somewhat since a maximum
      number must also be considered (Damas, "The Distribution and Habits,"
      n.d.).

134 NA, RG 18, Acc. 85–86/048: Annual Report, Year Ending 31 December
      1955.

135 Ibid., Conditions Amongst Eskimos, Generally, Annual Report for 31 De-
      cember 1956.

136 Ibid., Annual Report for Year Ending 30 June 1957.

137 Ibid.

138 Ibid.

139 Ibid.

140 NA, RG 18, Acc. 85–86/048: Annual Report for Year Ending 30 June
      1958.

141 Ibid.

142 Ibid., Conditions Amongst Eskimos, Chantrey Inlet, 12 February 1960.

143 Ibid., Annual Report for Year Ending 30 June 1959.

144 Ibid., From A/Corporal Spence Bay Detachment to Fort Smith. Re: Conditions Amongst Eskimos Living Close to DEWline Sites, E4 Spence Bay District, 21 March 1956.

145 Ibid. However, at one of the sites, fraternization of women with men of the sites and use of liquor caused the station to be declared out of bounds "except when men were working there." There was, at this site, however, an arrangement whereby men were alternated week by week in DEWline employment in order to allow time for hunting and trapping (Conditions Amongst Eskimos Along DEWline E4, Spence Bay District, 4 July 1956).

146 NA, RG 18, Acc. 85–86/048: Eskimo Conditions Along the DEWline in E4, Spence Bay District, Re: Father Van De Velde, Roman Catholic Missionary, Pelly Bay, NWT, 8 April 1957.

147 Ibid., R.A.J. Phillips, Chief Arctic Division, 28 June 1957.

148 Steenhoven, *Leadership and Law*, 63.

149 NA, RG 18, Acc. 85–86/048: Annual Report for Year Ending 30 June 1957.

150 Balikci, *Development of Basic Socio-Economic Units*, 71.

151 NA, RG 18, Acc. 85–86/048, Officer Commanding "G" Division from J.S. Craig, Fort Smith. Spence Bay, HBC, RCMP, and Federal Day School, 27 April 1960.

152 Abrahamson et al., *The Copper Eskimos*, 105 (materials taken from File 401–22–5, Northern Administration Branch).

153 Ibid.

154 Records of the Catholic Mission, Bathurst Inlet, NWT (Permission of Father Louis Men'ez, OMI).

155 Ibid.

156 NA, RG 85, Vol. 119/150, File 1000, Pt. 1. To C.O. Fort Smith, Destitution Eskimos, Bathurst Inlet, 2 January 1955.

157 Ibid. Extract from Report of J.P. Richards, 10 May 1956, on investigations Central Arctic Region, period March – April 1956.

158 Hudson's Bay Company records at Bathurst Inlet Post.

159 NA, RG 85, Vol. 1119, File 1000/180/150(1): Destitution at Perry River, 24 January 1954.

160 Ibid., L.A.C. Hunt District Administrator to Cunningham, Sealing at Perry River, 16 March 1954.

161 Ibid., Hunt to Cunningham, 29 March 1954.

162 Ibid., Cpl in Charge, Cambridge Bay Detachment to Hunt, n.d.

163 Ibid., Hunt to Cunningham, 29 March 1954.

164 NA, RG 18, Acc. 85–86/048, Box 56, File TA 500–1–30, Conditions Amongst Eskimos, Generally, Cambridge Bay Detachment Area, 11 May 1948.

165 Ibid., A.L. Adams, A/Chief Arctic Division to H.A. Larsen, Commanding Officer "G" Division Re: Conversation with Matt Murphy, trapper Contwoyto Lakes, 11 October 1955.

166 Ibid.

167 Ibid., Conditions Amongst Eskimos, Perry River, NWT, 31 January 1959.

168 Author's field notes, Perry River, 1963.

169 Collinson, *Journal of H.M.S. Enterprise.*

170 Jenness, *The Life of the Copper Eskimos*, map at end of book.

171 Abrahamson et al., *The Copper Eskimos*, 118–19.

172 NA, RG 18, Acc. 85–86/048, Conditions Amongst Eskimos, Generally, Cambridge Bay Detachment Area, 11 May 1948.

173 Abrahamson et al., *The Copper Eskimos*, 120.

174 Author's field notes, Cambridge Bay, 1963.

175 Abrahamson et al., *The Copper Eskimos*, 120.

176 Ibid., 121.

177 NA, RG 18, Acc. 85–86/048: Annual Report, Year Ending 31 December 1956, Cambridge Bay Detachment.

178 Ibid., Annual Report, Year Ending 31 December 1958.

179 Ibid., Conditions Amongst Eskimos, Douglas Bay, King William Island, 21 January 1958; 27 February 1958.

180 Ibid., Sivertz to Larsen, 10 March 1958.

181 Ibid., Annual Report, Year Ending 31 December 1958.

182 Author's field notes, Cambridge Bay Area (including Bathurst Inlet and Perry River, 1962–63).

183 Usher, *Economic Basis and Resource Use*, 57, 63–5. The western and southwestern parts of Victoria Island were served by trading posts at Holman Island and, until 1962, Read Island. While patrol reports from the Coppermine detachment give information on these regions for the 1930s and 1940s, they contain little information for the 1950s. The RCMP report from the Coppermine detachment for the year ending 31 December 1951 indicates good conditions at Holman as well as at Read Island, except that caribou were rare on Victoria Island, and hunters from Read crossed to the mainland to hunt the animal. (NA, RG 85, Vol. 1118, File 1000/145(2). Condon, *The Northern Copper Inuit*, devotes little space to the 1950s, although he indicates that "from 1940 to the early 1960's the permanent Inuit population of Holman fluctuated between four and seven families" (131). Major settlement changes took place in the 1960s, which I shall treat in a later chapter.

184 NA, RG 18, Acc. 83-84/048, G567-24G, Coppermine reports 1932-63.

185 NA, RG 85, Vol. 1118, File 1000/145(2). Conditions in inland settlement in the river and lakes country between Coppermine and Bathurst Inlet can be gained from the report of the patrol of early 1949 [NA, RG 18, Acc. 83–84/068 G567–24(1)], as well as from Harrington, *The Face of the Arctic*, 79–136.

186 NA, RG 85, Vol. 1118, File 1000/145(2): Coppermine Detachment to Fort Smith, 24 June 1949.

187 Ibid., Welfare Report, Coppermine, November 1952.

188 Ibid., Memorandum to E.N. Grantham from J. Cantley, 11 December
1952. The estimate of 109 Inuit appears to agree with the figure of twenty
families "engaging in seal hunting and trapping out from settlement" for
the previous winter (To Officer Commanding, Fort Smith Division,
8 February 1951).

189 Ibid., Welfare Report, Coppermine, December 1952.

190 Ibid.

191 NA, RG 85, Vol. 118, File 1000/145(2): Welfare Report, February 1953.

192 Ibid., Welfare Report, April 1953.

193 Ibid., Welfare Report, May 1953.

194 Ibid., Welfare Report, August 1953.

195 Ibid., Welfare Report, November 1953.

196 Ibid., Welfare Report, December 1953.

197 Ibid., Telegram from Welfare Teacher, Coppermine, to Cunningham, Director Northern Administration and Lands Branch, 5 January 1954; NA,
RG 85, Vol. 1234, File 251–1(3), P.A.C. Nichols, Manager Arctic Division,
HBC to Mr Cunningham (reference to letter from Post Manager, Coppermine, 12 February 1954).

198 NA, RG 85, Vol. 1234, File 251–1(3): (quotation from Manager's letter).

199 Ibid., Cantley to Sivertz, 21 April 1954.

200 Ibid., Sivertz to Cantley, 31 May 1954.

201 NA, RG 85, Vol. 1118, File 1000, 145(1): To Commanding Officer from
Constable I/c Coppermine Detachment, 30 June 1954.

202 Ibid., To H.A. Larsen from Constable in charge Coppermine Detachment, 7 May 1854.

203 Ibid., part 3, Conditions Amongst Eskimos, Year Ending Dcember 31,
1954.

204 Ibid., part 4, Welfare Report, January 1956.

205 Ibid., Welfare Report, February 1956.

206 Ibid., To Officer Commanding, Fort Smith from Acting Constable, Coppermine Detachment, 15 May 1956.

207 Ibid., Conditions Amongst Eskimos, Generally, (RCMP report, 7 January
1957).

208 Ibid., Welfare Report, for April 1957; Welfare Report for May 1957.

209 NA, RG 85, Vol. 1266, File 1000/145(5). W.W. Mair Chief, Canadian
Wildlife Service to Chief, Arctic Division, 21 July 1958; Reply by R.A.J.
Phillips (copy to H.A. Larsen and memorandum to Jameson Bond),
19 August 1958. Reply to Phillips by Bond, 24 September 1958; Report
on Fishing Undertaken for the Purpose of Conserving Caribou, 29 August 1958 by Frank S. Bailey, Game Officer, Fort Simpson; Memorandum
for the District Administrator from J.C. Bryant, Superintendent of Game,
19 December 1958. This last report indicated that by mid September,

2,000 to 2,500 fish had been caught which "would take the place of about
100 to 125 caribou."

210 NA, RG 85, Vol. 1266, File 1000/145(5), to Fort Smith from RCMP Detachment Coppermine, 30 April 1959. This report indicated that seven
families, who usually lived inland, had spent the previous winter at Coppermine but were, by spring, requesting assistance in order for them to
return inland. The residents for the centre at this time comprised eleven
families "except in several months when they are sealing and fishing."
This same file at another date (26 March 1957) provided one of the few
reports on the Holman district, indicating six families living at the post, a
number that is consistent with Condon's figures cited in n184.

211 NA, RG 18, Vol. 1985–86/048, Box 56, Economic Conditions of Eskimo
at or near DEWline Sites, Coppermine Detachment Area, 30 May 1959.

212 NA, RG 85, Vol. 1266, File 1000/145(6), Game Conditions Coppermine
District, 17 July 1960.

213 Jenness, *The Life of the Copper Eskimos*, map at end of book.

214 Hearne, *Journey from Prince of Wales*, 96–112.

215 Rasmussen, *Intellectual Culture*, 70.

216 The frequent occurrence of caribou just to the west of Coppermine was
likely due to the presence of the Great Bear Herd, which occupied for
much of each year a largely uninhabited region, except for being visited by
the Coppermine people. Abrahamson et al., *The Copper Eskimos*, 68, map 6.

CHAPTER FOUR

1 Brack and McIntosh, *Keewatin Mainland*, vii–viii.

2 Usher, *Fur Trade Posts*, 141.

3 Bird, *Southampton Island*, 55.

4 Ibid., 64.

5 VanStone, *The Economy and Population*, 2.

6 Ibid.

7 Ibid., 5–6.

8 To gain some appreciation of the impact of the DEWline wages on the
local economy, VanStone, *The Economy and Population*, 9, notes that "in
1957–58 the Hudson's Bay Company store had total sales to the amount
of $91,627, while the value of the fur collection was only $21,832. Local
employment would not be sufficient to account for this difference."

9 Ibid.

10 Author's field notes, Repulse Bay, 196.

11 NA, RG 18, Vol. 3662, File G567–21(2): Patrol to Repulse Bay, Pelly Bay
and Igloolik by dogteam and RC Mission Plane, Submitted 14 April 1948.
This patrol stopped at Repulse Bay on 19 March 1948, which was Easter
Sunday that year. *The World Almanac, 1998*, 656.

12 NA, RG 18, Acc. 85–86/048, File TA 500–8–1–4: Annual Report, Year Ending 31 December 1958, Chesterfield Inlet Detachment.

13 Ibid., To "G" Division, Re: Conditions, Chesterfield Inlet, From Sergeant in Charge, Period 29 July to 30 November 1947.

14 Ibid.

15 Ibid., Conditions Amongst Eskimos, Generally, Education – Chesterfield Inlet District, 16 January 1952.

16 Devine, "Chesterfield Inlet."

17 NA, RG 18, Acc. 85–86/048, File TA 500–8–1–4: Conditions Amongst Eskimos, 16 January 1952.

18 Ibid., Larsen to Director, Northern Administration and Lands Branch, 7 February 1952.

19 Ibid., Conditions Amongst Eskimos, Generally, 15 March 1952.

20 Ibid., Annual Report, Year Ending 31 December 1951. (Submitted 24 April 1952.)

21 Ibid., Annual Report, Year Ending 31 December 1952.

22 Ibid., Annual Report, Year Ending 31 December 1953.

23 Ibid., Annual Report, Year Ending 31 December 1954.

24 NA, RG 85, Vol. 1266, File 1000/158: Chesterfield Inlet, General File (Including Repulse Bay), Memorandum to the Chief of the Arctic Division from Northern Service Officer – Churchill, 1 February 1955.

25 Ibid., Sivertz to Kerr, 19 July 1955.

26 Ibid., To Officer Commanding "G" Division from Constable in Charge, Chesterfield Inlet Detachment, 2 August 1955.

27 Ibid., Larsen to Director, Northern Administration, 17 April 1955.

28 A.C.L. Adams, Acting Chief, Arctic Division wrote to Superintendent H.A. Larsen, on 22 August 1955: "We quite agree with Constable Boone and yourself that the tendency of the Chesterfield Eskimos to congregate around the settlement should be discouraged, but we have come to the conclusion from past experience that unless the local missionaries are prepared to co-operate, the detachment alone would not have much success in making any change" (NA, RG 85, Vol. 1266, File 1000/158).

29 NA, RG 85, Vol. 1266, File 1000/158: To RCMP Chesterfield Inlet Detachment from W.G. Kerr, Re: Discussion held 30 August 1955 between R.C.M.P., R.C. Mission, DNSO, 31 August 1955.

30 Ibid., Memorandum to the Chief of the Arctic Division, Re: Eskimos Chesterfield Inlet, NWT, 25 November 1955.

31 NA, RG 18, 85/86/048 TA 500–8–1–4, RCMP, Annual Report, Year Ending 31 December 1955.

32 Ibid.

33 Ibid., Annual Report, Year Ending 31 December 1956.

34 Ibid.

35 Ibid., From Constable in Charge, Chesterfield Inlet Detachment, to Officer
    Commanding "G" Division, 29 August 1957.
36 Ibid., Annual Report Chesterfield Detachment, Year Ending 31 December
    1957.
37 Ibid.
38 Ibid., Annual Report, Year Ending 31 December 1958. This report de-
    scribes the houses built by the mission as being "well constructed and very
    comfortable." This assessment agrees with my impression of them in 1968,
    when a number were still being occupied (author's field notes, Chester-
    field Inlet, 1968).
39 Ibid., Annual Report, Year Ending 31 December 1959.
40 Included were the groups of the Qairnirmiut, the Harvaqtuurmiut, and the
    Hauniqtuurmiut (Arima, 447–8).
41 While the people of the lower Back River–Chantrey Inlet region were part
    of the Netsilik "tribe" (Balikci, "Netsilik," 415), by the 1950s those of
    the upper Back River came from Netsilik and Copper Eskimo groups
    (NA, RG 18, 85–86/048).
42 Usher, *Fur Trade Posts*, 144.
43 NA, RG 18, Vol. 3662–G567–21, File Y21, Patrol Reports, Chesterfield Inlet
    Detachment; NA, RG 18, Vol. 3661, File G567–8, Patrol Reports, Baker
    Lake Detachment.
44 NA, RG 18, Vol. 3662–G567–21.
45 Ibid., Vol. 3661, File G567–8.
46 NA, RG 18, Vol. 3661, File G567–8: Report of Patrol to Garry Lake by
    Norseman Aircraft, 25 March 1949.
47 Ibid., Report of Patrol to Garry Lake by Norseman, 4 April 1949.
48 NA, RG 18, Acc. 85–86/048, Vol. 55, File TA 501–8–1–(2). Annual Report,
    Baker Lake Detachment, Year Ending 31 December 1951.
49 NA, RG 18, Vol. 3661, File G567–8. Patrol to Kazan River District and Re-
    turn, 21 February 1951.
50 NA, RG 18, Acc. 85–86/048, Vol. 55, File TA 1500–8–1(2): Annual Report,
    Year Ending 31 December 1951.
51 Ibid., Annual Report, Year Ending 31 December 1952.
52 NA, RG 18, Vol. 3661, File G567–8. Report of Patrol, Baker Lake to Aber-
    deen Lake and Return, 3 April 1953.
53 NA, RG 18, Acc. 85–86/048, File TA 500–8–1(2), Vol. 55: Annual Report,
    Period Ending 31 December 1954.
54 Ibid.
55 Ibid. It is not clear whether this report of deaths is based on rumour, or, if
    true, what proportion was due to sickness and what to starvation. Vallee,
    Kabloona and Eskimo, 5, lists thirty-seven deaths from starvation in the
    period 1949–58 in the Baker Lake trading district. If one deducts the sev-
    enteen lost in 1958, the difference may indeed refer to this report.

56 Tester and Kulchyski, *Tammarniit*, 238–73; several files in Record Group 18 (RCMP Reports) and Record Group 85 (Northern Administration) contain information on the situation around Garry and Pelly Lakes for 1957–58.

57 The scattering of people in the district created one of the difficulties of this tragedy, that of reaching Inuit for the purpose of relieving possible destitute conditions.

58 Flights to the region were made to this airstrip, and a building had been erected there to hold the supplies which were flown in. The fire that destroyed it was later described as one of the chief factors of the tragedy (see the main text).

59 NA, RG 18, Vol. 3661, File G567–8(1): Patrol Report via RCAF, Garry Lake Destitute Relief Assistance, 22 March 1954.

60 Ibid., Report dated 2 April 1955.

61 Ibid.

62 NA, RG 18, Vol. 3661, File G567–8(1): Patrol Report, Baker Lake Detachment area, 27 March 1956.

63 Ibid., Patrol Report, 7 May 1956.

64 Ibid., Part 2, Patrol Report, Baker Lake to Garry Lake and Return, 2 April 1957.

65 Ibid.

66 NA, RG 85, Vol. 1447, File 1000/159, 10 August 1957.

67 Ibid., 13 August 1957.

68 Ibid., 4 December 1957.

69 NA, RG 85, Vol. 1447, File 1000/159(3). Memorandum for Chief, Arctic Division: Garry Lake Eskimos, from D.E. Wilkinson, NSO Baker Lakes, NWT, June 1958.

70 While Tester and Kulchyski, in *Tammarniit*, in my opinion, come down too severely upon the principals in government service involved in this tragedy, they have injected a note of moderation in their analysis. After assigning blame to several officials, they write: "But then, it is easy through the distance and comfort of archival documents to reach such conclusions. That it was far more difficult in the cold, dark winter circumstances of Baker Lake in 1958 to know where the greatest priorities should lie, especially given the events which preceded this starvation, is without doubt" (271).

71 NA, RG 18, Acc. 85–86/048: Annual Report, Year Ending 31 December 1955.

72 Ibid., Annual Report, Period Ending 31 December 1956.

73 Ibid.

74 NA, RG 18, Acc. 85–86/048: Conditions Amongst Eskimos, Aberdeen Lake, NWT, 8 February 1958.

75 Ibid., Annual Report, Year Ending 31 December 1958; also reports of 2 February and 1 March 1959.

76 NA, RG 18, Vol. 3661–8(2). To O.C. "G" Division From Constable in Charge, Baker Lake Detachment, 16 April 1959.

77 Ibid.

78 After the famine of 1958, the Garry–Pelly Lake people, with the exception of two families, were moved to a camp about ten miles from Baker Lake, but in September 1959 they expressed the wish to return (NA, RG 85, Vol. 1382, File 1012–13(5), NSO S.A.H. Dobbs to Regional Administrator, Churchill, 4 September 1959). However, at year's end it was reported that no one lived at the lakes (NA, RG 18, Acc. 85–86/048, Vol. 55, File TA 500–8–1(2), Annual Report, Period Ending 31 December 1959.

79 NA, RG 85, Vol. 1382, File 1012–13(5), Relocating of Eskimos to Schultz Lake NWT, 7 October 1959.

80 NA, RG 85, Vol. 1382, File 1012–13(5), Relocation of Eskimos to Schultz Lake, NWT, 7 October 1959.

81 NA, RG 18, Acc. 85–86/048, Vol. 55, Annual Report, Year Ending 31 December 1959

82 Ibid.

83 NA, RG 85, Vol. 1382, File 1012–13(5), Patrol to Baker Lake area, 15–21 December. Report by R.L. Kennedy, NSO, 22 December 1958.

84 Birket-Smith, *The Caribou Eskimos*, Part I: 59–66, and the map in the flyleaf indicate only the Padlirmiut (or Padliqmiut) as inhabiting the southern interior. Gabus, *Vie et Coutumes*, is credited with identifying the Ahiarmiut; see also Arima, "Caribou Eskimo," 447; Burch, "The Caribou/Wild Reindeer," 366.

85 Usher, *Fur Trade Posts*, 141–2.

86 NA, RG 18, Vol. 3991, File G567–8, Patrol Reports, Baker Lake Detachment.

87 NA, RG 18, Vol. 3663, File G567–31, Patrol Reports, Eskimo Point Detachment.

88 Ibid.

89 Harper, *Caribou Eskimos*, 51–3. This account deals with the organization of relief flights out of Brochet, Manitoba by Dr Robert F. Yule. The large amounts of food and equipment brought in to alleviate this famine were remarkable (NA, RG 18, Vol. 3663, File G567–31(1), Patrol by Airplane Eskimo Point to Nueltin Lake, Upper Kazan River and Return, 24 August 1948).

90 NA, RG 18, Acc. 85–86/048, File TA 500–8–1: Conditions of Natives, Eskimo Point, 4 February 1950.

91 Ibid., Conditions of Natives, Eskimo Point, 20 January 1951.

92 Ibid.

93 Usher, *Fur Trade Posts*, 141.

94 NA, RG 18, Acc. 85–86/048: Conditions of Natives, Annual Report, Year Ending 31 December 1951.

95 Ibid., Annual Report, Year Ending 31 December 1952.

96 Ibid., Annual Report, Year Ending 31 December 1953.

97 Ibid., Annual Report, Year Ending 31 December 1954.

98 Ibid., Annual Report, Year Ending 31 December 1955.

99 The files can be found in Record Groups 18, 22, and 85 of the National Archives, as well as in the Alexander Stevenson Fonts of the Prince of Wales Heritage Museum in Yellowknife, NWT. Published works include Mowat, *The Desperate People*, Tester and Kulchyski, Marcus, and Csonka.

100 This estimate is based on census material from the beginning of the 1950s, before Inuit from other regions moved to Eskimo Point and before the exodus of Caribou Eskimo to Rankin Inlet, as revealed in disk list registrations for the E1 or Eskimo Point subregion. Thus, a 1 January 1951 census showed 499 Caribou Eskimo (NA, RG 85, File 66, 1951 census, 1 February 1951). To these numbers can be added a few people who were living in the Yathkyed Lake district, who are listed in the E2 or Baker Lake subregion.

101 This summary is based on the following sources: NA, RG 85, Vol. 1349, File 1000/179(3) (see especially Memorandum from L.C.A.O. Hunt to Mr Cunningham, 26 January 1959); Sivertz to Deputy Minister, 9 March 1959; NA, RG 18, Vol. 3663, File G567–31, Part 2, Patrol Reports Eskimo Point Detachment, 1956–58; PWNHC, Stevenson Fonts (especially Memorandum for Director, 20 October 1958, Re: Starvation among Eskimos in the winter of 1957–58, Box 24–6).

102 Usher, *Fur Trade Posts*, 141, 143.

103 NA, RG 85, Vol. 1511, File 179(2), Kerr to Chief, Arctic Division, 12 May 1957.

104 NA, RG 22, Vol. 545, Memorandum for the Deputy Minister from G. Rowley, 22 January 1958.

105 PWNHC, Stevenson Fonts, File 24–2. Memorandum for Mr Kerr, Eskimos, Henik Lake, from J.P. Richards, 7 March 1958: "I agree that in the circumstances, moving the Eskimos to Eskimo Point was the desirable thing to do."

106 For Yathkyed Lake, this estimate is given for 1959 (NA, RG 18, Acc. 85–86/044, Box 55, Conditions Amongst Eskimos, 18 March 1959). For Padlei, the number relates to 1960 (NA, RG 85, Vol. 1951, File A1000/150, Memorandum for the Administrator of the Arctic, from R.L. Kennedy, Regional Administrator, Churchill, 9 May 1960).

107 NA, RG 18, Acc. 85–86, Vol. 56, File TA – 500–20: Game Conditions Eskimo Point, for Year Ending 30 June 1958.

108 Ibid., Game Conditions for Year Ending 30 June 1959.

109 NA, RG 85, Vol. 1951, File A1000/150, Report on Padlei by Joan Ryan, n.d.

110 VanStone and Oswalt, *The Caribou Eskimos*, 22.

111 NA, RG 18, Acc. 85–86/044, Box 55, Conditions Amongst Eskimos, 18 March 1959.

112 Oswalt and VanStone, "The Future of the Caribou Eskimos," 28.

113 Ibid., 7.

114 Ibid., 4–8.

115 Ibid., "The Future of the Caribou Eskimos," 162.

116 Burch, "The Caribou Inuit," 131.

117 Dailey and Dailey, *The Eskimo of Rankin Inlet*, 1.

118 Ibid., 4.

119 NA, RG 85, Vol. 1268, File 1000/184(1), Rankin Inlet, General File: A. Kelso Roberts to Hon. Robert E. Winters, 21 April 1953; Roberts to Winters, 18 May 1953; E.P. Murphy, Deputy Minister, Department of Public Works to General Young, 18 August 1953; Young to F.K. Smith, Chairman, National Harbours Board, 13 October 1953; Murphy to Young, 27 October 1953.

120 Williamson, *Eskimo Underground*, 91.

121 NA, RG 85, Vol. 1268: File 1000/184(1): To Officer in Charge "G" Division from A/Cpl. I/C Chesterfield Inlet Detachment, 11 March 1956.

122 Ibid., B.G. Sivertz to H.A. Larsen, 12 April 1956.

123 Ibid., W.G. Kerr to Chief, Arctic Division, Re: Employment of Eskimos – Rankin Inlet, NWT, 16 April 1956.

124 Ibid., Kerr to Chief, Arctic Division, 23 April 1956.

125 Ibid., Kerr to Chief, Arctic Division, 16 November 1956.

126 Ibid., Cunningham to Deputy Minister, 26 February 1957.

127 Ibid., Kerr to Chief, Arctic Division, 30 March 1957.

128 Ibid., Memorandum for Mr Phillips, Interim Report by D. Snowden, 12 April 1957.

129 NA, RG 85, Vol. 1268, File 1000/184(2): W.W. Weber to R.G. Robertson, 1 April 1957.

130 Ibid., C.B. de Capelin, Chief, Minings and Lands Branch, Memorandum for the Director, 23 April 1957.

131 Ibid., Memorandum for Mr Phillips, Mining Operations – Rankin Inlet (Report of Meeting, Director and Dr W.W. Weber), 25 April 1957.

132 Ibid., J. Patry to W.J. Wood, Regional Superintendent, Indian and Northern Health Services, 31 May 1957; A. Easton to W.J. Wood, n.d.

133 Ibid., W.J. Wood to Director, Department of National Health and Welfare, 14 June 1957.

134 Ibid., W.W. Weber to Robertson, 22 October 1957.

135 Ibid., Kerr to Chief, Arctic Division, Re: Conference with Easton, 20 November 1957.

136 Ibid.

137 NA, RG 85, Vol. 1268, File 1000/184(2): Monthly Report for the Month of December 1957, from Welfare Teacher, Rankin Inlet.

138 Ibid., Report of Dr Patry, from W.J. Wood to Director, Arctic Division,
     June 1957. This report indicated 169 at Rankin as compared to "about
     100 at Chesterfield"; by August, the estimated population of Rankin was
     200 (Ibid., W.W. Weber to Director, DNA and ND, 30 August 1957) and
     continued to grow in the autumn of 1957.

139 Ibid., W.W. Weber to Robertson, 3 January 1958.

140 Ibid., Reference to the following: Robertson to Weber, 6 January 1958;
     J.P. Richards to R.A.J. Phillips, 16 January 1958; Dr P.E. Moore to Direc-
     tor, Northern Administration and Lands Branch, 17 January 1958; Sivertz
     to Moore, 21 January 1958.

141 Dailey and Dailey, *The Eskimo of Rankin Inlet.*

142 Ibid., 10–19.

143 Ibid., 20.

144 Ibid., 63.

145 Ibid., 66.

146 Ibid., 65.

147 Mowat, *The Desperate People*, 283–6.

148 Dailey and Dailey, *The Eskimo of Rankin Inlet*, 78.

149 Ibid., 95.

150 Ibid., 104.

151 PWNHC, Stevenson Fonts, Box 35–8, Rankin Inlet, P.W. Grant, Area Ad-
     ministrator, 29 November 1959.

152 Ibid.

153 PWNHC, Stevenson Fonts, File 24–6, Relocation, Keewatin Inuit, 1956–
     60, Memorandum to the Cabinet, from Minister, Department of North-
     ern Affairs and National Development, 9 May 1958.

154 NA, RG 85, Vol. 1659, File NR 4–2–4.

155 Ibid., First Meeting of Keewatin Committee, 23 May 1958.

156 PWNHC, Stevenson Fonts, Minutes of the Ninth Meeting of the Commit-
     tee on Eskimo Affairs, 26 May 1958.

157 Ibid., Comments by Father Ducharme and Bishop March.

158 Ibid., Comment of B.G. Sivertz.

159 Ibid., Comment of R.A.J. Phillips.

160 NA, RG 85, NR 4–4–4: Minutes of Second Meeting of the Keewatin Com-
     mittee, 27 May 1958.

161 Ibid., Minutes of Third Meeting of the Keewatin Committee, 30 May 1958.

162 Ibid., Minutes of the Fourth Meeting of the Keewatin Committee, 9 June
     1958.

163 Ibid., Minutes of the Fifth Meeting of the Keewatin Committee, 20 June
     1958.

164 PWNHC, Stevenson Fonts, File 13–1, Memorandum for members of the
     Keewatin Committee, Report on Proposed Sites for Keewatin Community
     at Tavani and Whale Cove, by F.J. Neville, 11 August 1958.

165 Ibid.

166 Brack and McIntosh, *Keewatin Mainland*, 75. They comment on game conditions in the Whale Cove district as follows: "The site was chosen for its several favourable attributes. The floe edge is normally 1 ½ to 3 miles off ... The Tavani area has long been reported to be a wintering ground for caribou, herds or bands numbering up to 2000 having been recorded. Within a radius of about 30 miles of the settlement are many lakes in which fish are plentiful, and the mouth of the Wilson River is also reported to be a good fishing area. Whales frequent the vicinity of Whale Cove during the summer months."

167 NA, RG 85, NR 4–2–4. Minutes of the Sixth Meeting of the Keewatin Committee, 28 July 1958.

168 Vallee, *Kabloona and Eskimo*, 49.

169 NA, RG 85, NR 4–2–4. Minutes of the Sixth Meeting of the Keewatin Committee, 28 July 1958.

170 Tester and Kulchyski, *Tammarniit*, 286–90.

171 Williamson, *Eskimo Underground*, 94.

172 NA, RG 85, Vol. 1071, File 251–6(2). Memorandum for Mr Walton – Great Whale River – Whale Cove, from Alexander Stevenson, 30 October 1958.

173 Ibid., Distribution of Whale Cove Families as of 14 October 1958, by D.W. Grant.

174 PWNHC, Stevenson Fonts, File 24–6, Memorandum for the Director, Keewatin Re-establishment Project from C.M. Bolger, 24 February 1958.

175 Ibid.

176 Ibid.

177 NA, RG 18, Acc. 85–86/048, TA 500–8–1–6, Conditions Amongst Eskimos, Eskimo Point Detachment, Conditions Amongst Eskimos, Whale Cove, 7 October 1959.

178 Tester and Kulchyski, *Tammarniit*, 305.

179 Vallee, *Kabloona and Eskimo*, 51.

180 For example, Tester and Kulchyski, *Tammarniit*, 274–305.

181 Ibid., 305.

182 NA, RG 18, Acc. 85–86/048: Conditions Amongst Eskimos, Whale Cove, 7 October 1959.

183 Ibid.

184 NA, RG 18, Acc. 85–96/048, Conditions Amongst Eskimos, Whale Cove, Patrols to Whale Cove 10–12–59 and 11–12–59, 12 December 1959.

185 PWNHC, Vol. 1/17 Minutes of the Special Meeting of the Council of the Northwest Territories, 20 January 1949.

186 Banfield, "Preliminary Investigation," 38.

187 NA, RG 85, Vol. 1250, File 401–22–5(1), W. Winston Mair, Chief, Canadian Wildlife Service to F.D.G. Cunningham, Director, Northern Adminis-

tration and Lands Branch, 25 November 1956; Technical Committee for Caribou Conservation, Agenda of First Meeting 26 February 1956.

188 NA, RG 85, Vol. 1251–401–22(5), Minutes of the Third Meeting of the Administrative Committee of the Caribou Conservation Committee, 3–4 October 1957.

189 Ibid.

190 NA, RG 85, Vol. 1251, File 401–22(5), R.G. Robertson, Commissioner of the Northwest Territories to Alvin Hamilton, Minister of Northern Affairs and National Resources, 25 November 1957.

191 Clarke, *A Biological Investigation*, 194.

192 Clancy, "Caribou, Fur and the Resource Frontier."

193 Burch, "The Caribou/Wild Reindeer," 366.

194 MacKinnon, "The 1958 Government Policy." 165. As MacKinnon notes on page 166, among the policy changes brought about by the tragedies was the encouragement of in-gathering at the villages on the west coast of Hudson Bay.

CHAPTER FIVE

1 This version, as agreed upon by the council, represents a streamlining of the act, which was passed by Parliament as follows: "An Act to provide for Family Allowances (assented 15 August 1944) to provide the following monthly sums: $5.00 for children under the age of 6; $6.00 for children ages 6–9; $7.00 for those 10–12; and $8.00 from age 13 through 15." *Canada Yearbook*, 1945, 341–2.

2 NA, RG 85, File 1125/163(1), Family Allowances, NWT, General and Policy. Made at meeting of the NWT Council 23 March 1946.

3 *Canada Yearbook*, 1950, 271.

4 NA, RG 85, Vol. 1125, File 163(1): Cantley to Gibson, 6 April 1946; Gibson to Cantley, 9 April 1946; Cantley to Gibson, 11 May 1946; Gibson to Cantley, 17 May 1946; Cantley to Gibson, 1 February 1947; Gibson to Cantley, 7 February 1947.

5 Ibid., Wright to Craig, 16 May 1946.

6 Ibid., Gibson to Cantley, 17 May 1946.

7 Ibid., Reference to Bill 308, "An Act to Amend The Family Allowances act of 1944."

8 Ibid.

9 NA, RG 85, Vol. 1125, File 163(1): Gibson to Chesshire, 17 February 1947.

10 Ibid., Gibson to D.J. Masters, Officer Commanding "G" Division, 28 February 1947.

11 Ibid., Reference to meeting held in Moore's office, Wright to Gibson, 21 March 1947.

12 Ibid.

13 Ibid., Gibson to Commissioner, RCMP, 5 April 1947.

14 Ibid., Extracts from the minutes of the 171st Session of the Northwest Territories Council held on 15 April 1947.

15 NA, RG 22, Vol. 254, File 40–8–1(4), Minutes of the Fifth Meeting of the Committee on Eskimo Affairs, 29 November 1954; PWNHC, Stevenson Fonts, File 17–7, Minutes of the Twelfth Meeting of the Committee on Eskimo Affairs, 10–11 April 1961. It was my observation in the field that in the more remote trading districts, where effective administration remained in the hands of the traders, the voucher system remained in effect into the 1960s.

16 Damas, "The Contact-Traditional Horizon," 122. The data is from HBCA, AG 3/35–1, and HBCA, AG 3/35–4.

17 Ibid., 123.

18 To give some idea of the growth in applying the Old Age Assistance Act, together with its austere implications, a Special Meeting of the Council of the NWT, held 20 May 1948, is revealing. It was indicated that $8 a month was being issued to "115 Eskimos" at that time. The next year at the meeting, 187th meeting of the Council, on 20 January 1949, it was concluded that this amount "has met with general satisfaction in the field" but, that the age of eligibility "should be lowered 10, or at least 5 years, due to the strenuous life they lead."

19 Newman, *Renegade in Power*, 218. (citation of Diefenbaker's campaign speech, 12 February 1958).

20 Ibid., 317.

21 Comments on the "vision" made by Newman are appropriate: "the results never came within a light-year of the expectation aroused by the Prime Minister's 1958 campaign oratory" (ibid., 218); "one irony of the vision's brief flowering was that Canada's Eskimos, who might have expected to be among its prime beneficiaries, were only slightly better off at the end of the 'Diefenbaker Years'" (ibid., 233). Nevertheless, the following years' increasing budgets, the legacy of the Diefenbaker years, rapidly improved conditions in the north by the end of the 1960s.

22 PWNHC, Stevenson Fonts, Box 13, Minutes of the Tenth Meeting of the Committee on Eskimo Affairs, 25 Mai 1959.

23 *Canada Yearbook*, 1969, 1061.

24 Rea, *The Political Economy*, 352.

25 NA, RG 85, Vol. 1059, File 251–1. Conditions on Southampton Island. This report of 30 April 1943 by T.H. Manning, who had been appointed as liaison with U.S. Forces and civilians around Coral Harbour, listed the following concerns: (1) indifference to scabies; (2) neglect during a meningitis epidemic; (3) lack of education facilities for the Inuit; (4) traders exploiting the Inuit. D.L. McKeand, then deputy commissioner of the Bureau of Northwest Territories and Yukon, was the author of the remark regarding

"rumour" and "gossip" in a memorandum to Gibson. He was, however, concerned with the accusation that the local trader was allowed to "exploit the Eskimos" (ibid., 6 May 1943). R.H. Chesshire finished his response to Gibson's conveyance of the American complaints with: "In conclusion, may I say that we are probably just as qualified to express opinions upon the conditions and circumstances of negroes and sharecroppers in the Southern States as are these casual visitors in expressing their opinions concerning the Eskimos of the North" (ibid, Chesshire to Gibson, 10 June 1943).

26 Cantley dismissed the Danish administration as being "based on the ideal of a self-contained native community, almost completely segregated from derogatory outside influences and peacefully pursuing its primitive native ways." He pointed out that the Greenlanders were "really a hybrid race that is much more European than Eskimo" ("Survey of Economic Conditions," 6). With regard to the U.S. administration of its natives, he thought that the administration had been "aided by large, private involvement" (ibid).

27 Rea, *The Political Economy*, 357.

28 NA, RG 22, Vol. 254, File 40–21(3). Memorandum for the Deputy Minister from Cunningham, Eskimo Loan Fund, 18 March 1953.

29 NA, RG 85, Vol. 1382, File 1012–13(3). Memorandum for the Director. Creating new Communities, from W. Rudnicki, Chief, Welfare Division, 13 December 1960.

30 This was entirely consistent with the original intent of the fund as a revolving and self-sustaining fund (NA, RG 22, Vol. 847, File 40–8–7, Enclosure, n.d.). But see discussions in Marcus, *Relocating Eden*, 202–6, and Tester and Kulchyski, *Tammarniit*, 166–74.

31 NA, RG 22, Vol. 254, File 40–21, Pt. 3, Memorandum for Deputy Minister from Director Cunningham, Eskimo Loan Fund, and reply by Robertson, 17 February 1954.

32 NA, RG 22, Vol. 847, File 40–8–7(4): To Governor General from Minister of Northern Affairs and National Resources, Granting of Power to Commissioner of Northwest Territories on 28 August 1963.

33 Ibid., Summary of Eskimo Loan Fund (Enclosure), 1 April 1966–31 March 1967, n.d.

34 Ibid.

35 NA, RG 22, Vol. 847, File 40–8–7(4), Pt. 4: To Minister from E.A. Cote, Deputy Minister, 14 April 1967.

36 Ibid., Eskimo Loan Fund, 1 April 1969 to 31 March 1970.

37 Ibid., To Minister from E.A. Cote, Deputy Minister, 14 April 1967.

38 Grygier, *A Long Way From Home*, 67.

39 PWNHC, Vol. 1/13 Northwest Territories Council, 160th Session, 13 February 1945.

40 Grygier, *A Long Way From Home*, 67–8. Beginning in 1949 the western Central Arctic was being reached out of Aklavik as far east as Spence Bay by

aircraft. Between 1950 and 1960, 28,709 x-rays were taken in the Canadian Arctic (ibid., 82).

41 PWNHC, Vol. 1/1 Northwest Territories Council, 13th Session, 15 January 1930.

42 NA, RG 85, Vol. 1871, File 550–1(2): Bishop Flemming to Gibson, 15 January 1944.

43 Ibid., Doyle to McKeand, 2 February 1944.

44 PWNHC, Stevenson Fonts, File 38–2, Eastern Arctic Patrol 1929–49. Considerations in Planning Medical Care of Eskimos by J.G. Wright, 17 January 1945.

45 Ibid. It should be noted that Dr Otto Schaefer, who served as physician at the Pangnirtung Hospital in 1955–57, travelled many miles by dogsled visiting Inuit in outlying camps (Grygier, *A Long Way From Home*, 25–6, 28).

46 NA, RG 85, Vol. 298, File 40–8–1: R.G. Robertson, Discussion with Bishop Marsh, 11 January 1954; Bishop Donald B. Marsh to Louis St Laurent, Prime Minister of Canada, 10 November 1954.

47 Ibid., Memorandum for Deputy Minister from B. Sivertz. Comments on Bishop Marsh's letter to Prime Minister, 26 November 1954.

48 Grygier, *A Long Way From Home*, 55.

49 At the twentieth session of the Council of the Northwest Territories held in Ottawa 16–24 January 1961, Dr P.E. Moore, Director of Indian and Northern Health Services, outlined the difficulties of attracting medical men to the north: "it would be necessary to provide a more adequate income than offered by the Civil Service Commission for salaried and professional staff." Later, in the January 1962 or twenty-second session of the Council, the figure of $31,474 was presented. It should be noted that this figure included overhead expenses of $12,064, so that the actual salary proposed was $19,350. It was argued that this figure compared well with DEWline salaries, which were represented as $18,000.

50 Northern Health Services, "Record of Health Conditions," 9.

51 Graham-Cummings, "Northern Health Services," 524.

52 Author's field notes, Perry River Region, 1963.

53 Northern Health Services, "Record of Health Conditions," 9.

54 Among these were the sputum surveys, Mantoux tests and home chemotherapy and chemoprophylaxis. Grygier, *A Long Way From Home*, 135.

55 Department of Northern Affairs and National Resources (Indian and Northern Health Services), "Eskimo Mortality and Housing."

56 Ibid., 5.

57 Ibid.

58 Ibid., 6.

59 Ibid., 31, 48.

60 Ibid., 52.

61 Ibid., 58–60, 67–9.

62 Ibid., 61–5; 60–70; PWNHC, Stevenson Fonts, File 49–8. Report of Branch Housing Committee, Policy Paper on Housing for Northern Residents, n.d.

63 PWNHC, Stevenson Fonts, File 13–2, Minutes of the Twelfth Meeting of the Committee on Eskimo Affairs, 10–11 April 1961.

64 Ibid., File 49–8. Report of Policy Paper on Housing.

65 Ibid. Report of Policy Paper on Housing.

66 Ibid. Report of Policy Paper on Housing.

67 Ibid. Report of Policy Paper on Housing.

68 PWNHC, Stevenson Fonts, File 13–2. Minutes of the Tenth Meeting of the Committee on Eskimo Affairs, 29 May 1959.

69 Ibid., Minutes of the Twelfth Meeting of the Committee on Eskimo Affairs, 10–11 April 1961.

70 Ibid., Minutes of the Tenth Meeting of the Committee on Eskimo Affairs, 29 May 1959.

71 Ibid.

72 Thomas and Thompson, *Eskimo Housing as Planned Cultural Change.*

73 Duffy, *The Road to Nunavut,* 45–6.

74 NA, RG 85, Vol. 1505, File 600–1–1 (2): Report of an Educational Survey Conducted in the Mackenzie District of the Canadian Northwest Territories During the Months of July and August 1944.

75 Ibid.

76 Ibid., Cummings to A.J. Baxte, 3 January 1945.

77 Ibid., Baxte to Cummings, 6 January 1945; Cummings to Gibson; Deputy Minister to Moore, 9 January 1945; J. Troceillien to Moore, 15 July 1945.

78 Ibid., J.C. Wright to Gibson, 19 November 1946.

79 NA, RG 85, Vol. 1506, File 600–1–1 (2A): Gibson to Cummings, 26 August 1946.

80 Ibid., Wright to Gibson, 19 November 1945.

81 Ibid.

82 Ibid., Gibson to Mielke, 2 December 1947.

83 Ibid.

84 NA, RG 85, Vol. 1506, File C00–1–1 (3): E.A. Grantham to Mr Doyle, Expenditures on Education in the Northwest Territories and Northern Quebec, 5 February 1951.

85 Ibid., Gibson to Wright, 27 January 1950; Gibson to Superintendent of Education, Yellowknife, NWT, 14 January 1950.

86 Ibid., Eastern Arctic Inspection Flight by S.J. Bailey, 9 April 1950.

87 Ibid.

88 NA, RG 85, Vol. 1506, File 600–1–1 (4), Gibson to Wright, n.d. (probably early 1951).

89 Ibid.

90 Ibid., Jacobson, "Eskimo Education," 27 October 1954.

91 Dates for the east Central Arctic and the Keewatin District are from Mouat, "Education in the Arctic District," 4, and for the west Central Arctic, from Treude, "Studies in Settlement Development," 56. (Note Treude's alternate usage of the area designations used here.)

92 NA, RG 85, Vol. 1435, File 600–1–1(4): Memorandum, for Director from the Administrator of the Mackenzie, 6 January 1964.

93 Correspondence included: Memorandum to Administrator of the Mackenzie from Director: School and Hostel Building Plan on the Arctic Coast, 12 February 1964; Memorandum for the Director from the Administrator of the Mackenzie, 20 February 1964; Director to Administrator of the Mackenzie, 13 March 1964, and 16 March 1964; Acting Director to Mr Thorsteinson, 13 May 1964; Administrator of the Mackenzie to Mr. Gillis, 27 May 1964; Hodgkinson to Director; 8 June 1964; Thorsteinson to Chief, Engineering Division. 15 June 1964; Director to Adminstrator of the Mackenzie, 15 June 1964; For Director from E.J. Orange, 29 June 1964.

94 Ibid., Director to Administrator of the Mackenzie, 28 July 1964.

95 NA, RG 85, Vol. 1435, File 600–1–5(5), Stevenson to Director, 9 December 1964.

96 NA, RG 85, Vol. 1985/220, File A 1000/138(2), General File, Igloolik.

97 PWNHC, GFNA, File T101–5, Vol. 1: Branch Policy Directive No. 32, n.d.

98 Ibid.

99 Ibid.

100 Ibid.

101 Ibid., Branch Policy Directive No. 1, 6 May 1959.

102 Ibid., Branch Policy Directive No. 3, n.d.

103 Ibid., Branch Policy Directive, No. 10, 23 June 1961.

104 Ibid.

105 Ibid., Branch Policy Directive No. 12, 21 September 1961.

106 Ibid., Branch Policy Directive No. 13, 25 October 1961.

107 PWNHC, Stevenson Fonts, File 17–7, Policy Inuit, 1935–1959. In this vein, Stevenson wrote, "The objective of the government policy ... is relatively easy to define, ie; to give Eskimos the same rights, privileges and opportunities and responsibilities as all other Canadians – in short, to enable them to follow the national life of Canada" (4 October 1962).

108 PWNHC, GFNA File T101–6, Vol. 1: Branch Directive No. 18, n.d.

109 Ibid., Branch Policy Directive No. 32.

110 PWNHC, GFNA 2/197, Town Planning Council, General File, Community Planning Group, 15 October 1962.

111 Ibid.

112 Vallee et al., "Contemporary Canadian Inuit," 670.

CHAPTER SIX

1 NA, RG 18, Acc. 85–85/048, File TA 500–8–5, Conditions Amongst Eskimos, Grise Fiord.
2 Marcus, *Relocating Eden*, 67–123; Tester and Kulchyski, *Tammarniit*, 102–
204.
3 Freeman, "The Grise Fiord Project," 676–82; "Adaptive Innovation Among
Recent Immigrants," 769–81; Paine, "Tolerance and Rejection of Patron
Roles in an Eskimo Settlement," in *Patrons and Brokers in the East Arctic*, 34–54.
4 Freeman, "The Grise Fiord Project," 678.
5 Rick Riewe, "Inuit Land Use," 236, describes the regions around Grise
Fiord as "the polar desert, probably the least productive land in North
America." However, with further reading of this and other writings by
Riewe, it becomes apparent that he is referring to the terrestrial rather
than the marine potential of the region. Marcus, *Relocating Eden*, 209, ex-
trapolates Riewe's comparison of Port Harrison with Eskimo Point with regard to resources based on correspondence of latitude. This comparison
cannot stand because of the superior caribou populations on the west side
of Hudson Bay, whereas caribou on the east side had been depleted for
some years before the relocation project. In spite of their generally negative view of the High Arctic relocations, Tester and Kulchyski, *Tammarniit*,
156, concede that the hunting ranges of the Grise Fiord colony "were the
richest in the high Arctic."
6 Freeman, "Tolerance and Rejection," 39–40.
7 NA, RG 18, Acc. 85–86/048, Vol. 53, File TA 500–8–1–5, Grise Fiord Detachment: Annual Report, Year Ending 31 December 1959.
8 Ibid., Annual Report, Year Ending 31 December 1962.
9 Freeman, "The Grise Fiord Project," 679.
10 NA, RG 18, Acc. 84–86/048, Vol. 53, File TA 500–8–1–5, Grise Fiord Detachment: Annual Report, Year Ending 31 December 1967.
11 Ibid., Annual Report, Year Ending 31 December 1962.
12 Ibid., Annual Report, Year Ending 31 December 1967.
13 Ibid., Annual Report, Year Ending 31 December 1966; also comments in
Reports of 1967 and 1968.
14 Ibid., Annual Reports of 1961, 1962, 1963, 1964, 1966, 1967, 1968.
15 Freeman, "The Grise Fiord Project," 681.
16 Ibid., 682.
17 Ibid., 677. The table in Freeman was taken from RCMP records cited in an
unpublished report by Riewe, "Inuit Land Use."
18 NA, RG 18, Acc. 85–86/048, Box 55, File TA – 500–8–14.
19 Bissett, *Resolute*.
20 NA, RG 85, Vol. 254, File 40–8–1 (3), Memorandum for the Deputy Minister, Eskimo Loan Fund, 18 March 1953.

21 NA, RG 18, Acc. 85–86/048, Vol. 53, File TA 500–8–1–5, Grise Fiord Detachment: Annual Report, Year Ending 31 December 1966.

22 Ibid.

23 Bissett, *Resolute*, 107. Before 1963, there were no skidoos in use. By 1966–67, there were eighteen, as compared to only three dog teams.

24 Bissett, *Resolute*, 123–4, 129–30.

25 Ibid., 76–7, 84.

26 Tester and Kulchyski, *Tammarniit*, 167–8.

27 NA, RG 18, Acc. 85–86. Vol. 55, File TA – 500–8–14, Annual Report, Resolute Detachment Year Ending 31 December 1968.

28 Ibid.

29 Bissett, *Resolute*, 65.

30 NA, RG 18, Acc. 85–86. Vol. 55, File TA – 500–8–14, Resolute Detachment. Annual Report, Year Ending 31 December 1963.

31 Bissett, *Resolute*, 65. However, the annual report of 31 December 1961 makes a reference to this: "Morale has been very high this year. Two Eskimo families at their own request were allowed to return to Resolute as they found life there more to their liking than at Churchill. (Name omitted) reluctantly moved to Port Harrison because his step father and father-in-law asked him to. He expressed a desire to return to Resolute in the future." The difficulty in returning to Port Harrison was due to the roundabout routing via Montreal and the attendant expense.

32 Bissett, *Resolute*, 89.

33 Ibid., 90.

34 NA, RG 18, Acc. 85–86, Vol. 55, File TA 500–8–5, Annual Report, Grise Fiord Detachment, Year Ending 31 December 1965.

35 Bissett, *Resolute*, 85.

36 NA, RG 18, Acc. 85–86, Vol. 55, File TA – 500–8–14, Annual Report, Resolute Detachment, Year Ending on 31 December 1961.

37 Tester and Kulchyski, *Tammarniit*, 136–204; Marcus, *Relocating Eden*, 67–123. Tester and Kulchyski, *Tammarniit*, 204, recognize that "the 1960s brought about many significant changes. No longer could native people be moved about at the behest of northern administration and Hudson's Bay Company officials." The authors attribute these changes to the influence of Inuit on associated policy. I would differ in this regard since, in my view, it was not until much later that this was true. Rather, shifts in policy that were, in largest measure, initiated from within the civil service were behind these and other changes in the sixties.

38 NA, RG 18, Acc. 85–86, Vol. 55, File TA 500–8–14. Conditions Amongst Eskimos, Generally Annual Report of the Resolute Detachment, Year Ending 31 December 1960.

39 The friction between the two elements of the Inuit population described in chapter 3 appeared to be less of a problem as the sixties advanced: "The

friendship between the Port Harrison and Pond Inlet groups has improved due to marriage between the two groups" (NA, RG 18, Annual Report of the Resolute Detachment, Year Ending 31 December 1963).

40 Higgins, *South Coast–Baffin Island*, 102.

41 NA, RG 18, Acc. 85–86/048, Vol. 55: Conditions Amongst Eskimos, Annual Report, Lake Harbour Detachment, Cape Dorset, Year Ending 31 December 1961.

42 Ibid., Annual Report, Year Ending 31 December 1962.

43 Ibid., Annual Report, Year Ending 31 December 1963.

44 Ibid.

45 Ibid.

46 NA, RG 18, Acc. 85–86/048, Vol. 56, File TA 500–8–1–17: Cape Dorset Detachment, Conditions Amongst Eskimos, Generally, 12 January 1966. (This detachment officially opened on 25 November 1965.)

47 Ibid, Annual Report, Year Ending 31 December 1961.

48 NA, RG 18, Acc. 85–86/048, Vol. 56, File TA 500–8–1–1: Conditions Amongst Eskimos Generally, Cape Dorset Detachment, Year Ending 31 December 1966.

49 Ibid., Annual Report, Year Ending 31 December 1967.

50 Ibid., Annual Report, Year Ending 31 December 1968.

51 Higgins, *South Coast – Baffin Island*, 103.

52 NA, RG 18, Acc. 85–86/048, Vol. 56, File TA 500–8–1–1, Annual Report, Year Ending 31 December 1968.

53 Higgins, *South Coast – Baffin Island*, 110.

54 Ibid, 175.

55 Graburn, *Lake Harbour*, 6.

56 Ibid.

57 Ibid., preface.

58 NA, RG 18, Acc. 85–86/048, Box 55, Annual Report, Lake Harbour Detachment, Year Ending 31 December 1962.

59 Ibid.

60 Ibid.

61 NA, RG 18, Acc. 85–86/048, Box 55, Annual Report, Lake Harbour Detachment, Year Ending 31 December 1966.

62 Ibid.

63 Ibid.

64 NA, RG 18, Acc. 85–86/048, Box 55: Annual Report, Lake Harbour Detachment, Year Ending 31 December 1967.

65 Ibid., Annual Report, Year Ending 31 December 1968.

66 Ibid. However, this represents a rise from $2.00 compared to the previous year.

67 NA, RG 18, Acc. 85–86/048, Vol. 56, Conditions Amongst Eskimos, Cape Dorset Detachment, Year Ending 31 December 1968.

68 NA, RG 18, Acc. 85–86/048, Vol. 55, File TA 500–8–1–8: Conditions Amongst Eskimos, 5 April 1960. Frobisher Bay Detachment.

69 Ibid., Annual Report, Year Ending 31 December 1961.

70 Ibid.

71 Ibid.

72 Ibid.

73 Ibid.

74 NA, RG 18, Acc. 85–86/048, Vol. 55, File TA 500–8–1–8: Annual Report, Year Ending 31 December 1962.

75 Ibid.

76 Honigmann and Honigmann, *Eskimo Townsmen*, 54–63.

77 Ibid., 68

78 Ibid., 136, 138, 148–51.

79 Ibid., 196–215.

80 Ibid., 229–48.

81 Ibid., 96.

82 Ibid., 85.

83 NA, RG 18, Acc. 85–86/048, Vol. 55, File TA 500–8–1–8: Annual Report, Year Ending 31 December 1963.

84 Ibid., Annual Report, Year Ending 31 December 1964.

85 Ibid., Annual Report, Year Ending 31 December 1965.

86 Ibid., Annual Report, Year Ending 31 December 1966.

87 NA, RG 85, Box 15, 85–86/220, File A1000/169, Vol. 2 Frobisher Bay, General, Regional Administrator to Administrator of the Arctic, 12 November 1968.

88 Ibid.

89 NA, RG 18, Acc. 85–86/048, Vol. 55, File TA 500–8–1–11. Annual Report, Pangnirtung Detachment, Year Ending 31 December 1960.

90 Usher, *Fur Trade Posts*, 130.

91 Anders et al., *Baffin Island – East Coast*, 150.

92 NA, RG 18, Acc. 85–86/048, Vol. 55, File TA 500–8–1–11, Annual Report, Pangnirtung Detachment, Year Ending 31 December 1961.

93 Ibid.

94 Ibid.

95 Ibid.

96 NA, RG 85, Vol. 1952, File A1000/170(1). Memorandum for the Regional Administrator, Welfare Survey – Pangnirtung, from H. Zuckerman, 13 February 1962.

97 NA, RG 18, Acc. 85–86/048. Vol. 55, File TA 500–8–1–11. To Officer Commanding, Eastern Subdivision, from RCMP Detachment, Frobisher Bay, Conditions Amongst Eskimos, Pangnirtung, 8 March 1962.

98 NA, RG 85, Vol. 1952, File A1000/1700, Memorandum for Regional Administrator, 13 February 1962.

99 Ibid.

100 NA, RG 18, Acc. 85–86/048: Vol. 55, File TA 500–8–1–11: Conditions Amongst Eskimos, Pangnirtung, 8 March 1962.

101 Ibid., Conditions Amongst Eskimos, Pangnirtung Detachment, 3 May 1962.

102 Ibid.

103 NA, RG 85, Vol. 1952, File TA 1000/170(1): Memorandum for the Regional Administrator, Welfare Conditions – Pangnirtung, from H. Zuckerman, 9 March 1962.

104 Ibid., Memorandum for B.G. Sivertz, Director, Northern Administration from Director, DNA, 15 May 1962.

105 NA, RG 18, Acc. 85–86/048, Vol. 55, File TA 500–8–1–11: Memorandum for the Regional Administrator, Frobisher Bay, Situation at Pangnirtung, 16 January 1963.

106 Ibid.

107 NA, RG 18, Acc. 85–86/048, Vol. 55, File TA 500–8–1–11: Annual Report, Year Ending 31 December 1962.

108 Ibid., Annual Report, Year Ending 31 December 1963.

109 Ibid.

110 NA, RG 18, Acc. 85–86/048, Vol. 55, File TA 500–8–1–11: Annual Report, Year Ending 31 December 1964. Regarding subsistence in the regions stretching from Cumberland Sound north to Clyde River, Anders et al., *Baffin Island–East Coast*, 94, write as follows: "Food production in 1956–66 in the three study areas was about 1,200 pounds per person. It is assumed that probably 58% of all edible food products were used to feed dogs. The remaining food would, therefore, provide each inhabitant in the survey region with about 1.4 pounds of edible food per day."

111 NA, RG 18, Acc. 85–86/048, Vol. 59, TA 500–8–1–3: Annual Report for Padloping and Broughton Island, Year Ending 31 December 1964. This total of 238 compares with that of 236 given by Anders et al., 152, for this coast.

112 NA, RG 18, Acc. 85–86/048, Vol. 55, TA 500–8–1–3, Annual Report, Pangnirtung Detachment, Year Ending 31 December 1965.

113 Ibid.

114 Ibid.

115 NA, RG 18, Acc. 85–86/048, Vol. 55, File TA 500–8–1–3, Annual Report, Pangnirtung Detachment, Year Ending 31 December 1966.

116 Ibid.

117 Ibid.

118 Ibid.

119 Ibid.

120 NA, RG 18, Acc. 85–86/048, Vol. 55, File TA 500–8–1–3: Annual Report, Pangnirtung Detachment, Year Ending 31 December 1968.

121 Ibid., Annual Report, Cape Christian Detachment, Year Ending 31 December 1960.

122 Ibid.

123 NA, RG 18, Acc. 85–86/048, File 55, TA 500–8–1–3, Conditions Amongst Eskimos Generally, 29 June 1962.

124 Ibid.

125 NA, RG 18, Acc. 85–86/048, Vol. 55, File TA 500–8–1–3: Annual Report, Year Ending 31 December 1962.

126 Ibid., Annual Report, Year Ending 31 December 1963.

127 Ibid.

128 Ibid.

129 NA, RG 18, Acc. 85–86/048, Vol. 55, File TA 500–8–1–3, Annual Report, Year Ending 31 December 1965.

130 Ibid.

131 NA, RG 18, Acc. 85–86/048, Vol. 55, File TA 500–8–1–3: Annual Report, Year Ending 31 December 1966.

132 Ibid., Annual Report, Year Ending 31 December 1967.

133 Ibid., Annual Report, Year Ending 31 December 1968.

134 Ibid.

135 Wenzel, "Recent Changes in Inuit Summer Residence," 296–7.

136 Ibid., 300.

137 Anders et al., *Baffin Island*, 90.

138 NA, RG 18, Acc. 85–86/048, File TA 500–1–12, Annual Report, Pond Inlet Detachment, Year Ending 31 December 1960.

139 Ibid.

140 NA, RG 18, Acc. 85–86/048, File TA 500–1–12: Annual Report, Year Ending 31 December 1961.

141 Ibid., (Arctic Bay Area).

142 Ibid.

143 Ibid.

144 NA, RG 18, Acc. 85–86/048, File TA 500–1–12: J.T. Parsons, Officer Commanding "G" Division to RCMP, Frobisher Bay, NWT, 6 June 1962.

145 Ibid.

146 Ibid.

147 NA, RG 18, Acc. 85–86/048, Vol. 55, File TA 500–1–12, Annual Report, Pond Inlet Detachment, Year Ending 31 December 1963.

148 Ibid.

149 NA, RG 18, Acc. 85–86/048, Vol. 55, File TA 500–1–12: Annual Report, Year Ending 31 December 1965.

150 Ibid., Annual Report, Year Ending 31 December 1966.

151 Bissett, *Northern Baffin Island*, 9.

152 NA, RG 18, Acc. 85–86/048: Vol. 55, File TA 500–1–12 Annual Report, Year Ending 31 December 1967.

153 Ibid., Annual Report, Year Ending 31 December 1968.

154 NA, RG 18, Acc. 85–86/048, annual reports, years ending 31 December 1959 and 1966.

155 Bissett, *Northern Baffin Island,* 83.

156 Damas, *Igluligmiut Kinship,* 92–7.

157 Ibid., 97.

158 Ibid., 71–92.

159 Author's field notes, Iglulik Area, 1960–61.

160 NA, RG 18, Acc. 85–86/048, Vol. 55, File TA 500–1–12: Annual Report, Pond Inlet Detachment (Igloolik Area), Year Ending 31 December 1962.

161 Ibid., Annual Report, Year Ending 31 December 1963.

162 NA, RG 18, Acc. 85–86/048, Vol. 56, File TA 500–8–1–10: Annual Report, Year Ending 31 December 1965, Igloolik Detachment. This detachment was opened 24 November 1964.

163 Ibid, Annual Report, Year Ending 31 December 1968.

164 Ibid, Annual Report, Year Ending 31 December 1967.

165 Ibid, Annual Report, Year Ending 31 December 1968.

166 Ibid., Annual Report, Year Ending 31 December 1966.

167 Crowe, *A Cultural Geography,* 94.

168 NA, RG 18, Acc. 85–86, Vol. 55, File TA 500–1–12, Pond Inlet Detachment, Annual Report Year Ending 31 December 1963.

169 NA, RG 18, Acc. 85–86, Vol. 56, File TA 500–8–1–10, Igloolik Detachment, Annual Report, Year Ending 31 December 1967.

170 NA, RG 18, Acc. 85–86, Vol. 55, File TA 500–1–12, Pond Inlet Detachment, Annual Report, Year Ending 31 December 1959.

171 Vestey, "Iglulik Eskimo Settlement and Migration," 203.

172 Ibid, 204.

173 Ibid., 137–8.

174 Ibid., 181.

175 Ibid.

176 NA, RG 18, Acc. 85–86, Vol. 56, File TA 500–8–32, Annual Report, 26 August 1960. Spence Bay Detachment.

177 Ibid.

178 Ibid., Annual Report, Year Ending 30 June 1959; P.E. Moore, Director, Indian and Northern Health Services, to Superintendent W.G. Fraser, Officer Commanding "G" Division, 5 April 1960; to J.S. Craig, Fort Smith, 27 April 1960.

179 Ibid., To Officer Commanding "G" Division from J.S. Craig, 21 April 1960; B.G. Sivertz to W.G. Fraser, 15 June 1960.

180 Ibid., Annual Report, 26 August 1960.

181 Ibid.

182 NA, RG 18, Acc. 85–86/048, Vol. 56, File TA 500–8–32: Conditions Amongst Eskimos, 8 October 1960.

183 Ibid., Excerpt from Patrol Report of 13–3–61; Conditions Amongst Eski-
     mos, Levesque Harbour, 4 July 1961.
184 Ibid., Annual Report, Year Ending 30 June 1961.
185 Ibid.
186 NA, RG 18, Acc. 85–86, Vol. 56, File TA 500–8–32: Annual Report, Year
     Ending 30 June 1962.
187 Ibid., Annual Report, Year Ending 31 December 1963. During 1963, the
     year for reporting from Arctic posts was changed from 1 July to 30 June to
     the calendar year.
188 Ibid., Conditions Amongst Eskimos, Pelly Bay, 5 March 1964. As indi-
     cated in chapter 3, at the end of the fifties the Pelly Bay population had
     comprised two settlements, one at the mission and one just across the bay
     from the mission.
189 Ibid, Annual Report, Year Ending 31 December 1963.
190 Ibid., Annual Report, Year Ending 31 December 1964.
191 Ibid., Annual Report, Year Ending 31 December 1965.
192 Author's field notes, Gjoa Haven Region, 1965.
193 Ibid.
194 Ibid.
195 Author's field notes, Spence Bay Region, 1965.
196 NA, RG 18, Acc. 85–86, Vol. 56, File TA 500–8–32, Annual Report,
     Spence Bay Detachment, Year Ending 31 December 1965.
197 Author's field notes, Spence Bay Region, 1965.
198 Ibid.
199 NA, RG 18, Acc. 85–86, Vol. 56, File TA 500–8–32, Annual Report,
     Spence Bay Detachment, Year Ending 31 December 1967.
200 Ibid.
201 Ibid.
202 Villiers, *The Central Arctic*, 84.
203 Ibid., 118.
204 Treude, "Studies in Settlement Development," 53 – 66. The reader will
     note that Treude's "Eastern Central Arctic" (see 78) corresponds to the
     delineation of the Netsilik area.
205 Ibid., 59.
206 Ibid.
207 Ibid., 56.
208 Author's field notes, Cambridge Bay Region, 1965.
209 Treude, "Studies in Settlement Development," 60.
210 Ibid., 63.
211 NA, RG 18, Vol. 85–86/048, Vol. 56, File TA 500–1–30. Cambridge Bay
     Detachment, Annual Report, Year Ending 31 December 1960.
212 Ibid.
213 Ibid.

214 Ibid.

215 NA, RG 18, Acc. 85–86/048, Box 56, File TA 500–1–30: Conditions, Perry River, 1 March 1961. On the basis of my information gathered in the field, no such aggregation had any duration at that time.

216 NA, RG 18, Acc. 85–86/047, File TA 500–20–10–1: Game Conditions, Cambridge Bay Detachment, Year Ending 30 June 1960; NA, RG 18, Acc. 83–84/048, File 20, G567–14(3), Patrol to Bathurst Inlet, 24 March 1961.

217 NA, RG 18, Acc. 85–86/048, Box 20, G567–14(3), Patrol to Bathurst Inlet, 24 March 1961.

218 NA, RG 18, Acc. 83–84/048, File TA – 500–20–20–10–1, Game Conditions, Year Ending 30 June 1962.

219 Author's field notes, Bathurst Inlet, 1962–63.

220 Roman Catholic Church, Records of Roman Catholic Mission, Bathurst Inlet, 1955–61.

221 Author's field notes, Bathurst Inlet, 1962–63.

222 Author's field notes, Perry River Region, 1963.

223 Author's field notes, Bathurst Inlet, 1962–63.

224 Author's field notes, Perry River Region, 1963.

225 Author's field notes, Cambridge Bay, 1963.

226 Abrahamson et al., *The Copper Eskimos*, 21.

227 NA, RG 18, Acc. 85–86/048: Annual Report, Cambridge Bay Detachment, Year Ending 31 December 1963.

228 Ibid. Annual Report, Year Ending 31 December 1964 and Annual Report, Year Ending 31 December 1965.

229 Ibid., Annual Report, Year Ending 31 December 1967.

230 Farquharson, "Inuit Land Use," 49.

231 Author's field notes, Cambridge Bay, 1965.

232 NA, RG 18, Acc. 85–86/048, Vol. 56, File TA 500–1–30, Annual Report, Cambridge Bay Detachment, Year Ending 31 December 1967.

233 John Stanners, personal communication, 9–10 August 1963.

234 Author's field notes, Bathurst Inlet, 1963.

235 NA, RG 18, Acc. 83–84/048, File TA 500–20–20–1: Game Conditions, Cambridge Bay, Year Ending 30 June 1963.

236 Ibid., Game Conditions, Year Ending 30 June 1967.

237 Ibid., Game Conditions, Year Ending 30 June 1968.

238 Ibid., Game Conditions, Year Ending 30 June 1969.

239 Ibid., Game Report, Year Ending 30 June 1970.

240 PWNHC, File 1/495, Eskimo Hunting Camps, A.G. Gordon, Area Administrator, Cambridge Bay to Regional Administrator, Yellowknife, 20 March 1968.

241 Farquharson, "Inuit Land Use," 49.

242 Ibid., 41, 52.

243 NA, RG 18, Acc. 85–86/048, Vol. 56, File TA 500–1–30, Conditions Amongst Eskimos, Coppermine, NWT, 1945–1969; Annual Report, Year Ending 31 December 1962.

244 Usher, *Fur Trade Posts*, 115.

245 NA, RG 18, Acc. 85–86/048, Vol. 56, File TA 500–1–30: Annual Report, Coppermine, Year Ending 31 December 1962.

246 Ibid., Annual Report, Year Ending 31 December 1963.

247 Abrahamson et al., *The Copper Eskimos*, 70.

248 Ibid.

249 NA, RG 18, Annual Report, Coppermine, Year Ending 31 December 1965.

250 Ibid.

251 Ibid., Annual Report, Year Ending 31 December 1966.

252 Ibid., Annual Report, Year Ending 31 December 1967; PWNHC GFNA, File 1/495, Eskimo Hunting Camps, M.M. Petersen, Area Administrator, Coppermine to Regional Administrator, Yellowknife, 19 February 1968. In this correspondence, it is reported that at the above date there remained only three "permanent camps" in the Coppermine trading district, totalling a population of thirty-two Inuit. However, it is also stated that in the summer months, June to October inclusive, 60 per cent of the Coppermine people lived in camps.

253 NA, RG 18, Acc. 85–86, Vol. 56, File TA 500–1–30: Annual Report, Coppermine, Year Ending 31 December 1966.

254 Ibid., annual reports, years ending 31 December 1967 and 31 December 1968.

255 NA, RG 18, Acc. 85–86, Vol. 56, File TA 500–1–30: Annual Report, Year Ending 31 December 1968.

256 Ibid., Annual Report, Year Ending 31 December 1966.

257 Ibid., Annual Report, Year Ending 31 December 1968.

258 Usher, *Fur Trade Posts*, 113, 115–16.

CHAPTER SEVEN

1 Oswalt and VanStone, "The Future of the Caribou Eskimos," 162.

2 Ibid.

3 NA, RG 85, Vol. 1951, File A1000/153: Memorandum for the Regional Administrator, Churchill, from Welfare Officer, Eskimo Point, 23–31 December 1960.

4 Ibid., Report on Padlei, NWT, by Joan Ryan, n.d.

5 Ibid., Patrols to Padlei People at Maguse Lake, 28–31 December 1960.

6 Ibid.

7 NA, RG 85, Vol. 1951, File A1000/153, Memorandum for the Administrator of the Arctic from R.L. Kennedy, 15 February 1961.

8 Brack and McIntosh, *Keewatin Mainland,* 57.

9 NA, RG 18, Acc. 85–86/048, Vol. 56, File TA 500–20–10–2: Game Conditions, Eskimo Point, Year Ending 30 June 1960, 30 June 1961, and 30 June 1963.

10 NA, RG 18, Acc. 85–86/048, Vol. 56, File TA 500–20–10–2: Game Conditions, Eskimo Point, Year Ending 30 June 1963.

11 Ibid., Game condition reports, years ending 1964, 1965, 1966, 1967, 1968 (all years ending 30 June).

12 NA, RG 18, Acc. 85–86/048, Vol. 55, File TA 500–8–1–6, Eskimo Point: Annual Report, Year Ending 31 December 1962.

13 Ibid., Annual Report, Year Ending 31 December 1963.

14 Ibid., Annual Report, Year Ending 31 December 1964.

15 Ibid. On the other hand, Burch reported in a personal communication that as late as 1968 people were moving from inland.

16 NA, RG 85, Vol. 85–86/220, Box 15, File A 1000/153: Eskimo Point Settlement and Area, to Regional Administrator, Churchill, from Area Administrator, 2 March 1967.

17 Ibid., District Housing Co-ordinator to Mr Mielke, Eskimo Point, 10 March 1967.

18 NA, RG 18, Acc. 85–86/048, Box 55, File TA 500–8–1–6, Annual Report, Eskimo Point, Year Ending 31 December 1968.

19 Welland, "Inuit Land Use," 97.

20 NA, RG 18, Acc. 85–86/048, Vol. 55, File TA 500–8–1–2: Conditions Amongst Eskimos, Generally, Baker Lake District, 17 March 1960.

21 Ibid., To Officer in Charge "G" Division, Re: Conditions Amongst Eskimos – Baker Lake, NWT, 25 February 1960.

22 Ibid., Conditions Amongst Eskimos, Generally, Baker Lake District, 17 March 1960.

23 Ibid., Annual Report for Period 1960–61.

24 Ibid., Conditions Amongst Eskimos, 28 February 1961.

25 Ibid., Conditions Amongst Eskimos Generally Period 1960–61; NA, RG 85, Vol. 1951, File 1000/59.

26 NA, RG 18, Acc. 85–86/040, File TA – 500–20–10–2. Game Conditions, Year Ending 30 June 1961.

27 NA, RG 18, Acc. 85–86/048, Annual Report, Year Ending 31 December 1961. The report was written in January 1962 and the amount of relief relates to that month.

28 Ibid.

29 NA, RG 18, Acc. 85–86/048, Annual Report, Year Ending 31 December 1962.

30 NA, RG 18, Acc. 85–86/040, Game Conditions, Year Ending 30 June 1963.

31 NA, RG 18, Acc. 85–86/048, Annual Report, Year Ending 31 December 1963.

32 NA, RG 18, Acc. 85–86/040, Game Conditions, Year Ending 30 June 1964.

33 NA, RG 18, Acc. 85–86/048, Annual Report, Year Ending 31 December 1964.

34 Ibid.

35 Ibid.

36 NA, RG 18, Acc. 85–86/040, Game Conditions, Year Ending 30 June 1965. Another large herd estimated at 250,000 to 300,000 was reported along the south shore of Baker Lake in 1965. Ibid., Annual Report, Year Ending 31 December 1965.

37 NA, RG 18, Acc. 85–86/040: Annual Report, Year Ending 31 December 1965.

38 Ibid., Game Conditions, Year Ending 30 June 1966.

39 NA, RG 18, Acc. 85–86/048: Annual Report, Year Ending 31 December 1966.

40 Ibid., Annual Report, Year Ending 31 December 1967.

41 Ibid., Annual Report, Year Ending 31 December 1968.

42 Ibid.

43 Ibid.

44 Welland, "Inuit Land Use," 105.

45 The information on Repulse Bay is taken from my field notes, and includes data from the Inuit of the community, and also from Frs Didier and Riviore and the post manager, Henry Voisey (author's field notes, Repulse Bay, 1967). Information also comes from an interview with Mr Voisey in Ottawa, 30 May 1968.

46 There is some uncertainty regarding the date the Wager Bay region was abandoned, and consequently the time when full centralization took place at Repulse Bay. Brack and McIntosh, *Keewatin Mainland*, 77, report thirteen people at Wager Bay in the summer of 1961. Brice-Bennett, "Land Use in the East-Central," 89, puts the same year as the time these people moved to Repulse Bay. On the basis of my inquiries, it would seem to have been a year or two later.

47 This industry was in part subsidized by government funds. Lest this income be judged as large, it actually amounted to only $60 or $70 average income for each of the more than thirty nuclear families of the community.

48 Brack and McIntosh, *Keewatin Mainland*, 85.

49 Ibid., 86.

50 Ibid., 90. Proceeds from employment were $22,800 of the total community income of $32,654, and welfare was given to four families and totalled $3,221 (figures apparently for the year 1961–62).

51 Ibid., 89.

52 Ibid., 85.

53 Ibid., 86.

54 Author's field notes, Chesterfield Inlet, 1968.
55 Ibid.
56 Ibid.
57 Ibid.
58 Brack and McIntosh, *Keewatin Mainland*, 75–83.
59 Ibid., 77.
60 Ibid., 79. The survey gives a total income (presumably for the year 1961–62) of $11,920 from trapping. This can be compared to $3,729 for Chesterfield (90).
61 Ibid., 77.
62 Ibid.
63 Ibid., 79.
64 Ibid., 81.
65 Ibid., 83.
66 Welland, "Inuit Land Use," 98–102.
67 Ibid., 100.
68 Ibid.
69 Brack and McIntosh, *Keewatin Mainland*, 82, note that "by all accounts the various Eskimo groups pull together although there is some aloofness here and there."
70 Brack and McIntosh, *Keewatin Mainland*, 102.
71 Foster, "Rankin Inlet: A Lesson in Survival," 38.
72 Ibid.
73 Ibid.
74 Jansen, *Eskimo Economics*, 25.
75 Williamson, "The Keewatin Settlements," 114.
76 Foster, "Rankin Inlet: A Lesson in Survival," 38.
77 Much of the following account is based on my field notes, Rankin Inlet, 1968.
78 Jansen, *Eskimo Economics*, 26.
79 Welland, "Inuit Land Use," 104.
80 Williamson, *Eskimo Underground*, 136.
81 Williamson, "The Keewatin Settlements," 14, gives the following population figures for the settlements for 15 May 1970: Eskimo Point 549, Whale Cove 193, Chesterfield Inlet 220, Rankin Inlet 474, Coral Harbour 338, Repulse Bay 220, Baker Lake 620.
82 Jansen, *Eskimo Economics*, 25.
93 Brack and McIntosh, *Keewatin Mainland*, 72.
84 Ibid, 79.
85 Ibid.
86 Ibid, 96–7.
87 NA, RG 18, Acc. 85–86/048, Annual Report, Baker Lake Detachment, Year Ending 31 December 1961.

88 Brack and McIntosh, *Keewatin Mainland*, 99.

89 Ibid, 67.

90 Ibid, 72.

91 NA, RG 85, Acc. 85–86/220, File A100/153, Eskimo Point Settlement and Area, To Regional Administrator, Churchill, Manitoba, 2 March 1967, from Area Administrator, Eskimo Point, NWT.

92 Ibid.

93 Foster, "Rankin Inlet: A Lesson in Survival," 40.

94 Ibid., 38.

95 Ibid., 40.

96 Grygier, *A Long Way From Home*, 135.

97 Ibid., 135–6.

98 Brack and McIntosh, *Keewatin Mainland*, ii.

99 PWNHC, GFNA, File 1/495, Eskimo Hunting Camps.

100 Ibid., Crowe, "Eskimo Camps: A Sociological Viewpoint."

101 Ibid., Committee on the Future of Eskimo Hunting Camps, Report No. 1. "The Spence Bay Area," compiled by P. Cressman, n.d.

102 Ibid., Summary and Conclusions, n.d.

CHAPTER EIGHT

1 Duffy, *The Road to Nunavut*, 22–3.

2 Lieber, *Exiles and Migrants in Oceania*, 345, notes that in Pacific Island cases of relocation, the character of the move "ranges from forced relocation ... to a series of delicate negotiations that result in a joint decision." In the High Arctic relocations, and the relocation of the Ennadai Lake people to Henik Lake, the government's position has been largely that negotiation was prominent, while the critics of these resettlements perceive forced relocation.

3 Marcus, *Relocating Eden*, 77–8, has described those arranging the High Arctic relocations as avoiding "the word 'relocation', which might imply dislocation or intervention. Instead, the rather benign word 'transfer', and the more distinctive word 'migration' were used." Whether or not these usages were indeed an attempt to avoid using "relocation" is not clear. However, by the late 1950s, there was no such reluctance within governmental circles. A series of memoranda and other correspondence were entitled "Relocation [or Re-location] of Eskimos." (NA, RG 85, Vol. 1070, File 251–4, Sivertz to Deputy Minister, 6 June 1958; RG 85, Vol. 1382, File 1012–13(5): Memorandum for Director, 22 December 1958; Cpl in Charge, Resolute Bay to Officer Commanding "G" Division, 26 September 1959; C.M. Bolger, Memorandum for Director, 15 November 1960).

4 Tester and Kulchyski, *Tammarniit*, 7.

5 Brody, *The People's Land*, 167.

6 Mathiasson, *Living on the Land*, 141.

7 Rasing, *Too Many People*, 165.

8 Ibid. Rasing's example is not quite accurate regarding the dates when the pressures were said to have been applied – for instance, the date of establishment of a school – and the role of the RCMP in the matter of settlement policy. It appears that whatever pressures were applied came after the implementation of the housing programs at Igloolik and Hall Beach.

9 Vestey, "Igloolik Eskimo Settlement," 162. This case involved pressure to move to Hall Beach because of hospital proximity.

10 Brody, *The People's Land*, 166–7. Two of the three examples he cites were dated 1966 and 1967 respectively, when housing was well established throughout much of the Central Arctic, though the exact locations for these examples are not given.

11 A number of references to generalized "nomadism" among Inuit in the period just before centralization can be found in government correspondence, some of which have been noted in earlier chapters. This generalized conception has also found its way into published material. Tester and Kulchyski, *Tammarniit*, 3, use the term in a highly general sense to describe conditions of settlement just prior to centralization. They also depict a "nomadic lifestyle" for the Garry Lake people just prior to relocation (ibid, 239). They do, however, employ the more accurate "semi-nomadic" designation to the Ennadai Lake people (ibid, 206). While Marcus, *Relocating Eden*, 136, writes of the "nomadic nature of Ahiarmiut life," his description of the seasonal movement between camp sites conforms to the semi-nomadic mode (ibid, 129). Indeed Murdock's scouring of the literature on the Caribou Eskimo places this major grouping within his semi-nomadic classification (*Ethnographic Atlas*, 103). In lean winters when meat was in short supply, it was necessary for the Inuit to depart from winter encampments of the more permanent sort in order to seek better hunting locales. Under these circumstances, a closer approach to true nomadism can be recognized.

12 The categories of nomadic, semi-nomadic, and semi-sedentary as used here are based on Murdock, *Ethnographic Atlas*, 51.

13 It seems likely that a transitional phase from truly nomadic to semi-nomadic characterized the years immediately after the establishment of trading posts. Such a circumstance appears to have been the case in the Bathurst Inlet region (author's field notes, Bathurst Inlet, 1962–63).

14 PWNHC, Stevenson Fonts, File 17–7, Policy Inuit, 1935–1959, n.d.

15 Diubaldo, "You Can't Keep the Native Native," 183, comments on the work of the administrators of the Department of Northern Affairs as follows: "The most sensitive of government planners were a new breed who would have to contend with outworn or incorrect perceptions of the Inuit. The

likes of R.A.J. Phillips, Bent Sivertz, Vic Valentine, and Graham Rowley all played a part in this change in attitude." References to several of these figures leads me to support, in general, Diubaldo's statement. However, such reference also must imply that these men did not always represent monolithic stances. As well, as in the case of Stevenson, several of these individuals also showed evolution in their thinking as the process of centralization advanced.

16 Treude, "Pond Inlet, Northern Baffin Island," 95–122.
17 Ibid., 95-119.
18 Ames et al., *Keeping on the Land.*
19 Ibid., xvii.
20 Ibid., xxiv.
21 Wenzel, "Inuit Subsistence," 9–10.
22 Wenzel, *Animal Rights, Human Rights.*
23 Condon et al., "The Best Part of Life," 32.
24 Ibid.
25 Ibid.
26 Rasing, *Too Many People.*
27 Author's field notes, Iglulik.
28 Rasing, *Too Many People*, 186, map 7: Igloolik Settlement (Ikpiakjuk) 1986–1987.
29 Damas, *Igluligmiut Kinship*, 97.
30 Author's field notes, Iglulik.
31 Rasing, *Too Many People*, 167.
32 Ibid.
33 Damas, *Igluligmiut Kinship*, 103.
34 Rasing, *Too Many People*, 188, table 3: Igloolik Population by Family Units (as of 31–12–1986).
35 Author's field notes, Iglulik.
36 Rasing, *Too Many People*, 193, table 6.
37 Ibid., 194.
38 Ibid., 273.
39 Author's field notes, Iglulik.
40 Rasing, *Too Many People*, 201.
41 Author's field notes, Iglulik.
42 Rasing, *Too Many People*, 192.
43 Author's field notes, Iglulik.
44 Rasing, *Too Many People*, 195–6, 236–89.
45 Ibid., 196–9.
46 Ibid., 195, 224.
47 Ibid., 209–65.
48 Author's field notes, Iglulik.

49 Rasing, *Too Many People*, 216 (table 7), 242. The local courts were the Youth Court, 248, and the Justice of the Peace Court, 248–9.

50 Ibid., 215.

51 Ibid., 225.

52 Ibid.

53 Ibid., 224–5.

54 Author's field notes, Iglulik.

55 Rasing, *Too Many People*, 230.

56 Ibid., 231.

57 Ibid., 232.

58 Nunavut Implementation Commission, *Nunavut's Legislature*, appendix A1.

59 The estimate for 1951 is based on census material for that year, (NA, RG 85, File 66), which shows some ambiguity, however, regarding the districts involved.

60 Nunavut Implementation Commission, *Nunavut's Legislature*, appendix A1.

61 Ibid., appendix A2.12.

62 Ibid., appendix A2.25.

63 Ibid., appendix A2.19.

64 Ibid., appendix A2.20.

65 Ibid.

66 Ibid., appendix A2.18.

67 Ibid., appendix A2.22.

68 Vallee et al., "Contemporary Canadian Inuit," 668.

69 Ibid.

70 Ibid.

71 Petersen, "The Pan Eskimo Movement," 724–8.

72 Freeman, "The Grise Fiord Project," 682.

73 Royal Commission on Aboriginal Peoples, *The High Arctic Relocation*, 2:553–5.

74 Ibid., 2:555.

75 Ibid.

76 Reports included those of Gunther (2:564–5); Soberman (2:560–7); and Hickling Corporation, "A Report on the 1953–55 Relocation," 2:181).

77 Ibid, 2:555–6.

78 Bell, "What are the Exiles Signing?" 2; Bell, "Exiles Denied Apology," 14.

79 Bell, "Exiles Denied Apology," 14.

80 Vallee, *Kabloona and Eskimo*, 671.

81 Minister of Indian Affairs and Northern Development, *Agreement Between the Inuit.*

82 Ibid.

83 See discussion in Saladin et al., "The Inuit People," 13–19; Fenge, "Political Development," 118–42; Fenge, "Inuit Land Ownership," 147–50.

84 Minister of Indian Affairs and Northern Development, *Agreement Between the Inuit.*
85 Malone, "Irwin Report," 14.
86 Nunavut's Implementation Commission, *Main Estimates* 1999–2000. The actual breakdown of revenue for the fiscal year ending 31 March 2000 is as follows:

Formula Financing Grant	81.8%
Tax Revenues	5.8%
Other Transfers	8.5%
Other Own Source Revenues	3.5%

Bibliography

PUBLIC DOCUMENTS

Canada, Dominion Bureau of Statistics. *Canada Yearbook*, 1929, 1930, 1938, 1940, 1945, 1950, 1956, 1957, 1962, 1964, 1965, 1966, 1969, 1970–71.
– Northern Health Services. "Record of Health Conditions in the Northwest Territories," 1962.
– The Minister of Indian Affairs and Northern Development and the Tungavik Federation of Nunavut. *Agreement Between the Inuit of the Nunavut Settlement Area and Her Majesty in Right of Canada*, 1993.
Department of Northern Affairs and National Resources, Arctic Correspondence
Department of Northern Affairs and National Resources. "Eskimo Mortality and Housing," Indian and Northern Health Services. Ottawa: Northern Administration Branch, 1960.
Department of the Interior. Annual Reports for the Fiscal Years Ending March 31, 1923, March 31, 1924, March 31, 1933. Ottawa: Department of the Interior, 1923, 1924, 1933.
Hudson's Bay Company Archives (HBCA)
  AG 3 Post Journals and Annual Reports
  RG 2 Internal Correspondence
  RG 3 Introduction, and Annual Accounts
  RG 7 Correspondence, Eskimo Welfare
National Archives of Canada (NA)
  RG 18 Royal Canadian Mounted Police Records
  RG 22 Department of Indian Affairs and Northern Development
  RG 85 Northern Affairs Branch Program Records
National Film Board of Canada, "Coppermine," 1992.
Nunavut's Implementation Commission. *Nunavut's Legislature, Premier and First Election.* Iqaluit: 1996.

– *Nunavut, Government of Nunavut Main Estimates,* 1999–2000.
Prince of Wales Northern Heritage Centre (PWNHC)
    NALB Files of the Northern Administration and Lands Branch
    GFNA Files of the Northern Administration Branch
    Alexander Stevenson Fonts, N–1992–023
– Council of the Northwest Territories: Minutes of Meetings for 23 June 1924;
    23 June 1925; 15 June 1930; 23 March 1937; 13 February 1945; 23 March
    1946; 20 May 1948; 26 June 1948; 20 January 1949; and National Library
    (NL) Sessional Papers, January 1959, January 1961, January 1962.

REFERENCE MATERIAL

Abel, Perry and Jean Friesen, eds. *Aboriginal Resource Use in Canada.* Winnipeg:
    University of Manitoba Press, 1971.
Abrahamson, G., P.J. Gillespie, D.J. McIntosh, P.J. Usher, and H.A. Williamson.
    The Copper Eskimos: An Area Economic Survey. Ottawa: Department of North-
    ern Affairs and National Resources, 1964.
Ames, Randy, Don Oxford, Peter Usher, Ed Weick, and George Wenzel. *Keep-
    ing on the Land.* Ottawa: Canadian Arctic Resources Committee, 1989.
Amundsen, Roald. *The Northwest Passage.* 2 vols. London: Archibald, Constable
    and Company, 1908.
Anders, G., A.A. Haller, D.C. Foote, and P.D. Cove. *Baffin Island – East Coast: An
    Area Economic Survey.* Ottawa: Department of Indian Affairs and Northern
    Development, 1967.
Arima, Eugene Y. "Caribou Eskimo." In Damas, ed., *Arctic, Handbook of North
    American Indians, Vol. 5.* Washington: Smithsonian Institution, 1984.
Balikci, Asen. *Development of Basic Socio-Economic Units in Two Eskimo Communi-
    ties.* Ottawa: National Museum of Canada Bulletin 202, 1964.
– "Netsilik." In Damas, ed., *Arctic, Handbook of North American Indians, Vol. 5.*
    Washington: Smithsonian Institution, 1984.
Banfield, A.W.F. "Preliminary Investigations of the Barren Ground Caribou."
    Ottawa: *Wildlife Management Series 1,* No. 10A, 1954, 1–79.
Bell, Jim. "What are the Exiles Signing?" *Nunatsiaq News,* year 24, no. 7
    (15 March 1996): 2
– "Exiles Denied Apology." *Nunatsiaq News,* year 24, no. 7 (15 March 1996): 5
Bird, J. Brian. *Southampton Island.* Ottawa: Department of Mines and Technical
    Surveys, Memoir, no. 1, 1953.
Birket-Smith, Kaj. *The Caribou Eskimos,* Parts I and II. Report of the Fifth Thule
    Expedition 1921–24, Vol. V. Copenhagen: Gyldendalske Boghandel, 1929.
Bissett, Don. *Northern Baffin Island: An Area Economic Survey,* Vol. I. Ottawa: De-
    partment of Northern Affairs and Northern Development, 1967.
– *Resolute: An Area Economic Survey.* Ottawa: Department of Indian Affairs and
    Northern Development, 1968.

Boas, Franz. "The Central Eskimo." Bureau of American Ethnology, Washington, *Sixth Annual Report*, 1888: 399–669.

Brack, D.M. and D. McIntosh. *Keewatin Mainland Area Survey and Regional Appraisal.* Ottawa: Department of Northern Affairs and National Resources, 1963.

Brice-Bennett, Carol. "Inuit Land Use in the East-Central Canadian Arctic." In Freeman, ed., *Inuit Land Use and Occupancy Project.* Vol. I. Ottawa: Department of Indian and Northern Affairs, 1976.

Brody, Hugh. *The People's Land.* Harmondsworth, England: Penguin Books, 1973.

Burch, Ernest S. Jr. "The Caribou/Wild Reindeer as a Human Resource." *American Antiquity* 37 (1972): 339–68.

– "Muskox and Man in the Central Canadian Subarctic 1689 – 1974." *Arctic* 30, no. 3 (1977): 135–54.

– "The Caribou Inuit." In Morrison and Wilson, eds., *Native Peoples, The Canadian Experience.* Toronto: McClelland & Stewart, 1986.

– "Knud Rasmussen and the 'Original' Inland Eskimos of Southern Keewatin." *Etudes/Inuit/Studies* 12, nos 1–2 (1988): 81–100.

– Letter to author, n.d.

Burch, Ernest S. Jr. and J. Ellanna, eds. *Key Issues in Hunter – Gatherer Research.* Providence: R.I. Berg Publishers, 1994.

Cantley, James. "Survey of Economic Conditions Among the Eskimos of the Canadian Arctic." Ottawa: Department of Resources and Development, 1950.

Clancy, James P. "Caribou, Fur and the Resource Frontier: A Political Economy of the Northwest Territories to 1967." Unpublished Ph.D. thesis, Department of Political Science, Queen's University, 1985.

– "The Making of Eskimo Policy in Canada 1952 – 62." *Arctic* 40, no. 3 (September 1987): 191–7.

Clarke, C.H.D. *A Biological Investigation of the Thelon Game Sanctuary.* Ottawa: Department of Mines and Resources National Museum of Canada, Bulletin No. 96, 1940.

Clifton, James, ed. *Introduction to Cultural Anthropology.* Boston: Houghton, Mifflin, 1968.

Coates, Kenneth S., and William S. Morrison, eds. *For Purposes of Dominion: Essays in Honour of Morris Zaslow.* North York: Captus University Press, 1989.

Collinson, T.B., ed. *Journal of H.M.S. Enterprise.* London: Sampson, Low, Morton & Rivington, 1889.

Condon, Richard G. *The Northern Copper Inuit.* Toronto: University of Toronto Press, 1996.

Condon, Richard G., Peter Collings, and George Wenzel. "The Best Part of Life: Subsistence Hunting, Ethnicity and Economic Adaptation Among Young Adult Inuit Males." *Arctic* 48, no. 1 (March 1995): 31–46.

Crowe, Keith. *A Cultural Geography of Northern Foxe Basin, N.W.T.* Ottawa: Department of Indian Affairs and Northern Development, 1969.

– "Eskimo Camps: A Sociological Viewpoint." In *Eskimo Hunting Camps.* PWNHC, File 1/495, Eskimo Hunting Camps, A.G. Gordon, Area Administrator, Cambridge Bay to Regional Administrator, Yellowknife, March 20, 1968.

Csonka, Yvon. *Les Ahiarmiut: A Lecart des Inuit Caribous.* Neuchatal, Switzerland: Éditions Victor Attinger SA., 1995.

Dailey, Robert C. and Lois A. Dailey. *The Eskimo of Rankin Inlet: A Preliminary Report.* Ottawa: Department of Northern Affairs and National Resources, 1961.

Damas, David. *Igluligmiut Kinship and Local Groupings: A Structural Approach.* Ottawa: National Museum of Canada, Bulletin No. 196, 1963.

– ed. "Characteristics of Control Eskimo Band Structure" *Contributions to Anthropology: Band Societies.* No. 228. Ottawa: National Museums of Canada, Bulletin No. 228, 1969.

– ed. "Environment, History and Central Eskimo Society" *Contributions to Anthropology: Ecological Essays.* No. 230. Ottawa: National Museums of Canada, Bulletin No. 230, 1969

– ed. *Arctic, Handbook of North American Indians, Vol. 5.* Washington: Smithsonian Institution, 1984, William C. Sturtevant, General/Editor.

– "The Contact-Traditional Horizon of the Central Arctic: Reassessment of a Concept and Reexamination of an Era." *Arctic Anthropology* 25, 2 (1988): 101–38.

– "Shifting Relations in the Administration of the Inuit: The Hudson's Bay Company and the Canadian Government." *Etudes/Inuit/Studies* 17 no. 2 (1993): 5–28.

– "From Ethnography and History to Ethnohistory in the Central Arctic." *Arctic Anthropology* 35, no. 2 (1998): 166–76.

– "The Distribution and Habits of the Ringed Seal and Central Eskimo Settlement Patterns." Unpublished ms, n.d.

Damas, D. and Ives Goddard. "Introduction." In Damas, ed., *Arctic, Handbook of North American Indians, Vol. 5.* Washington: Smithsonian Institution, 1984.

Devine, Marina, ed. *NWT Data Book: 1981.* Yellowknife: Outcrop Ltd., 1981.

Diubaldo, Richard J. "You Can't Keep the Native Native." In Coates and Morrison, eds., *For Purposes of Dominion: Essays in Honour of Morris Zaslow.* North York: Captus University Press, 1989.

Duffy, R. Quinn. *The Road to Nunavut.* Kingston and Montreal: McGill-Queen's University Press, 1988.

Farquharson, Don R. "Inuit Land Use in the West-Central Arctic." In Freeman, ed., *Inuit Land Use and Occupancy Project.* Vol. I. Ottawa: Department of Indian and Northern Affairs, 1976.

Fenge, Terry. "Political Development and Environmental Management in Northern Canada: The Case of the Nunavut Agreement."*Etudes/Inuit/Studies* 16, no. 1–2 (1992): 115–42.

– "Inuit Land Ownership: A Note on the Nunavut Agreement." *Etudes/Inuit/Studies* 17, no. 1 (1993): 147–50.

Finnie, Richard. *The Lure of the North*. Philadelphia: David McKay, 1940.

Foster, Terence W. "Rankin Inlet: A Lesson in Survival." *The Musk – Ox* 10 (1972): 32–41.

Freeman, Milton M.R. "Adaptive Innovation Among Recent Eskimo Immigrants in the Eastern Canadian Arctic." *Polar Record* 14, no. 93 (1969): 769–81.

– "Tolerance and Rejection of Patron Roles in an Eskimo Settlement." In Robert Paine, ed., *Patrons and Brokers in the East-Central Arctic*. 34-54. Memorial University of Newfoundland, 1971.

– ed. *Inuit Land Use and Occupancy Project*. Vols I, II, and III. Ottawa: Department of Indian and Northern Affairs, 1976.

– "The Grise Fiord Project." In Damas, ed., *Arctic, Handbook of North American Indians, Vol. 5*. Washington: Smithsonian Institution, 1984.

– "The Grise Fiord Project." In Damas, ed., *Arctic, Handbook of North American Indians, Vol. 5*. Washington: Smithsonian Institution, 1984.

Fryer, A.C. "Eskimo Rehabilitation Program at Craig Harbour." *RCMP Quarterly* 20, no. 2 (October 1954): 139–42.

Gabus, Jean. *Vie et Coutumes des Equimaux*. Paris: Pqyot, 1944.

Gilder, William H. *Schwatka's Search*. New York: Charles Scribner's Sons, 1881.

Glover, Richard. "Introduction." In Williams, ed., *Andrew Graham's Observations on Hudson's Bay, 1767–1794*. London: Hudson's Bay Company Record Society Publication 27, 1969.

Graburn, Nelson, H.H. *Lake Harbour, Baffin Island*: Ottawa: Department of Northern Affairs and National Resources, 1963.

Graham-Cummings, C. "Northern Health Services." *Canadian Medical Association Journal* 100 (15 March 1969): 526–31.

Grant, Shelagh. *Sovereignty or Security?* Vancouver: University of British Columbia Press, 1988.

Grygier, Pat Sandiford. *A Long Way from Home*. Montreal and Kingston: McGill-Queen's University Press, 1994.

Hall, Charles F. *Life with the Esquimaux*. London: Sampson, Low and Marston, 1864.

Hanbury, David T. *Sport and Travel in the Northland of Canada*. New York: The Macmillan Company, 1904.

Harper, Francis. *Caribou Eskimos of the Upper Kazan River, Keewatin*. Lawrence: University of Kansas Press, 1964.

Harrington, Richard. *The Face of the Arctic*. London: Hodder & Stoughton, 1952.

Hearne, Samuel. *A Journey from Prince of Wales Fort in Hudson's Bay to the Northern Ocean in the Years 1769, 1770, 1771 and 1772*. (1975). Richard Glover, ed. New York and Toronto: The Macmillan Company, 1958.

Helm, June and David Damas. "The Contact-Traditional All-Native Community of the Canadian North." *Anthropologica* 5, no. 1 (1963): 9–21.

Higgins, M. *South Coast – Baffin Island: An Area Economic Survey.* Ottawa: Department of Indian Affairs and Northern Development, 1967.

Hoare, W.B.H. *Report of Investigations Affecting Eskimo and Wildlife, District of Mackenzie, 1924–26.* Ottawa: Department of the Interior, 1927.

Holland, Clive. *Arctic Exploration and Development, c. 500 B.C. to 1915.* New York: Garland Publishing, Inc., 1994.

Honigmann, John J., ed. *Handbook of Social and Cultural Anthropology.* Chicago: Rand McNally and Company, 1973.

Honigmann, John J. and Irma Honigmann. *Eskimo Townsmen.* Ottawa: University of Ottawa, 1965.

Hudson, Charles. "The Historical Approach in Anthropology." In Honigmann, ed., *Handbook of Social and Cultural Anthropology.* Chicago: Rand McNally and Company, 1973.

Hudson's Bay Company. Journal of the Bathurst Inlet Post, permission of Mr John Stanners.

Jansen, William Hugh II. *Eskimo Economics: An Aspect of Culture Change at Rankin Inlet.* Ottawa: National Museums of Canada, Mercury Series, 1979.

Jenness, Diamond. *The Life of the Copper Eskimos.* Report of the Canadian Arctic Expedition, 1913–18, Vol. 12. Ottawa: F.A. Acland, 1922.

– *Eskimo Administration, II: Canada.* Montreal: Arctic Institute of North America, Technical Paper No. 14, 1964.

Lieber, Michael, D., ed. *Exiles and Migrants in Oceania, ASAO Monograph No. 5.* Honolulu: University Press of Hawaii, 1977.

Lofthouse, Joseph. *A Thousand Miles from a Post Office or Twenty Years Life and Travel in the Hudson's Bay Regions.* London: Society for Promoting Christian Knowledge, 1922.

Low, Albert P. *Report of the Dominion Government Expedition to Hudson Bay and the Arctic Islands on Board the D.C.S. Neptune, 1903–1994.* Ottawa: Government Printing Bureau, 1908.

Lyon, George F. *The Private Journal of Captain G.F. Lyon of H.M.S. Hecla During the Recent Voyage of Discovery Under Captain Parry.* London: John Murray, 1824.

MacKinnon, C.S. "The 1958 Government Policy Reversal in Keewatin." In Coates and Morrison, eds., *For Purposes of Dominion: Essays in Honour of Morris Zaslow.* North York: Captus University Press, 1989.

Malone, Marc. "Irwin Report: The View from Yellowknife." *Northern Perspective* 17, no. 1 (January – March 1989): 13–20.

Manning, T.H. "Remarks on the Physiography, Eskimos, and Mammals of Southampton Island." *Canadian Geographical Journal* 24, no. 1 (January 1942): 17–33.

- "Notes on the Coastal District of the Eastern Barren Grounds and Melville Peninsula From Igloolik to Cape Fullerton." *Canadian Geographical Journal* 26 (February 1943): 84–145.

Marcus, Alan R. *Relocating Eden.* Hanover and London: University Press of New England, 1995.

Markham, Albert., ed. *The Voyages and Works of John Davis the Navigator.* London: The Hakluyt Society, 1880.

Markham, Clement R., ed. *The Voyages of William Baffin.* London: The Hakluyt Society, 1881.

Mathiassen, Therkel. *Archaeology of the Central Eskimos,* Part I. Report of the Fifth Thule Expedition 1921–24, Vol. 4. Copenhagen: Gyldendalske Boghandel, 1927.

- *Material Culture of the Iglulik Eskimos.* Report of the Fifth Thule Expedition 1921–24, Vol. 6, No. 1. Copenhagen: Gyldendalske Boghandel, 1928.

Mathiasson, John S. *Living on the Land.* Peterborough, Ontario: Broadview Press, 1992.

McCartney, Alan P., ed. *Thule Eskimo Culture: An Anthropological Perspective.* Ottawa: National Museum of Man, Mercury Series Archaeological Survey Paper No. 88, 1979.

McClintock, Francis, L. *The Voyage of the Fox in the Arctic Seas.* London: John Murray, 1879.

McGhee, Robert. "Speculations on Climatic Change and Thule Culture Development." *Folk* 11–12 (1969/70): 173–84.

- *Copper Eskimo Prehistory.* Ottawa: National Museum of Canada, Publications in Archaeology 2, 1972.

- *Canadian Arctic Prehistory.* Toronto: Van Nostrand Reinhold, 1978.

- "Thule Prehistory of Canada." In Damas, ed., *Arctic, Handbook of North American Indians, Vol. 5.* Washington: Smithsonian Institution, 1984.

Morrison, R. Bruce and C. Roderick Wilson, eds. *Native Peoples, The Canadian Experience.* Toronto: McClelland & Stewart, 1986.

Mouat, W. Ivan. "Education in the Arctic District." *The Musk – Ox* 7 (1970): 1–9.

Mowat, Farley. *The Desperate People.* London: Little, Brown, 1959.

Murdock, George P. *Ethnographic Atlas.* Pittsburgh: University of Pittsburgh Press, 1967.

Newman, Peter C. *Renegade in Power: The Diefenbaker Years.* Toronto, Montreal: McClelland & Stewart, 1964.

Nourse, J.E. *Narrative of the Second Arctic Expedition Made by Charles F. Hall.* Washington: Government Printing Office, 1879.

Osborne, Sherard, ed. *The Discovery of the Northwest Passage.* Edmonton: M.G. Hurtig, 1969 (originally published in London: Longman, Brown, Green and Longman, 1856).

Oswalt, Wendell and James W. VanStone. "The Future of the Caribou Eskimos." *Anthropologica* 2 (1960): 154–76.

Paine, Robert, ed. *Patrons and Brokers in the East Arctic.* Memorial University of
Newfoundland, Social and Economic Paper No. 2. Toronto: University of
Toronto Press, 1971.

Park, Robert W. "Thule Winter Site Demography in the High Arctic." *American
Antiquity* 62, no. 2 (1997): 273–84.

Parry, Sir William E. *Journal of a Second Voyage for the Discovery of a Northwest Passage from the Atlantic to the Pacific: Performed in the Years 1821–22–23, in His
Majesty's Ships Fury and Hecla.* London: John Murray, 1824.

Petersen, Robert. "The Pan Eskimo Movement." In Damas, ed., *Arctic, Handbook of North American Indians, Vol. 5.* Washington: Smithsonian Institution,
1984.

Rae, John. *Narrative of an Expedition to the Shores of the Arctic Sea in 1846 and
1847.* London: T. and W. Boone, 1850.

Rasmussen, Knud. *The Netsilik Eskimos: Social Life and Spiritual Culture.* Report of
the Fifth Thule Expedition 1921–24, Vol. 8 (Parts 1 and 2), Copenhagen:
Gyldendalske Boghandel, 1931.

– *Intellectual Culture of the Copper Eskimos.* Report of the Fifth Thule Expedition
1921–24, Vol. 9. Copenhagen: Gyldendalske Boghandel, 1932.

Rasing, W.C.E. *Too Many People: Order and Nonconformity in Iglulingmiut Social
Process.* Nijmegen: Recht & Samenleving, 1994.

Rea, K.J. *The Political Economy of the Canadian North.* Toronto: University of Toronto Press, 1968.

Report of the Fifth Thule Expedition, 1921–24, Copenhagen: Gyldendakse
Boghandel. Vols 1–10, 1927–52.

Riewe, Rick. "Inuit Land Use and the Native Claims Process." In Abel and Friesen, eds., *Aboriginal Resource Use in Canada.* Winnipeg: University of Manitoba Press, 1971.

Robinson, J.L. "Eskimo Population in the Canadian Eastern Arctic." *Canadian
Geographical Journal* 29 (1944): 129–42.

Robinson, Samuel I. "The Influence of the American Whaling Industry on the
Aivilingmiut, 1860–1919." Unpublished master's thesis, Department of So-
ciology and Anthropology, McMaster University, 1972.

Robson, Joseph. *An Account of Six Years' Residence in Hudson's Bay from 1733 to
1736 and 1744 to 1747.* London: Payne and Bouquet, 1752.

Roman Catholic Church. Records of the Bathurst Inlet Mission. Permission of
Father Louis Menez.

Ross, Sir John. *Narrative of a Second Voyage in Search of a North-West Passage, and of
a Residence in the Arctic Regions During the Years 1829, 1830, 1831, 1833.* Philadelphia: E.L. Corey and H. Hart, 1835.

Ross, W. Gillies. *Whaling and Eskimos: Hudson Bay 1860–1915.* Ottawa: National
Museum of Man, Publications in Ethnology, No. 10, 1975.

– "Commercial Whaling and Eskimos in the Eastern Canadian Arctic 1819–1920." In McCartney, ed., *Thule Eskimo Culture: An Anthropological Perspective*, 242–66. Ottawa: National Museum of Man, 1979.

– "Whaling, Inuit, and the Arctic Islands." In Zaslow, ed., *A Century of Canada's Arctic Islands, 1880–1980*. Ottawa: The Royal Society of Canada, 1981.

Rowley, Susan. "Population Movements in the Canadian Arctic." *Etudes/Inuit/Studies* 9, no. 1 (1985): 3–22.

Rowley-Conway, Peter, ed. *Animal Bones: Human Societies*. Oxford: Oxbow Books, 2000.

Royal Canadian Mounted Police (RCMP). *Annual Report for Fiscal Years 1922, 1923, 1924, 1925, 1926*. Ottawa: F.A. Acland.

Royal Commission on Aboriginal Peoples. *The High Arctic Relocation*, 3 parts. Ottawa: Minister of Supply and Services Canada, 1994.

Saladin d'Anglure, Bernard, and Francoise Morin. "The Inuit People, Between Particularism and Internationalism: An Overview of Their Rights and Powers." Peter Frost, trans. *Etudes/Inuit/Studies* 18, nos 1, 2 (1992): 13–19.

Savelle, James M. "Information Systems and Thule Eskimo Bowhead Whaling." In Rowley-Conway, ed., *Animal Bones and Human Societies*. Oxford: Oxbow Books, 2000.

Savelle, James M. and Alan P. McCartney. "Geographical and Temporal Variation in Thule Eskimo Subsistence Economies: A Model." *Research in Economic Anthropology* 10 (1988): 21–72.

Stanners, John. Conversation with author, 9–10 August 1963.

Steenhoven, Geert van den. *Leadership and Law Among the Eskimos of the Keewatin District, Northwest Territories*. The Hague: Ungeverij, 1962.

Stefansson, Vilhjalmur. *My Life With the Eskimo*. New York: The Macmillan Company, 1913.

– *The Stefansson – Anderson Arctic Expedition of the American Museum*. Preliminary Report. New York: Anthropological Papers of the American Museum of Natural History, 1919.

– ed. *The Three Voyages of Martin Frobisher in Search of a Passage to Cathay and India by the North-west, A.D. 1576–8*. From the original 1578 text of George Best. London: Argonaught Press, 1938.

Sturtevant, William C. "Anthropology, History and Ethnohistory." In Clifton, ed., *Introduction to Cultural Anthropology*. Boston: Houghton, Mifflin, 1968.

Tester, Frank J. and Peter Kulchyski. *Tammarniit: Mistakes*. Vancouver: UBC Press, 1994.

Thomas, D.K. and C.J. Thompson. *Eskimo Housing as a Planned Cultural Change*. Ottawa: Department of Indian Affairs and Northern Development, 1971.

Treude, Erhard. "Studies in Settlement Development and Evaluation of the Economy in the Eastern Central Arctic." *The Musk – Ox* 16 (1976): 53–66.

– "Pond Inlet, Northern Baffin Island: The Structure of an Eskimo Resouce Area." *Polar Geography* 1, no. 3 (1977): 95–122.

Tyrrell, James W. *Across the Sub-arctics of Canada.* Toronto: W. Briggs, 1897.

Tyrrell, Joseph B. "Report of the Doobaunt, Kazan, and Ferguson Rivers and the Northwest Coast of Hudson Bay." *Canada: Annual Report of the Geological Survey* n.s.9(F) Ottawa: S.E. Dawson, 1988.

– *Report on the Doobawnt, Kazan and Ferguson Rivers.* Ottawa: Geological Survey of Canada, 1898.

Usher, Peter J. *Economic Basis and Resource Use of the Coppermine – Holman Region, N.W.T.* Ottawa: Department of Northern Affairs and National Resources, 1965.

– *Fur Trade Posts of the Northwest Territories 1870–1970.* Ottawa: Department of Northern Affairs and Northern Development, 1971.

Vallee, F.G. *Kabloona and Eskimo in the Central Keewatin.* Ottawa: Saint Paul University, 1967.

Vallee, F.G., Derek G. Smith, and Joseph D. Cooper. "Contemporary Canadian Inuit." In Damas, ed., *Arctic, Handbook of North American Indians, Vol. 5.* Washington: Smithsonian Institution, 1984.

VanStone, James W. *The Economy and Population Shifts of the Eskimos of Southampton Island.* Ottawa: Department of Northern Affairs and National Resources, 1959.

VanStone, James W. and Wendell Oswalt. *The Caribou Eskimos of Eskimo Point.* Ottawa: Department of Northern Affairs and National Resources, 1959.

Vestey, Jennifer. "Igloolik Eskimo Settlement and Mobility, 1900–1970." Unpublished master's thesis, Department of Geography, McGill University, 1984.

Villiers, D. *The Central Arctic: An Area Economic Survey.* Ottawa: Department of Indian Affairs and Northern Administration, 1969.

Voisey, Henry. Interview with author. Ottawa, 30 May 1968.

Weissling, Lee. "Inuit Redistribution and Development: Process of Change in the Eastern Canadian Arctic 1922–1968." Unpublished Ph.D. thesis, Department of Geography, McGill University, 1984.

Welland, Tony. "Inuit Land Use in Keewatin District and Southhampton Island." In Freeman, ed., *Inuit Land Use and Occupancy Project. Vol. I.* Ottawa: Department of Indian and Northern Affairs, 1976.

Wenzel, George W. *Clyde Inuit Ecology and Adaptation: The Organization of Subsistence.* Ottawa: National Museums of Canada, 1981.

– *Animal Rights, Human Rights.* Toronto: University of Toronto Press, 1991.

– Review of *Living on the Land* by John S. Mathiasson. *Etudes/Inuit/Studies* 17, no. 2 (1993): 152.

– "Recent Changes in Inuit Summer Residence Patterning at Clyde River, East Baffin Island." In Burch and Ellanna, eds., *Key Issues in Hunter-Gatherer Research.* Providence, R.I.: Berg Publishers, 1994.

– "Inuit Demographic and Ecological Relations Along Northeast Baffin Island, Circa, 1920–1960." Unpublished manuscript submitted to Ethnology Division, National Museum of Man, n.d.

– "Inuit Subsistence and Hunter Support in Nunavut." Unpublished manuscript, n.d.

Williams G., ed. *Andrew Graham's Observations on Hudson's Bay, 1767–1794.* London: Hudson's Bay Record Society Publication 27, 1969.

Williamson, Robert G. "The Keewatin Settlements: A Historical Review." *The Musk – Ox* 8 (1971): 14–23.

– *Eskimo Underground: Cultural Change in the Central Arctic.* Upsala: Institutions for Allaman Och Jamforrande Ethnografie, 1974.

Willmott, William E. *The Eskimo Community at Port Harrison.* Ottawa: Department of Northern Affairs and National Resources, 1961.

World Almanac Books. *The World Almanac.* Mahwah, New Jersey: World Almanac Books, 1998.

Zaslow, Morris, ed. *A Century of Canada's Arctic Islands, 1880–1980.* Ottawa: The Royal Society of Canada, 1981.

– *The Northward Expansion of Canada 1914–1967.* Toronto: McClelland & Stewart, 1988.

Index